# PLANETS AND POSSIBILITIES

Susan Miller is also the author of
*The Astrology Book of Days*
available from Warner Books

# PLANETS AND POSSIBILITIES

*Explore the Worlds Beyond Your Sun Sign*

*Susan Miller*

WARNER BOOKS

A Time Warner Company

Warner Books, Inc., 1271 Avenue of the Americas, New York, NY 10020
Visit our Web site at www.twbookmark.com
Ⓦ A Time Warner Company

Printed in the United States of America
First Printing: January 2001
10 9 8 7 6 5 4 3 2 1

ISBN: 0-446-52434-4
Library of Congress Card Number: 00-109235

Book design by Fenix Design, Inc.

*To my mother and to my daughters, Christiane and Diana*

# ACKNOWLEDGMENTS

All successful people have many other successful people behind them. Producing a book is a lengthy process involving the caring contribution of many wise and thoughtful people. This book was born out of talks with Maureen Egen, president of Warner Books, who first urged me to write a detailed book on astrology. I remember sitting opposite Maureen in her office, presenting various ideas for my book and crossing my fingers in hopes that she would select my first (and most ambitious) concept, *Planets and Possibilities*. She did, and provided the loving encouragement to make this book possible. In this, my second book with Warner Books, I can only thank my lucky stars that I have such a supportive publisher behind me. I would like to thank Frank Weimann, my agent, for his kind support as well.

I thank my hardworking editor, Jackie Joiner, whose instincts always were similar to mine. Part of Jackie's talent is her ability to preserve a writer's voice, soul, and spirit. Jackie did that and much more, and for her hard work and exceptionally good nature I am so appreciative.

I owe a tremendous debt to my longtime friend Jackie Meyer. Jackie's steadfast faith in me has had (and continues to have) an enormous influence on my life. Jackie gave me the opportunity to write my first book, *Astrology Book of Days*, with Warner Books in 1996, and she also gave me the opportunity to present my ideas for a Web site to Time Warner. As a result, I was able to give birth to Astrology Zone® on Time Warner's Web site Pathfinder. Three years later, I moved Astrology Zone to its present home on the Disney Internet Group, with Time Warner's blessings and encouragement. Without the opportunities Jackie provided me, my life would have taken a very different (and less exciting) course. In the figurative sense, Jackie will always provide the lilting, lyrical music to the background of my life.

In the astrologic field, I would like to thank Wendy Ashley, astrologer-mythologist, who first opened my eyes to the importance and enjoyment of learning the myths underlying each of the astrologic signs. Wendy's lectures were unforgettable and made me thirst for more. Her knowledge about the myths is encyclopedic and wise, and she delivers her expertise with all the colorful enthusiasm of a storyteller at a campfire. In the years since first hearing Wendy speak, I've discovered a number of valuable books both here and in Europe that helped to expand my knowledge and interest in this area. I also owe a debt to the equally erudite author/historian/lecturer Robert Hand, whose lectures inspired me to go back in time to study the genesis of astrology. Judi Vitale, astrologer colleague and trusted member of Robert Hand's Project Hindsight team, gets my sincere thanks for being a consultant to the historical section of my book.

A million heartfelt thanks go to my dear close friend Edward Rubinstein for his steadfast personal support of me over the years, in ways too numerous to count, and for his never-ending help on whatever facts I needed checked. Edward, I enjoyed our long sessions spent looking up and debating ideas together. My assistant, Pleasant Cragie, lent her talent and love of history by helping me check some of the historical facts, and she always made the process fun. Special thanks too go to Daryl Chen and Christopher Sandersfeld, who worked methodically and enthusiastically on making the actual corrections to the manuscript in the final edit. It is enormously comforting to work with such a talented team of individuals.

Finally, my family deserves an expression of gratitude too. I send thanks to my two daughters, Christiane and Diana, who got used to eating take-out food for many months as I worked on the book long into the evening without breaks. Chrissie and Diana are the best children on the planet.

Further, I would like to thank my mother, Erika Redl Trentacoste, who opened my eyes to the planets, the Moon, the Sun, and the stars and, in so doing, to the vast and humbling beauty of our universe and of the blessing that is life. Dear little Mom, I love you.

—SM

# CONTENTS

# INTRODUCTION

# MY UNUSUAL INTRODUCTION
# TO ASTROLOGY

When I was little and couldn't sleep, late at night I would creep into the living room to see if anyone was up. Invariably, I would find my mother curled up on the couch reading her astrology books or studying her charts. In those wee hours of the morning my father would be asleep, but Mom, as the busy mother of two young children, would try to use the only time she had to concentrate on her serious hobby. Astrology was not her only interest. She (along with my father) devoured three newspapers a day, had friends, and also helped my father in his specialty grocery store. But astrology deeply intrigued Mom, and she studied it every chance she got. Her penetrating mind sought to figure out why astrology always seemed to work, and her study also offered her creative clues to life's mysteries. My mother's biggest challenge, however, both in life and in astrology, would be to figure out how to help me with a debilitating and mysterious birth defect in my left leg.

She asked me not to tell anyone about her interest in and knowledge of astrology, saying it should be for "just us" and never for those outside our family. Times were different then, and she did not want to invite criticism about her hobby from either new acquaintances or old friends. Still, she said, "It's always good that I know the cycles, Susan—I can help you go with the cosmic tide, not try to swim against it."

I remember having lunch with Mom when I was little at the dining-room table. She would always sit down next to me, wearing her apron, and cheerfully keep me company. A Gemini, she'd make lots of interesting conversation. It was fun to be with Mom. I would eat my tunafish sandwiches, and sometimes she would talk about astrology. She said I would look at her with big eyes and swing my legs while I chewed. Today she laughs and says, "I used to talk to you but you never said much, dear Susie, so I thought you weren't listening. Now I know that you heard every word!"

My mother discovered astrology by accident. Her elder sister (my wonderful aunt) Harriet, the eldest of five, suddenly became interested in the subject and, wanting to have someone with whom she could talk about it, tried to get my mother involved. My mother was initially skeptical about astrology and resisted my aunt's suggestions. I think that is a very common and healthy first reaction by everyone who comes to study astrology. I don't think anybody is a born "believer." Later, Mom, as a young girl of eighteen, moved to New York City and Aunt Harriet remained upstate, but they both took a home correspondence course in astrology. It was something the two sisters could still do together even though they lived apart. Mom continued to study over the next two or three years and become better and better at her hobby and more drawn to investigating the full spectrum of what the ancient art could offer. Its complexities fascinated her, and its richness never bored her active mind. My mother wrote letters to my aunt to debate certain shadings of current planetary aspects.

When my mother was thirty-five years old, Aunt Harriet suddenly became very ill with ovarian cancer and died a very slow and painful death at the age of forty-five. (At the time, I was five years old.) This was a terrible and devastating event in my mother's life. At the reading of the will, my mother learned that Aunt Harriet had left all her favorite astrology books to her as a special gift. When my mother received them, she found inside one of the covers a letter from my aunt, apparently written when she was aware that she did not have long to live: "Erika, study astrology—you will go far, much further than I was meant to go with this subject. You are innately mathematical and you deal with symbolism superbly. Don't give it up." Hence my mother found herself the new owner of some of the best books on the subject. From that point on, my mother dove even more deeply into astrology, probably as much out of curiosity as well as to remain psychologically close to her sister.

My involvement with astrology would also start almost by accident and certainly was fueled by my birth defect. I was born with a debilitating and mysterious illness that caused excruciating pain in my left leg; I had sudden, inexplicable attacks that felt like thick syrup was falling into my knee. The attacks would come about twice a year and would leave me bedridden for six to eight weeks. Doctors were mystified, and in the absence of any hard data they said I had made up the illness to stay out of school. The doctors who did believe me suggested all kinds of cures, including radiation treatments which we rejected. The leg was so terribly tender and painful to the touch that I didn't want to risk having anything done to it, and even as a child I begged my mother simply to "let me be." After any one of my sudden "attacks," as long as I remained perfectly still (not moving an inch in bed for weeks), I always recovered perfectly.

I felt unjustly accused when the doctors called my illness psychosomatic, and after a time I didn't want to see any more doctors. A mother's intuition is strong—Mom knew something was very wrong with me, so she became my protector, comforting me with the assurance that someday someone would figure out what was wrong and help me. She even predicted a change of status in my health when the ruler of my ascendant, Mercury, would go direct in my progressed chart when I turned age *fourteen*. She surmised that I would simply outgrow the illness, so she wasn't too anxious to hurry me into an unnecessary operation. It was clear that she was confident that my ordeal was going to have a happy ending. My father was supportive too, but they nevertheless agreed that we had to continue to see new doctors no matter what the charts said.

As things turned out, Mom was astoundingly right about the timing of my health breakthrough. When I was exactly thirteen years, ten months, three weeks, and two days old, I had the worst attack of my life. Bedridden again, I patiently waited two months for a recovery that never came. Something was different about this attack. The pain was much worse and the swelling greater. Still, I did not want an operation. We tried one doctor, who put me in traction and made everything worse. My father, horrified by the pain I was in, carried me out of the hospital, saying quietly that we needed a new doctor. Exasperated, I begged to celebrate my birthday at home, and I blew out the candles on the cake in bed.

I was now fourteen, the exact age my mother had predicted for the end of my health difficulties. Two weeks later, I agreed to surgery performed by a new young doctor and brilliant scholar. The protégé to the chief of a different hospital, he solved my case, and he is still my doctor to this day.

The secret of my illness was that I had had recurring life-threatening internal bleeding. I was born with veins in my left leg from the hip to the knee that were malformed and turning to tissue paper. The vessels would simply vanish. There was nothing for the surgeon to tie or hold on to, so for any doctor operating on me, a condition like this is a nightmare. Today such a condition is still rare — I am told that there are only forty-seven known cases in medical history. I am one of the very few survivors because my condition was located in the lower body. Had the malformed veins been near my head or my heart, the illness would have killed me. The doctor said it was better that we had waited for surgery, surmising that part of the problem was that during my growth periods, my vessels didn't grow along with me. Now that my growth (at age 14) was nearly over there was less chance that I would experience fresh internal bleeding. Even so, the doctors went the whole nine yards to see that my attacks never happened again.

I spent eleven months in the hospital when I was fourteen as doctors revamped my veins, arteries, muscles, and bone, and I even had a skin graft. A nerve was severed during the difficult surgery and I had to go through therapy to regenerate it, a process that took three years. During those years I could not actually attend high school, so I studied in the hospital and later at home, taking my state exams and SATs. I graduated high school and then at age sixteen entered New York University and later received a B.S. degree in business with honors. Studying by myself had helped my self-discipline. Through these years Mom told me, "Susie, get used to not having friends. They will understandably get tired of you being sick. Read, sweetheart, and for now let books be your friends. Later, when you walk again, you will have friends again." She was, as ever, right.

During this period of recovery, no one was sure if I would ever walk again. With a severed nerve, I had no sensation or movement in the lower part of my left leg. Although my doctor never wavered in his cheerful predictions, the hospital residents were not so sure—and would privately tell me not to keep my hopes up.

I was highly motivated to find out what was going to happen next, and I needed a big dose of hope quickly. It was then that astrology entered the picture for me. I wrote a letter to the editor of *Horoscope* magazine, a publication I used to see my mother read occasionally. I asked the editor if she would do my chart and tell me if I would ever walk again. (I could have asked my mother, but I figured she might not tell me the whole truth if the answer was no.) In the letter I included my month, day, and year of birth, as well as the city and exact time of my birth, knowing from my mother's afternoon lunch conversations that this information was critical for doing a chart. I knew my time of birth because my mother so often talked about it. Much to my surprise, my letter was published! My mother, amazed that I had written to the magazine, sat down next to me and read the answer aloud. After a long analysis, the astrologer-editor said yes, she felt I would walk again and that I would eventually fully recover!

At the time I was still very, very ill and needed braces and crutches to get around, but I was very encouraged by the answer though still a little cautiously skeptical.

Instantly, I made up my mind that I wanted to know more about astrology and figure out exactly what the editor had seen — I wanted to do my chart for myself. Not being able to walk, I certainly had time to read and study. But I would have an unexpected obstacle: My mother surprised me by saying she did not want me to study astrology. She explained that astrology demanded a full and intense commitment, something I was still too young to know if I would be able to carry out. "A little knowledge is dangerous, Susan," she would often say. She felt that novices often think they know more than they actually do, leading them to jump to conclusions. She warned, "Don't start, Susan. Leave it alone. If you aren't ready to study for twelve years straight, don't begin." Of course, tell teenagers not to do something and that's precisely what they will do.

In those teen years, I could not get out of bed by myself; I was weak from many blood transfusions, and my hip was so swollen it was hard even to sit up. There was no TV or phone in my room. In our house, the TV stayed in the living room, the phone in my parents' bedroom or the kitchen. This situation was good because I had no distractions. My mother would go to the library and get me stacks of classic books to read, which I enjoyed.

Yet I also wanted my mother's astrology books. During that summer, when I was finally home from the hospital, my little sister, Janet, then eleven, would secretly bring my mother's books into my room. We would hide them under my bed's dust ruffle. I studied a great deal after I got my homework done but I did not tell my mother, and I kept this secret for years. In fact, my interest was only revealed twenty years later when one day I had to ask my mother for a written recommendation to an astrological research association that she belonged to. "You aren't ready," she responded. Then I had to reveal that I had been writing a small column for a magazine and told her the full extent of my research. But before she would write the recommendation she took my articles home with her and did charts for all the months I had written about. She studied whether I was giving the right advice or not. I am lucky she was such a tough teacher, and I'm also lucky that I passed her test.

My true calling, however, had not yet formed. When my two daughters were still babies, I started my own business as an agent for commercial photographers but continued to write two astrological columns on the side. I became very successful as an agent, representing talent in London and the United States. I was happy with life, though the bones in my left foot were clearly wearing down (the severed nerve had left that leg a little weaker). Just walking a few blocks would give me teeth-grinding pain. Still, I was determined to persevere no matter what. In 1992 another bout with the leg scared me—on a total eclipse, out of the blue, I broke my left thighbone for the third time. This last bout was the worst. I received seventeen blood transfusions in one night during an emergency operation. It was a defining moment, for I was to be reminded again how fragile life can be. My original doctor saved me—but both of us agreed that I could not endure more surgery. I now had steel lining my femur and was able to walk again after I recovered.

A few years later, in connection with my work as a photo agent, I was calling on Warner Books and offering to do an occasional chart if someone asked me to do one. My reputation for accuracy was growing. My mother's insistence on my doing research in astrology for twelve years before I was to read a single chart outside the family was starting to pay off in peer respect. Not surprisingly, I was getting my readings right. I turned to writing more and more, and the magazine work kept growing bigger. Warner Books gave me a chance to be editor of my own astrology Web site in December of 1995, and thus Astrology Zone® was born. My first book, *Astrology Book of Days*, appeared a few months later. I was well on my way to a new career.

It turned out that the difficulties with my leg bestowed unanticipated and enormous side blessings. I became religious, reflective, and philosophical. Like most people who go through an ordeal, it also made me very compassionate toward others who suffered.

I am reminded of a little incident that was to forever change the way I viewed difficulties in life. It remains as crystal clear today as the day it happened. One morning when I was nine years old, I was at my grandmother's house in the country. My father had brought my sister, my mother, and me upstate for the summer. I shared a room with my sister in the attic. Within a day or two of arriving, I suffered one of my mysterious attacks. I knew I would be in bed the rest of the summer.

That morning my mother was changing the sheets with me in the bed, a routine we used to do as I couldn't get up. I couldn't even move from one side of the bed to the other, no more than an inch, because the pain was so intense. After my mother spent about an hour slowly pushing the new sheet under me and the old sheet off the other side, I had cool, smooth, new sheets and pillowcases. My mother was putting another pillowcase on another pillow to prop up my back when I saw through the open window a verdant oak tree with a bluebird on a branch. The sunshine was bright, and the air was warm. Suddenly overwhelmed by the prospect of spending the whole summer in the attic in bed, I blurted out to my mother: "Oh, this old leg. I wish I didn't have this old problem. I wish somebody else had it!" I guess it was typical of what a nine-year-old would say, but it was kind of unusual for me actually to voice such a thought. My mother spun around with the pillow in her hand and looked a bit surprised. "What did you say? Did I hear you say that?" I repeated my lament. She came over to the side of the bed and said very gently, "There is a reason for everything. What if you knew you were absorbing some of the ills of the world with your pain? How would you feel about it then? What if there were worldly reasons for your pain that transcended you? You should never say you wish you didn't have it—it is your cross to bear but you must do so gladly. God chose you for this difficulty. We know nothing about life or of God's will, Susan. We must not suppose we know all about the universe. Reasons may be revealed in time." Her words struck a deep chord in me; I was stunned into silence. But her words taught me about the concept of pain having a noble value. This was an idea I had not considered, but she inspired me to think outside myself. I wanted to find out my life's role and determine whether I had a mission to fulfill.

My mother's words echoed in my heart for years as I continued to have many bad bouts with my health. It is only now that I have an inkling of what she may have meant. She told me that it is through compassion that one's pain can absorb others' pain, but at nine I was too young to understand that empathy is one of the world's most human and valuable gifts. This is something I see with greater clarity and depth as I get older. Life has many twists and turns, and often we have no idea why we are going through a particular phase until years later.

My mother's deeply philosophical nature and steadfast optimism in the face of all odds was to have a profound influence on my view of the world and, I think, on my readings and predictions, too. She taught me to see the value in challenge, and for that I will always be grateful. My dear father was also highly encouraging. He sparked my determination to explore all aspects of life. He also helped me to realize that material objects are ephemeral and hold no candle to spiritual values. Both parents helped me not only to become a happier person but also to look beyond the surface, to look deeply into events and conditions to try to find clues as to why there is suffering. My hard start in life and many subsequent challenges shaped me as a person and as an astrologer. I realized that "bad" aspects weren't necessarily all bad—they had value too. As my mother would say, "We learn nothing from times of ease, Susan. It is in times of difficulty that we come face to face with who we are and what we want to be. We will always have the opportunity to build our character to its full potential—it is never too late to begin."

# THE HISTORY OF ASTROLOGY

LIFE IN MESOPOTAMIA

Astrology is nearly as old as mankind. Some of the very first written records—in cuneiform characters, created by pressing wedge-shaped implements into soft clay—date back approximately to 3000 B.C. in Sumer. It was in this region of Mesopotamia, as well as in the other "cradles of civilization" (Egypt, China, the Indus Valley, and Meso-America), that the study of astrology as we know it today began.

When humans evolved the first agrarian societies, life was very precarious. It was a world without modern medicine, a time when people could not expect a long life. If starvation or disease was not a problem, there was always the danger of a surprise attack from an enemy. When inclement weather destroyed crops, bringing pain, suffering, and even death, community leaders would scan the sky, as much to discover a better way to forecast weather conditions as for omens of upcoming events. The ancients spent a great deal of time studying the heavens, where, they believed, their gods and goddesses lived and oversaw the care of mortals below. It is important to note that unlike today the ancients believed that the planets *were* their gods. Through observation over time, they decided that certain planetary activity correlated with particular traits and events, and to explain their insights in a way that people could understand them (and to make them vivid and memorable), they associated these findings with certain myths. These were the first steps in the creation of the vast body of work called astrology.

What is surprising is *not* that the ancients developed a system of forecasting, but that they designed it to be the rich, complex, and creative tool it remains to this day. Astrology has proven to be relevant and flexible enough to encompass the vast changes that mankind has experienced over the centuries and across geography. As you come closer to astrology, the textual depth of the subject becomes even more remarkable because it is based on a sophisticated combination of mathematics and mythological meaning. Astrology reveals itself slowly, for there are layers of meaning that can be translated from various symbols underlying the horoscope. Each chart is unique and dynamic too, encompassing not only natal planets' positions but also the continual motion of the planets astrologers call "transits" in relation to those natal planetary positions. Some planetary aspects form common and recurring patterns, while others are rare, once-in-a-lifetime events. Some aspects are rewarding, others are challenging — but both teach us about ourselves and the world where we live.

The ancient people saw the same stars and constellations that we do now, a thread that links all generations and nationalities in one human family. Without the dense atmospheric conditions, bright lights, and tall buildings that we have in our cities, the average citizen in ancient times could see the stars and planets clearly. On the other hand, now we have the *Voyager* programs from the 1970s and the Hubble Space Telescope, which, since its launch in April 1990, has sent back thrilling photographs of the planets, stars, and galaxies. Hubble's photographs have pushed back the boundaries of deep space. It is exciting to realize that we are the first generation of people to see all the planets up close and in great detail.

## THE CULTURES ASSOCIATED WITH ASTROLOGY'S DEVELOPMENT

The astrology of the Western world (as opposed to Chinese, Vedic, Indic, or Native American astrology) is based strongly on the astrology developed by the Babylonians. The Greeks, Romans, Egyptians, and Persians were also instrumental in our understanding of astrology, as virtually all these ancient peoples presented different cultural contributions for astrology to draw upon. Scholars believe that cultures developed versions of astrology independently from one another, and that the influence of travel and exploration as well as the building of empires through military conquest both blended and edited parts of these versions over time. This, though, is an oversimplification. Let's take a look at some of astrology's key moments so that the intricate evolution of this ancient art and science can become clearer.

## THE OLDEST EVIDENCE WE HAVE UNEARTHED
## COMES FROM BABYLONIA

It was in Babylonia, around the second millennium B.C., that one of the first codifications of astrologic information was compiled. This was the *Enuma Anu Enlil*, a catalog of the celestial gods that was etched into clay tablets. Archaeologists have not been able to recover all of the tablets. The ones that have been discovered were found at the library of King Ashurbanipal, a seventh-century B.C. Assyrian leader who had the forethought to make copies of the original Babylonian tablets.

Another important collection of clay tablets were the *Venus Tables of Ammizaduga* (the probable date of this information is still the subject of debate), which contain information about the movements of Venus's position in relation to the Moon and, to a lesser degree, the Sun. The Babylonians referred to Venus as the "mistress of the heavens" and carefully tracked Venus's whereabouts in the sky. It is important to note that the Babylonians felt that the position of the Moon in a horoscope was even more important than the position of the Sun. The Babylonian calendar was based on lunar months too.

The Chaldeans, who at about 700 B.C. populated the southern region of Babylonia in Mesopotamia (now roughly Iraq) and were considered "latter-day" inhabitants, were particularly keen observers of the skies. The Chaldeans noticed that among the stars they saw above, a few of them actually moved—those were the planets. The twelve constellations provided perfect fixed points from which to watch the movements of these "wandering stars" (literally, planets), and those constellations allowed the Chaldeans to track how fast the various planets were traveling. The Chaldeans carefully collected much information about the movements of all five of the known (and visible) planets, namely Mercury, Venus, Mars, Jupiter, and Saturn, as well as the movement of the Sun and Moon. So important was their contribution to astrology that people in those days referred to astrologers generically as "Chaldeans." The Chaldeans are credited with developing some of the key foundations of astrology that are still in use today.

## THE CONSTELLATIONS

A word about the constellations seems appropriate here. The constellations are the fixed points from which ancient astrologers could track the paths of the planets. They are the primary navigational points, for it is the planets that give the constellations their significance, not the other way around. In ancient astrology these constellations played a much greater role than they do today. In those days, for example, farmers knew it was wise to plant in the spring and reap in the fall, but in some regions the seasons were not as easily distinguished as they were in others. So those farmers looked to the constellations to tell them what month it was. For example, in the Northern Hemisphere, Scorpio is visible in the evening sky only in the summer. Hence, the constellations provided a convenient calendar in the sky.

In the 4,000 or 5,000 years that constellations have been recorded by man, their numbers have grown. The International Astronomical Union has recently approved boundary lines that define eighty-eight official constellations. In ancient times, eighteen constellations were selected for astrological purposes, but in time these were narrowed down to twelve classic constellations. The progress of the transiting Sun was tracked through the twelve signs of the zodiac that the Egyptians adopted and later handed down. Of the zodiac constellations, Taurus, the then sacred Bull, is thought to be the oldest, and Libra is the most recently added of the twelve.

Libra was not part of the zodiac in Babylonia but made its appearance as a separate and distinct zodiac sign by the time of the Egyptians. (Previously Libra was part of Virgo and of Scorpio, varying by culture.)

## CHALDEAN DISCOVERIES

The Chaldeans realized that the planets did not travel all over the sky but in one area within a very narrow belt—the path called the ecliptic. The Chaldeans also noted that the constellations move thirty degrees, or one-twelfth of a circle, every two hours. This is the basic foundation of the modern horoscope. The Chaldeans put special emphasis on the phases of the Moon and on eclipses, just as astrologers do today. (Astrologers agree that eclipses are important, for when they occur within certain degrees of natal and transiting planets, they bring swift changes of status or condition in the house where they fall.) By the end of the fourth century B.C., the Chaldeans had compiled tables of the planetary and lunar movements, which are the precursor to the modern-day *ephemeris* (which means "diary" in Latin).

## ASTROLOGY'S PURPOSE THEN AND NOW

When the Babylonians began practicing astrology, it was not intended to be a personal tool. Instead, astrology was the preserve of the king and heads of state to prepare for future events. Astrologers were highly educated mathematicians and astronomers whose skills and services were beyond the reach of the common man. Aristotle recorded that the Chaldeans forecast Socrates' death from his horoscope. It is also said that Euripedes' father requested that the Chaldeans erect his then unknown son's chart when he was born (480 B.C.). Both of these occurrences are reported in the writings of historian and biographer Diogenes Laertius in the third century A.D.

The Babylonian Chaldeans are owed a great deal of credit for the development of astrology as we know it today. In early birth charts, the oldest dating from 410 B.C., the positions of planets were used but they did not yet have a house system quite as developed as ours. That came in Ptolemy's time (approximately A.D. 170, in Greece). Instead, the ancients used the zero to thirty degrees of each sign as "places" in the same way we use "houses" today. Although this system was simpler, it did incorporate a calculated ascendant (see "Your Road Map to Understanding the Basics of Astrology") and sophisticated mathematical calculations, which astrologers still use to achieve special insight into a horoscope.

## MODERN HOROSCOPE-BASED ASTROLOGY EVOLVED IN EGYPT BY CHALDEANS

Most experts, including the respected astrologer-historian Robert Hand, consider Egypt to be the place where modern astrology evolved toward its present-day form. Hand suggests that there were two events in Egypt that fostered astrology's progress. One was the conquest of Egypt by the Persians, and the other was the conquest of both Persia and Egypt by Alexander the Great. In both instances, Egypt was brought under the same regime that ruled the Babylonians. Hand writes, "In the case of the Persian Empire, the Persians themselves became ardent devotees of astrology which no doubt assisted the movement of astrological ideas into Egypt." These two conquests caused a great assimilation of ideas among all peoples in that region.

## ALEXANDER THE GREAT PLAYED A ROLE IN ASTROLOGY'S PROGRESS

The conquests of Egypt, Turkey, Mesopotamia, Afghanistan, Persia, and the northern edges of India by Alexander the Great (356–323 B.C.) spread Greek astrology throughout the region, effectively fusing East and West. By the time the Babylonians' Moon-based astrology arrived in Egypt, the Egyptians already had a Sun-based form of astrology, which is believed to have originated in approximately 1200 B.C. The Egyptians are credited with the development of our present-day solar-based calendar of 365 days, different from the Mesopotamian calendar, which was lunar-based. Astrology would use the Sun as a key player in the chart, considering it slightly more important than the Moon. The Egyptians, despite their mathematical prowess, did not use horoscopic astrology. The Chaldeans introduced their lore-based methods of divination using the symbolism of planets in signs, while the Egyptians contributed their ability to calculate the rising degree.

The Egyptian practice of aligning their monuments and tombs to correspond with the positions of the fixed stars was astonishingly accurate. The Pyramids are but one example. It is presumed that the Egyptians did this to create greater harmony between their world and that of the heavens. Robert Hand points out that the Egyptians did not yet have the proper mathematical techniques for constructing a horoscope—that would come much later from the Arabs, with the addition of zero and the decimal point.

## ASTROLOGY IN GREECE

Around 250 B.C., another important event in the development of astrology took place. The Chaldean astrologer and scholar Berossus set up the first astrologic school on the Greek island of Cos and, in so doing made astrology available to a wider audience. Over the next 400 years the Greeks enthusiastically converted the Chaldean form of astrology to their own traditions.

In about 200 B.C. two Egyptians named Petosiris (a priest) and Nechepso (a pharoah) compiled what had been discovered about astrology in what may be the earliest astrologic manuscript. The zodiac as we know it, originally called the Circle of Animals and now called the Circle of Life, was somewhat different in those early astrological records, but it gradually evolved. As the constellations were narrowed down into the twelve classic signs of the zodiac, some of the traits of the eliminated constellations were combined with the remaining ones. For example, the qualities of the bear (food, hibernation, and good memory) once situated as a neighbor to the crab, were combined with the other qualities of the crab into the description of Cancer, cautious, self-protective.

## PTOLEMY, GREEK MATHEMATICIAN

By A.D. 170 astrology had taken a great scientific leap forward due to the theories, writings, and teachings put forth by Ptolemy (or Claudius

Ptolemaeus), a key figure in astrology. Ptolemy was a Greek mathematician, geographer, and astronomer who wrote what is regarded to be the first "modern" astrology manuscript, *Tetrabiblios*. Ptolemy emerged as the spokesperson for astrology in his age by explaining it in concrete terms that could be understood by the scientific establishment. As a respected member of the community, he gave credence to the system of astrologic aspects based on geometric angles that form the basis of modern astrology. Ptolemy, like others of his day, started to experiment with the horoscope house system by superimposing a mathematically constructed partitioning of the chart over the twelve signs of the zodiac. This was one of the first modifications to the more primitive method already in place.

## THE HOUSE SYSTEM OF ASTROLOGY

The house system, whereby a horoscope delineates various areas of life, is a basic part of astrology to this day. Specifically, Ptolemy wrote that the first house covers self, life, and vitality; the second house, money or poverty; and the third house, brothers and sisters (it now also includes short trips and communicative efforts). The fourth house ruled, as it does now, parents and home, as well as "the end of all matters," presumably because this house is found at the very bottom (foundation) of a chart. The fifth house covered children and lovers (later astrologers added creativity and leisure activities). The sixth house covered servants (we now call these people our assistants and colleagues) and health matters. The seventh house ruled (and still does rule) all committed relationships, such as those to one's spouse or even business partners. The seventh house also ruled "open enemies" (as opposed to those who remain hidden, which is a twelfth-house matter).

In Ptolemy's day, the eighth house ruled death, but it was gradually redefined to include such things as legacies (money of the dead) and business deals that require other people's money. Both sex and surgery are now also included in this eighth house, for it is the area of the chart given over to regeneration and transformation of energy. Continuing on, the ninth house, once devoted exclusively to religion, now includes long-distance travel, publishing, and moral and legal matters, as well as higher education. The tenth house covered "dignities" (known today as the house of fame, career, honors, and advancement). The eleventh house was the house of "good fortune." It ruled Platonic relationships, or friendships (all group-oriented activities and charitable efforts are now included in this house). The twelfth house was known then as the house of hidden enemies. Now the meaning has been expanded to include the subconscious, intuition, certain medical treatments and efforts to heal the body and mind, secrets, and all things that happen behind the scenes in confidence, as well as what the ancients referred to as "self-undoing." These assignments are still true to this day.

## ASTROLOGY'S REBIRTH DESPITE ROME'S FALL

After the Romans conquered Greece, Greek astrology was ardently absorbed into the Roman society during the reigns of Augustus Octavian (27 B.C.–A.D. 14), Tiberius (14–37), and Hadrian (117–138) and was used by rich and poor alike. During this period the Latin poet Manilius wrote *Astronomica,* a literary tome in several volumes that put astrologic information in verse.

In A.D. 395 the Roman emperor Constantine established Constantinople as a second seat of power of the Roman Empire. As Rome declined after 410, this region developed into the Byzantine Empire, with Constantinople as its center. During the time of Rome's decline, the Church attacked astrology's temporary state of corruption and emphasis on superstition, and so the study of astrology also declined. However, the Greek astrological writings were safely preserved in Constantinople, as Greek, along with Latin, was widely spoken. The Byzantine Empire declined in the eighth century after the Islamic culture rose and dominated the Middle East and North Africa. In the ninth century, Constantinople turned over the entire library of Greek writings, including all the work of Ptolemy, to the caliph of Baghdad as part of a peace treaty.

Instead of astrology suffering or even dying out completely when it reached Persia, the opposite was true. Astrology actually flourished, mainly because it appealed to the Islamic love of allegory and symbolism and because this culture was so advanced in the study of mathematics. The Islamic culture quickly translated the Greek work into Arabic and eagerly applied astrology for personal use, such as choosing the right date to start a business or to get married. So after astrology reached the Islamic culture, prediction became much more precise and targeted. The use of Arabic numbers, including recognition of the concept of zero, was responsible for astrology's increasing precision. Some experts feel that astrology's survival was due largely to the new contributions to the field made by the advanced Islamic cultures of North Africa, as well as those based in the eastern portion of the Mediterranean, who had been using astrology since the eighth century.

## ASTROLOGY BLOSSOMS IN EUROPE—AGAIN

Greek-inspired astrology returned to Europe through the work of the famous ninth-century Islamic astrologer Abû Ma'schor (A.D. 805–850). He wrote the important document *Introductorium in Astronomiam* and is credited with the revival of astrology in the Middle Ages. Some three to four centuries later, his work was brought to Moorish Spain, where it was translated into Latin. Wrote Abû Ma'schor, "As the motions of these wandering stars [i.e., the five known planets plus the Sun and Moon] are never interrupted, so the generations and alternations of earthly things never have an end. Only by observing the great diversity of planetary motions can we comprehend the unnumbered varieties of change in this world."

Then, in the sixteenth century, astrology had a great revival with the birth of the Renaissance in Italy. Astrology was taught as part of the curriculum from as early as A.D. 1125 at many universities, including the University of Bologna, where Dante and other Renaissance luminaries studied. Indeed, astrology was so well regarded at this time that this university established a chair of astrology. Other universities in Europe paid astrology similar respect.

## JOHANNES KEPLER, GERMAN MATHEMATICIAN

Astrology changed little until German-born Johannes Kepler (1571–1630) made mathematical calculations of the orbits of the planets when he was appointed Imperial Mathematician to the court of Rudolf II in 1601. Kepler was also an astrologer who made important modifications to the Ptolemaic version of astrology. He placed the Sun in the center of the solar system, in agreement with Copernicus's theory, which was published in 1543. In modern circles, Kepler is highly regarded for his work.

## ISAAC NEWTON, BRITISH ASTROLOGY ADVOCATE

When the British scholar Sir Isaac Newton published *Philosophiae Naturalis Principia Mathematica* in 1687, he opened the era of modern astronomy. Many critics point to Copernicus's discoveries and Newton's advancement of astronomy as causing astrology's decline in the nineteenth century. While it is true that astrology did go into a temporary decline, it is not true that Newton completely rejected astrology. Newton was well grounded in astrologic technique, and reports are that he never lost his respect for the truths inherent in its precepts. Today all planetary movement and positions are calculated from their relation to Earth, and astrology still holds true to the foundation laid down by Ptolemy, which is that the horoscope is seen when we look up to the heavens from Earth. There are also branches of astrology that are Sun-based (heliocentric), so again astrology proves to be flexible enough to deal with astounding changes in man's understanding of the universe around him.

## ASTROLOGY IN THE TWENTIETH CENTURY AND BEYOND

In the twentieth century, psychiatrist Carl Jung wrote extensively about astrology, and it is well documented that he used astrology in his study of personality and human motivation. Today many magazines and newspapers carry horoscope columns, bringing astrology to a mass audience.

Most people today know their Sun signs, and many people know more than that about their horoscopes. The proliferation of the personal computer and the Internet has engendered a powerful revival of astrology. If the credo of the new century is "Information should be free," this goal is currently being met, crossing lines of gender, geography, and economic and social strata. More people can afford to have their personal natal charts cast (if only by computer) and, for the small monthly cost of Internet service, to have fast and easy access to a wider variety of astrologers' in-depth writings. Astrology at the start of the twenty-first century is more alive than ever, truly accessible to one and all.

# YOUR ROAD MAP TO
# UNDERSTANDING THE BASICS
# OF ASTROLOGY

### WHAT IS ASTROLOGY?

Astrology, as it is referred to here and elsewhere, is the study of the planets and stars with the help of certain mathematical tables to construct a horoscope. The study of omens without the use of a horoscope is not considered astrology.

### THE PLANETS AND THE MYTHS ARE THE KEYS TO ASTROLOGY

If you look at the sky on a clear night far from city lights, you will see what the ancients saw: stars that appear to stay fixed while others move along on a special path. The ancients called these moving bodies *planets* which means "the wanderers." When you get to know your Sun sign and perhaps a little bit more about your chart, you begin to realize that the symbolism of each of the zodiac signs is acquired from its ruling or guardian planet.

### IN THE BEGINNING THE SIGNS WERE RULED BY OLYMPIANS, NOT PLANETS

In the very beginning, when astrology was being formed in Greece, the zodiac signs were ruled not by planets but by the Olympians, the mythological gods and goddesses who formed the Greek pantheon. It is important to study the myths to learn the archetypes that form the very genesis of those signs.

The Greek astrologer and mathematician Ptolemy, in A.D. 150, set up a system with the five (known) planets plus the Sun and Moon designated as the rulers of the various signs.

In Ptolemy's day, there were not enough heavenly bodies to go around the zodiac so some signs shared planets, and although science has since discovered three more planets, some signs still share a ruling planet.

To understand some of the nuances of your signs in a colorful and memorable way, it is critical to know the Greek and Roman myths. If you are an Aries, for example, you will note that you are influenced strongly by Mars. Appropriately called the Red Planet by scientists and the "warrior planet" in mythology, Mars gives Aries courage, daring, and a restless nature to hurl new endeavors continually into being. As an Aries, you will note that your chapter includes the myth of Jason and the Argonauts. That myth does not necessarily mean that Jason *was* an Aries but that he *personified* the qualities of Aries in a particularly effective way. Jason's actions summed up the fearless, courageous persona that your sign exudes. If you think deeply enough, you might be able to add a new interpretation or slightly different shading to the qualities of your sign that others have missed up until now.

### The Rulerships of the Signs

| | |
|---|---|
| *Aries* | is ruled by Mars. |
| *Taurus* | is ruled by Venus. |
| *Gemini* | is ruled by Mercury. |
| *Cancer* | is ruled by the Moon. |
| *Leo* | is ruled by the Sun. |
| *Virgo* | is ruled by Mercury. |
| *Libra* | is ruled by Venus. |
| *Scorpio* | is ruled by Pluto (Mars is the secondary ruler). |
| *Sagittarius* | is ruled by Jupiter. |
| *Capricorn* | is ruled by Saturn (once ruled by the "night house" of Saturn). |
| *Aquarius* | is ruled by Uranus (once ruled by the "day house" of Saturn; Saturn is still considered a subruler). |
| *Pisces* | is ruled by Neptune (Jupiter, the secondary ruler). |

*Did You Know?*

*Your sign name is simply a way to refer to the degrees of the wheel.*

*Many people are surprised to realize that the names of the signs are simply a convenient way to refer to specific portions of the sky. For example, rather than saying "the portion of the sky that is found between 331 degrees and 360 degrees" we simply say "Pisces" or instead of "0 degrees to 59 degrees" we say "Aries."*

## THE HOROSCOPE AS A MAP OF YOUR LIFE AND A MIRROR OF MANKIND'S EVOLUTION TO MATURITY

According to the dictionary, horoscope comes from the Greek word *horoskopos*, meaning "one who observes the hour of birth for the purpose of astrology." (*Hora* means "hour" and *skopos* is "watcher," from *skopein*, meaning "to view.") Specifically, a horoscope tracks the position of the planets and stars in relation to one another at a given time and place, usually at a person's birth (but not always—companies and endeavors have charts too) that is used to divine current and future conditions.

## FATE AND FREE WILL

The issue of fate versus free will was discussed very early on, most notably by Plotinus (c. A.D. 205–270), a Neoplatonist, in the *Enneads*. Wrote Plotinus, "The movements of the stars announce the future for all things, but they do not shape the future. . . . Celestial movements are indications, not causes," which is a viewpoint astrologers agree with today. Astrology does not suggest that events are inevitable or predestined, but that there are positive or negative trends or influences that will offer you a choice of action. Everyone has free will. Taking responsibility for our actions is a very basic and important part of astrology's focus in the twenty-first century.

## THE ZODIAC AS CIRCLE OF LIFE

The word *zodiac* comes from a Greek root meaning "circle of animals," with *zo* meaning animal. Although *zodiac* means Circle of Animals, the zodiac is not composed only of animals. It also contains three fully human signs and, interestingly enough, all three are the intellectual "air" signs,

*The Special Number Twelve*

*Have you ever noticed how often you come across the number twelve as significant in life? There were twelve apostles, twelve tribes of Israel, and twelve gates to Jerusalem. In mythology there were twelve Titans, one of a family of giants who were born of chaos and were the fathers of the twelve gods and goddesses of Mount Olympus. Hercules is said to have gone through twelve Labors. Recovering alcoholics follow a twelve-step program. There are twelve chromatic tones in a Western musical scale. The twelfth day of Christmas followed by Epiphany is called the Twelfth Night. We send twelve roses to the one we love. There are, of course, twelve months of the year, and our days contain two equal parts of twelve hours each. The number twelve suggests completion of sorts, one that will require a certain journey or set of tasks before one can experience the whole. That is certainly true of the richly complex horoscope, which reflects all of life.*

Gemini (the twins), Libra (the scales), and Aquarius (the water bearer). You might also add Sagittarius, the centaur, who is half man and half horse. Accordingly, many astrologers prefer to call the zodiac the Circle of Life.

## WHAT HAPPENS WHEN A NEW PLANET IS DISCOVERED?

When a new planet is discovered, astrologers judge its influence by looking at the events prevalent in the world at the time of discovery. The rationale is that planets are located at a time when society is most ready to expand or shift its consciousness and is able to assimilate the new information fully. For example, Pluto was discovered in 1930, near the inception of the atom bomb, World War II, and the Holocaust, so astrologers assigned Pluto's influence to death and destruction but ultimately to full transformation. These influences were already associated with Scorpio, so Pluto was made the ruler of Scorpio, and Mars was associated as a sub-ruler. Similar decisions were made when Uranus and Neptune were found, and they were assigned to Aquarius and Pisces, respectively.

## WHAT ABOUT ASTEROIDS AND CHIRON (THE MOON OF PLUTO)?

In recent years you might have noticed that some forecasts mention some newly discovered asteroids or Chiron, Pluto's moon. I don't acknowledge these celestial bodies here or in my Internet column. I am a purist and feel Chiron, although important, cannot be "weighted" with the same influence as a planet. The Sun, the Moon, and the planets exert the most powerful influence in a horoscope. I realize this view is somewhat controversial.

## WHY DOES THE SUN MATTER MORE THAN THE PLANETS?

The Sun holds a special place in the horoscope because the Sun is the center of our solar system, the brilliant star that creates and sustains all life on Earth. All the planets in our solar system orbit around the Sun. The Sun is the reflector of ego and determination and shows in a chart where you will shine. Thus, we read "Sun signs" for a very good reason: The Sun is the key that an astrologer notices first when a chart is cast.

## WHAT IF I WAS BORN ON THE CUSP OF TWO SUN SIGNS?

I get hundreds of letters from readers asking me what happens if they

### What Is the Difference Between the Personal Planets and the Outer Planets?

*The so-called personal planets are those that stay closer to the Sun, such as Mercury, Venus, the Moon, Mars, Saturn, and Jupiter. Those were the ones the ancients saw with their naked eye, and the closer planets are to the Sun the more quickly they move. Those planets have a very direct yet short-lived influence on your life.*

*The distant planets, Uranus, Neptune, and Pluto, have wider and longer influence, because they take a longer time to orbit the Sun. As these slow-moving planets inch along the sky degree by degree, they occupy a longer visit to each of the constellations of the zodiac they visit, thus yielding a deeper and more indelible influence on us. These three outer planets affect entire generations, setting up questions and themes that societies work on as a whole. But they also have a long-term major impact on our personal lives. They are the "heavy hitters" of the zodiac, affecting both individuals and society as a whole.*

can't quite figure out which sign they are because they were born on the cusp, in the middle of two adjacent signs. "Which sign should I read for?" readers ask. The answer is that there are no sharp divisions in the sky. If you are born on the cusp of a sign you are quite lucky, because you are a true blend of *both* signs. For example, if you are a Gemini-Cancer, you have the superb reasoning of a journalist but also the heart of a romantic, and are quite intuitive. Thus this mingling of signs should help the Gemini side of you find that "whole truth and nothing but the truth" by letting hunches and feelings guide you closer to full discovery. Many "cuspers" have the best of both signs.

Probably the only way to know for sure which sign you most resemble is to have your horoscope chart cast. Keep in mind that Mercury, Venus, and the Sun often travel close together, so chances are you may have more planets in one sign or the other. That, too, would tip the scales one way or the other. The best way to tell which sign to read for without having your chart cast is to look over the descriptions of both signs and see which seem to fit you more closely.

Be aware that the dates of demarcation of the signs can change very slightly from year to year, depending on the exact moment the sun moves into that constellation at zero degrees. One book may list Aquarius as starting on January 20, and another may say it starts on January 19. The reason for this discrepancy is that although a year is 365 days long, it takes the Sun 365 days, 4 hours, 35 minutes, and 12 seconds to make a complete rotation through all twelve signs of the zodiac. Every four years we correct this slight variance with a leap year, and we further add the provision that in centuries not divisible by 400 there won't be a leap year. So one year one Sun sign might begin at 11:55 P.M. but the following year it may not begin until 12:01 A.M. of the following day. (This may even vary by time zones.) Magazine and book publishers simply take the most common demarcation date because that's the only reasonable way to do it. However, don't get too "stuck" on the dates of the signs—figure out which sign sounds more like you and reasonates more powerfully within you. There is no right or wrong answer.

Finally, remember what a wonderful ring that expression has, to be "on the cusp" of anything in life—in everyday language we use this term to mean being on the verge of something new, and that alone can denote plenty of energy and vitality. Indeed, that probably describes you well!

## What if I Don't Know the Exact Time of my Birth?

*If you don't know your time of birth, the astrologer will do a sunrise chart, which places your Sun on the ascendant. It is the best she or he can do until you find out the actual time you were born (you will need the hour and minute of birth). If that is going to be impossible, there is something called chart rectification, where an astrologer uses major events in your timeline to ascertain your true time of birth, working through the chart backward in time. Because a chart is based on mathematics, any astrologer can go backward or forward in time by studying the ephemeris, or book of tables of planetary orbits.*

## WHAT IS A RISING SIGN?

The rising sign or ascendant (as it is also called) is the sign of the constellation that was dominant on the eastern horizon at the moment you were born. Some people know their rising sign because they had their horoscope chart cast to the year, month, day, and exact time (to the minute) and converted that information to Greenwich Mean Time. All astrologers need your place of birth so that they can convert your chart to the same spot on Earth, as a common denominator. Because of the rotation of the Earth, a new sign rises on the Earth's horizon approximately every two hours, so the exact degrees of your rising sign also matter.

The rising sign, or ascendant, explains why people of all signs are not alike. We are all a blend of *both* the rising sign and the Sun sign, and knowing both signs is important. For instance, if you were born in August, you will be a Leo Sun sign forever, and should always read for Leo, but if you have Scorpio rising, you will always be part Scorpio as well and should also read for that sign. This is somewhat of an oversimplification, for all the planets of a chart have to be noted (especially the Moon, the repository of emotions), but the rising sign is so vital that once you discover it you should never forget it. Remember it as faithfully as you would your telephone number, because you will get a much more three-dimensional view of your chart when reading your personality profile and forecasts of both the ascendant and rising sign. It is said the ascendant sign reflects the qualities you accepted naturally and blend with your Sun sign.

## What Is My Ruling Planet?

Each person has two ruling planets, the planet that rules the Sun sign and the planet that rules the rising sign. Both planets impart a strong influence on your personality. (The only exception to this is when the Sun sign and the rising sign are the same.) When your astrologer makes a forecast for your current trends, the comings and goings and meetings and communications between your ruling planets and other planets have to be noted. Whatever your ruler happens to be doing has special bearing on your life.

All the planets continually move, and when they are positioned at special angles in relation to one another (within a very narrow band of specified mathematical degrees), they start a "conversation" that lasts for a certain length of time. This is called a planetary aspect, and it may linger for a day or for several weeks, until the two (or more) planets spin off on their separate ways. If the conversation is one that sets up a good trend, then your astrologer will urge you to act within that narrow window of time.

## Why It Is Harder to Have Aquarius Rising than Libra Rising?

The concept of long and short ascension of the rising sign is quite fascinating. One might assume that you have an equal chance of having any one of the twelve signs as a rising sign. However, because of the curvature of the Earth and the angle of its axis, some signs, the signs of long ascension, require more time to rise above the horizon than do the signs of short ascension. In the Northern Hemisphere, the signs of short ascension are Capricorn, Aquarius, Pisces, Aries, Taurus, and Gemini; therefore you would be less likely to see these signs rising than the others. In the

Southern Hemisphere, the signs of short ascension are Cancer, Leo, Virgo, Libra, Scorpio, and Sagittarius.

## WHAT DOES IT MEAN WHEN PEOPLE SAY THEY ARE A DOUBLE PISCES OR A TRIPLE SCORPIO?

When people say they are a double Pisces, they mean they have a Pisces Sun sign and also have Pisces rising. In other words, the Sun sign and the rising sign are in the same sign. Those who say they are a triple Scorpio mean they have both the Sun and a rising sign as well as the Moon in the same sign of Scorpio, which is an unusual occurrence.

## HOW CAN I BEST LEARN ABOUT MY CHART?

There are no bad signs or good signs. Everyone is a blend of ten heavenly bodies, a rich and complex blend of symbolism in a horoscope that defies off-the-cuff, cookie-cutter descriptions. Once you know the basic descriptions and mythologies of the various signs and you have had your horoscope chart read, you can fuse your understanding of the signs with your understanding of each planet. Learning astrology is a long and enjoyable process that can't be rushed; it unfolds to show the great beauty underlying the mathematics of the universe.

## HOW A CAPRICORN COULD BE MORE LIKE A TAURUS (TRANSLATION: WHY ARE SOME PEOPLE NOT TYPICAL OF THEIR SIGN?)

The horoscope wheel represents the signs of the zodiac with twelve slices called houses that cover various areas of life. Each house is "owned" by a different sign of the zodiac—this is that sign's piece of real estate. The first house (found where the number 9 would be on the face of a clock and symbolizing the eastern horizon) is ruled by Aries. Proceeding counterclockwise to the second house, we find the house that is "owned" by Taurus. The third house belongs to Gemini, and so forth, as we go counterclockwise through all the signs, ending with Pisces, the sign found at the very end of winter.

For demonstration, let's say you are a Capricorn but have several planets in the second house. This configuration would indicate a strong Taurus shading to your personality simply because you have such a heavy concentration of planets in the part of the horoscope that is considered Taurus's home base. (This is important to note once you have your customized chart.) This is an example of the brilliant way astrology works. You don't have to be born in May to have a personality very similar to a Taurus, and this is applicable to anyone of any sign, thus explaining why some people claim that they are not typical of their sign.

## LOOKING AT THE HOROSCOPE WHEEL: NOTING IF MOST PLANETS FALL ABOVE OR BELOW THE HORIZON, AND EAST OR WEST

When an astrologer looks at a horoscope wheel, one of the first things he or she will notice is whether most of the planets fall above or below the "horizon" line. (If the horoscope were the face of a clock, the horizon would be the line that would stretch across from the numbers 9 to 3). People with planets above the horizon have planets "in daylight." People with this configuration tend to be more interested in developing their leadership qualities and are slightly more extroverted and objective. Those below the horizon deal better in the realm of intuition and instinct, are more interested in developing their creativity, and tend to be slightly more private. This division of the horoscope wheel is tied to the signs of the zodiac, with Aries through Virgo falling below the horizon and Libra through Pisces falling above the horizon.

The wheel of the horoscope is again divided in half vertically (if it were the face of a clock, imagine a string that spans from the "12" on the top to the "6" on the bottom). Planets on the left side of the wheel are said to be easterly and engender more self-reliance, while planets on the right side are called westerly and would give a person talent with working in collaborative, team situations.

### A Map of Life: The Four Major Quadrants
### of the Wheel

If you look at the four quadrants of a chart,
you will see a mirror of the progress of man
in those quadrants. The cross itself is a symbol of matter being manifested, and thus, the
horoscope is a wheel of life.

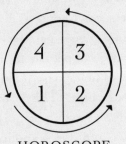

HOROSCOPE

The first quadrant is symbolized by Aries, Taurus,
and Gemini, and encourages individual development, the understanding of
one's sense of self, gaining a sense of possession and a handle on language
and communication. The second quadrant, still on the lower part of the
horoscope but now on the right or western side, rules Cancer, Leo, and Virgo,
and this quadrant covers mankind's important relationships as we start to
mature, such as the interrelationships with parents and children, teachers,
and co-workers, and even how we experience our first, fresh love affair as we
venture out into the world.

Proceeding in a counterclockwise fashion, we come to the third quadrant,
and in this quadrant for the first time we are now above the horizon. This
signals a point in time when we are "coming out of ourselves" and are now
more aware of our responsibility to others: spouse, business associates,
merchants, teachers, and those we meet when we travel far from home.
This area of the chart is one of cooperation in a one-on-one mode and
marks a special stage in mankind's development as well as an individual's.

Finally, on the left side of the upper part of the chart, we come to the
final, fourth quadrant, ruling Capricorn, Aquarius, and Pisces. By the
time the wheel has turned to the fourth quadrant, man is aware that he
is part of a larger whole. He is aware of the society or group to which he
belongs, and there is a growing awareness within him of the need to give
something back to the world, whether in thanks or to leave a mark.

This quadrant requires that we give something back to society through charitable efforts, leadership on the job, artistic works, or by setting a good example.

## WHEN IT COMES TO SUN SIGNS, OPPOSITES ARE LINKED

Each of the signs of the zodiac is also linked in a special way to its opposite sign on the same axis. For example, if you are a Cancer, there are qualities that complement the sign that falls six months from your birthday, which would be Capricorn. While at first glance the two signs may seem to have nothing in common, if you look closer you will see they work on some of the very same issues. For example: Cancer starts life, and its polar opposite, Capricorn, sustains it. (Cancer is the crab that comes up from the sea of creation, while Capricorn is the hardworking and ambitious goat that has big goals and achieves much—a father figure who can provide for his family and for the community.)

Astrologers call your opposite sign your polar opposite. That opposite sign represents some of the unrealized or unmanifested qualities you may want to develop, consciously or unconsciously. Carl Jung, one of astrology's greatest modern thinkers, wrote about the bright and dark sides that form the whole of personality. Each sign has something to gain by learning from its polar opposite. Aries symbolizes the life force and is necessarily self-absorbed, to bring ventures forth. Libra, its opposite, is "outer-directed" and puts the wishes and feelings of partners first. Aries has to be self-absorbed to hurl those figurative life-forms into being, but it would be wise for Aries to take a page from Libra's notebook concerning effective partnering—Libras are brilliant collaborators. Similarly, Libras put others' wishes first so often that it might be wise for them to become more conscious of their own needs, in a way that Aries can teach. So you see that each sign has its contribution to make. If you learn from your opposite sign, you will complete your sign's personality in a particularly effective way.

## ADJACENT SUN SIGNS CONTRAST ONE ANOTHER AND
## CORRECT FOR WHAT'S MISSING

There is even more elegance to the zodiac. Each sign corrects for the qualities of the signs that come before and after it. For example, Sagittarius balances Scorpio's awesome deal-making business intensity by being curious about more academic pursuits in the field of higher education, publishing, and travel. Scorpios are able to concentrate their awesome power, but they are not known to be highly social. In fact, Scorpio likes to be alone a great deal. However the sign that precedes Scorpio, charming, easygoing Libra, is one of the most social signs of the zodiac. Libra is a sign that likes to partner with others and likes to make introductions. Each of the signs comes to the table with gifts to share with the others, and each sign contributes a necessary and

important insight. When reading about your sign, keep in mind that everyone possesses a broad spectrum of traits but what we describe astrologically are the dominant ones, the ones your friends and family might list first when they characterize you. These dominant traits are reflected most strongly in your Sun sign and rising sign, and also in your Moon sign.

## ASTROLOGY IS BASED ON THE
## SYMBOLISM OF THE SEASONS OF
## THE NORTHERN HEMISPHERE

You will see references to the moods of nature of the Northern Hemisphere reflected in the description of your sign. The soft colors and verdant fertility of nature we see in May, for instance,

*Northern Hemisphere vs.*
*Southern Hemisphere*

*If you were born (or live) in the Southern Hemisphere, will your chart and an astrologer's forecasts be correct for your sign?*
*No matter where you happen to have been born on this planet (or where you live now), the personality profiles of the various signs and the forecasts for those signs should still be relevant to you. There is a strong consensus in the astrologic community that this is true. Whether you live in India, America, Africa, New Zealand, or even the South Pole, your sign's description (as well as my forecasts on the Internet) should ring true for you.*

are reflected in Taurus's love of comfort and sensuality. As another example, the harsh, frozen landscape and bright clear skies of January encourage Capricorn's rock-solid realism and energetic determination to overcome obstacles. On a larger scale, the Sun moves through the months of the year, and the seasons symbolize the stages of mankind.

At the spring and fall equinox (*equinox* is a Latin word meaning "equal" or "balanced"), the days have equal daylight and evening light. In the spring, the days get longer, and after the fall equinox they get shorter. In astrology, daylight symbolizes individuality and singularity, while evening or night symbolizes our link to the community and universal thinking. People born in Aries (at the spring equinox) are more involved with developing their truest sense of self or ego, while Libras, born at the opposite time, the fall equinox, would be more attuned to their alter ego and be especially interested in developing productive partnerships. Yet both are born at the time of year when daylight and nighttime are fairly equal (as are those born at the later parts of Pisces and Virgo). This means that these four signs would have a finger on the pulse on the collective consciousness and would resonate in an uncanny way to what people value and need. A sign like Gemini would tip slightly more toward individuality. Its opposite sign, philosophical Sagittarius, is concerned with learning, reflecting on, and preserving the information that Sagittarius's opposite sign, Gemini, collects (figuratively). Thus, Sagittariuses are more fully immersed in the world community (the whole), in protecting the information in the libraries and other repositories in the world. There is an elegant symmetry in astrology on every level.

## MASCULINE AND FEMININE SIGNS: FINDING OUT IF YOU ARE A "LOVER" OR "BELOVED" TYPE

Signs alternate between masculine and feminine energies. The term *masculine* signifies a positive, aggressive, pioneering charge. The term *feminine* refers to a negative, receptive, or more passive charge. So, starting with Aries, the sign is masculine; next is Taurus, which is feminine; followed by Gemini, another masculine sign; and so forth through the zodiac to Pisces, which is feminine, receptive, and magnetic (rather than assertive and pioneering). Be aware that if you are a man with a feminine sign, such as Capricorn, you aren't any less of a man. These influences are very subtle. It simply means you have a charming way that allows you to attract others to you rather than having to go out and sell your ideas aggressively. If you are a woman with a masculine energy, you simply have plenty of "get-up-and-go." You like to control your fate more energetically than some other signs. The world is divided into lovers (those who work to impose their ideas on the world) and beloveds (those who get to pick and choose among the ideas presented). Everyone is more comfortable with one or the other. Your horoscope, including your Sun sign, will tell you which you happen to be. Keep in mind that one should take all the planets in a chart into account, but the Sun sign and ascendant do matter a great deal.

## Why Astrology Works

Nobody knows why astrology works—yet. The world and our bodies are known to resonate to various cycles, and it is known that the Moon rules the tides, and that various species seem to be strongly influenced by the Sun and the Moon. For example, oyster's shells open and shut at regular intervals, and this timing was once presumed to be matched to the tides of the sea. Through recent experiments by the scientist J. R. Brown, when oysters were transported in sealed tanks and brought to his laboratory in Evanston, Illinois (near Chicago), approximately1,000 miles from the sea, the batch of oysters behaved as if they were still in the sea, opening and shutting their shells on a schedule that matched their home tides. However, two weeks later the oysters had reset their internal clocks to coincide with the phases of the Moon in the city where they now lived, proving that the Moon, not the tides, controlled the cycles of the oysters. Scientists also know that solar flares and storms interfere with radio transmissions on Earth, and they have also discovered that there is an increase in auto accidents—up to four times the usual rate—just prior to and after these storms.

One interesting theory about how conditions in the universe influence our personalities points to magnetic fields that may be intensified by the Sun and then imprint signals on a baby's nervous system, acting as an antenna to prevailing frequencies at the moment it is born. Most astrologers proscribe to the axiom in astrology that allows for synchronicity in the universe. The universe is alive and whole, so things that happen here on Earth are but a microcosm of what is occurring in the heavens.

## WHAT DOES THE "AGE OF AQUARIUS" MEAN?
## WERE THERE OTHER "AGES"?

The world is now entering the Age of Aquarius, a phenomenon that refers to the Earth's orbit or movement backward (in "retrograde" motion) into the constellation of Aquarius. The Earth will spend time in each constellation. From the birth of Christ to now, the Earth has been in the Age of Pisces and, prior to that, in the Age of Aries. It will take the Earth 25,868 years to visit all twelve signs. Dividing 25,868 by twelve signs will give you roughly 2,100 years to a particular "age." Thus, we will remain in the Age of Aquarius for over 2,000 years.

The "precession of the equinoxes" that underlies this principle was first discovered by the Greek astronomer Hipparchus of Nicaea (c. 160–125 B.C.) and is due to a slight wobble in the Earth's rotation. This also means that the dates encompassing the signs have shifted somewhat from the original dates. The *precession of the equinoxes* is a term that describes the constellation that lies behind the Sun at the vernal equinox, which changes gradually over time. Rather than negate the dates of the Sun signs, this precession adds a unique tone to each of the signs; a new and subtle blending of personality characteristics seems to be underway. Classical astrologers do not feel that the precession of the equinoxes changes the inherent qualities of the signs. Just as world events are looked at when choosing the influence of new planets and do not change, it is possible that because astrology was discovered at a certain time and place, those descriptions of the signs were meant to endure and remain unchanged.

## WHEN, APPROXIMATELY, DID THE AGE OF PISCES EXIST AND WHAT IS ITS SYMBOLISM?

During the past approximately two thousand years, the world has been going through what we the call the Age of Pisces because the Earth has been spinning in retrograde motion through the constellation of Pisces. Astrologers don't quite agree on the exact date when one age ends and the new one begins (some astrologers feel we are in the Age of Aquarius now, and others say we are still a few hundred years away). Nevertheless, everyone agrees that the past one thousand years was the Age of Pisces, a time when the age of Christianity came alive.

When astrologers speak about the Age of Pisces or the Age of Aquarius, they are referring to the Earth's movement backward (or in retrograde motion) into one of the twelve signs of the zodiac. As stated in the previous section (p. 39), the Earth spends roughly 2,100 years in each particular "age."

Since the Earth is moving in retrograde motion, the age we have just left (or are about to leave) is the Age of Pisces, which marked the years from A.D. 1 to A.D. 2000, and that coincides with the age of Christ and Christianity. Pisces is considered the last sign of the zodiac, a compilation of all the signs that came before it. As the sign known for universal love, compassion, and altruism, Pisces know the truth of the universe but can't quite say why they know it. Pisces know that the concept of "truth" is always in flux. To Pisces, an introspective sign, what lies within the human heart is trustworthy, for feelings reveal the soul. This mode of approaching the world colored everything new people encountered during that period, and part of the Age of Pisces was also called the Age of Faith.

The emphasis on the washing of the feet as a significant ritual signifying purification of spirit ties into Pisces' symbolism, for Pisces rules the feet. Pisces "carry" the cares of others and often have sore feet. Christ spoke of his role as servant to his flock. Again, we see this as a very Pisces notion;

Pisces says, "I believe" (whereas Aquarius, the age we are in now or will soon enter, says, "Prove it to me scientifically").

Mary, Christ's mother, embodied all the qualities of Pisces' polarity to Virgo, namely, modesty, commitment to service, and passive acceptance of what must not be changed. In Pisces there is a strong need for individual seclusion, and Christianity puts value on retreats, convents, cloisters, or spiritual pilgrimages—the places inhabited by monks and nuns as well as deeply religious people. Conversely, as we move into the Age of Aquarius there will be more emphasis on group activities and community, thus we have the Internet and the eye of the global village that we call television. Aquarius is very social. Pisces likes people too, but needs regular time away to rinse themselves of the troubles of others they unconsciously keep collecting.

As discussed in "Pisces Personality," abstinence is appropriate at the time of Pisces' birth, for it is a time when the Earth rests in preparation for the coming spring. Food provisions, once abundant at the autumn harvest, are at their lowest point by March, for it is the end of winter.

Further evidence of Pisces' links to spirituality is the fact that the Christians chose the fish as a secret symbol to identify themselves as followers of Christ. (Pisces, as ruler of the twelfth house, also rules secrets and underground activities.) Jesus asked his followers to be "fishers of men," and the word *Bethlehem* means, literally, "House of Bread." In one parable Jesus washes the feet of Mary Magdalene, and Christians interpret that to demonstrate Jesus' humbleness and the kind message that all people are welcome in the kingdom of God.

Neptune, Pisces' ruler, will always be the planet to suggest areas in any chart where there will be faith, love, charity, and hope, for each of us has Neptune placed somewhere in our charts. It will also suggest a blurring of edges or softening of lines, even a dissolution and general unraveling of a situation. Neptune's effects are, like water, slow and gradual. Think of water slowly wearing down the sharp edges of a rock to make it smooth to the touch. Neptune gives Pisces, and in a wider sense each of us, creativity and inspiration. As the higher octave of Venus, Neptune teaches us to take love to a higher, more spiritual realm. One wonders what Earth would be like without this lovely planet of inspiration that teaches us not only to reach for the stars but also to reach out to each other in our hour of need.

As we move into the Age of Aquarius we won't simply discard all we have learned in the past two thousand years, but hopefully we will carry it with us and use it as we become more developed and enlightened. No matter what religion or way of life one chooses, Pisces urges mankind simply to believe, deeply, in the universal power of love.

## DO AQUARIUSES FEEL ESPECIALLY HAPPY DURING THEIR OWN AGE?

It is possible that members of this sign feel strongly in tune with events, moods, and fashions of the day. (That is always the case whenever a number of planets move into your sign—there's a feeling of more cosmic support, and more planets tend to be in your sign near the time of your birthday.) Aquarius is the sign of new inventions, high technology and scientific advances, strong social justice, and a sense of community—all areas due for vast development in years to come. Keep in mind, however, that the influence is subtle, like gentle background music, because the sign of an age affects the overall focus and direction of society.

During the Age of Aries, 2000 B.C. to A.D. 7, man learned about self-defense, while during the Age of Pisces, which lasted from the birth of Christ to A.D. 2000, the focus was on religion. Is what is learned lost when leaving one age and entering another? Hopefully not: Our knowledge and sensitivity keep increasing and evolving to an ever better place.

## DO THE PLANETS COMPEL OR MIRROR WHAT IS HAPPENING?

Is astrology the study of what influences the planets may have on our lives, or the study of how planets reflect, like a mirror, what is going on in our lives?

The answer is a little bit of both and yet actually neither, because
you get to make the final decisions. Studying the horoscope shows how the
planets are behaving—what communications they are making to one another
at certain times. Not all communications are equally important; some are
more vital than others. The movement of the planets sets up circumstances
that either reward or challenge. Astrology is the study of cycles that reoccur
regularly over time at differing intervals, although some of those cycles are
once-in-a-lifetime occurrences and others happen much more frequently. It is
fascinating that certain aspects help us revisit long-term issues over and over
so that even though the problem looks new, it is actually rooted in a similar
condition that happened some time ago. By studying the cycle we can get
clues about the core of the problem by examining what came before. Once
that is done, we can use our experience and apply what we learned to the
new one, to help us deal with the present more effectively.

Because the planets send signals to each other as they rotate along their
paths, they continually set up changing patterns and conditions. As above in
the heavens, so too, below here on Earth. We are a microcosm of what those
vibrations suggest. Yet the study of astrology is the study of the conditions we
face, not the decisions we make. Those choices will always be up to us.

The planetary "snapshot" for the day (mentioned in any astrologer's forecast)
will always be unique. The exact degrees and placements of each of the ten
heavenly bodies will never be repeated again in exactly the same way. This
goes for the day you were born: Your natal planetary patterns will never exist
again in the same way, even for others born on that day, for longitude and lat-
itude enter into the equation as well. This puts enormous responsibility upon
us to use our gifts to their best advantage. Anyone who has ever parented a
child knows that the specific traits and gifts given to that child are sacred; the
child is to be honored and valued for his or her precious individuality.

## THE VALUE OF THINKING LONG-TERM

Hearing my predictions about my life as a child did set up certain expecta-

tions and a sense of possibility within me. Seeing the big picture was important because it helped me visualize the future the way I wanted it to be.

The actual journey and quest have been, so far, even more exciting than
hearing those predictions, because neither my mother (who was making
those predictions) nor I could have imagined precisely how some of those
planetary influences would play out. Why? Because I, like you, have a
hand in what finally occurs and the direction my life is to take. I must
admit that working through life's struggles has been interesting so far,
even during those times when life was hard and didn't feel at all like fun.

If an astrologer suggests to you, for example, that you could live in
Europe, you might stop and think about that possibility. Some people may
say to themselves, "No thanks. I like it here." That is okay—you've given
it thought and rejected that option. Others may say, "How interesting! I
have always wanted to do that, but I never realized how much doing
something like that meant to me. I disregarded it because it seemed like a
pipe dream!" The latter person will be more encouraged to do something
about that goal. If your chart suggests that going for that dream would be
met with favorable opportunities, it will be more easily accomplished for
someone with good aspects than for someone without them.

In short, the aspects will suggest, but you get to decide. The fact is, it is
up to us to figure things out, and we can't shirk that responsibility. The
stars offer benefits, like ripe fruit from a tree, to choose either to take or
leave, and so too with challenges; to confront or avoid.

## THE FORCE OF PERSONALITY IS ALL
The point is that the force of your personality determines everything you
do and the outcome of all endeavors and relationships. Astrology makes
this clear to us, for the first house of the horoscope drives the entire chart
in whatever direction the person wants to take it. If you've ever written a
story or poem, cooked a new dish, taken photographs, composed a song,

or painted a canvas, you learned a little more about yourself through the creative process. That feeling of discovery can be exciting and intoxicating. The process of living is hugely creative too, for you constantly learn more about who you are and what you are capable of doing and giving to the world, not only in the career, money, or charitable sense, but in terms of close personal relationships as well.

Your nature is revealed through the decisions you make as well as through the people and things you value along the way. If we are doing things in accordance with the universe, we learn to enjoy and celebrate the differences in ourselves as well as in others. If we aren't getting things right, the universe nudges us back on track. The point is, the journey is fascinating and beautiful, and certainly not predetermined.

## WHAT ARE THE ELEMENTS? EARTH, FIRE, AIR, AND WATER

All the astrological signs are evenly divided into four main elements of earth, fire, air, and water. Knowing which element rules *you* will help explain some of your basic temperamental qualities. Knowing which element predominates in other people will help you understand and communicate with them better. Keep in mind that we are studying only Sun signs. A professional astrologer would assess *all* the elements of your planets, including your rising sign and various planets. However, the Sun is very important in the horoscope—it is the lead luminary in our universe around which all the other planets orbit, so of course it does merit extra attention.

### Earth: Taurus, Virgo, and Capricorn

Earth signs possess the gift of making dreams and plans real and tangible. Highly ambitious, earth signs have their feet firmly planted on the ground and know what it takes to get things done. They understand deadlines, teamwork, and budgets, and are marvelous producers and builders of things because they always get results. While an earth sign might not be drawn to start things in the way a fire sign might, earth's awesome talent is in making existing structures more sturdy, established, and secure, often building endeavors to the next level. Earth also understands power and influence. Earth signs are also quite sensual. They use their five senses in a powerful way. They usually love beautiful objects and take very good care of them. Earth signs are also reserved, and don't need the spotlight; in fact, they often prefer to work offstage, because they know that this is very likely where the real influences lies.

### Fire: Aries, Leo, and Sagittarius

Fire signs are highly creative and enjoy playing with new concepts. They are warm-hearted, enjoy being the center of attention, and like the stimulation of being with others. Their energy often burns brightest when they exchange ideas with others and, because fire needs room to breathe, they like being their own boss. Fire signs are known to be impulsive, spontaneous, sometimes even a bit eccentric. These signs are enthusiastic too, "catching fire" to new ideas and plans. Often natural leaders, they don't mind being the very first to try new things. Fire signs are the zodiac's trendsetters.

### Air: Gemini, Aquarius, and Libra

Air signs are highly intelligent. They love to analyze facts and make judgments. Curious, playful, and very verbal, they are the pure communicators of the zodiac. They sparkle in a crowd because they know lots of juicy news and information. They are meant to be out and about, socializing—they seem to know *everyone* and they increase their energy by being around others. Breezy and easygoing, air signs get along with many types of people. They rarely hold grudges; rather, they say what they need to say to "clear the air" and then forget the matter completely. These are the "people persons" of the zodiac, truly interested in others. Air signs are able to form very close personal relationships and often have friends for life.

### Water: Cancer, Scorpio, and Pisces

Water signs are more emotional and more intuitive than other signs, often displaying psychic ability. Having sharply honed emotions makes them compassionate, caring, and nurturing. Water purifies and cleanses and could even be a bit mysterious too, so water signs reveal themselves more slowly than the others. There is always something going on inside that they have to think about a little more before they are ready to share those thoughts. These signs *feel* events around them, and those instinctive feelings are usually right. Their skill at reading body language is remarkable. Water signs easily pick up on the true emotions and moods of others. Being so giving and sensitive can sometimes be exhausting, so the gentle water signs need to be alone occasionally, to recharge and refresh themselves, before going back into the world. Water signs are, like fire signs, often very creative.

## WHOM DO YOU GET ALONG WITH BEST?

*If you are an earth sign (Taurus, Capricorn, or Virgo)* you will get along with other earth signs or water (Pisces, Cancer, and Scorpio). Fire and earth don't cut the mustard, since earth puts out fire's brightness. Earth and air simply coexist, but the relationship is nothing special.

*If you are an air sign (Gemini, Aquarius, or Libra)* you will get along great with other air signs, as well as water (Pisces, Cancer, and Scorpio), or even with fire (Sagittarius, Leo, and Aries). Earth, however, will suffocate you.

*If you are a fire sign (Leo, Sagittarius, or Aries)* you will click with other fire signs as well as air signs (Gemini, Aquarius, and Libra). Water will put out your lights, as will earth.

*If you are a water sign (Pisces, Cancer, or Scorpio)* you groove with other water signs or air signs (Gemini, Libra, or Aquarius), or with earth (Taurus, Virgo, or Capricorn). Fire and water isn't a good mix.

If the special person you like isn't right for your sign, *don't despair;* we all have *several* planets in our horoscopes, so the Sun sign is only one of many planets that needs to be on your wavelength. There is still a very good chance this person might be right for you.

## WHAT ARE THE QUALITIES?
## THE CARDINAL, FIXED, AND MUTABLE SIGNS

As you delve into astrology, you will find that the human attributes are based on the natural rhythms of nature. So each sign is put into a category that is assigned a special role to play in relationship to its placement within the four seasons. These qualities or modes have been part of astrology since Ptolemy wrote about them in early Greece. Like the elements, the qualities seem to be a Greek insight. There seems to be no mention of them before then. The number twelve, which is so prevalent in astrology, comes up here too, when one considers that there are four elements and now three qualities (cardinal, fixed, and mutable); three times four equals twelve and represents a full balance of masculine and feminine energies.

### The Cardinal Signs: Aries (Spring), Cancer (Summer), Libra (Autumn), and Capricorn (Winter)

If you are a cardinal sign, your sign's job is to initiate the season, to be the leader sign that *brings forth* that season. In fact the word *cardinal* means "first" or "principal." The word comes from the Latin *cardinalis*, meaning "principal" or "pivotal," and, interestingly, is related to the word *cardo*, a root word that means "hinge."

Cardinal signs are pioneering and enterprising. They need a cause or endeavor to channel their excess energy or they will get restless and even frustrated. People born with cardinal signs are go-getters and respond favorably to change. They like to start projects and are also very goal-oriented. Some astrologers have likened cardinal signs to firstborn children because cardinal signs make terrific leaders. They certainly like to take initiative because they are born with a strong sense of urgency.

### The Fixed Signs: Taurus (Spring), Leo (Summer), Scorpio (Autumn), and Aquarius (Winter)

If you are a fixed sign, your sign's job is to maintain and make indelible the qualities of the season when you were born. The fixed signs consolidate and make permanent that which the cardinal signs began and are very determined and able to concentrate exceedingly well. Basically loners, they have a high level of self-assurance. The downside of fixed signs is that they usually don't like to change their viewpoint or lifestyle. Nevertheless, fixed signs ultimately achieve much success due to their strong persistence and perseverance.

The word *fixed* comes from the latin *fixus*, the past participle of *figere*, meaning "to fasten," or "to latch on to." Fixed signs follow the cardinal signs and, as the ones found in the middle of the season, they express the truest, perhaps most pure, form of that season. Fixed signs concentrate energy and solidify ideas. They are enormously stable.

In early Christianity, the four writers of the gospels became associated with the fixed signs. Matthew was typified as the man (a man is also a symbol for Aquarius); Mark was the lion (his symbol was the lion of Saint Mark, the emblem of Venice, and is also the traditional icon for Leo). Luke was personified as the ox, also a Taurus icon, and finally John was the eagle, Scorpio's symbol. Fixed signs are known for their great endurance and fortitude in the face of all odds.

It is interesting to note that the middle degree of the fixed signs (since there are thirty degrees in a sign, fifteen degrees is the midpoint) is the strongest and represents the maximum force of power. (That would refer to those fixed signs born approximately on the sixth of the month.) When a fixed-sign planet moves into that fifteenth degree, it is considered very significant because important ideas or promises that are related to structure always come up then.

### The Mutable Signs: Gemini (Spring), Virgo (Summer), Sagittarius (Autumn), and Pisces (Winter)

Finally, we have the mutable signs, and if that describes you, your sign is the third (and final) month within each season. The word *mutable* comes from the Latin *mutabilis*, and *mutare*, "to change." *To mute* and *mutate* are other forms of the word. The role for these signs is to prepare for the transition to the next season.

Mutable signs make great communicators and teachers. They are highly flexible, visionary people full of innovative ideas and concepts. Mutable signs prepare us for the next season, hurrying us along and assuring us not to worry about what is coming. These signs enjoy change and are focused on what comes next.

The mutable signs, born at the end of each season after the cardinal and fixed signs, mark the end of the old and the beginning of the new, and they are the most flexible of signs. Strongly verbal, analytical, and intellectual, these signs excel in social situations. When they are upset they express their views openly. They are excellent in crisis situations, for they quickly perceive what needs to be done, and, being highly adaptable, they can respond to shifting conditions. They are talented at coming up with alternate methods to overcome obstacles. These are the signs that have the ability to turn on a dime in times of difficulty, a trait so necessary for survival and ultimate success. Mutable signs realize that nothing is more constant than change, and therein lies their power.

## IS ASTROLOGY AN ART OR A SCIENCE?

Astrology is a beautiful blend of science and art. In its use of mathematics, cycles, and patterns, it acts as a science, and with its emphasis on the decoding of planetary symbols and ancient myths, it acts as an art. Hence, astrology utilizes both the left and right hemispheres of the brain and forces us to integrate both. Success in astrology depends on both technical ability and artistry, and the study of astrology takes years to get right. Even so, new insights will continually occur. Because astrology is an art, the astrologer must be experienced enough to blend many aspects at once, unlike computers, which look at only one aspect at a time and sometimes come up with conflicting interpretations. A human can more effectively weigh all the aspects and integrate them into a cohesive whole.

The astrologer strives to pinpoint upcoming trends and to forecast the best ways to take advantage of them and, in times of stress, to minimize discomfort and maximize options and growth. The astrologer also strives to delineate the delicate shadings of the personality, looking to understand the psychology of the person he or she is reading so that fresh insights can emerge. The horoscope holds overlapping cycles—it is truly three-dimensional, so all charts are complex and hold certain riddles. Cracking the code is a fascinating process.

## YOUR STORY IS NEVER FINISHED

When we feel we have seen our darkest hour—and nobody escapes feeling hardship and sadness at times in life—the magic and truth about the process is knowing that as long as you are alive, your story is never done. Miracles can—and do—happen all the time. Your indomitable spirit will always prevail, because it reveals your will, the pure energy that drives your life.

# HOW TO USE ASTROLOGY

Almost all people are curious about the future, and this has been true through the ages of man, across time and geography. Carrying a sense of hope and optimism each day is very important, as a bright outlook allows us to control our lives more effectively in an active, energetic way.

Like the scores of generations that have come before, we long to have a better understanding of and perspective on the challenges life presents. We yearn to know when certain difficulties will end, and astrology can give us clues. However, that does not prevent us from taking action, for not acting is still a decision in itself. To answer your most pressing questions, step out of yourself. View yourself as the star of a very important story, the story of your life.

Astrology is not predestination, nor does any astrologer purport to know exactly what you will choose to do. As students of astrology, we consider mathematical *probability*—not absolutes—and those pertain to the trends, not the final outcome. Astrology isn't fortune-telling, nor do astrologers speak of life being fated. As agents of free will, we always have choice. We need to drive our lives in the direction we choose or else risk having life's events control us. We usually have more choices than we think we do; our horoscopes can easily suggest possibilities that may have been overlooked.

We all want to live interesting lives that are filled with positive, enriching experiences, with new paths sprouting from time to time that delight and fascinate us. We also want plenty of love in our lives, both the romantic love from a mate or a special someone and the genuinely warm platonic love we receive from family and friends. In the process of living we also hope to be confirmed as unique individuals who have a purpose and place in this world. In a quest to live harmonious lives, we seek insight.

Traditional religious beliefs can provide inspiration and insight into how to live life in the ethical and moral sense, and through prayer, religious people can also find tremendous hope and comfort. I believe deeply in the power of prayer, and my religion will always play an enormously important role in my life. Astrology is not meant to be a replacement for religion or spirituality. Indeed, this very part of life is reflected in the ninth house of the horoscope wheel.

Astrology helps us think and grapple with life's mysteries by challenging us to ask such questions as: How can I allow myself to feel safer and more protected? What kinds of talents might I contribute to the world in my lifetime? What is special about me? Am I lovable? How can I be more generous, caring, or giving? Can I gain a perspective on a situation that has been hurtful? Have there been unrecognized recurring patterns in my life? Can I have happier relationships?

While astrology can't answer these questions directly, it can help find many answers by being a tool for self-discovery. By getting in touch with yourself and having a firmer, surer sense of who you are, you can better plan for the future. Astrology provides an organized system for creatively dealing with life's great questions. When it is time to act, astrology can offer you just the right amount of confidence to help you take that first step.

The best way to use astrology is as a creative brainstorming tool, to consider new possibilities. I call this book *Planets and Possibilities* because the planets offer us many more choices than we might otherwise see at any given time. When we're busy focusing on the details of our lives, most of us unconsciously continue to repeat our old formulas for success. Applying the same solutions to the same problems will only yield the same results. To affect a breakthrough, we need to consider new, sometimes rather random solutions. Opening up new lines of thinking will lead you to explore whole new worlds. Cast a wide net by asking, "What if?" and "Why not?" Let your horoscope chart speak loudly to you by bringing up all your options.

Astrology can help you work with the cycles of the universe. The beauty of the mathematical cycles that form the underpinnings of both the universe and astrology are fascinating and awe-inspiring. It has been said that the more you study math, the closer you come to religion. To me, God created the planets for a purpose, for nothing in nature is extraneous; nature is very conservative of energy.

Like acupuncture, astrology helps you work more effectively *with* the energy flow of the universe. Accept the wisdom of the universe, work with its rhythms, change what you can, and accept what you cannot. Remember that no matter how stressful a period might be, there will always be areas of opportunities in a chart. Few situations are all bad. Unless we take a proactive approach to our lives, many situations will be taken out of our hands and chosen for us. Make a decision, any decision. Don't be passive.

In terms of your personality, astrology can make you aware of your unique gifts and help you shape a clear view of your individuality. Your chart might even suggest latent talents that should be developed. We all want to be confirmed as unique and valuable, and astrology can provide that assurance. Certainly we are all born distinctive, for the planets, the Sun, and the Moon will never be configured in exactly the same way again. (Even twins are born a few minutes apart, which means the degrees of those planets are different.) Astrology can make you optimistic, calm, focused, and certainly much more reflective.

Some conditions can be changed; others need to be accepted. It is important to know the difference, and here again, astrology might give clues not only to the events in question but also to your present psychological outlook. Sometimes we create problems for ourselves, and when we self-undo, we need to acknowledge our mistakes and make a course correction, but we also need to avoid becoming so paralyzed with guilt or regret that we can't move forward. Astrology can suggest a variety of favorable actions to take for making a fresh start.

Astrology gives us the bird's-eye view of our lives that few of us would normally have the time to see. Its study can give you the confidence to test your wings and experiment with different ideas and concepts. Astrology can help you see the full flowering of your abilities by providing the confidence that you can ultimately make a difference to the world. To begin, however, you must make the effort. If you do, the universe will help you every step of the way.

# THE HEAVENLY BODIES

*What Science Tells Us and What Astrology Tells Us*

# THE SUN

## WHAT SCIENCE TELLS US ABOUT THE SUN

The Sun, found in the outer part of the Milky Way galaxy, is the source of Earth's energy, warmth, and light, and it creates and sustains life on Earth. All nine known planets in our solar system revolve around the Sun: Mercury, Venus, Earth, Mars, Jupiter, Saturn, Uranus, Neptune, Pluto, and their respective moons. Classified as a star, the Sun is a large mass of gas held together by its own tremendous gravity. The force of gravity presses inward, and the Sun's central pressure is strong enough to support its own weight and keep it from collapsing. Formed from material processed inside a supernova, the Sun's light and heat emanate from thermonuclear conversion of hydrogen into helium in its interior. Internally, continuous nuclear reactions convert an estimated 5 million tons of matter per second — a negligible portion of the Sun's total mass. In other words, the energy released by the Sun equals 100 billion one-megaton hydrogen bombs exploding every second.

Remarkably, the Sun is a stable source of energy, varying no more than 1 percent in heat or light at any given time, and it will probably burn at its present brightness for another 6 billion years. This stability is the reason life flourishes on Earth, for indeed, all the foods and fuels found here ultimately depend on plants that get their energy from sunlight.

## WHAT ASTROLOGY TELLS US ABOUT THE SUN

When astrology first became known around 2000 B.C., the prevailing worldview was that the planets revolved around the Earth. However, ancient astrologers decided to give the Sun a central role nevertheless, with its brilliant light as a key element in a chart. As the heavenly body that an astrologer will check first, the Sun reveals intriguing clues as to where a person will shine brightest in life. Our Sun sign refers to the constellation that the Sun falls in on our birthday. In a horoscope the Sun describes personality, spirit, ego, talents, and individuality. It is the face we show to the world, how we are known. The Sun also reveals temperament and overall outlook on life, self-confidence, sense of self-worth, and the ability to be self-sufficient. Astrologers discover clues about a person's ambitions by seeing the way the Sun fits into a chart or how it relates to other planets. For example, if a person has the Sun in the tenth house, the house of fame and honors, career will be very important to that individual throughout his or her life. That person's ego and sense of identity will be tied to his or her professional accomplishment. Conversely, if a person has the Sun in the fourth house, home and family, this person will stress lifestyle and the family unit much more than the person in the first example. For this person, home is not only where the heart is, it is where the ego resides too. Willpower, determination, strength, resilience in the face of adversity, and the ability to conquer goals are all characteristics revealed by the Sun in an astrological chart.

The placement of the Sun in a chart also indicates leadership qualities, the degree of desire for power and authority, the *relationship* with people in authority, reputation, and a sense of pride and honor (as well as honors bestowed). Also shown are the playful, experimental, and creative urges; the ability to bring new ideas and forms into existence; the capacity for pleasure, joy, and happiness; and health, specifically a person's vigor and strength as well as his or her recuperative powers. And finally, the Sun also rules over masculinity and over the prominent males such as a father, husband, or steady boyfriend in a woman's chart; or a male boss or other important male figure in anyone's life.

The part of the body ruled by the Sun is the heart and blood, providers of life. The Sun's symbol is a circle of unlimited potential brought into focus. Leo, symbolized by the Lion, is ruled by the Sun.

# THE EARTH

## WHAT SCIENCE TELLS US ABOUT EARTH

From a distance of 93 million miles, Earth is the third planet orbiting the Sun and is the fifth largest of the planets in diameter. The Earth is not perfectly round but slightly oblate (flattened at the poles). Rotating at approximately 1,000 miles per hour, the Earth rotates on its axis once every 23 hours 56 minutes. Traveling through space at about 66,000 miles per hour, it completes an orbit of over 583 million miles around the Sun once every 365 days.

## WHAT ASTROLOGY TELLS US ABOUT EARTH

Typically, Earth is not placed in a classic horoscope chart because we live on Earth. (Heliocentric astrology does use the Earth in the chart, but it is practiced by far fewer astrologers.) However, it is simple to find Earth's proper place in a chart. To find Earth in a horoscope, count six months to the day from your birth sign—180 degrees—and that is where Earth is found, in perfect opposition to the Sun sign. (Therefore, if you are born a Pisces on March 7 you have a Sun sign of sixteen degrees Pisces, Earth is located at 182.5 days away, at sixteen-degrees Virgo.) The Earth's effects in a chart are still being studied.

Ancient astrologers created a symbol for Earth: a cross enclosed by a circle. The cross suggests the quartering of the universe, separating humanity from the divine, and the inner world from the "real" outer world. Correspondingly, the cross represents our plane of existence, the material world. The circle represents the human spirit encasing this material world, or symbolizes that the spirit influences the entire view of the world at large. This symbol crystallizes astrology's view that the individual has mastery over his environment and must take responsibility for his actions.

# THE MOON

## WHAT SCIENCE TELLS US ABOUT THE MOON

The Moon is the Earth's natural satellite and has two major cycles. The first cycle is the sidereal period (its relation to the stars), the 27 days, 7 hours, and 43 minutes it takes to make a complete revolution through the constellations of the zodiac. The second cycle is called a synodic period, referring to the time between one new Moon and the next one, completing one lunar cycle in a slightly longer period: 29 days, 12 hours, and 44 minutes. This is commonly called the lunar month. Due to the Earth's daily rotation and its annual motion around the Sun, the Moon appears always to move west, though in fact it moves slowly east, rising later each day and passing through its four phases: new, first quarter, full, and last quarter. Just like Earth, half of the Moon is always in sunlight, half is always in darkness. Depending on the particular phase of the Moon, all to almost none of the sunny side can be seen at any one time. Although the Moon appears bright, it reflects only 7 percent of the light that falls on it. But at the phase of the new Moon it looks dark. A week later, the Moon moves to its first quarter, and a beautifully lit half-circle is seen. Two weeks after the new Moon (and a week after the first-quarter Moon), the full Moon appears as a silvery white circle. During that phase, the Moon is located as far from the Sun as it will ever be. In its last quarter, a week later, it is again in half-circle. The Moon is said to be waxing when the new Moon becomes fuller. As the Moon moves away from the full Moon to a new Moon, it is said to be waning.

## What Astrology Tells Us about the Moon

The Moon in a horoscope is very important, second only to the Sun, because it is thought to reflect the true character of the soul. The Moon rules the inner part of the person that can be seen only when someone knows that person well. Being a heavenly body viewed mainly at night, the ancient astrologers designated the Moon to be in charge of the "inner" life, including dreams and subconscious mind, as well as habits, intuition, and instinctual actions.

Long before the Moon was discovered to rule the tides on Earth, the ancients gave the Moon governance over all bodies of water as well as a person's most private feelings and emotions. The Moon has no light of its own but instead reflects light, suggesting that it imparts to us the ability to be influenced by the emotions of other people.

The Moon is also the repository of memories. In a chart, it represents imagination and the feminine, receptive side, as well as the urge to nurture, maternal instincts, fertility, possible pregnancy, birth, and nurturing of children (for a male, it refers to his wife's ability to conceive and care for children). The Moon also has bearing on other key creative projects, as does the Sun. The Moon rules our impressionable side but also sharpens imagination through its strong link to the subconscious. Related to this, the Moon reveals in a chart what is needed emotionally to feel secure, the state of domestic conditions (the person's inner private life), and especially reveals the early relationship with one's mother. As the person grows, the Moon also suggests close relationship with a steady girlfriend or wife (in a male chart) or one's future (or present) relationship with children. In fact, the Moon governs the key females, such as a girlfriend in a man's chart, or female boss or important female client in anyone's horoscope. The Moon can even give an indication of a person's future and present personal parenting style.

In everyday life, the phases of the new Moon and the full Moon should be noted, for they are times to harness important energy. As the light of a new Moon increases, astrology considers this a time to plant seeds for new beginnings. A week later, the quarter Moon suggests a period of overcoming obstacles and continuing on the path to growth. Always two weeks after the new Moon, the full Moon is a time of fruition and culmination. Energy runs high on full Moons, allowing for enormous productivity and completion of current projects. The waxing Moon (moving from new Moon to full Moon period) accents everyday matters of life, and indicates a good time to act instinctively and spontaneously and to experience solid growth.

The waning Moon (coming after the full Moon and moving toward the new Moon) accents subconscious creative urges, and helps to clarify inner values through reflection on recent events. The waxing Moon is a time of high activity, while the waning Moon (coming directly after the frenzied full Moon) is one of release and rest, a time to take in what has happened and gather energy for the next new Moon.

☽ The symbol of the Moon is the crescent, which is the symbol selected by the ancient astrologers to express a person's soul. This complements the Sun's representation of one's spirit or outer manifestation of personality.

The Moon governs the stomach (and for women, the breasts) and has always been considered a fruitful celestial body, encouraging reproduction and the nurturing care of children. The Moon rules the sign of Cancer.

# MERCURY

## WHAT SCIENCE TELLS US ABOUT MERCURY

Discovered 5,000 years ago, Mercury is a small planet, only 3,030 miles wide at its diameter, with a density similar to that of Earth. Difficult to see, Mercury is rough, dark-colored, porous, and rocky, and although it is the closest planet to the Sun, it does not reflect sunlight well. It is called either a "morning star" or an "evening star," depending on whether it is seen just before sunrise or just before sunset. Mercury orbits the sun every eighty-eight days at an average speed of 29.8 miles per second.

## WHAT ASTROLOGY TELLS US ABOUT MERCURY

Mercury, or "the messenger of the Gods," named after Hermes in Greek mythology, is considered the most objective planet in the chart. The only planet without a masculine (positive) or feminine (negative) charge, it is completely neutral. When Mercury is at a particular angle to another planet, Mercury helps to convey that planet's wisdom more accurately and lucidly. A person is considered quick, adaptable, or clever when Mercury is prominent in a chart. Mercury is by default prominent for Gemini and Virgo—Mercury rules both of these signs—but anyone can have a prominent Mercury for any number of reasons.

Mercury rules intelligence, the way the mind works, language, and all communication and interpretation. It also governs reasoning ability, adaptability, and versatility. Rules and procedure, as well as teaching, researching, reporting, answering, and responding, are all found in

Mercury's domain. New and old, rare documents, autographs, handwriting, speeches, agreements, and contracts are also ruled by this planet. Mercury encourages listening and responding, learning and reflecting. Other functions influenced by Mercury include modes of travel as well as commerce, including sales, bartering, importing, and exporting.

If there is a lot of influence of Mercury in a chart, small motor skills increase dramatically. Mercury rules the hands and fingers, so these people are talented in carpentry, furniture restoration, drawing and illustration, sewing, needlepoint, knitting, piano playing, typing, and other skills and artistic crafts using the hands. Those with Mercury influencing their charts will even talk vividly with their hands. Other people will exhibit strong mechanical ability, or will have beautiful handwriting.

 The symbol of Mercury is similar to Venus, a circle with cross under it and a half crescent over the circle. This icon suggests manifested (crescent) spirit (circle) over matter (cross), and indeed, Mercury's job is to link the spirit to everyday matters to facilitate the process.

# VENUS

## What Science Tells Us about Venus

Venus is the second planet from the Sun after Mercury, and due to the distance of the orbits of Venus and Earth from the Sun, it can be seen only three hours before sunrise or three hours after sunset. Venus generally transits across the face of the Sun only twice a century—the next occurrences will be in 2004 and 2012. When it is possible to see Venus, it is the most brilliant object in the sky other than the Sun and Moon.

Venus is 67 million miles from the Sun, with an orbit that takes 225 days. Unlike the other planets, which are flattened somewhat at their poles, Venus is a nearly perfect sphere. Venus requires 243 days to complete one revolution. This slow spin allows Venus to retain an almost perfectly circular (rather than elliptical) course, more so than any other planet. Venus also spins in a different direction from other planets. If you could stand on her North Pole, you would see that instead of going counterclockwise like the other planets in our solar system (except Uranus), Venus spins clockwise. This means if you were able to see through the thick clouds covering Venus's surface, the Sun would rise in the west and set in the east. Venus is 94.9 percent the size of Earth at the diameter, and her mass is 81.5 percent of Earth's. Her density is 5.24 grams per cubic centimeter; Earth's is 5.52. Venus's orbit is such that she always shows the same "face" to Earth at their closest approach. The reason for this isn't completely understood, but it may be linked to the influence of Earth's gravity on Venus.

## WHAT ASTROLOGY TELLS US ABOUT VENUS

Venus, ruler of the signs Taurus and Libra, was one of the five planets
known in ancient times. Discovered by the Babylonians in about 3000
B.C., Venus appears in the astronomical records of several other ancient
civilizations: China, Egypt, Greece, and Central America. In ancient
times when Venus shone in the east at sunrise she was called Lucifer or
Phosphorus. If Venus was seen in the evening, she was called Hesperus.

The role of Venus in a chart is to add love, friendship, and beauty into the
mix. Without Venus, life would be a dreary existence, for Venus governs
tenderness, joy, and harmony, and even the capacity for humor. She also
governs esthetic taste and all social interactions on every level. Venus
shows that humans were meant to have fun in this world. Venus can also
bring added self-esteem and confidence, thus encouraging people not only
to love openly but to receive love too. When Venus is highlighted in a
chart in a positive way, there will be benefits from women, because in a
chart Venus symbolizes femininity or relations with women.

Financial benefits are another positive aspect of Venus, and this lovely
planet governs money and gifts as well as sensuous indulgences, such as
jewels, fine wines, gourmet foods, imported chocolates, silks, perfumes,
music, or painting. There is a decorative quality about Venus, as well as a
feeling of abundance or luxury. Additionally, Venus is linked to creation,
reproduction, and fertility. (Conception of a baby will always have to
involve the Moon as well.) Hence the purpose of Venus is to bestow creativity and new life, along with the aim of bringing greater pleasure into
the world.

Yet Venus's most important role will be in romance and love, as a guide to
the deepest layers of the unconscious mind to find the kind of love the
psyche craves. Venus will give clues to the overall qualities needed in an
ideal lover and how the love affair should proceed. Indeed, Venus's primary role is enormously important: to insure that the initial spark of love

will prevail, and then to encourage the long-term enjoyment of the lovers if they are truly compatible.

For a man, Venus indicates the type of women he would love as well as the nature of his romantic relationship. For a woman, Venus indicates the overall type of romantic relationships she needs—its tone and intensity, and the kind of balance between independence and intimacy she intuitively seeks. The man she would love and/or marry would likely be indicated by Mars, not by Venus. On another level, Venus is said to make a friendship deeper, or strengthen the bond between a child and a parent, or bring popularity to a ruler. The way friendship is influenced by this happy planet and its placement suggests whether you need many or few in your circle of friends.

♀ In the paintings by the Old Masters, Venus is often seen nude, reclining on a bed of silky satin, gazing in a hand mirror, while cherubs circle above her, holding bows of red and pink roses. The image of the hand mirror is ironic. It looks like the glyph for Venus, a circle with a tiny cross under it, and some have pointed out that this symbol looks like a mirror. In fact, Venus's symbol is the circle above a cross, the symbol for the female, and it connotes spirit (the circle) over matter (the cross). This image is quintessentially Venus; beauty, grace, desire, luxury, adornment, love, and harmony all come under the domain of this lovely, joyous planet. What on Earth would life be like without Venus?

# MARS

## WHAT SCIENCE TELL US ABOUT MARS

Mars is the fourth planet from the Sun at 141 million miles away, and it takes almost two years to revolve through all the constellations. Relatively small compared to the other planets, Mars is about half Earth's diameter and has a tenth of Earth's mass. Through a telescope, Mars looks red-orange, hence it is known as the Red Planet. Mars was originally named for the Roman god of war because it has always appeared fiery bright in the night sky. Because of the relative movements of Earth and Mars around the Sun, Mars seems to travel backward in the sky for a short time. When this phenomenon occurs, astrologers call it a Mars retrograde.

This feisty planet has a very interesting geological feature: It holds the largest volcano in the solar system, Olympus Mons, which is about twice the size of Mount Everest. Near it are three other volcanoes that are almost as large but appear to be dormant if not extinct. Mars has seasons but, unlike ours on Earth, they are uneven in length due to the rotation of its axis. Mars also has small permanent polar ice caps that increase when one or the other of Mars' hemispheres is in winter.

For over 100 years people have wondered whether there was life on Mars. This has led scientists to send the *Viking* (1975) and *Pathfinder* (1996) space missions to investigate. So far no organic material has been found on Mars; however, it has been theorized that a meteorite found in Antarctica in 1984 contains fossilized bacteria that originated on Mars about 4 billion years ago. There is also some recent evidence that water may have existed on Mars. The quest for truth continues as the twenty-first century begins. Mars has certainly ignited the imagination of people everywhere in this modern age.

## WHAT ASTROLOGY TELLS US ABOUT MARS

Aggressive, assertive, passionate, forceful, energetic, courageous, fearless, competitive, and daring, the Red Planet governs the whole spectrum of traditionally "masculine" events from sex to combat, strenuous athletics, and nerves-of-steel risk-taking. It is not surprising that Mars is also known as the warrior planet, due to its courage and pure strength and its ability to outlast and outdistance adversaries.

Mars is called the timekeeper of the zodiac, because it points out where your best and purest energies can be put, depending on where Mars happens to be traveling in a horoscope.

Another side of Mars reveals one's sexual drive. Mars is bold, forceful, experimental, and exciting, symbolizing a thrilling lover. Mars causes things to "happen." Bringing endurance, ambition, determination, and even a survival instinct, Mars' energy can enable us to keep on going even when the road gets rough.

Certainly Mars brings noise, movement, and plenty of activity to whatever house of the horoscope it visits. If there is too much energy coming from Mars, there is danger of accidents. Hotheaded outbursts are also possible too when Mars is at a tough angle to other planets. Mars rules sharp instruments, fire, and anything combustible. Mars can, through force, destroy matter. Yet Mars can, conversely, bring passion, spirit, zest, and energy to whatever it touches. It is, in the end, a matter of proportion and the quality of expression of the person who is being influenced by Mars at the time. Some people learn to harness and direct Mars' influences especially well.

Mars takes approximately two years to make a complete revolution around the Sun, usually staying in each sign for six weeks, but if it retrogrades (appearing to travel backward in the sky), it can settle in for as long as seven or eight months. When any planet retrogrades, its powers are said to be reduced. The symbol for Mars is masculinity, a circle with an arrow pointing upward, indicating that Mars works on an almost entirely material plane. There are no crescent circles indicating spirit; Mars deals with the here and now. The arrow indicates action and sexuality—thinking and reflecting are left to Mercury, as Mars is not weighed down with too much reflection to slow it down. It is the natural ruler of Aries, and the co-ruler of Scorpio.

# JUPITER

## WHAT SCIENCE TELLS US ABOUT JUPITER

As the fifth, and by far the largest, planet orbiting the Sun, Jupiter was aptly named. As a matter of fact, Jupiter, 88,640 miles wide at its diameter, is bigger than all the other planets in our solar system combined. After the Sun, Moon, and Venus (and at time Mars), Jupiter is the next brightest object in the Earth's sky, more than three times brighter than Sirius, the brightest star in the night sky. Located 484 million miles from the Sun, Jupiter takes 11.9 years to revolve around the Sun through all the signs of the zodiac.

Scientists postulate from Jupiter's makeup that it was actually formed from the same cloud of material as the Sun. Its small core is made up of rock and iron. However, this planet has no solid surface but rather is a dense ball of gas made up of the lightest elements, hydrogen and helium. Consequently, it is less than one-fourth the density of Earth, with a diameter 11.2 times greater than Earth's, and its volume is more than 1,300 times that of Earth.

Easily seen from Earth are Jupiter's four brightest moons: Io, Europa, Ganymede, and Callisto, named for mythological figures associated with Jupiter. Io comes from the Greek word *ion*, meaning "wanderer" or "travel," and is particularly well named because Io has an indirect influence on the ionosphere of Jupiter (unbeknownst to the ancient astronomers who named it). Europa is covered with a blanket of water-ice that cracks and vents heat. Exobiologists, scientists who study possible life on other planets, believe that these vents might support primitive forms of life. Io and Europa appear dense and rocky, like Mercury, Venus, Mars, and Earth, while the other two big moons, Ganymede and Callisto, positioned farther from Jupiter, are composed of less compact materials, similar to Neptune and Uranus.

Finally, scientists have discovered that Jupiter has a system of rings (like Saturn) and its own internal heat source, which actually emits *more* energy than it receives from the Sun. (It had always been believed that only stars generate energy, not planets.) Additionally, Jupiter has the strongest magnetic field of any planet in our solar system. And one more interesting note: Jupiter is a source of intense bursts of radio noise, with some frequencies occasionally radiating more energy than that of the Sun.

## WHAT ASTROLOGY TELLS US ABOUT JUPITER

How appropriate that the biggest planet of this solar system, the planet that scientists think perhaps narrowly missed becoming a sun itself, should rule good fortune and happiness. Jupiter brings hope, honesty, spirituality, and compassion to a chart and is known as the fortuitous planet because it expands or creates opportunities wherever it touches in the horoscope sector it is visiting. Additionally, Jupiter brings broad vision, a comprehensive, inclusive feeling toward others, faith, optimism, loyalty, justice, confidence, and even wisdom both to a chart and to those sectors within a chart it visits. Jupiter paints a broad picture and makes you want to think big.

From its assorted scientific properties, Jupiter's nature can be characterized as radiation of energy. Jupiter expands everything it touches. Jupiter also rules wealth and tangible, solid financial gains, for Jupiter is the giver of gifts and luck. At the same time, Jupiter rules philosophy, philanthropy, scholarship, and all academic pursuits, ethics and morality, religions of all cultures, medicine (Jupiter is also called the great healer), as well as government service for the purpose of setting standards and for the good of the whole community. Finding one's higher purpose for being alive is also considered a pervasive Jupiter influence. This curious, boundless planet encourages the creation of ideas across all nations, colors, races, and even timelines, and rules the publishing industry as well as the judicial system. Finally, Jupiter encourages long-distance travel and investigation into diverse cultures.

 Though the Romans named Jupiter after their chief god, Jove, and the Greeks named the planet Zeus after their chief god, the astrological attributes of Jupiter do not reflect this fearsome image. Instead, Jupiter's symbol is the half-circle above the cross, signifying the triumph of spirit over matter. Jupiter takes twelve years to circle through the zodiac, so while the Jovian planet is the natural ruler of Sagittarius, Jupiter gives each sign a turn at its bountiful luck for one year.

# SATURN

## What Science Tells Us about Saturn

Saturn, the sixth planet from the Sun, had been observed from Earth by the naked eye since prehistoric times. At 887 million miles from the Sun, Saturn's full orbit requires 29.46 years. It is the second largest planet in the solar system after Jupiter—74,900 miles in diameter—yet it is important to note that although Saturn is huge, its mass is three times smaller than Jupiter, and thus it has the lowest density. However, compared to Earth, Saturn's mass is 95.13 times greater and its volume is 766 times larger.

The weight of Saturn's atmosphere causes the atmospheric pressure to increase toward its interior, where the hydrogen gas condenses into a liquid. Closer to the center of the planet, the liquid hydrogen is compressed into metallic hydrogen, which is an electrical conductor. The electrical currents in this metallic hydrogen are responsible for the planet's magnetic field.

Saturn's most notable property is its rings, the most impressive in the solar system. The rings consist of particles of rock, frozen gases, and water-ice, ranging from .0002 of an inch to 33 feet wide in diameter, from pulverized dust to chunky boulders. In addition to the seven main rings of Saturn, more than 100,000 very thin ringlets were discovered by the *Voyager 2* space probe. Many people feel that Saturn is the most beautiful of all the planets.

## What Astrology Tells Us about Saturn

Saturn is the planet of thoughtful concentration, permanence, tangible rewards, tenacity, ambition, and productivity. This taskmaster planet also rules caution, delay, constriction, limitation, responsibility, rules and regulations, pain, fear, separation, anxiety, learning the hard way, authority, discipline, control, and denial. Before you say, "Ugh!" consider this: Without Saturn there would probably be no progress, because there would be no discipline, no standards, no controls, no final tangible evidence of hard work—just chaos.

Named after the Roman god of agriculture, known to Greeks as Cronus, father of Zeus, Saturn is not a planet that tolerates shortcuts, nor does it let us get away with anything. It grabs us by the collar and forces us to face up to things, especially things we have been avoiding. Whatever Saturn is currently touching in your chart will go through a kind of slowdown or freeze. Saturn rules the element lead, so you get the picture. But because of its slowed-down nature, Saturn teaches the value of maturity, patience, prudence, and sacrifice, either for later gratification or for the good of someone else. Saturn is also serious, mature, reserved, temperate, and devoted. It brings longevity and true commitment to whatever it touches and rules valuables from the past (historical, artistic, or archaeological). This planet rules teeth and bones, the building blocks of the human body. In fact, Saturn rules all foundations, from the skeleton of the body to the organizational hierarchy of a company.

When an individual has a "Saturn return," this means Saturn returns to the place it occupied at birth—something that happens every twenty-nine years. At this time a person "grows up." Thus, in astrology, the age of true maturity is twenty-nine, and great wisdom is reached at fifty-eight, a time when Saturn has gone around the individual's wheel twice. (Some people are luckier yet to reach eighty-seven, a third Saturn return of enormous experience, sagacity, and insight.) Whenever a Saturn return happens, the individual makes an adult decision—to get married, have a baby, take a big job, buy a house, or other decisions that will help to provide roots and stability to one's life. It is also true that the more a lesson from Saturn is needed, the harsher the life's lesson will be. Once we have learned much, Saturn will teach less and less with each turn around the wheel. Thus, Saturn rules old age, while Uranus rules youth. As we age, we have a harder time with Uranus's transits, but an easier time with Saturn's transits through our charts. The reverse is true for young people.

♄ The symbol for Saturn is a cross, representing the material world (over a half-circle) ruling over the mind, and this planet's ability to crystallize and stabilize whatever it touches. Saturn's job is to turn ideas into reality. Saturn takes twenty-nine years to pass through the zodiac, staying in each sign for 2½ years, and is the ruler of Capricorn.

# URANUS

## What Science Tells Us about Uranus

Seventh in line from the Sun, Uranus is a blue-green planet of low density and a large size that makes it among the four giant planets. It is composed primarily of hydrogen and helium with water and other volatile compounds. Located 1.78 billion miles from the Sun, Uranus is 31,771 miles wide at its diameter and takes eighty-four years to revolve around the Sun.

Perhaps the most interesting quality of Uranus is that its rotation axis is tilted at a ninety-eight-degree angle relative to its orbit axis so it spins on its side. Not only that, but Uranus rotates differently from every other planet except Venus. This planet spins clockwise, whereas other planets move around the Sun while rotating in a counterclockwise direction. In forty-two years, half of Uranus's cycle, the Sun moves from being over one pole to being over the other. This unusual condition may have been caused by a violent collision billions of years ago during the formation of the solar system.

## What Astrology Tells Us about Uranus

The unusual rotation of Uranus may explain the surprising attributes it holds in astrology. Innovative, resourceful, and experimental, Uranus is meant to bring creativity, surprise, and even genius to whatever it touches. This planet breaks up established patterns of thinking, creating sudden—even radical—change, by replacing what "was" with something newer and better. Uranus is the planet of the future, and new technology falls under Uranus's domain.

Uranus rules space exploration, the Internet, computers, telecommunications, aviation, broadcasting, and video and digital photography. This revolutionary planet also promotes all kinds of breakthrough medical research and engineering, from transplants to cloning, biology and biophysics as well as X-ray, laser, and electromagnetic technology. Astrology, psychic experiences, acupuncture, and other new forms of homeopathic, holistic forms of healing all fall under Uranus.

People with a strong Uranus influence in their charts are trailblazers, pioneers, reformers, and forerunners in society. The impetus for social change and social good arises from Uranus, for its dominion covers social issues of global consequence, including humanitarian, philanthropic, charitable, sociological, and environmental issues. In addition to all these worthy attributes, Uranus leads to a strong impulse for rebellion, independence, and even shock. Exciting, liberating, invigorating, erratic, unusual, and odd, Uranus is definitely not routine or predictable. Uranus is intuitive, instinctive, imaginative, inventive, investigative, curious, nonconformist, willful, and intellectual in its influence.

In spite of its nonconformist properties, Uranus is scientific, objective, rational, and unemotional, ever seeking truth. This planet is considered the "higher octave" of Mercury. While Mercury portrays the normal mental processes of looking, perception, reading, writing, speaking, and listening, Uranus will go to a higher level, employing intuition gleaned from wisdom gained from experience. While Uranus has been called the Great Awakener because it sees deficits in society others are too blind to see, it is also called the Great Synthesizer, because its work is to blend the information gathered by the other planets into a new and massive whole. Uranus imparts the ability to customize and individualize concepts and ideas.

Uranus is like a lightning bolt in its effects—sudden, surprising, and unexpected. For this reason, Uranus is said to rule youth (while Saturn rules old age). When one reaches a half cycle of Uranus, at age forty-two (actually occurring anytime between thirty-eight and forty-two, depending on the speed of Uranus's orbit in an individual's chart), one experiences an important life crisis. In fact, what is occurring is that Uranus opposes the place it took in the natal placement in a birth chart. This mid-life crisis that the ancients spoke of will occur in everyone's chart in those years and will help clarify one's life's goals and strengthen one's sense of purpose and individuality.

 The symbol for Uranus is two half-circles on either side of a cross above a circle. The cross, in the middle of the symbol, is matter, and on either side are crescents, which are spirit. This planet stays in a sign for seven years and therefore takes eighty-four years to travel through the zodiac. Uranus rules the sign Aquarius.

# NEPTUNE

## WHAT SCIENCE TELLS US ABOUT NEPTUNE

Neptune is the eighth planet from the Sun, with a 164.8-year solar orbit. About the size of Uranus, 30,700 miles in diameter, it is almost four times larger than Earth. Like Jupiter, Saturn, and Uranus, Neptune is a gaseous planet consisting of hydrogen, helium, and, to a much lesser degree, methane (3 percent) which is responsible for Neptune's deep blue color. Her orbit is nearly circular (similar to Venus's). The discovery of Neptune in 1846 is considered one of the triumphs of mathematical astronomy. Disturbances in Uranus's orbit indicated that a huge mass was influencing it. That mysterious force was found to be Neptune.

Because Neptune is so far from Earth, it is never bright enough to be seen without a telescope and so was difficult to examine. Only recently have scientists come to know more about it.

## WHAT ASTROLOGY TELLS US ABOUT NEPTUNE

Whenever a planet is discovered, astrologers note world events and the nature of the times to discern the qualities of that planet. Neptune was discovered during the period of Romanticism, a movement that counteracted the Enlightenment, with its stringent emphasis on logic and the scientific method. Thus Neptune stands for idealism, altruism, self-sacrifice, and dreams, and all that logic and science cannot explain, confirm, or dictate.

Neptune's role is to help us transcend everyday reality, to bring us to a more meditative and spiritual place where ideas have wings and dreams feel so real you could touch them. Compassion, kindness, empathy, and an unselfish, giving nature are Neptune's most important gifts. Neptune's strength comes from its very lack of preciseness. Through its gauze we see the outline, the long view, or concept of the dream rather than the dream's specifics. By masking specific details, Neptune emphasizes the universal and all-encompassing elements of whatever it touches. Neptune helps us receive information from the imaginative and visual right brain, bypassing the intellect and speaking directly to the intuition, soul, or unconscious heart, using scenes, pictures, music, dance, photography, paintings, poetry, or illustrations rather than more concrete language. Neptune whispers "I believe" rather than "I know," for truth is found within the heart. Neptune keeps its eyes on eternity.

As the "higher octave" of Venus, Neptune expands upon Venus's cultural appreciation of beauty and love. Where Venus fully enjoys the lightness of love and erotic sexuality, Neptune loves so deeply that it will sacrifice for that love and shifts the emphasis from "me" to "thou," thereby adding the quality of love's selflessness to Venus's more strict definition of beauty and enjoyment. Venus wants to enjoy love, while Neptune is cognizant of the responsibilities that come with love. Venus may define certain standards of beauty, but Neptune elevates those standards beyond culture, fashion, or a moment in time.

Neptune deals in abstract and conceptual terms, not the specific, therefore this planet is known to add poetic, creative, artistic, elusive, idealistic, and ethereal overtones to whatever it influences. Psychic, clairvoyant, intuitive, instinctive, subtle, and mysterious, this enchanting planet enlarges imagination by building alternate realities. Neptune rules the subconscious, the psychological, and all things mystical.

Neptune's waters cleanse any planet it "speaks to" (called making an aspect, or, in other words, coming into certain mathematical degree), leaving it purer than it was before. Like Uranus and Pluto, the other powerful "outer" planets, Neptune creates vast change. Yet Neptune's changes are so subtle as to be imperceptible—Neptune works nearly invisibly in a slow and gradual way, like water washing slowly and gently over rocks, continually, methodically, and rhythmically. Water dissolves, washes away, obscures, and blurs in its amorphous realm.

Neptune cannot bear anything too brash, too coarse or mundane, for it would bruise the planet's delicate sensibilities and lofty concentration on the ideal. Neptune carefully keeps its dreams alive and lives in what can be rather than what is. When reality becomes too cruel, Neptune creates a refuge, an escape, a daydream to embrace until things get better. Ironically, Neptune teaches us that things are neither as good nor as bad as they seem. Neptune doesn't leave us there, but inspires us to build a better version of the world through our visions. Neptune governs the foundation of knowledge about the world around us, and yet in the process still leaves us believing in miracles and magic.

Ψ The symbol of Neptune is Greek god Poseidon's trident, related to the Roman god Neptune's pitchfork, used to spear the elusive fish. Fittingly, Neptune is the ruler of Pisces, and travels 146 years through the zodiac, staying about fourteen years in each sign.

# THE HEAVENLY BODIES

*The Planets, the Sun, and the Moon*

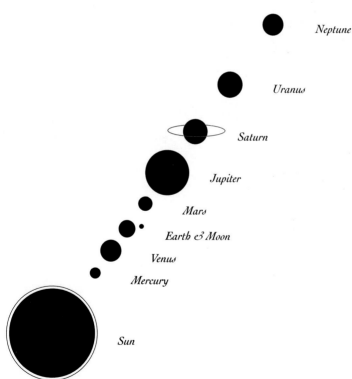

Pluto

Neptune

Uranus

Saturn

Jupiter

Mars

Earth & Moon

Venus

Mercury

Sun

### The Ruler of Leo

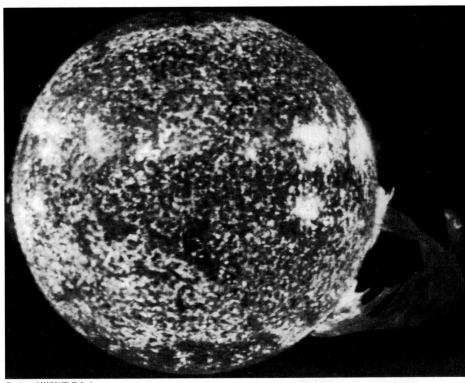

Courtesy of NASA/JPL/Caltech

The Sun is a star located in the outer part of the Milky Way Galaxy and is the center of our solar system. The energy the Sun releases is comparable to the explosion of 100 billion one-megaton hydrogen bombs going off every second. The Sun is a very stable source of energy, varying no more than one percent.

Astrology tells us the Sun symbolizes determination, will, ambition, pride, power, authority, leadership, self-expression, and confidence. The Sun is a creative, life-giving, vitalizing, elevating, illuminating, and masculine influence.

# Mercury

## The Ruler of Gemini and Virgo

Mercury is a small planet that moves nearly 30 miles a second. A year on Mercury is only 88 Earth days long. It is the planet that is closest to the Sun; it is never more than 27°45" away.

Astrology tells us Mercury symbolizes communication. This planet covers language, the gathering of any and all information through observation and listening, reading and writing. Devoid of emotion, Mercury seeks truth.

Courtesy of NASA/JPL/Caltech

# Venus

## The Ruler of Taurus and Libra

Unlike other planets that are flattened at the poles, Venus is a perfect sphere. While other planets have elliptical courses, Venus' course is perfectly circular. Venus is the only terrestrial planet to hide its surface features under a veil of clouds and is almost as reflective as snow.

Astrologers call Venus the planet of love, elegant beauty, pleasure, adornment, gifts, festivity, and especially magnetic attraction.

Courtesy of NASA/JPL/Caltech

## *Moon*

### The Ruler of Cancer

Courtesy of NASA/JPL/Caltech

The moon is the Earth's only satellite and rules the oceans' tides. A quick moving body, the moon is always half in light, and half in darkness. The same side of the moon is always facing Earth; the other side is never seen. The moon, having no light of its own, reflects the light of the Sun.

Astrology tells us the moon symbolizes the fine-tuning of our character, the part hidden in others that is revealed only when we know them well. The moon also rules emotions, memory, moods, imagination, dreams, habits, intuition, and sympathy.

## *Mars*

### The Ruler of Aries, Ancient Ruler of Scorpio

Courtesy of NASA/JPL/Caltech

Mars is nicknamed the Red Planet because of its red-orange color, and its brilliant appearance in the night sky. Mars is home to the largest volcano in our solar system. Photographs reveal a large scar on Mars' face, probably due to collisions with other planets or asteroids it has encountered in its path.

Astrologers call Mars the Warrior, planet of action, energy, passion, sexuality, courage, and sometimes strife.

## The Ruler of Sagittarius, Ancient Ruler of Pisces

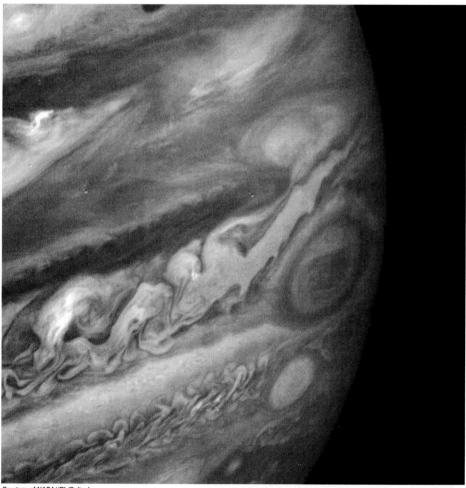

Courtesy of NASA/JPL/Caltech

Jupiter is bigger than the sum of all the other planets in our solar system. As one of the only planets with its own inner heat source, Jupiter emits more energy than it receives from the Sun. Scientists postulate that Jupiter only narrowly missed becoming a sun in its own right.

Astrologers say that Jupiter is the expansive planet of happiness, opportunity, faith, medicine and law, broad vision, financial prosperity.

# *Saturn*

## The Ruler of Capricorn, Ancient Ruler of Aquarius

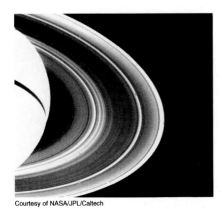

Courtesy of NASA/JPL/Caltech

Saturn is about 95 times larger than Earth and is known for its beautiful rings. Saturn's rings are 84,650 miles wide, yet at some points are only 16.4 feet thick. They consist of rock, frozen gases and water ice, ranging in size from .0002 of an inch (pulverized dust) to boulders up to 33 feet wide in diameter. More than 100,000 ringlets have been attributed to Saturn.

Astrologers say that Saturn is the planet of restriction, limitation, responsibility, ambition, hard work, maturity, and lessons learned. Its job is to manifest goals into a tangible reality. Although Saturn brings fear and caution, it also brings a sense of organization and structure.

Courtesy of NASA/JPL/Caltech

# *Uranus*

## The Ruler of Aquarius

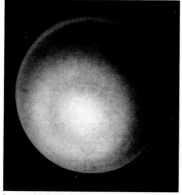

Science tells us that Uranus tilts at an unusual 98-degree angle so it spins on its side. Uranus and Venus are the only planets that orbit clockwise around the Sun.

Astrology calls Uranus the planet of independence, rebellion, disruption, surprise, chaos, and creativity. Uranus' job is to challenge the established order and replace it with something else.

Courtesy of NASA/JPL/Caltech

# *Neptune*

## The Ruler of Pisces

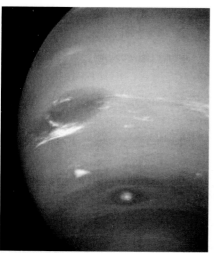

Deep blue and mysterious, Neptune teeters on the far edges of our solar system. Neptune's reflectivity is high but because it is so far from Earth it is never bright enough to be seen without a telescope. It is only one-fifth as bright as the faintest star visible to the naked eye.

Astrology tells us that Neptune is the higher octave of Venus, symbolizing universal love and the dreams of the collective unconscious. Neptune

Courtesy of NASA/JPL/Caltech

is spiritual, giving, idealistic, intuitive, imaginative, and subtle. It can be escapist, evasive or confused, but in its highest order it is giving and extremely compassionate.

## *Pluto*

### The Ruler of Scorpio

Courtesy of NASA/JPL/Caltech

Small, very dark and dense, Pluto is difficult even for space probes to photograph. Found in deep space, 3.67 billion miles from Earth, some feel it is remarkable that Pluto was ever discovered. Pluto is so far from the Sun that it takes five hours for sunlight to reach its surface.

Astrology tells us Pluto raises the energy of Mars an octave. Pluto symbolizes destruction, obsession, decay and elimination, but, more importantly, transformation and complete rebirth. Pluto also rules massive power and the ability to rebound against all odds.

# PLUTO

## What Science Tells Us about Pluto

At 3.67 billion miles from the Sun, Pluto, the ninth planet, takes nearly 248 years to complete its orbit. Pluto is the solar system's smallest planet. With a diameter of only 1,440 miles, it is less than half the size of Mercury and merely two-thirds the size of the Moon. Being the farthest away from the Sun, it is a very dim planet. Pluto's orbit is so elliptical that at times it trades places with Neptune (whose orbit is nearly circular), becoming closer to the Sun than Neptune.

In 1905, Percival Lowell hypothesized the existence of Pluto and instituted a search for it after he noted disturbances in the gravitational fields of Uranus and Neptune. However, Lowell died before actually locating Pluto. Incredibly, in 1930, after astronomer Clyde Tombaugh discovered the planet, its small size suggested that Pluto could not have caused the gravitational disturbances on a regular basis in the first place, therefore it was considered a remarkable coincidence that it was ever found.

## What Astrology Tells Us about Pluto

Pluto was named for the god of the underworld in Roman mythology. (In Greek mythology, the god is called Hades.) This planet is so far into deep space that sunlight takes five hours to reach it. By comparison, Pluto gets only 1/1,600 of the sunlight received on Earth. So the name is appropriate. When Pluto was discovered in 1930, the world was going through a very hard time. To decipher Pluto's meaning, astrologers looked at world events and saw the Depression, fascism, and communism, and World War II and the atomic age loomed shortly ahead. Obviously, Pluto had some heavy duty associations attached to it.

Cold, icy, dark, Pluto seems impossibly distant and enigmatic. Yet Pluto is also associated with rebirth, regeneration, rejuvenation, basically any kind of metamorphosis. It allows us to reinvent ourselves in new forms, as dramatically, yet as gradually, as when a caterpillar becomes a butterfly. Pluto is associated with death as the ultimate transformation of life's energy. Yet Pluto also rules life's other "deaths" too, in terms of important endings or even in terms of surgery. (The surgeon cuts out an unneeded part of the body to heal.)

While Pluto puts an end to things, it also often shows the hidden reasons for those endings and usually provides a path for new growth too. Pluto's influence is occasionally so massive and overpowering that it can make us feel out of control, and sometimes when we experience a certain vibration from Pluto we simply need to accept whatever is being presented. However, as seen earlier, Pluto helps us to reinvent ourselves when we most need change—not sudden change (like Uranus) but, rather, change that is more gradual.

Pluto is so powerful because it is the slowest planet in the solar system, staying in a sign for thirteen to twenty-five years and exerting a powerful influence over each sign. In astrology, the farther away a planet is from the Sun, the more powerful the planet. The reason the distant planets are more powerful than the others is that those outer planets take longer to orbit the Sun. As a result, the slow-moving planets (Pluto, Neptune, and Uranus) inch along the sky, degree by degree, and as they occupy each of the zodiac constellations they hover there longer than other planets. This causes a deeper and more indelible experience than planets that move quickly through the signs (such as the Moon, Venus, or Mercury). Pluto particularly affects the members of whole generations, setting up questions and themes that societies work on together.

Pluto also rules the psychological and subconscious aspects of life (especially obsessions), known or unknown, including phobias and fears, and feelings of alienation, isolation, and separation. In fact, Pluto's closest neighboring planet, Neptune, is 856 million miles away. Its link to reproduction makes Pluto the planet of sexuality too, in terms of both its pleasurable or reproductive applications and its taboos and difficulties.

Appropriately, enigmatic Pluto is the lord of Scorpio, the eighth house of the horoscope, a house of not only death but regeneration, including debt, taxes, insurance, loans, and other shared resources. Money is located in this sector, which shouldn't be a surprise, as money can be inherited after death. Before Pluto was discovered, Mars ruled the eighth house and retains some influence. However, Pluto was deemed a more appropriate ruler because it rules transformation and mutation of all kinds—money is generated from work performed or inherited; sexual expression leads to birth. These are all appropriate activities to be included in the eighth house and ruled by Pluto.

Pluto's massive influence explains why it also rules power bases of all kinds, whether that is the government of a nation or of a behemoth global corporation. When people feel like they are "fighting City Hall," there is probably a large Pluto influence at play in their horoscope.

Additionally, Pluto will also indicate what must be brought to light and possibly discarded (Pluto rules waste and elimination, among other things) so that we can move forward with more strength and higher energy. Pluto's association with the underworld qualifies it to be the planet of secrets, strategies, and plots, as in investigative journalism and espionage.

Pluto possesses unusual strength and an ability to rebound against all odds. More than any other planet, Pluto symbolizes the miraculous ability of the human will to triumph over all odds, like the mythological Phoenix rising, reborn and renewed, from the ashes of defeat. While Mars brings energy, Pluto, as the higher octave of Mars, directs this energy inward for spiritual growth and enlightenment. Furthermore, while Mars will destroy matter, Pluto will cause a transformation, a rebirth, a concept beyond the scope of Mars.

 Pluto's symbol is a cross (matter) with a crescent (soul) over it, and over that, a circle (spirit). This means spirit contained by soul, as if "floating" within it, and both are situated over the cross. In other words, soul and spirit are triumphant over everyday matter—quite an upbeat and optimistic symbol.

# THE SUN SIGNS

*Personality and Myths*

# ARIES PERSONALITY

**Aries**
March 21–April 19

---

*Guiding Principle*
"I Want"

*How This Sign Feels Joy*
Finds joy in taking a proactive, energetic
approach and in imposing their pure will
upon their environment.

*In the New Millennium, Your Contribution to
the World Will Be . . .*
Your adventuresome, entrepreneurial spirit
will be encouraged and rewarded. Your
usual way of hurling endeavors into motion
with daring energy will show, by example,
that change is good. You'll also find innovative ways to contribute your talents to
humanitarian causes.

*Quote That Describes You*
"A LEADER DOES NOT DESERVE THE NAME UNLESS
HE IS WILLING TO STAND ALONE."

—HENRY KISSINGER, a *Gemini*

Lucky you, Aries, to be given the cosmic gift of pure energy, an enormous reserve of life-giving strength, ready to be accessed and used in any way you please. Born at the beginning of spring, Aries epitomizes new beginnings. Your sign is always bursting with new ideas and looking for ways to create fresh starts. For this reason, many Aries become entrepreneurs or especially effective leaders, pioneering into new and uncharted territories. Winning is very important to you. You love being first, fastest, and, most of all, you love being proven right or best. You simply don't take no for an answer. Aries governs the first house of the zodiac, which rules identity, ego, confidence, and self-esteem—all qualities given to you in abundance.

When you move toward a goal, you take not small steps but giant strides. You create a powerful vortex of energy around whatever you do. Your sign embodies the first bolt of energy necessary to initiate any new project—Aries starts the process of spinning everything else into motion. After a while, your endeavors take on a life and momentum of their own. That pulsing drive within you is part of the powerful primal life force that created you and everything else on Earth, and it pushes you ever forward. Your enormous enthusiasm provides the first spark that lights your bonfire. Don't underestimate your charismatic and powerful magnetism, Aries. Others notice this in you and want to be part of your sparkling light. It is one of your most lovable, irresistible qualities.

## SYMBOLS

The symbol for Aries is the Ram—a male sheep—that climbs to the highest peaks, a challenge you choose to take on often just because it's there. Your glyph is the symbol of the horns of the Ram, horns to use if necessary to protect yourself during your arduous ascent to the summit. You relish the challenge of climbing up the mountain as much as you do the reward: by surveying the view. Each part of the effort is enjoyable for you, and so drives you to keep climbing ever more peaks.

♂  Your glyph for Mars is a circle and arrow, optimistically pointing
   upward, symbolic of your need to assert your life-giving will upon
the world.

## PLANETARY INFLUENCES

Originally, Aries and Scorpio both shared Mars as their ruling planet.
However, in 1930, when Pluto was discovered, astrologers decided that
Pluto was a more appropriate ruler for Scorpio, with Mars remaining
Scorpio's secondary ruler and your primary ruler, Aries. The differences
and similarities of the two signs, Aries and Scorpio, are interesting to note.
Both signs are highly energetic, though each exerts its energy differently.
Aries has the short, sprinter kind of energy that bursts forth all at once,
while Scorpio has the "marathon" kind of energy that starts less bright
but lasts longer because Scorpio's power is often directed within. Though
Scorpio has more endurance, Aries marshals its strength and uses it all at
once in a very powerful way.

Aries rules the first house of the horoscope, symbolizing the individual.
The Sun in Aries encourages an outward expression of energy. Therefore,
it is very important for Aries to leave its mark upon the world. Aries
is quite gregarious, and is invigorated by having people around. Aries'
bountiful brand of energetic idealism makes them enormously popular
leaders. They have a charismatic charm that people want to follow, unlike
fellow Mars-ruled Scorpios, who have a deep, mysterious, and silent quality
and are far more emotional. Sometimes Scorpios appear to be brooding or
deliberating about something. Scorpios can be hard to read. In contrast,
Aries are easy to read, being an extroverted sign that speak their mind
and let people know where they stand on any issue. A bright, impetuous,
creative fire sign, you can easily generate ideas that dazzle like diamonds
(your birthstone) as they burst from your fertile mind.

Being ruled by the warrior planet, Mars, Aries is able to withstand substantial pain—whether emotional, physical, or financial—on the path to

fame and glory. In fact, the honor of victory means more to you than the
financial compensation. To you, glory is its own reward, and while money is
fun, the thrill of achievement really motivates you. You have a will of iron,
and you have no problem sacrificing for a goal. An Aries has twice the energy of most signs and can accomplish as much in half the time. You are busy
"having it all"—career, marriage, children, friends, travel, hobbies, and
whatever else you crave, confounding everyone who knows you.

## Cosmic Gifts

Nothing is tentative about you, dear Aries. The cosmos gave you the
precious and important gifts of decisiveness and strength of conviction.
Without these qualities you would be filled with good ideas but have no
power to execute them. You know you can do nothing great without a certain
audacity to pull it all together—even in times of enormous adversity;
perhaps *especially* in times of adversity.

Inside your chest is the brave and passionate heart of a true hero, a person
who can find the resourcefulness to bounce back when others are betting
you are down for the count. I have seen Aries beat all odds when it would
take a miracle to turn things around—physically, financially, professionally,
or emotionally. Aries is never down for long. Perhaps it is your persistent
optimism that acts as your self-fulfilling prophecy, allowing you always to
land sunny side up, sometimes immediately and sometimes later. The timing
doesn't matter. Whether you are fully cognizant of it or not, a magical
reservoir of energy is available to you to tap into whenever it is needed.
Yet this amazing energy is both an asset and a responsibility, for to use
your talents well you have to direct your energies with discipline—it would
be all too easy to squander such a precious natural resource. Being impetuous and spontaneous by nature, you could spread yourself in too many
directions. Harness your enormous power and you could make a substantial
contribution to the world.

As the first sign of the zodiac, your sign symbolizes the birth of man. Think of Aries as the newborn infant. Who has purer survival instincts than a newborn? Babies don't think about their vulnerability—they shout out what they want. Like a newborn, Aries let others know what they need to do to move an endeavor forward. You use charm, persuasiveness or persistence, or become annoying enough so others will do exactly what you want them to do just to keep you quiet. You are good at thinking up ingenious methods to get your own way.

Aries is a cardinal sign. Cardinal signs lead their particular season and prepare us for the coming new environment (*cardinal* literally means "first"). Aries, the first sign of the zodiac, initiates spring. (The other cardinal signs are Cancer, initiator of summer; Libra, autumn; and Capricorn, winter.) Your role is always to be a pioneer of new frontiers, including those areas so dangerous and treacherous that only the most courageous leader would venture first.

You are highly competitive, especially when you can vie with others whom you deem your equal or better. (Going up against an unworthy competitor, to you, is a waste of time.) You continually test your moral, physical, and emotional strength, even unconsciously. Some Aries turn their love of competition into a pastime, whether in business, by playing a real-life Monopoly game, or on a personal level, for instance by competing in difficult sports and taking on hard-to-accomplish fitness regimens.

Your ability to take risks is legendary, and you realize that the only way to score big is to take some judicious gambles, backed up with an intense, wholehearted effort. It isn't just professional interests that attract your I'll-try-anything spirit. You play hard too, often being the first one in your crowd to try a new roller-coaster ride, a bungee jump, or whitewater rafting. A daredevil lives inside every Aries and always emerges at some point. When you're scared, you overcompensate for your fear by putting up an especially strong front. (After all, you can feel just as vulnerable as the rest of us. A little comforting praise from others is always appreciated—right, Aries?) You, more than most astrological signs, understand the advantage of "psyching out" your opponent. You also believe that the best defense is a strong offense, and you will attack to divert attention from any weakness you think you possess. You are a master of the preemptive strike in business, sports, combat, or wherever you need an advantage.

Can you be a bit boastful at times? Sure, but you're also smart enough to know you should watch that tendency. The more evolved Aries know that it's not in their interest to distance other people by displaying arrogance, so smart Aries zip-shut their urge to shout about their accomplishments.

Hopefully, while you were growing up, no one tried to diminish your self-confidence. If you had supportive parents, you began to see the strength of your self-sufficiency and your talent for finding opportunity in situations that others overlook. Even if you did not have that childhood parental support, you can still restore your self-esteem later in life. It is as much a part of you, Aries, as your DNA code. Aries have the most interesting lives because they are courageous enough to propel themselves into new situations others would be afraid to consider.

Thinking big is one of your most attractive qualities. Your innocent optimism enables you to start those large, bold projects. You proclaim, "I want to be either President of the United States or, failing that, CEO of my own company." An Aries would never say he or she wants to make just enough money to pay the rent, but rather, "I want to make my first million by the time I'm thirty." Even when leading a charity effort Aries doesn't cross his fingers and say meekly that he hopes to meet last year's figures. Instead, Aries will go out on a limb and declare: "Not only will we beat last year's donations—we'll double them!" You see what I mean? How can anyone resist following you? Your enthusiasm and your strong self-confidence help you succeed. And you are resilient enough to bounce back, if necessary, from any setback, to begin anew.

Sometimes friends or family tell you that you are a little too self-absorbed, even selfish, because you are always talking about your favorite subject: yourself! Perhaps the universe wanted you that way. Your projects and enterprises need enormous amounts of energy to lift off, and plenty of courage and skill to start in the first place. Being single-minded about your goals and confident in your abilities helps you succeed because you can focus intently on your target. You understand that you have to concentrate all your attention and not waste your energy. Being self-absorbed helps keep your eyes firmly focused on your goal while you also rally others. Just don't carry this theme to the extreme, dear Aries, or you won't have any friends!

It can, at times, be a lonely trek up to the top of your personal Mount Everest. You may feel the pressure of being a leader with much of the responsibility for coming up with original ideas on a consistent basis and the strain of battling the ever-present obstacles that naturally occur on the road to achieving your goals. Isolation always does you a world of good, especially in strategizing new plans and dreams. But being the sociable and warm people person that you are, you might not find time to be alone as often as you should. Choose to schedule some regular dream-fantasy time. Even though it may feel like play, it could be the most productive time you give yourself.

As a fire sign, you rely on your superb instinct and intuition to tell you which endeavors are worth pursuing and to show you how to enlist other people. However, the bean counters around you won't want to hear about how you operate from your gut and hunches. They will want to see the documented research for your latest inspirations and will impose certain structures that may frustrate you initially. It's a shame the accountants won't put as much credence in your intuition as you do—they should. Sometimes your ideas are too revolutionary to be tested accurately by market research because the rest of the world usually lags behind you. When this happens, hang on to your dream, dear Ram. Luckily, you have

a bottomless well of enthusiasm. Don't reward their pedantic cynicism —
instead prove your critics wrong!

Rules bother you, but the world will insist that you follow certain procedures. Your motto is "Rules are meant to be broken." You love being
the exception, and you persuade people easily, but your Aries passion
and charm may not be enough. Be tenacious, disciplined, thorough, and
prepared — then you'll win.

Realize that within your Aries personality is the propensity to battle
almost any obstacle. Even when there is no serious threat you readily go
into defense/offense mode. Sometimes Aries will stir the pot to see what
will bubble up. You also like it best when the volume of life is turned up
high. To you life often seems like opera, and, like the child who "acts up"
at school simply to relieve the monotony of routine, you often need more
drama in your life than most people.

Odd as it sounds, inactivity can drive you crazy and action can calm you
down. When you face an adverse situation — personally or professionally —
the hardest thing for you would be to do nothing while you await an
outcome. Instead, you often find you must *do something*. This is a good
quality in Aries, because if faced with a reversal, you can ride out the
storm in the blink of an eye. While others are still debating options, you
are busy stunning everyone with your bold, decisive actions. Your talent
for cutting to the core of a problem shocks others into admiration. You
prefer simplicity and have no patience with too much theoretical thinking
and circular arguments. Living in the extreme present moment and having
substantial fervor propels you to cut through life's complexities and then
act. For Aries, self-discovery is always achieved through action.

This active drive leads people to call you too brash, too bold, lacking in
direction, impatient, undisciplined, and, at times, foolhardy or self-destruc-
tive. You might even agree that you have some of these qualities. Don't

make moves when unprepared, overly emotional, or without being circum-
spect. Aries would do well to cultivate a little reflective meditation and a
sense of philosophy. If you do learn to stop, look, and listen, with your
guts, street smarts, and energy you could conquer the world. However,
some Aries have to go through a period of sowing wild oats and defeat
before they finally hit on their best individual formula for success.

One of your most likable qualities is your complete lack of pretension.
You are a straight shooter; it is a rare Aries who puts on airs. No beating
around the bush for you. You don't have a trickster bone in your body,
and people soon appreciate your unvarnished honesty. Besides, covering
up your feelings or acting stealthily would require guile or patience that
you don't possess. However, when someone does rile you up, watch out!
You have a temper, Aries, and will show it by yelling, slamming doors,
even breaking dishes. Your ruler, Mars, isn't called the Red Planet for
nothing. Those who know and love you also know that your anger, like
your element, fire, quickly burns out. You certainly aren't vengeful, as
it takes too much energy to hold on to old resentments. A great stress
reliever for you is sports—the more aggressive and strenuous the better.
Channeling your energy into a regular outlet is a good idea.

## RELATIONSHIPS

In your closest romantic relationships, you exude that same verve that your
friends and business colleagues find so attractive. Most Aries men prefer a
modern, self-sufficient woman who is a confident and equal partner rather
than a clinging vine. Even so, the Aries male enjoys being the hero of his
lady's life and will find ways to save his damsel in distress (even if she doesn't
need rescuing). Never let your Aries lover know he doesn't measure up to
the hero in your gothic novels—what harm is there in letting him continue to
think he does? Lots of Aries women find themselves naturally gravitating
toward athletes or self-made men because of their strength and courage.
However, make no mistake, the Aries woman is quite accomplished in her
own right. She is modern, independent, and not likely to sit by the phone

patiently waiting for him. She knows there are other fish in the sea. Or if he's special enough, she'll just pick up the phone and call him.

For both males and females of this sign, the need to experience various challenges can delay marriage. The love of the chase is intoxicating, and once in a serious relationship an Aries will love his or her sweetheart with an incredible depth of passion. Aries is a red-hot lover. Red is Aries' color, and also the color of passion and loyalty. Your intense magnetism relates to your raw, primal, erotic sexual drive. In lovemaking you tend to be experimental, much to your partner's delight. With your sign ruling the pure life force, it is easy to imagine how much you enjoy sex.

A piece of advice to those admirers who hope to win your heart: You won't want to be compared with other lovers. Your Aries sense of individuality would be wounded—you want your lover to see you as completely unique in the world. Also, Aries prefers to have an equal partnership or to be the dominant partner, especially males. When you begin dating, you are disappointed if a new relationship develops too easily because your ever-present sense of competitiveness requires a chance to prove your mettle, even in love.

Once in an established relationship, you will still want to keep alive some of the early freshness, that cat-and-mouse fun, from your early days. You can't ever stand dull routine in any part of your life. You value humor and spontaneity, and if life becomes too predictable you will grow restless. If you can manage to maintain a lively relationship, both you and your partner will benefit. Even though you may resist settling down initially, once you decide you've found the right partner, you can become an extremely loyal, loving, and sexy lifetime mate.

Activities you would enjoy as a couple include international travel to new and exotic places, attending political rallies and debates, playing sports (especially brand-new or exciting), or being a spectator at sports events. You would enjoy investigating new hobbies and interests because your sign is so closely aligned with the creation of new things. Some couples might also find it fun to develop a new business plan together—just realize that if you are married to an Aries, the Aries will still want to be the boss, even if the business idea was yours.

If you are married to an Aries (or are planning to be), be aware that Aries can be headstrong at times, so diplomatic negotiating skills will come in handy. Often Aries' bark is far worse than their bite, so don't be intimidated if they start shouting. In marriage, if you become too practical or staid—if you allow your spirit to be crushed by the weight of life's obligations—it could make your Aries restless or even stray. Not all Aries will have a roving eye, of course, but to keep your marriage secure, you should recognize your mate's need for stimulation, plenty of attention from you, and a strong need for discovery. In return, you will be rewarded with an exciting life filled with surprise and adventure. You will never know what's around the next corner—each day will seem shining new.

## FINANCE

Financially, you can be either stingy or wildly generous, cleverly talking your friends into paying for your lunches or drinks, or almost literally throwing money out the window. This propensity for extremes seems to live within every Aries. On one hand, you have practical Taurus on the cusp of your second house of earned income, giving you the propensity to hold on to every dollar. On the other hand, your need for thrills and entrepreneurship could lead to some crazy financial risks, sometimes with terrible results. When you gamble, you would rather bet on yourself than on anyone or anything else. But when you leap headfirst into one business opportunity after another, you are always in danger of losing money. You may be guilty, too, of impulsively throwing good money after bad. You will doggedly find more capital to keep your project alive during the very difficult start-up phase. You will never give up on your idea. In terms of your money management, to be safe, always have a wise financial adviser, perhaps to slow you down a little before writing those checks.

## CAREER

One gift the cosmos gave you was a fascination with starting new endeavors, and so you are, as stated before, the classic entrepreneur. However, you will quickly discover that you need to hire practical, detail-oriented executives for your team, people who know how to build complex organizations. You won't want to mess with detail. It is not your forté. Rather than get bogged down with the nitty-gritty, your role should be to oversee the larger effort and continually lead the way into the future. The most difficult start-up phase requires raw courage, determination, and street-smart savvy—your best attributes. After this phase is completed you should entrust your business to a practical earth sign–type for your president or CFO. For example, Taurus, Virgo, or Capricorn would make good candidates. This person will have the patience you lack and will develop your endeavor into something more permanent.

Aries is not a sentimental sign, so you probably won't form an emotional attachment to your business. Therefore it is easy for you, Aries, to release your business when it is ready to go public or be merged, sold, or given over to more qualified managers. You are more objective about the value of your creation, and this helps you build wealth. For an Aries, this objectivity lets you continually concentrate on your main talent: starting up more new enterprises. You have an instinct for the right moment to cash out—you don't let grass grow under your feet. No doubt your eye is already firmly fixed on your next big project with the venture capital already in place.

Aries are well suited to work for themselves. If not as the CEO of their own start-up then on a smaller scale, as an independent shopkeeper or the owner of a service-related company. Corporate structure isn't for you, for you view the endless rounds of meetings big companies favor as simply a waste of time. The whole concept of an organization hierarchy above you sticks in your craw, for Aries likes to be boss. (Your style of management is closer to dictatorship than democracy, but somehow it works for you.) For those Aries who are employees, inside your head you are just as smart or smarter than your boss. You also sense that soon you will have his or her job. You have to keep moving; you can't stagnate in one position for long. Aries knows that power is rarely given—it has to be seized.

Besides being a whiz at business, Aries usually does well in a career in the armed forces, thanks to your rulership by Mars, the warrior planet. Aries succeeds in the use of sharp instruments or weapons. The necessary strategic thinking comes easily and could turn you into a brilliant leader. And although corporate hierarchy bothers you in the civilian world, in the armed forces you expect to be promoted more rapidly. Certainly, you would spend your time working toward leading your own platoon or division. Nothing pleases an Aries more than a quick rise through the ranks. Being courageous and strong, you might like being a firefighter or a policeman, detective, FBI agent, or other law-enforcement or security official. Being skilled with sharp instruments, you might also consider becoming a surgeon or a dentist, professions where Aries also excels.

When deciding on a career, also think about doing something that would involve a strenuous physical effort to capitalize on your awesome inner strength. For example, Aries is often brilliant in sales because you are persistent, you've got a superb business sense, and you possess the strength to call more prospective clients than any other salesperson on the team. You also like being out and about, master of your own fate, free to call on whomever you choose. Also requiring strong self-discipline is a career as a professional athlete or dancer, fields you could do well in. Being smartly aggressive in the marketplace comes naturally to you, as would a career as a strategist/planner, perhaps in the marketing or advertising industry. Aries make great explorers and adventurers, too, because they enjoy the discovery process. Doing something unusual or daring, such as working as a storm chaser, a spy, or stuntperson, might also be perfect.

Some Aries are attached to technical jobs, and in that case you could do well as an engineer, mechanic, software designer, producer, or contractor. Aries rules the head, and accordingly some Aries become talented hairstylists

(owning and running their own salon, of course) or designers or manufacturers of hair accessories or hats. You need to express yourself in a pure,
unfettered way, and the freedom to call your own shots will always be of
prime importance to you.

## BODY, MIND, AND SPIRIT

Aries rules the head, and when you have a great idea your head can
physically hurt until you give birth to it. Since teeth are part of the head,
it is vital that you see the dentist frequently, because tooth pain is probably
the number-one pain for Aries. Another possible area for difficulty is fever.
Mars, your guardian planet, is known to bring them on sometimes—the
Red Planet can inflame or overheat you. Unfortunately, some Aries also
suffer from migraine headaches.

Aries also rules the hair. Make no mistake, this sign is *very* interested in
how their hair looks. Male and female Aries alike will tell their sweethearts before going out, "I just need to check my hair, you go ahead—get
the elevator/get the car/meet me at the restaurant"—whatever. And Aries
will be miserable until it looks right. If your Aries sweetheart asks if he or
she can get a haircut, you should answer yes quickly. Aries puts a premi-
um on having stylish hair and loves buying hair products and spending an
inordinate amount of time on hairstyling. Don't discount how important
his or her hair is to your Aries friend, lover, mate, relative, or child.

## SUMMARY

In astrology, each sign's characteristics make up for qualities lacking in
the sign that precedes it. Aries, the sign that begins the zodiac, symbolizes
spring and flows after Pisces, the last sign, born of winter. It is also a sign
that rules the universal; in Pisces there are no boundaries, just all-encompassing love. Through its rulership by Neptune, Pisces is the symbol of
primordial waters of creation itself. Out of the womb of life, the collective
consciousness of mankind, Aries must emerge to assert his or her will
powerfully upon the world. This is part of your destiny, dear Ram, so it is

up to you to leave a very precise, individual stamp "out there" in the cosmos, in the most fearless and pioneering way you can. Your enthusiasm and strength will inspire the rest of us to think big and to attempt endeavors we never thought we were capable of. In the end, your best role will always be one of a passionate and creative visionary.

# THE MYTHS OF
# ARIES AND MARS

At the time of the year when you were born (March 21 to April 19), there are equal amounts of daylight and darkness. This is true six months from your birthday, in October, for Libra too, yet there is a big difference: In the springtime, in the northern latitudes, the Sun is increasing in light, while in the fall the days are gradually growing shorter. In astrology, the force of daylight is symbolized by the Sun—thus, as the Sun grows in importance in your chart, so too does the importance of your individuality. Therefore, it was logical that the ancient astrologers designated Aries as the sign ruling ego and the formation of the personality.

Easter, one of Christianity's biggest and most joyous holidays, symbolizing the triumph of the spirit over the body (matter), comes in the spring. Thus, you are born at the time of the year when many different civilizations celebrate growth, regeneration, and rebirth. Logically, the sign of Aries would prize identity, self-esteem, and independence of the individual.

## ZEUS, METIS, AND ATHENA
Aries is symbolized by the ram, and rules the head. In Greek mythology, there is a wonderful myth that has a lot to do with your creative side, Aries, and the goddess of wisdom, Athena. When Zeus heard that his lover Metis had become pregnant and would soon bear a child that would ultimately dethrone him, Zeus ate her. Not a bit happy about this, Metis

hammered inside Zeus's head day and night, making a helmet. This caused Zeus unbearable headaches. He asked Hephaestus, god of tools, to split open his head. When he did, out came Athena, child of Metis and Zeus, fully dressed and grown and wearing a brilliant helmet. Thus, from this myth comes the astrological saying that Aries should always allow creative ideas to blossom forth, for if they remain locked inside the head they will literally cause this sign's head to hurt until those ideas are given life.

## JASON AND THE GOLDEN FLEECE

Perhaps the most famous myth associated with Aries is Jason and the Golden Fleece. Phrixus and Helle, children of King Athamas and stepchildren of Ino, are to be sacrificed. At the last moment, Zeus sends a winged ram adorned with a golden fleece and saves them. The fleece is given to the king of Colchis, who hangs it on a tree in a sacred grove guarded by a dragon that never sleeps. Jason is chosen by Queen Hera to reclaim the fleece.

Jason represents the quintessential Aries—independent and adventuresome. He rallied a who's-who of Greek action heroes and together they built the *Argo,* the first ship. After a journey fraught with danger, Jason and the Argonauts, with the help of the sorceress Medea, are able to secure the prized Golden Fleece and bring it home.

The story of the Golden Fleece is important because it shows how Jason, through danger and adversity, realizes his courage, strength, and the range of his skills, attributes he could draw on for future explorations. Aries are known to put themselves in difficult, demanding, or even dangerous situations from time to time throughout their lives to test their own mettle on a physical, emotional, or even financial level. They compete not only with others, but also within themselves, always looking to establish their next personal best.

A theme that materializes often in myths that involve Aries-like figures is rebellion against father figures. Some astrologers feel that one way many male or female Aries attain their independence is by coming to terms with a complex relationship with their father. You may have had to question whether you should follow the path your father took in his work, marriage, or other goals, and it's likely that you have discovered, after reflection, that you need to be a trailblazer, even if it means breaking with family tradition. This sense of rebellion ultimately will encourage your biggest growth. Also, the myths suggest that the female Aries probably grew up watching a wounded male in her family suffer—a father, a stepfather, or perhaps a favorite uncle. Her determination to become especially strong and independent in her own life may have been to avoid some of the ordeals this person had to endure.

## MARS THE WARRIOR

The ruler of Aries, Mars, has a rich mythology. To the Romans, Mars was the god of war, and was so esteemed that the only god of greater importance was Jupiter. In Greek mythology, Mars was named Ares and was their god of war too, but wasn't as highly regarded as in Roman mythology. The Greeks thought he was rebellious, hot-tempered, and an all-around troublemaker. However, they did credit him for his courage, passion, and good intentions.

Ares loved but did not marry Aphrodite (Venus), but he did father five children with her, four of whom were Eros (desire and passion), Anteros (desire that is either unreciprocated or unrequited), Phobus (panic), and Deimus (terror). The last child, Harmonia (harmony), was irresistibly beautiful and was Ares' favorite child. Her soft sweetness and grace would soothe this warrior's savage breast. This shows that Mars needs the same influence of calmness and peacefulness that everyone needs.

It is interesting to note that Ares/Mars was not really the movie action hero that we might expect. The myths express the determination he had to succeed and how hard he strove for his successes. In one story Ares battled Otus and Ephialtes, the giant sons of Poseidon, and when they finally trapped him inside of a bronze jar, it was a year before Hermes, messenger of the gods, found a way to release him. In another battle with Hercules, Ares was knocked down four times and finally chased off the battlefield. There are several other stories, but the point is that defeat did not tarnish Ares' image; he was still revered as one of the major gods on Olympus.

Other duties were associated with Mars. In early Rome, Mars' festivals celebrated agriculture. Some mythologists believe that Mars' original function was to reign over land, and later he took on the role of chief warrior and protector. This makes sense because the harvest was such a means of survival to the community, and it was important for it to be protected and defended. Who better for the job than Mars?

According to another myth, the ancient city of Rome was founded by the twin brothers Romulus and Remus, the sons of Mars and Rhea. Romulus and Remus were abandoned on the mountaintop but saved by the woodpecker and nursed by a she-wolf. These sacred animals were sent by Mars, and the children were later sheltered by shepherds. This myth explains how the Romulus-Remus offspring could be called children of the wolf, or children of Mars.

As you see, Aries, you have an enormously powerful planetary ruler. Mars' role in the zodiac as self-confident and powerful protector of the community and of agriculture, using whatever aggression or resourcefulness are necessary to succeed, is why Aries is thought to be blessed with uncommon strength, courage, and optimism. Keep those bright dreams of yours always in sight, dear Aries, for without them the world would be a dreary place. You are the original action hero, the Superman or Superwoman of the zodiac, quite sure you will always land sunny side up. Invariably, you do just that!

# TAURUS PERSONALITY

*Taurus*
April 20–May 20

*Guiding Principle*

"I Maintain"

*How This Sign Feels Joy*
Finds joy in material possessions, in having a
nest egg, and in building established, secure
structure, often by fortifying existing ones.

*In the New Millennium, Your Contribution to
the World Will Be . . .*
As the first earth sign, you are the practical
and patient builder of the zodiac. You will
dance on the edge of all that is relevant to
new technology and enjoy the social change
it brings. You will be relied upon to create
stability.

*Quote That Describes You*
"STRENGTH DOES NOT COME FROM PHYSICAL
   CAPACITY. IT COMES FROM AN INDOMITABLE WILL."

—MOHANDAS K. GANDHI, a *Libra*

Do you think that only a few people know the real, inner you? If yes, it's because you happen to have a more reserved nature than most of the other signs, so it takes a little more time to get to know you, dear Taurus. Unlike some signs that chatter more, or are flashier, or possess bigger egos, you reveal yourself slowly. When you do, we find a powerful inner calm at your center, and self-contained assurance about yourself that is terribly attractive. You have an awesome talent to magnetize people to you, an erotic charm so subtle and yet at the same time so strong that without so much as lifting a finger, the subject of your fascination is often powerless to resist you.

## SYMBOLS

Ancients saw the bull as a highly erotic and sensual creature, one of great fertility. If you were to draw the outline of the bull's face and horns on a piece of paper (an upside-down triangle with horns), you may be surprised to see the outline of a womb and fallopian tubes too, the very symbol of female procreation. In keeping with Taurus's place as formerly first in the zodiac, some historians speculate that the source of the first letter of our alphabet, *A* (also used in the Hebrew alphabet), may have come from that very image of a bull's head, written upside down. Some mythologists have also pointed out that the horns of the bull resemble the crescent moon, an ancient symbol of growth and regeneration, and indeed, many of the monuments in the ancient world were of the bull's horns. (In Crete, near 4000 B.C., a plethora of stone images of bull's horns, called *bacrania*, were made by farming people.) In Egypt, the hieroglyph for Taurus and the word *bull* were both depicted with the image of a phallus. Today we say that Taurus rules the neck, and Scorpio the reproductive organs. Scorpio falls exactly six months from Taurus, and therefore lies on the same axis as the sign of Taurus, which is considered significant because signs on the same axis are complementary.

In the astrologic glyph for Venus, ruler of Taurus, which looks a little like a hand mirror, a circle rests over a cross. The cross is said to represent matter and the circle over it the soul, and in this image we see that the soul has the power to transform matter into something more: spiritual beauty.

## PLANETARY INFLUENCES

So much of who you are, Taurus, is due to your ruler, Venus. Venus is diplomatic, delicate, reserved, pleasure loving, and always desirable, even spellbinding. Venus doesn't try too hard because it isn't necessary. Being as captivating as she is, she just waits for others to come to her, just as you do, dear Taurus, whether you are a male or female. Venus gets her most effective results by combining seductive allure with serene composure, luring her subject sweetly, subtly, as if with a magical, imperceptible, yet intoxicating scent. Just as importantly, Venus urges you to deliberately allow room for the other person to respond. Your ruler, Venus, doesn't have to exert much effort—her focused allure works nearly every time.

Your sign is closely tied to the Earth, to agriculture and fertility. Your personality is virtually a mirror of nature's beauty and of the cycles of the seasons. At the time you are born, Taurus, the Earth is particularly verdant and abundant. It is a time when Mother Nature virtually bursts open in celebration of life. It is not surprising, then, for your sign to be one that especially appreciates the land and all of Nature's gifts.

The Bull stands fixed, heels dug in, and refuses to move unless an outside force causes him to do so. He moves only when the time is right, and this is also true of the farmer and gardener—the seeds must be planted at just the right time, nurtured "just so." We cannot make seeds grow faster by shouting at them or doing anything else to speed their progress. Seeds grow and mature at their own pace, and no outside force can rush the process—does this all sound like your personality, Taurus?

By summer, it will be time to slow down and enjoy the fruits of your labors. Taurus does not move around quickly, rather, the Bull moves slowly for both purpose and pleasure. In the fall, it will be time to anticipate the coming winter and carefully preserve the harvest to ensure survival. Later, Taurus knows it will be time to sell off the extra crops for profits so that you and your loved ones can make it through the barren winter without fear of running out of provisions or money. Better than most, Taurus understands the necessity of anticipating future needs. This all relates to the Taurus qualities of provider and to your skill at the appropriation of assets and the building of wealth, qualities you have in abundance. As a Taurus you won't squander assets. By winter, you know you will have to be prudent and patient while the ground rests under icy cover. Few signs are in such special harmony with the land and nature and, when you look at the year as a whole, you can see how your personality echoes the rhythm of the Earth and celebrates its gifts.

## COSMIC GIFTS

One of your most attractive qualities is your ability to really listen to what other people have to say. Your fans say that your earnest attention is madly flattering. Your interest is one of the best compliments you could possibly give someone, and you do it all the time. You are a superb observer and miss very little of what is going on. Moreover, because you are so reflective by nature, when you have something to say, you command quite a bit of attention because you are always sure your view is relevant to what is being discussed. You think deeply and form opinions, and because you are so slow to come to a firm decision, you are usually stubborn about changing your views later. Nevertheless, in our increasingly noisy and fast-moving environment, so full of commotion, general static, and overall pandemonium, you are a beacon of consistently calm, comforting strength and a symbol of steadfast devotion. On "planet Taurus" everything is reasonable, logical, and carefully thought out.

Do you get mad sometimes? Of course you do. You are human, after all. When the Bull sees red, it gets very angry, but it takes a whole lot to get you to "lose it." However, once done, you are hard to stop. You rage, you rant, and you make everyone wish they weren't around. However, acting silent, withdrawn, and sullen or simply pouting is more your style. Again, here is Venus telling you to attract others to you rather than assertively seeking their attention. Yet if someone has pushed you over the edge by not respecting your feelings or if someone from the home team is disrespectful of you in front of others, the Bull can make quite a mess in that proverbial china shop.

On the positive side, you do have an uncanny ability for simplifying complex concepts to get at the meat of the matter, and then you will rarely lose track of it. As a practical sign, you don't get overly analytical—in your mind, things are fairly straightforward, if not clearly black and white, perhaps spanning just a few shades of gray. Not seeing thousands of shades in a debate can be an asset because you are less likely to become confused or distracted by minor issues in the mass of information. You are a remarkable realist who deals quite well with what is reality without wasting time moaning about what you hope can be.

Your strong will and dogged determination to achieve what you say you will do often engender admiration. When Taurus vows that something will happen, you can bet your house on it. Nothing—not rain, not snow, nor dark of night—will prevent you from delivering on a promise. Your endurance and pure stamina to fulfill goals are inspirational—you are not a quitter. This simple yet supreme personality trait is part of your secret for succeeding in what you set out to do. You wouldn't dream of letting anyone down.

Like the tortoise, Taurus goes about his work slowly and carefully, attending to detail, not overlooking promises made, and thus building a career and reputation conservatively and methodically. Like the hare, your competitors may drive into the fast lane and leave you temporarily back a few paces, but they are also more likely to burn out down the road. Your motto will always be "Slow and steady wins the race." Long after everyone has dropped out, you're still going, often confounding the critics by gradually pulling out in front.

Consistency is a gift, dear Taurus, as just about any expert will tell you, so you should never overlook its value. (Think about this: Without consistency, who could achieve success with diet and exercise? Or reach goals without a consistent advertising campaign? Try to become a popular elected leader without consistency—it is almost impossible.) In the process of achieving its goals, Taurus doesn't ask for acclaim or fanfare. You enjoy occasional praise, like everyone else, but if that praise doesn't come, you don't give any less to your endeavor; your motivation comes from within. This is part of the consistency that you have down to a science, and it reveals that you are ever mindful of your larger goals.

Your sign is also designated a fixed sign, which means that you stick to your guns and aren't easily convinced to change your opinion or your life's path. This can be good when setting goals. Other people might forget their New Year's resolutions, but you can check off every one of them on last year's list. If any sign can see a goal through to successful completion, it's you, but when you commit to one, you already know to your toes that you really want to do what you say you will do. However, sometimes you cling to outmoded ideas, refusing to listen to arguments that you consider changing your point of view. You see no reason to change for the sake of change. "If it ain't broke, don't fix it" is another motto of yours. Some people call you stubborn, and they could be right. In a crisis, you are likely to move too slowly. Keep a flexible Gemini, Virgo, Sagittarius, or Pisces nearby to give you advice— then remember to take it!

You find predictability comforting, because a steady routine reminds you of the enduring cycles of the seasons. You are persistent, patient, and ever so practical. You can also be quite affectionate and romantic, but your pragmatic viewpoint prevents you from being overly sentimental. Capriciousness is not welcome in your world, nor is taking any undue risks. Your lack of freewheeling spontaneity can, at times, drive those around you and those who love you a little crazy. If you can try it, it might be wise to fight this tendency when you find yourself *too* unwilling to accommodate new points of view or improved methods. Those who love you know this is a downside of a personality that also encompasses so much good, the best of which is your rock-solid stability.

Similarly, another quality relating to your propensity for inertia is your tendency to dig in your heels and stay put, both literally and figuratively. This can be a problem, and if you don't fight it you may be the last to know that you've fallen in a rut as deep as a pit and as dark as pitch. When this happens you feel stuck, and loved ones may find you a little boring. Your sweetheart asks: "Do you want peas or carrots? Cookies or pie? Do you want to rent a movie or go bowling, see Mom or go to the beach?" However, in response, all you say, while you continue to read the paper, watch TV, or stare down on your food, is "Hmmm, you decide," or, worse, "Whatever . . ."

If you do find yourself doing this, Taurus, stop and ask yourself what has made you such a passive person. If you don't snap out of this mood, your life will be colored a drab shade of dull gray. Oddly, the very thing you are guilty of here—passivity—you complain about in others. As you read this I can see your lips curling up into a little smile. You recognize this in yourself, don't you? You get away with it because you are so loyal and lovable. Yet life could be more fun, dear Taurus. No matter how old you are, you are too young to be acting this way.

Another of your less favorable qualities is that you don't like to exercise or exert yourself too much. To you, a perfect weekend is spent lolling around. Here's your perfect Saturday: Taurus adores affection in the morning, so you wake up and make passionate love to your partner. Then, with as many goose-down pillows as you can gather up in the house, you prop yourself up and curl under a cozy comforter, then catch up on your reading. Breakfast in bed with your sweetie is a bowl of big, luscious strawberries, perhaps a buttery croissant, and a glass or two of the best champagne you can afford. Later you'll switch on the TV to catch the weather, news, and stock report while someone else runs downstairs to get your mail. You linger over notes from friends and family. You glow as you check your recent statement of investments, stopping to admire the computer pie charts the bank provided to demonstrate the impressive growth you've achieved so far. A long, hot shower is next with a lightly scented body wash applied with a natural sponge, and then it's off to meet friends for lunch. After lunch, shopping is the order of the day. You catch that auction preview, followed by a long drive in the countryside with the top of your convertible down for fresh air. While you drive, you make reservations on your car phone at a four-star restaurant for a late dinner with your honey . . . and so it goes. Not much physical exertion for you! Gym? Not today; you say "No time!"

## RELATIONSHIPS

As a Taurus, you give other people plenty of space and time to make up their minds about you. Once the subject of your attention *does* initiate some action toward you, you know it's more likely that the other person is sure about his or her feelings. You hang back out of respect for others but also because it is a wise thing to do: You know the resulting relationship will be stronger if the other person is convinced, on his own, that he wants to be with you, too. Creating permanent, strong bonds is very important to you—when you link up, you want it to be forever. This slow process of forming relationships takes patience, but patience is one of Taurus's supreme virtues. You feel that time to build strong foundations is time well spent.

You are one of the most dependable, responsible, and trustworthy signs of the zodiac. This might sound boring until you think about being in a relationship with someone who *lacks* these qualities. Most of us have experienced at least one painful episode concerning a significant other (friend, partner, child, sweetheart, or spouse) who lacked some of those very mature and valuable qualities you have in such abundance. Indeed, responsibility and trustworthiness are two of the most important characteristics necessary to form a strong relationship. What close bond could survive without them? So, while your loveliest qualities may seem common, in time you will see they aren't all that common after all.

In a relationship, if you are committed, you stay that way and naturally allow for some moodiness in the other person. When things get too stirred up for you to handle, your first instinct is to stand quietly apart, confident that your sweetheart's emotions will soon settle down and normalize. They often do, perhaps because you don't push the panic button.

Surprisingly, you are often attracted to a partner who is opposite in temperament, thus completing you by possessing the very traits you lack. This might be a spouse or business partner who is quite spontaneous, flexible, adaptable, and versatile. However, you may later find that you have difficulty dealing with this person on a daily basis. You admire and seek out these qualities, but you often find that you can't live with them. Some problems can't easily be resolved, but you should try anyway because your initial instincts to balance out some of your more fixed tendencies were right.

Another natural outcome of being ruled by the refined planet Venus is your sensuousness. Your senses—sight, sound, touch, smell, and taste— are exquisitely heightened and mixed into a beautiful, integrated whole. As a matter of fact, no sign can hold a candle to your ability for the sensuous appreciation of the world around you. As we progress through the signs of the zodiac, the succession from the first sign to the last sign symbolizes the evolution of mankind. Infancy is related to the first sign of the zodiac, Aries, and in Taurus, the sign that follows, we find represented the next stage in human development, babyhood.

At this stage the child is able to sit up, and reach out and touch the world to explore. The baby is not yet able to walk, or talk, but he nevertheless is curious about the world and uses his senses to find out as much as he can on his own. The baby touches everything he can get his little hands on, turns an object over to examine it from all sides. The baby will put an object in his mouth next, and then will rattle it to see if it makes a noise. If it has a pretty smell, or if it is food and tastes sweet or sour, the baby will notice that, too. The baby will bring all senses into play to detect information about the world around him. You do the same, Taurus, only on a very much more mature, sophisticated, and less literal level.

Someone once said that the world is divided into two parts: those who are "lovers" and those who are "beloveds," meaning that lovers are more aggressive and actively seek approval from others, while the other half, the beloveds, prefer that people come to them. Your ruler, Venus, makes you a beloved, more passive and receptive than aggressive and forward. In other words, you aren't pushy. You'd rather sit back and let spunky Aries, chatterbox Gemini, expansive Leo, analytical Libra, persuasive Scorpio, or humanistic Aquarius press forward. You aren't a crusader and you're not about to talk anyone into doing anything. "You know where to find me," you might say at the end of an important interview. Other signs would write their phone number in large print for the interviewer and reiterate that they'll be waiting at their desk whenever the interviewer needs to call. You say to yourself, "My number is on the résumé. If I'm not in, I'm not in. I've got an answering machine." You prefer that people be pulled toward you by sheer magnetism or, in the professional sense, through admiration and respect.

Your predecessor, Aries, is often too busy to stop and smell the roses. Aries runs around and wants everything done in a flash. Since Taurus is meant to balance Aries and add to what Aries lacks, Taurus will not be rushed, whether in love or anything else. The Bull likes to stop, look, and listen and take in the world at a leisurely pace. This helps you see details others miss, and also allows for leisurely contemplation of various subjects. You not only meditate about personal dilemmas but also take time to ponder current events, too, and you like to consider carefully where you stand.

In love, you are steadfast and true, and also quite possessive. When you say "Be mine!" you mean it literally. This is your ruler, Venus, speaking, for Venus urges you to "take ownership" of things and, in some respects, also of people. You might ask yourself, Why look further if I've already found the light of my life? You love with your whole heart, which is why just the thought of losing what you feel to be yours can drive you into a jealous rage. Keep in mind that while *you* may have made up your mind, it doesn't mean your sweetheart has come to the same conclusion. If your decision comes early, it could put pressure on a relationship. Yet if this should happen, as a Taurus you will be quite patient, giving your partner time and space. As a matter of fact, you will wait forever if necessary—once you know in your heart that your partner is the one for you, that's all there is to it. You are not likely to propose living together as an experiment, because when you know, *you know*. When the time is right, you will exchange promises and rings without hesitation. Once you commit, you commit forever.

Venus is responsible for your enjoyment of lusty affection. Venus rules both Taurus and Libra, and the ancient astrologers assigned the more objective, intellectual side of love and the precepts of beauty to the cooler, more analytical sign, Libra. The more passionate side of love was given to Taurus. Your earthy, erotic sensuousness is always alive and operating (no matter how old you get), and your lovemaking is sure to be memorable. You may not come up with many variations of positions or novel ideas for places to make love, but you thoroughly enjoy the experience and bring more of your senses into play than almost any other sign. It is fair to say that after you have made love, the Earth has moved! The object of your affections should be sexually loyal to you—you do not accept or recover easily from an episode of infidelity. Your sweetheart is lucky to have you, Taurus, for few people have the fierce level of devotion you possess, and your actions attest to your deep feelings. Most of all, you crave unconditional love and, bless your heart, perhaps because it is so important to you, you often find the kind of legendary love you are seeking.

FINANCE

That baby will soon learn to exclaim "Mine!" when he sees something he likes and wants, and, like him, you too are known to be quite possessive, stemming from your basic instinct to acquire and hold on to things. No surprises here, for Taurus is placed in the second house of the horoscope, the house of possession and wealth. The concept of ownership, an outgrowth of the development of personal identity begun by Aries, is a very basic and early instinct of humans and is completely indigenous to you.

Each sign is said to make up for what the sign before it lacks. Unlike Aries, a sign motivated more by new ideas and concepts than money, Taurus is very interested in material wealth. Your sign's focus on the accumulation of things and money, combined with your stable qualities, makes you financially conservative, prudent and yet wise, able to build and amass riches on a grand scale if you put your mind to it.

You are quite talented in financial matters, and making money is very important to you; sometimes it seems like an enjoyable game. You occasionally hear of people who say that they are not interested in building a nest egg. This attitude puzzles you. Shaking your head and shrugging your shoulders, you accept their views as one of life's mysteries. You know *you* cannot operate that way. Taurus needs money in the bank to feel secure. Until you have it, you always feel a little uneasy and out of sorts. When you set out to build wealth, you take a cautious path, steering clear of wild gambles. You often like to pay in cash, too. Pulling out a hundred-dollar bill instead of a credit card shows confidence in a poised, self-possessed kind of way, and never more so than when your wallet is brimming.

With their comforting stability and trustworthiness, responsible Tauruses will treat other people's money with the same care they would give to their own. They make great financial advisers.

While a Taurus likes making money, Tauruses also like spending it—wisely. You are not a tightwad by any means; acquiring beautiful things interests you and is fun. One of your favorite investments is real estate, for Taurus rules the earth and the land, and you are happy to acquire an acre or two you can call your own. You like to own rather than rent, so if you live in town you could save up for a condo or cooperative apartment. A Taurus will usually try to find one overlooking a park or a garden plot.

Other items on your shopping list that any Taurus would give his or her eyeteeth to have stem from your sharpened sensuousness and love of beautiful, functional things. You crave real jewelry (to give or to get), artwork, fine furniture, imported rugs, a wine collection, stereo equipment, quality linens, a well-built automobile, and perhaps a gold watch. As a Taurus, it's fairly certain you won't be seen sporting the plastic watch with flashing LED time display. Add to that list a gorgeous new laptop, a collection of music for your CD player, a fine cashmere sweater—all are good examples of things high on your "must-have" list in the future.

Until you make your six-figure salary, you might start by giving yourself a small treat now and then, as you can afford them (Tauruses generally don't go wild with credit cards because their practical side tells them not to pay high finance charges). Some examples of treats could include a couple of tickets to a hit Broadway show, a sensuous massage after a stressful day, or a magnificent meal in a four-star restaurant to celebrate a victory. When you marry, it is important to you that you marry someone who has similar views about money and possessions, or there could be angry conflicts.

Are you a tad materialistic? Yes. But you work hard to attain your luxuries and enjoy them so thoroughly that we can't give you too hard a time about this inclination. Still, your love of possessions does have its downside. There is always the danger that you could become too attracted to beauty and greed and therefore this attraction could become a trap, a glittering, glamorous lure that remains out of touch. The more you love beauty, the more you want to take it home and own it (the object being a thing or even a person). But the most evolved Taurus realizes that the true gift is an *appreciation* of beauty, which costs nothing and is available to everyone.

## CAREER

Career-wise, you take your work seriously, and you recognize that what you produce is a tangible reflection of the inner you. Your reputation is important to you, and you want your name to be associated with the best you can be.

In your career, you establish yourself as a talented producer, organizer, or committee leader and can take something already begun and transform it into something more sturdy, solid, and permanent. You build things that last. While Aries is the sign best known to generate new ideas (a process that interests you less), Aries relies on Taurus to turn these ideas into a more established form after the initial start-up phase. Taurus can take almost any good idea and transform it into something far more solid and lasting.

One of your other talents is your pragmatic sensibility about new proposals. As an earth sign, you deal in the "real" world all the time; other signs should forget about showing you any overblown, Hollywood razzle-dazzle proposals. You know those kinds of deals won't likely get inked by your client any-way—not unless they make solid, money-in-the-bank sense and can be proven first. Why waste clients' time asking for a something they don't have the money for or even want? Taurus knows it would only get them mad, per-haps mad enough to walk. Taurus's instincts are right—why waste time? Your ideas, Taurus, are more likely woven into a much more doable plan, one that integrates form and function, beauty and durability, within a realistic budget and realistic timeline.

You are generally not as comfortable at the idea-generating, brainstorming stage of a project as you are in the second stage of establishing stability for an existing but fledgling idea. The conceptual stage is a little too fuzzy and unconcrete for you. Think of Aries as the imaginative screenwriter, for example, and Taurus as the one who gets the movie funded and produced. Many Tauruses' golden gift is expanding on someone else's idea by giving it form, function, and foundation. What good is an inspiration, you say if it doesn't eventually get produced? In other words, dreams must be materialized to exist. The Taurus gift is to make dreams a tangible reality. And that, dear Taurus, is no small talent.

There are a number of occupations at which Taurus will excel. These include real estate broker, CFO, insurance or stockbroker, financier or financial analyst, accountant, banker, or venture capitalist. Taurus's love of land and of real estate could inspire him to be an architect, agricultural biologist, botanist, landscape artist, surveyor, residential or commercial interior designer/decorator.

Your sensuous side and your good taste make you a natural as a perfume designer, wardrobe stylist, or clothing designer. Consider too being a wine broker or retailer, or a wine steward. You might choose to be a model or a modeling-agency owner, beauty editor, art director or graphic artist, or a textile designer. (Taurus is highly creative, a quality that flows from fertile and beauty-loving Venus.) Perhaps you might like being a masseur or masseuse, a florist, a nursery owner, auctioneer, recording studio owner, restaurateur, museum curator, jeweler, or jewelry designer. Add to the list a hair and makeup stylist/consultant, plastic surgeon, boutique owner, photographer, voice-over professional, or musician/conductor (Taurus loves music). Finally, Taurus rules the throat, and some of our most gifted singers—from opera to pop—were born under your sign.

Whatever you choose to do, make sure you can generate a steady paycheck. You cannot deal with a wildly fluctuating income as well as creative, freewheeling Pisces or gambling, entrepreneurial Aries. Taurus's cash flow has to be rock solid and as regular as the Sun and Moon. Nothing's wrong with that!

## BODY, MIND, AND SPIRIT

Taurus puts stock in creature comforts and sees no reason to be inconvenienced. After a grueling day at the office, you're happiest to shut the door and pull down the blinds, sit in your favorite chair or your personal side of the sofa (Taurus is quite territorial), and watch TV, remote control in hand. Perhaps you prefer to sit back and listen to your favorite music without interruption from telephones or needy friends and relatives. Taurus draws the line firmly and sets clear boundaries. While you are relaxing, some special sweets in a nearby dish would be nice (you love chocolate). A fragrant bouquet of flowers in a crystal vase wouldn't hurt either.

In your everyday life, you don't just enjoy being near to greenery—you *need* to be near it. You feel better—more alive and happier—in an environment that looks good. Beauty invigorates and stimulates you to do better work. Fresh flowers, healthy houseplants, or a sturdy indoor tree can soften the stark edges of your office. It would be ideal to live in a rustic area with plenty of nature for enjoying long walks in all seasons of the year. If you live in the city, you no doubt find ways to enjoy frequent weekend trips out of town or have plenty of plants in your apartment.

Your ruler, Venus, makes your taste refined and sophisticated. You are a fashionably dressed sign, and your presentation is likely to be clean and polished, even elegant and refined, but never loud, ostentatious, or flashy. Taurus wants classic designer trends that last. For instance, your jeans tend to be clean, never scruffy or dirty, and you wear them along with a freshly pressed, clean, and crisp shirt. You often notice the smallest details of style and beauty. As you converse with a friend, you may lean over to touch the sleeve of her jacket, commenting, "I love this marvelous fabric! Such a flattering color on you too!" Or upon greeting your sweetheart, as you warmly embrace, you immediately detect a sexy new scent and will quickly mention its pleasing quality. Taurus misses nothing. Bless your heart.

You do have your standards and little rituals that give your days a comforting routine. When it's time to eat, you want dinner, not mere fuel to keep you going. You want to sit in your chair and dine at the normal time. If your sweetheart asks to stop at a fast-food restaurant, you are incredulous at the suggestion. You reply in disbelief, "I don't think so. A greasy hamburger? Fast food is not dinner." You would rather go hungry than gulp down something you didn't enjoy or, worse, be forced to do it in a hurried manner. You like to savor food, chewing slowly so that you can enjoy every morsel.

You practically originated the term *couch potato*, Taurus. For this reason, Taurus often piles on pounds later in life. Try to keep moving, if only for health's sake. If you look up *inertia* in *The American Heritage Dictionary,* it reads "the tendency of a body at rest to remain at rest or of a body in motion to stay in motion in a straight line unless acted upon by an outside force." As you can see, there is hope—you can change the direction you are headed in. If you can manage to motivate yourself, there is nothing you can't accomplish. When a Taurus says he is going to kick a bad habit or start on a new path of self-improvement, this sign demonstrates a certain kind of drive that could break through a concrete wall. You've got the resolve if you want to conjure it up. Better yet, with your patience, the results are likely to be more *long-lasting* (even permanent) than those of other signs. So you see, dear Taurus, your fixed nature works both for and against you. You decide how it is to be used, positively or negatively, for better or for worse. You are in charge.

### SUMMARY
Trustworthy, loyal, reliable, steadfast, devoted, and true blue are all admirable qualities that describe you, dear Taurus. Lucky is the one who

loves you, for you will work your whole life to be an ardent provider for your family and a fair and true partner to your mate. You also have the sharpest and most developed appreciation of the senses of any sign, sure to help make your life a joy. Gradually and methodically, you will teach the people in your life to open their eyes to see the rich depth of beauty that the universe has to offer. In the end, what you have to give is an awesome talent to behold.

# THE MYTHS OF
# TAURUS AND VENUS

As a Taurus, you, like Capricorn, have the distinction of being born under one of the zodiac's oldest constellations. The sign of Taurus was and still is considered an astrological symbol of fertility and erotic pleasure, for at the time of Taurus's birth, nature is at her most voluptuous and abundant. You may be delighted to hear that your symbol was not just any bull but a sacred bull, one of the most revered symbols of fertility. Historians say that the constellation of Taurus was first named sometime between 4000 and 2000 B.C. In ancient days, there were a remarkable number of statues and other monuments to Taurus in Egypt, Crete, and Assyria, for these cultures, as well as that of the Romans, venerated the bull. The bull's link to fertility began when Egyptian farmers noticed that Taurus was rising in the evening sky at the time that the Nile receded back far enough to plow the fields with oxen.

In those early cultures, myths of the Bull and the Moon Goddess were intertwined, with the Bull acting as the male counterpart to the female Moon, for the ancients knew both were necessary for creation of new life and a new crop. Indeed, farmers believed that to have a successful crop it was best to plant on the waxing Moon (the period between the new Moon and the full Moon) rather than at the full Moon or on a waning Moon (the time between the full and the new Moon). Astrologically, we understand this timing because to this day we generally initiate endeavors on a new Moon and look to see results on the full Moon.

In ancient days, as the astrological zodiac was still being formed, Taurus was considered the first sign of the zodiac. How the shift occurred many millennia ago is not entirely clear. It could have been caused by the so-called precession of the equinoxes, meaning that in the early days of the zodiac, the vernal equinox fell in late April or May rather than in March, as it does now. However, whether Taurus is first or second in the zodiac's lineup doesn't matter. In tune with Taurus's enduring sensibilities, you are still considered one of the finest producers of the zodiac, with an extraordinary talent for creating tangible results and increased security for yourself and those who depend on you. So, although today Aries is deemed the zodiac's first sign, all the original attributes of Taurus remain constant.

A particularly bright star that was part of the Taurus constellation was and is still called Aldebaran—in fact it is considered the fourteenth brightest star in the skies—literally "the bull's eye" because it was found in the very center of the constellation, at fifteen degrees Taurus. (Each sign has thirty degrees.) The Romans felt that Aldebaran was a master star because it was *the* star that allowed astrologers to measure all longitude, allowing them to fix the beginning point of the zodiac band.

In Taurus we are reminded that in order to create the abundant crop, a personality that accepted responsibility was necessary. This understanding of what it takes to achieve results is present in all three earth signs (Taurus, Virgo, and Capricorn), but for Taurus particularly this idea is echoed in the image of the Bull's yolk. Astrologically, we know that Taurus doggedly remains fixed to its job, patiently seeing its goal through to completion, unfazed by whatever obstacles it may encounter. Taurus can surmount any and all odds simply by being determined and working in a slow, steady, and practical manner, a necessary attitude when it comes to agriculture. There is no need to get flustered, Taurus tells us—unless a red flag is waved in front of the Bull. In that case the Bull will become incensed. When this happens, some astrologers feel that Taurus's metamorphosis from sturdy and stable Bull to wild and impassioned Bull is more of an emotional "feminine" quality. Appropriately, in astrology Taurus is given a negative (feminine) charge. This does not mean that Taurus men and women are feminine. It simply means that in keeping with the Venus-ruled image of the sign, Taurus men would be more likely to enjoy the finer parts of life, such as special wines and gourmet food, and that sensitivity is considered a negative, or feminine, charge in a chart. Venus's rulership of Taurus makes this sign sophisticated and cultured and also tends to bestow artistic talents on its members, particularly in music and the visual arts.

Several of the myths that follow here will involve Taurus's well-known proclivity for sensuality. The tales, as we will see, focus on love and sex (perennial Taurus themes), as well as this sign's steadfast ability for overcoming obstacles. There is also a story about desire for material success that goes too far, a trap that some but, happily, not all Tauruses fall into.

## ISHTAR AND GILGAMESH

The Sumerians reverently called Taurus the Bull of Heaven. In one early myth, Ishtar (a lustier version of Venus) fell in love with a rugged and heroic male named Gilgamesh. Ishtar had a rather bad reputation as a lover—she was considered disloyal, volatile, and untrustworthy—so, not surprisingly, Gilgamesh rejected her advances. Ishtar, outraged, went directly to her father, Anu, king of the gods, to ask him to create a giant, awesomely powerful Bull of Heaven to kill Gilgamesh in punishment for rebuffing her. That bull was to be Taurus, and Gilgamesh did later face the bull and was victorious (one of many tests and challenges he was to face). Some experts feel that Gilgamesh represented a patriarchal way of life. Ishtar's inability to draw him to her pointed toward her future eroding power. (Gilgamesh was the first action hero of mythology and is discussed in more detail in "The Myths of Aquarius and Venus.")

## ZEUS'S LOVE OF EUROPA

From Greek mythology comes another tale that focuses on sexuality, but in true Taurus style, it contains great finesse and beauty. Zeus, the ruler of the heavens, fell in love with Europa, the daughter of the king of Sidon. Zeus (Jupiter) had fallen in love with many women, but clearly Europa was special. Indeed, she was breathtakingly beautiful as well as young and innocent. One day Europa woke from a troubling dream about "two continents" who took the form of women who wanted to possess her. One was called Asia and the other woman was nameless, but the latter one declared to Europa in the dream that Zeus would certainly allow her to give herself to him. Europa awoke from this troubling dream and decided to go off to the seashore to see her friends.

As the story goes on, Europa innocently collected all kinds of gorgeous flowers in that dawn hour, which were, like her, at the peak of perfection, and of various colors and incredibly beautiful, exuding a rich, fragrant scent. Unbeknownst to her, Zeus, the king of the heavens, was watching her and was enthralled by her beauty. At that moment Venus sent Cupid to pierce Zeus's heart, and he instantly fell in love with Europa. Zeus decided to seduce Europa. His wife, Hera, was away, but Zeus neverthe- less felt it was more discreet to disguise himself as a strikingly handsome bull. He transformed himself into one like none other, a bull that bore a silver circle on his brow and with horns shaped in the form of a young crescent moon. Attracted by his striking good looks and gentle demeanor, Europa and her friends caressed Zeus and enjoyed his heavenly, fresh scent. The bull knelt at Europa's feet, allowing her to put a wreath of flowers on his horns. Slipping on the back of the bull, she bid her friends to join her for a ride on the great animal, but before they could even reply, Zeus leaped up in a flash and rushed into the sea at full speed. The two rode on top of the waves, and as Europa and Zeus rode together, a whole variety of characters appeared to accompany them, including Zeus's brother, the god Neptune (Poseidon), Tritons blowing horns, and Nereids riding dolphins.

Europa was both terribly frightened and excited by all the activity and the turn of events. She clung to one of the bull's horns and held up her purple dress to keep it dry. It was apparent to the young Europa that her bull must be a god, but she was not sure of his identity. Unsure where she was going, she begged him not to leave her alone in a place far from her home. He gently told her not to worry, and he told her truthfully that they were going to Crete. Zeus made love to her there under the plane tree and Europa was to bear him three sons, two of whom, Minos and Rhadamanthus, would become well known, both later rewarded for their just behavior on Earth by being appointed judges of the dead.

## APHRODITE ON A HALF-SHELL

Venus's alternate name, Aphrodite, literally means "born from sea foam," and it is said that she rose out of the sea-green foam of the ocean on a half-shell, emerging from the frothy white-capped waves as a young, beautiful, and alluring woman with long, luxurious hair. The sea or ocean is thought to stand for the collective human unconscious as well as the waters of creation. According to the legends, Venus's lovers always spoke of her as "bathed in golden light," emphasizing her role as a goddess, helping her lovers enjoy their five senses as well as causing the initial spark of love. (Note that Venus's job was not to create marriage but initiate love—other planets would have to get involved for commitment to result, something we will discuss under Libra.)

## KING MINOS AND THE MINOTAUR

There is a myth about a Minotaur that explains some of the talent of a Taurus lover to strengthen his or her sweetheart's courage by helping the lover to confront fears. In the story, Poseidon (Neptune) sent an extraordinary, magnificent bull to King Minos and ordered him to sacrifice it. However, upon seeing the fine animal, King Minos couldn't obey this divine order, for the bull was too splendid to behold. Instead of sacrificing it, King Minos decided to keep it. Neptune and the gods became angry, so in retaliation they drove the king's wife, Queen Pasiphae, mad with lust. She mated with the bull and later gave birth to a monster, half man, half bull, called a Minotaur. Not knowing what to do, King Minos quickly hid the beast and asked Daedalus, a great inventor and architect to build a labyrinth, a place of no escape, to confine the Minotaur. Human sacrifices were brought to the maze for the beast to consume, but instead of being satisfied the monster continually grew more demanding, and more and more human sacrifices were needed as time went on.

Consider that King Minos represents a side of Taurus that is curious about intense, unbridled passion (thought to be the normal domain of Scorpio), but when this level of passion is encountered it often overwhelms, and Taurus finds he is unable to deal with it. King Minos's instinct in dealing with the monster was not an aggressive one, but rather passive: He locked it up. This is typical—Taurus's first instinct may well be to contain or bottle unrestrained passion. Taurus likes to remain calm because the Bull knows that a wild beast resides inside and that it may come out, a wild creature it can't seem to control—as happens when the Bull "sees red." However, continually choosing to remain passive isn't always a good thing, either. Tauruses can become imprisoned within their passivity; they sometimes find themselves unable to experience life to the fullest so instead they make do with life as is.

Continuing the story of King Minos, among the new sacrificial victims brought in from Greece to feed this terrible monster was a man called Theseus. Theseus wanted to kill the monster, so he asked Ariadne, daughter of King Minos (her name means "pure one"), for her help. Ariadne gave Theseus a magic thread in which to chart his way through the dark basement maze, and Ariadne, risking all, held a torch for him to light the way. In the end, Theseus was successful in slaying the Minotaur, but he abandoned Ariadne in a cold and heartless manner. Ariadne had helped and supported Theseus—and in so doing she even revealed to him his most heroic side—and without the slightest gratitude or feelings of hesitation, he left her. (She later found a new relationship with Dionysus.)

From this story, we see the Taurus talent to "light the way" or be a torchbearer to his or her lover, helping the lover find his or her full potential through the power of love. In ancient times, it was more likely to be the woman who stood by her man, aiding him through his trials and tribulations, but in modern times it may work out in reverse, with a man doing the same for a woman. Taurus often likes to play a supporting role, and often does so magnificently.

Yet still, Theseus's attitude toward Ariadne is troubling. This is another recurring theme in Taurus, specifically the question of being abandoned when one is no longer is useful, beautiful, or vital to the other person in a relationship. Venus prompts us to ask the question, What will happen when we are no longer fairest of the land? (Male Tauruses in fact have the same concern, even though this is generally thought to be more of a female problem.) This tale seems to warn that with Venus there is always a tendency to pay more attention to beauty, luxury, and possessions. Being too focused on superficial things may leave one (Taurus particularly) vulnerable. In the case of Ariadne, there was not much she could have done to change things, but the tale does seem to warn, "Life is not fair—plan accordingly." Taurus soon discovers that material goods cannot maintain a relationship that is falling apart at the seams. Hopefully, one can create a tighter spiritual bond rooted in mature and substantial values, qualities that will hold two lovers together in love long after the initial rush has subsided. Of course, this is not Venus's role (Venus starts relationships, but does not keep them going)—other planets will have to help, but it is a worthy goal.

## KING MIDAS AND HIS WORLD OF GOLD

There is one last myth that applies to Taurus, one that many schoolchildren know: the cautionary story of King Midas. King Midas, like Taurus, loved wealth but, unlike Taurus, he was materialistic beyond all reason. When King Midas wished for more and more gold, his wish was granted, but he was soon horrified to see that gold crowded everything else from his life. According to the tale, everything he touched—his food, clothing, even his child—all suddenly turned to gold. This fable warns Taurus not to put too much emphasis on possessions at the cost of human relationships because if taken to the extreme, those beautiful and glittering objects could add up to one very lonely life. The story seems to whisper Venus's guiding principle: Without human love, life is empty and useless.

The powerful Taurus ability to maximize resources will always be one of this sign's greatest gifts. The farmer works with the soil and by trying different methods he wisely finds ways to use what nature has provided to its best advantage. Growing things to fullness is a steady, slow process that requires enormous patience and forbearance, and surely Taurus is blessed with all these qualities. The important point, then, is not to focus on how many resources you are given, but on what to do with those you have. Some squander the greatest riches; others figure out how to multiply their meager resources. Taurus creates (and pushes hard for) ever-increasing growth but doesn't let it expand out of control. An Earth sign, Taurus will stabilize that growth, and in so doing bring the world a greater security though the abundance of food that Taurus grows, food that can sustain himself, his family, and his community through the coldest of winters. It is no wonder that Taurus is considered such an awesome builder, expanding the structures and enterprises he tackles while he secures the future for himself and for everyone else as well.

# GEMINI PERSONALITY

## Gemini
### May 21–June 20

### *Guiding Principle*

"I Think"

### *How This Sign Feels Joy*

Finds joy in being active on several fronts at once, actively gathering, testing, and sharing factual information as well as new concepts and ideas.

### *In the New Millennium, Your Contribution to the World Will Be . . .*

Your role in the future is as an ambassador. You will use your considerable gift for communication to forge unity and understanding among people of various countries, religions, and social classes.

### *Quote That Describes You*

"CURIOSITY IS, IN GREAT AND GENEROUS MINDS, THE FIRST PASSION AND THE LAST."

—SAMUEL JOHNSON, a *Virgo*

Geminis are like the White Rabbit in *Alice in Wonderland,* who chattered, "I'm late, I'm late, for a very important date. No time to say hello good-bye. I'm late, I'm late, I'm late." Of course the White Rabbit is late—he is squeezing too many things into his schedule, but if he's a Gemini, and I suspect he is, then that's Gemini's idea of life at its best. Gemini gets more done in a day than most people get done in a week. Part of your secret, Gemini, is your legendary ability for doing two things at once. A typical Gemini gets bored doing just one thing at a time. You write proposals while you watch TV, return phone calls while you're balancing your checkbook, dictate letters while you pedal your exercise bike. Not a moment to lose!

Gemini is the third sign of the zodiac, the sign after Aries and Taurus, and it symbolizes the stage of learning language and man's need to communicate with others. Aries, the first sign, symbolizes the self-contained bundle of energy, the primal life force. Aries is the zodiac's newborn that says "Me, me, me" and rules initiations of all kinds. Next comes Taurus, symbolized by the older baby, learning to crawl and reach out to touch all the marvelous things in the world. The Taurus baby says "Mine! Have it! Want it!" and in so doing mirrors a very early and basic instinct of man, which is the need to have as well as the need to investigate using all the senses. Your sign, Gemini, symbolizes a slightly older child, one who is able to speak, read, and write. The child keeps asking "Why?" impatiently, and when he travels he asks eagerly, "When are we going to get there?" There is a big world out there to explore, and Gemini can't wait to get going. Once language is developed, reasoning and analytical ability follow. Thus, Gemini is considered a highly thinking, reasoning, and intellectual sign.

Gemini is the first air sign, so it resembles a child learning everything it needs to learn all at once at breathtaking speed. The child's mind is wide open, and he finds learning easy. As a matter of fact, a child cannot get enough—he wants to know about everything he can as fast as he can. The two hemispheres of Gemini's brain analyze and digest information, bouncing data off each other rapidly, right and left, in the search for truth. The duality of the Gemini mind allows you to see various facets of a situation. You say, "On one hand, this is the case, but then again, on the other hand, the perspective changes." Or you say, "I am of two minds about this." This internal wrestling about an issue is so indicative of your personality. Your mind darts back and forth as you think with dazzling speed. Your highly developed nervous system makes the inner circuitry of your mind process information in unique ways. You approach everything with curiosity, as if for the first time, and you are intent on getting to know your subject inside and out.

## SYMBOLS

♊ The glyph for Gemini is the roman numeral II, to symbolize the sign of twin identities. According to the ancient astrologers, in Gemini there is no masculine or feminine energies per se as there are for other signs. Here we find neutrality—a merging of both the yin and yang for completeness. Gemini is regarded as androgynous and therefore has the capability for divine wholeness.

☿ The symbol of Mercury, ruler of Gemini, is a circle of spirit and the crescent of soul. The mind links the spirit, soul, and matter (body) together.

## PLANETARY INFLUENCES

Your talent is fostered by the rulership of the most objective and rational planet of our solar system, Mercury, the planet of intellect. Mercury is seen as being so objective that when it meets up with another planet it doesn't color that planet's energy but rather becomes colored by it, acting as if it were that planet's "spokesperson." Mercury is the ultimate intermediary, facilitator, and guide or mediator to other planets, helping to clarify the messages of those planets. As the guardian of Mercury or as "Mercury's child," you are given this talent too. Mercury's job in a horoscope is to be completely objective and rational, and to be as unemotional as possible. It is the planet in charge of finding truth, the whole truth, and nothing but the truth. This is why as a Gemini you are perfectly positioned to report the news objectively, without shading it with your own biases. While not all Geminis are reporters or jour-nalists, this sign always cares about what's going on "out there"—in their company, in the industry, in the local community, and on the world stage. Gemini is the sign most likely to keep an ear to the ground, so if you want to know what's going on, ask a Gemini. They have an uncanny way of always knowing the latest gossip, and what's more, they will be pleased to tell you.

The tie between language and Gemini runs quite deep. As man matured and gradually became more civilized, his need for the preciseness of language became more pressing, partly to transmit the laws of the land that everyone would understand. Your mythological ruler, Hermes, the messenger of the gods, is the reason your role is so often as town crier, a go-between, to disseminate information. Hermes's mythological back-ground and influence on you is discussed in "The Myths of Gemini and Mercury." Without agreements, procedure, rules, or laws there would be chaos in society, so language was imperative for man to conquer. Gemini is an air sign and, as with all air signs, its role is to analyze, hypothesize, and create a new world order, gleaned through communication. Air contin-ually moves like the wind, and so do you, Gemini. Your sign is restless and wandering, not yearning for roots but requiring just the opposite: complete freedom.

Ancients felt that there was something magical and sacred about one who has the ability to "name" an object or concept, because it would forever filter the way the rest of the group thought about that concept, thing, or person. And this was Gemini's main role: to name objects, things, and ideas, and to pioneer new avenues of thought. Being a thinker and reporter as well as a social animal, your key role is to gather information and send it out to the world. In this respect, the ancient astrologers felt that Gemini was similar to the magician, as one is often not able to "see" what has no name.

Mercury, your ruling planet, gives you another wonderful gift, and that is the gift of seemingly perpetual youth. Ancient astrologers wrote about how much younger Gemini always appeared as compared to the rest of the signs. It is true that you retain a certain radiance—a Peter Pan quality— and a razor-sharp alertness that often astounds others when they find out your true age. (Being mistaken as younger could be a bit irritating at age seventeen, but it's something to be grateful for at sixty-seven.) If you are a Gemini, you are lucky indeed. Remaining young in mind, body, and spirit has a lot to do with Gemini's ability to keep its inner child alive. This makes you not only more mentally active but more physically active too. Your abundant nervous energy makes you fidget, pace, participate in sports, react, and generally move and play around more than most signs.

Eternally inquisitive, your expression and even your mannerisms (*especially* your mannerisms) suggest a far younger person. This is proof that inner character and perspective can color outward appearances. Bless your heart, Gemini—your genuine curiosity about so many things and puckish sense of humor add to the overall impression that you remain ever young. You have been known to pull a little prank now and then, and this impish Tinker Bell in you keeps a bright twinkle ever present in your eyes.

## COSMIC GIFTS
Every sign makes up for the characteristics the sign before it lacks, so let's note the differences between those adjoining signs. The sign that precedes you is Taurus, known for its overall stability and yet also for inertia. Taurus is a sign strongly connected to the Earth and agriculture, the harvest. The field is readied with Aries (ruling new beginnings) but seeded in Taurus (ruling tangible results). With Gemini, there is no reason to hang out on the farm—the crop has been planted (so to speak), so Gemini is free to roam and seek stimulation elsewhere, which is why your sign is known to be the itinerant nomad. Geminis are known to like to travel so much that they may constantly live out of a suitcase—and enjoy every minute of it.

Unlike Taurus or Cancer, Gemini does not find comfort in the concept of permanence. A Gemini won't dream nostalgically of buying a house to live in until old age; to Gemini, thinking long-term is depressing. Gemini hopes there will be many houses; change is seen as a good thing. Gemini wants flexibility, not rigidity. Therefore, Gemini would more often prefer to rent an apartment rather than own one, just to keep the options open. After all, in Gemini's mind, a better offer may come along at any moment, or maybe there will be an opportunity to live in another city. Gemini wants to be ready, even if no such offer is even remotely on the horizon. This very concept of "keeping one's options open" is indigenous to Gemini, and it probably gets Geminis in trouble in matters of the heart. It isn't that Geminis are averse to marriage per se, but they are resistant to making any final, irreversible decisions about *anything* in life. Gemini has a real need to prepare for a change of mind, point to new directions, and explore new aspects of life to the fullest.

As you will see by studying the mythology of Gemini, Mercury, and Hermes in "The Myths of Gemini and Mercury," you are at your best when acting as an intermediary. There are many interchangeable terms we can use to describe this role: guide, middleman, conduit, agent, mediator, interviewer, gatekeeper, matchmaker, messenger, editor, spokesperson, or representative. Yet whenever you act as a catalyst or a facilitator of inter-action between two parties (or help to bridge two locations or events), you are often at your shining best. Cancer, the sign that follows yours, is closer in personality to Taurus than to you. After man has traveled here, there, and everywhere in the sign of Gemini, Cancer, the sign that follows, needs to seek refuge in a strong foundation of home and to build a cozy nest as a haven against the world.

With so much traveling, it is logical that the job of perfecting language would fall to Gemini. In his wanderings, meeting all sorts of people, the Twin would hear many languages and dialects, many kinds of word usage, grammar, and inflections, and in so doing polish his own skill with words by learning their subtle shadings. This will help you always to choose the perfect word to express your innermost whisperings and individuality. You learned well, dear Twin. Never discount the power you have to write, research, and speak effectively.

When it comes to word play, Gemini can run rings around anyone at any time. You know that you always win games of verbal Ping Pong, in any arena. Nimble and fast-moving, you know how to think on your feet and turn on a dime. If you find yourself in a jam where persuasion is the key to freedom or resolution, your gift of speech will always set you free. Some people know they can rely on family connections, money, or a good lawyer. Gemini knows he needs none of these, for his intellect will never fail him; the words always come when he needs them. You won't hide from any tough confrontation because you rely on your resourcefulness, which always comes to your rescue in the nick of time.

If you debate a Gemini, you will soon find that he has a quicksilver mind that moves at the speed of light. Try to trip Geminis up and they nimbly jump around you, and before you know it, they are yards ahead of you. They've played this chess game in their minds a zillion times before and have analyzed all your future moves. They are born captains of their debate team and can argue any side of an argument. Geminis are quick, alert, and funny, but sometimes they're a little hard to pin down. Just when you think you know where they stand, they'll change their minds — again. Debating is fun for your Gemini pals, but maybe less so for their opponents because Geminis are so well informed and so persuasive on any side of an issue they happen to be on at the moment.

Geminis are so good-naturedly cheerful and unflaggingly optimistic that it is hard not to like them even while you are disagreeing with them. They hardly ever get angry — in any debate they stay cool and calm and at their logical best. Although some say that the best lawyers are Libras (the sign interested most in justice), in fact, if truth be told, Geminis most often make the best lawyers because they can argue a case so well that few would disagree with their opening and closing arguments.

Gemini has a marvelous ability to see an opposing side of the argument too. This is why they win debates—they know the subject matter from the inside out and upside down because they have been there, in your place, at least once (or even as recently as yesterday). This is also why they often change their minds—to a Gemini, flipping his opinion from one side of the fence to the other is a sign of an open-minded person who can see two sides of every issue. Who is to say he's wrong? Being passionately wedded to one point could be thought of as taking a rigid stance—something you cannot lay on a Gemini.

If you plan to meet a Gemini at an appointed time and place and can't find him or her when you arrive, check the nearest phone booth. Chances are good that you will find Gemini standing there, totally engrossed in the call, oblivious that you've been searching high and low for him. Geminis get oxygen from hearing a dial tone. It enlivens them and keeps them perky. If they aren't there, check the nearby newsstand. Newspapers and magazines pull them in like a magnet. At a newsstand or a bookstore they get so absorbed that time simply flies and they forget where they should be.

It may take a few moments to actually find your friend, because Gemini will continue to wander around, leaving the newsstand and the phone booth, looking in the windows of the shops, keeping himself occupied until you show up. Never expect a Gemini just to stand there patiently in one spot until you appear. It simply never occurs to him that he *should*. There is also a good chance that your Gemini friend will be late—he always underestimates how long each of his many projects will take in a day and is continually playing catch-up. Yet he will show up, sooner or later, charming, saying how surprised he was to discover how bad the traffic was that day and apologizing about how long it took to get there. He will look boyish and full of wonder; he will tell you little anecdotes that happened on the way to your meeting, as well as a couple of things he read in the paper while in the taxicab. In the first two minutes he has made you laugh. How can you be mad at your Gemini friend? He is so adorable and kind you will want to hug him.

Gemini, you are exceptionally resourceful, witty, clever, objective, rational, flexible, versatile, persuasive, and multitalented—and curious. Gemini's ruler, Mercury, encourages this sign to find something fascinating in nearly any subject. As a Gemini, your ability to stay fresh and flexible is quite striking, especially when compared to Taurus, whose stability makes him fall into various ruts. You are very generous with your money (Gemini doesn't make budgets—those are too constricting), your time, and your talent. A busy Gemini is never too busy to help someone who needs his or her brand of expertise and good cheer.

If it is true that a person's home reveals his or her deepest values, then Gemini's ease with new concepts and ideas is very evident when you enter his space. The presence of the written and spoken word is immediately noticeable: Books line the walls, magazines overflow from baskets, and TV news is frequently on at all hours (TV sets are placed in various rooms). A typical Gemini can't quite settle down at night without the comforting ritual of hearing the news before bedtime. If something big happens in the media, Gemini gets on the phone to notify friends and family immediately. Later Gemini will want to be part of the global discussion about what happened, analyzing the events to the tiniest detail.

Geminis never want to hear "Where were you? I couldn't find you! I had such important news! Now it's too late!" Geminis break out in a rash when they hear things like this. You have to realize that Geminis don't go anywhere, not to the supermarket, the dentist, or even the library, without broadcasting to all those around them that they have their pager turned on should anyone need them. When they travel on a pleasure trip, they power up their cell phones and plaster their itinerary on walls all over the house and the office. Unlike Scorpio, who wants to move about incognito, Gemini wants to be found.

If you have been the lucky recipient of a letter from a close friend or relative who is a Gemini, you know how much fun those are to receive—their letters are chatty, well written, and usually include a newspaper clipping, a photograph, or a compelling piece of news. Sometimes there are little drawings in the margins. Gemini keeps cramming things into the envelope. When Geminis share data, they are showing a willingness to be connected to you. To a Gemini, the gift of information is always the best way to show love and concern.

Gemini also likes to talk—a lot. When Geminis find themselves in an elevator, train, or anywhere else where they are confined with other people, they instantly strike up a conversation—curious, of course, about the others who are riding with them. Before long, they know everything about everyone present and are introducing the strangers they've just met to one another, and it all is so effortless for gregarious Gemini. When watching a Gemini in action, it is obvious why everyone is instantly drawn to them. They have a friendly, engaging, warm style, and they use not only words and voice inflection to convey thoughts but also their hands and a whole host of facial and body expressions. Geminis frequently seem to know just about everyone, if only to wave at and say hi. They always have plenty of people around them, as they are always full of news and exude energy and excitement.

Tapping into their love of anything new, innovative and communicative or technological, Geminis love gadgets, electronics, and telecommunication devices. As a gift, give Geminis a key chain that beeps when you clap your hands (they can never find their keys). Give them a vibrating massage chair to calm them down and relax their shoulders, which are undoubtably tense from holding the phone on their shoulder all day. Give them an ultrawide rearview mirror for their car, because they spend a lot of time driving. Geminis, along with Aquariuses, are the wired signs. Gemini particularly loves electronic gadgets, the newer the better. Geminis think that people who have a single telephone line live in the dark ages and people without answering machines are social recluses.

Gemini worries about running out of postal supplies and keeps plenty of stamps around the house to use in daily correspondence. In fact, Gemini keeps all kinds of supplies in all sizes handy too, as well as laser paper and computer ink, brown wrapping paper, FedEx air bills, pens, legal pads—whatever—in close reach. They may have empty refrigerators, but they have lots of packing tape.

It isn't only stamps and shipping that interest you, dear Gemini. Saturday afternoons were made for Gemini to putter and shop in bookstores. No matter how many books you have, Gemini, there is always room for one more, because you find the smell of a new book sensuous and irresistible. You adore fine stationery too, and would love to have a box of elegant, letterhead engraved with your name or initials. A fine fountain pen would complete your list; you would use it to write your messages upon those gorgeous cards.

Your lovable qualities are abundant. As I said earlier, change doesn't frighten you—you embrace it. In fact, you enjoy finding ways to come up with new ways of doing things. It is in the realm of generating ideas where you truly excel, thinking outside the box, turning routine on its ear. You draw from both sides of your brain, both the analytical and creative sectors. One of your very unusual and valuable assets is that you find all ideas interesting. When trying to crack the code on a new problem, you are likely to brainstorm for a plethora of concepts. Like a treasure hunter who is looking for sparkling pebbles along a sandy beach, when an interesting one catches your eye you immediately pick it up and turn it over to examine it from all sides objectively and unemotionally.

If the person you are presenting to doesn't like one idea, you shrug and throw your treasured pebble back into the ocean because you understand (after discussion) that the idea was flawed. Your ability to detach from one idea and embrace another fairly quickly is a big part of your success. You won't argue—you know there are plenty of other interesting specimens along the beach to study. At the initial idea stage, your penetrating mind does not yet become wedded to a single solution; you cast a wide net, fishing for as many ideas as possible to consider.

Not only do you find all ideas interesting, but you find all *news* equally fascinating. You want to know about the car that crashed through a storefront window at 2:12 A.M. today as well as all the details on the diplomatic talks going on in China. You want to know the juicy gossip about your favorite movie star as well as be up to date on your latest stock prices and your favorite team's sports scores. You even find the Weather Channel fun and could sit in front of the TV for an hour watching a report on the century's worst hurricanes. Any and all news gets treated with the same respect and fascination.

There is a good reason for all this interest in the news. Mercury rules both Gemini and Virgo, but Virgo, a mutable earth sign, is endowed with a need to qualify and discriminate among various values. Gemini is not burdened with that quality, and the reason is easy to deduce. The universe deemed it important for you to gather any and all information so that you would have a broad spectrum to analyze. If you were given a certain disposition toward *some* news, you might choose not to report and analyze *all* news. It follows that the universe purposefully did not encumber you with the obsessive need to discriminate, rank, and prioritize information (as it did Virgo). Your role is to gather and disseminate information, and this role is too important to minimize. The universe made sure it wouldn't be!

Each sign is linked in a way to its opposite sign on the axis, and the sign six months away from yours is Sagittarius, also an intellectual mutable (meaning flexible and adaptable) sign. As a Gemini, you do a good job at amassing piles of tidbits of local, national, and international news and discoveries. Sagittarius's job will be to take all the information accumulated by you, Gemini, and teach others what can be gleaned from it.

Sagittarius's job is to be keeper of the keys of the libraries of mankind—it would fall to Sagittarius to make sense of the sweep of human consciousness across boundaries of time and nationality, to get closer to understanding the heart and soul of people everywhere. Sagittarius is the philosopher-professor, while Gemini is the journalist, traveler, and investigator-on-the-scene. Sagittarius tells Gemini that he gets too wrapped up in the topical moment and fails to step back to see the significance of the event within the context of human history. Gemini tells Sagittarius that he tends to remain too long in an ivory tower. Gemini feels that Sagittarius, being too philosophical and theoretical, is not a big enough part of the everyday scene. Both signs' contributions are valuable.

The third and ninth houses in a horoscope rule ideas and learning and also rule travel. Gemini rules the third house, and Sagittarius rules the ninth house. The wise, ancient astrologers knew that travel and learning were synonymous. While Sagittarius, the other travel sign, rules long-distance international travel, Gemini rules short-distance travel like those refreshing weekend trips. If you coop up Geminis in town for too many weekends in the summer you might as well measure them for a straitjacket. Both long- and short-distance travel will enliven your spirit, so keep packing those bags, Twin.

Your mind is so strong that you "live" in your intellect and sometimes forget that you have a body that needs continual care. Somehow you usually have plenty of energy, impressing people with your get-up-and-go, but partly this is because your nervous energy is looking for an outlet. You don't seem to need as much rest as the average person. Refocusing your attention on various topics and interests is often as refreshing and enlightening as a vacation. You simply can't do one thing at a time or view the world through one camera lens.

Gemini is classified as a mutable sign because it is the last of its season (spring), a sign that helps us prepare for the transition to the next season. This is why this sign is so flexible and adaptable. When Geminis are upset or angry they need to clear the air quickly. Geminis don't fester, nor are they likely to repress issues. They feel that it takes too much energy to hold things back. Gemini does express feelings as logically as possible to clear the air and then it's over—you won't bring up the subject again. This sign won't hold on to resentments or resort to sarcasm. These are two valuable qualities that make Gemini so loved.

Geminis are called scattered, superficial, vacillating, and overly restless. You may not have enough "stick-to-it" spirit; this may be something you have to work on. Unlike Taurus, which can be slow, steady, and deliberate, everything you do is lightning-fast. In your haste you sometimes carelessly miss details. Procrastination could be a problem, too. Are you inconsistent? You can be that way. When you waver, it often depends on your mood of the moment, a trait that drives your friends and colleagues crazy at times. Your child might whine, wanting a certain something that you respond to with a quick "No, no, no." However, an hour later you ask yourself why you are making such a big deal over the little tyke's request and cave in.

What others don't see is that you change your mind because you keep taking in information, thinking about what you have just read or heard and you learn from the experience of others. This process is never over, so naturally you come to new conclusions as you go along. Gemini keeps experimenting, trying new and better ways to do or understand things. The rest of us could learn a thing or two from you, Gemini.

Yet by the time you are a little older (thirty or so) life experience starts to kick in. You get more organized (a rather difficult task for some Geminis) and you begin to realize the need for strong follow-through. By knowing yourself better, you become less scattered and more enthusiastic about focusing in on what you like to do best. You no longer have such a driving need to experience everything at dizzying speed. Your communication skills also improve even more impressively with age. You are better able to weave your various interests and talents into your life's rich tapestry, and an interesting life it is.

## RELATIONSHIPS

By now you have a good idea of who Gemini is — but how about romantically and sexually? What are Geminis like in their most intimate relationships? Gemini is a master at playing hard-to-get in love. Their style is frothy, light, and flirtatious, at least at the start. Not a highly emotional sign, if you are a Gemini your head rules your heart. You take time to make an intelligent, rational decision rather than letting yourself be swept away. Thus, you can appear a little cool romantically, at least in the beginning. Some distance is necessary for you to retain a strong sense of your own identity. The best signs for you to pair with are other air signs such as Libra, Aquarius, and Gemini, or the fire signs of Aries, Leo, and Sagittarius, signs that instinctively understand your needs and may even share the same feelings. (If you have fallen in love with another sign not listed here, there may be some special configuration in the natal chart that is perfect for you, so don't despair.)

Gemini often opts to marry later rather than risk losing independence. Even within a marriage, you will make sure you aren't caged. Your sign has a powerful need for psychological space. Tell a Gemini she can't do something she has her heart set on (like travel) and she will be obsessed with doing exactly that.

Is Gemini fickle? Some say yes, because your need for variety, surprise, and stimulation is so strong. Truthfully, most Geminis want a sense of stability more than anything else, but when they find it, sometimes life becomes too predictable. This is a matter of balance, and much depends on your partner—if he or she remains as youthful and forward-looking as you, there should be no problem in remaining a loyal, dedicated couple. If your partner stops growing intellectually or emotionally, you will probably grow restless. Sometimes a change of routine helps the relationship—planning a few things to look forward to doing or working on a creative project together could be just the trick to keep a relationship growing.

As I said earlier, words light Gemini's passions. If you have a Gemini lover, send them notes, read passages from steamy novels, memorize poetry, and talk during lovemaking. Gemini's mind is their most erotic body part. Gemini's child-like curiosity keeps this sign looking far younger than they are, and they remain alluring to the opposite sex well into old age. Geminis may not be able to meet the level of outpouring of emotion of a water sign like Scorpio, Cancer, or Pisces, but Geminis will love in their own way. To Gemini, a water sign's emotions seem too deep, and too much. Gemini can still be loyal and emotional too, but their style is different. Before your Gemini will be in the mood for love, realize that they are highly strung and need a little time, so be patient. They also have a strong funny bone and admire cleverness, so don't be afraid to try a witty approach. Write e-mail to Geminis, read to them, or show them a new Web site—watch them take notice!

Finally, when it comes to matters of love, let's settle a burning issue: Is Gemini really two people? No. If you are a Gemini reading this, you are probably tired of the snide remarks you get at parties from people who think they know all about the astrological you. As much as some people might like to dismiss Gemini as two people, i.e., a bright, honest twin and a dark, evil twin, nothing could be further from the truth. While there are duplicitous people everywhere, I doubt there are more devious Geminis than any other sign.

What is true about Geminis is that this sign will change viewpoints and goals—and even their looks—from time to time, as I talked about earlier. This is due to an open mind that continues to process information even after it is (temporarily) made up. If you have a Gemini sweetheart, you will also likely discover that your Gemini unconsciously mirrors your style. He or she picks up your mannerisms, posture, or mode of speech when you are together to improve communication with you. This works quite effectively and explains why Geminis are such effective salespeople and writers—the buyer or the reader feels comfortable with Gemini because he is "just like me." But your Gemini is not trying to *become* you; he or she is simply trying just to *talk* to you effectively. So stop worrying about Geminis being two people; they are individuals. Remember, even twins do not think exactly alike.

Finally, Gemini's disarming unpretentiousness and breezy style may take getting used to. For example, if your Gemini sweetheart has something to hash out with you, don't expect him to make a big deal out of whatever it is and say, "Let's sit down tomorrow and discuss this." That won't happen, because planning to talk seems too stilted and rigid an approach to a Gemini—it surrounds the impending conversation with too much tension. Remember that Gemini is a sign that is open and impetuous. So instead, while you are there in your kitchen by the stove basting the turkey and getting ready for twelve guests, your Gemini sweetheart is likely to blurt out what's on his mind. "You hurt my feelings yesterday at the bank," or "I think we should have a baby." You never know *what* Geminis are going to say.

If you were hoping for the perfect romantic moment when your Gemini pops the question, forget it—you need a Cancer or Pisces for that. Once Geminis make up their mind, they will just spill the beans wherever they happen to be, whether standing with you at the post office, buying pineapple at the supermarket, or walking home with you from the subway. These ordinary moments are the most likely time for Geminis to bring up

the most earth-shattering questions and discussions. They can't hold anything in, so don't expect any planned moments. Yet what you are left with
instead may be a whole lot more precious and memorable: a bursting display of enthusiasm in the heat of the moment when he or she is happy—
and when Geminis aren't happy, well, they are just as full of unpretentious
disclosure.

## FINANCE

Have you ever noticed how you buy two of everything? Of course—you
need one for your symbolic "lost twin." The Gemini mother lovingly puts
two little ripe purple plums in her child's palms, saying, "Here, sweetheart—one for each hand." Gemini never thinks in terms of one. "Here's
your birthday gift," your Gemini pal might say to you, "but here is something else as well. I loved them both—I couldn't decide." Why think "one"
if you can double your fun? This gets expensive when you Christmas-
shop, Gemini. One gift for your sister, its match for you; something for
your parents' house, the same for you; the perfect item for your best
friend, ditto for you—and so it goes. You skip through the mall humming
a happy tune. If you happen to be a Gemini, you explain away that buying
two of everything is just a time-saver, but your need for "two" goes deeper
than that. The duality of Gemini is so instinctive that it asserts itself
unconsciously on a continual basis. You *need* to buy two, even if you aren't
sure why. If it were up to you, you'd have two houses, two children, two
professions, two cars, two computers, two phone lines, two of everything—and why not?

A Gemini should plan on making lots of money, not only to keep buying
two of everything but also to support all of his or her hobbies and interests. Gemini is eternally interested in the world and wants to know a little
something about everything—and then finds more things to investigate.
Some people accuse you of spreading yourself too thin and of having
superficial knowledge on too many subjects and not enough time to delve
deeply into any of them. It is true that you can be scattered, flighty, disor-

ganized, and forgetful. Sometimes you are a procrastinator, saying with a shrug, "Why do it today when I can do it tomorrow?" That can get you into trouble, but you already knew that, having thought about it but not yet put your insight into practice. Whether any of these things describe you depends on whether you have a few planets in earth signs in your natal chart to anchor you. An earthy influence, say the Moon, Mercury, or other prominent planet, in earthy Virgo, Taurus, or Capricorn, would keep you more organized and on point.

## CAREER

Gemini can be wonderfully imaginative, especially in writing, whether it's books, plays, advertising copy, or journalism. The ancients called Gemini the sign of the scribe or the storyteller. Many Geminis can relate a saga so rich in character, time, and location that by the time the story is done the audience feels the characters have come to life. This is why so many Geminis become novelists or authors of children's stories. Not surprisingly, a large number of Geminis have used pseudonyms. (Of course this makes sense—Gemini needs two names too.)

Gemini also does well in all areas of publishing, working as a writer, editor, publisher, circulation director, ad manager—even as a creative director. Gemini succeeds in related communication fields too, like broadcasting, computers, and the Internet, or working in public relations, sales, and marketing—even in teaching. Gemini's love of rare and historical documents and autographs make this sign especially suited to be gallery owners.

Some Geminis build careers in the express-mail or messenger-service industry; others find success working as post-office workers, in courier services, in trucking or shipping or as manufacturers, or as importers or shopkeepers of anything, but especially beautiful books and papers, envelopes, or rare pens and ink. Geminis can make great wardrobe stylists and decorators too, because they understand the value of accessories. Finally, Gemini also rules the travel industry, so members of this sign make

superb travel agents, pilots, flight and ticket attendants, air-traffic con-
trollers, railroad train conductors, automotive designers, and executives.

## BODY, MIND, AND SPIRIT

Watch that you don't get in the habit of not eating right or not getting
enough sleep. Gemini rules the fingers and hands, and you are particularly adept. You might have taught yourself to type very fast, play the piano
or guitar, or do any number of crafts, including needlepoint, calligraphy,
knitting, woodworking, or sewing. For many Geminis, their fingers get
most of the tension, not their neck, so you love having someone rub your
hands with a little warm hand lotion or scented oil. And your hands are so
busy that they probably get more than their share of cuts and bruises.

As a Gemini, besides being susceptible to jangled nerves and hand or finger soreness (watch out for carpal tunnel syndrome, dear Twin, and use
wrist rests when you type), you must also be careful about illnesses related to the lungs. Geminis must keep their lungs safe by not doing anything
that could harm them. Taking aerobics to increase lung capacity would be
an excellent idea. Gemini also rules the collarbones and shoulders, not so
surprising, as you figuratively carry a lot on your shoulders. The outside
world doesn't see the part of you that worries intensely about obligations—friends see the happy-go-lucky, optimistic side of you first—but it
is there, and that more mature, thoughtful side is revealed only later. You
say to yourself that you will stop overcommitting your time and talent, but
then you forget and instantly overbook your schedule again, enthusiastically cramming in as much as you can.

The rulership of Gemini over lungs is appropriate because you are an
air sign, symbolized by the Twins in flight. It is the air in your lungs that
seems to buoy you up, allowing you to feel that you can defy gravity and
soar through space. In mythology and in many fairy tales, the breath
symbolizes spirit. You want to fly, to be free as a bird, and to cover as
much ground in half the time. However, at times you seem to gasp and

gulp at life and sometimes feel like you bit off and swallowed too much in one huge gulp. You are inclined to that kind of nervous tension, and you get the hiccups because you literally swallow too much air. Slowing down would be good, but that is not what you really want to do most of the time.

## SUMMARY

Dear Gemini, you are a kaleidoscope of energy, ever changing and transforming. Some of your most outstanding assets are your supreme adaptability, your flexibility, and your versatile nature and awesome communication skills. If you've already done something one way, why repeat it? You say redundancy is unnecessary in this wide, wide world. Now that you find yourself in the information age, you are about to come into your own. Don't be surprised if the world comes to you for advice on how to handle it. After all, this is the world you envisioned and practically invented—this new world is about to feel very much like home. And that is a very good thing.

# THE MYTHS OF
# GEMINI AND MERCURY

If on a cloudless night you look into the heavens, you will, no doubt, be attracted to the part of the sky that contains two large stars situated right next to one another. One will be slightly brighter, but if you continue to watch this constellation, you will see that these two stars actually alternate in brightness, each taking turns to allow the other to be the bigger star. What you have found is the constellation of Gemini.

The mythology of your sign, Gemini, is particularly rich because it involves two sets of twins, one divine and one mortal, suggesting a certain remarkable completeness within you. One set of twins were brothers, the other twin sisters. The beautiful Leda, disguised as a gorgeous swan, laid two eggs that bore the two sets of twins. Not surprising in the tale of duality, the female and male twins were born of two fathers: Zeus, the most powerful god on Mount Olympus who fathered the brother and sister Pollux and Helen, and King Tyndareus, Leda's "human" husband, who fathered the mortals Castor and Clytemnestra.

## CASTOR AND POLLUX
The tale of Castor and Pollux is perhaps the most well known in ancient mythology, a tale of two brothers who were so close that they refused to be separated, even when one of them died. Castor and Pollux did everything together, and in the myths they were always in one another's

159

presence. Castor was known for his horsemanship and was a warrior, while Pollux was a famous boxer. The Spartan games were dedicated in their honor. Both Castor and Pollux participated in the story of Jason and the Argonauts, in Jason's quest for the Golden Fleece.

One day Castor, the mortal of the two, was killed, and Pollux, who was immortal, was overcome with grief. He begged Zeus not to separate him from his brother. Pollux did not want to accept his father's gift of immortality if it meant that Castor was compelled to remain forever in the underworld, a place Pollux could not visit. Zeus relented, and so it was decided that the twins would spend half their time in heaven and half their time in the underworld, which, incidentally, corresponds to periods when the constellation is visible in the sky (six months of the year).

## HELEN AND CLYTEMNESTRA

Meanwhile, on the female side, there was Helen and Clytemnestra, who were quite different in personality. Helen was the daughter of Zeus and Leda, and was, like her mother, exceptionally beautiful. Helen followed society's rules and never stepped outside the bounds of acceptable behavior. Some feel that her lack of resolution was largely responsible for the Trojan War. Her mortal sister, Clytemnestra, was not quite the "good" twin that Helen was, for Clytemnestra murdered her husband, King Agamemnon, after he returned from the Trojan War. As with all Greek myths, there is irony; Clytemnestra may have been the darker twin, but she had much stronger resolve and a feisty passion that was attractive. Helen was an exemplary goddess but was passive. In Gemini there seems to be mythological warnings that balance is needed and that to find it, one needs to look for clues in one's alter ego. (To look at one's twin is something like being able literally to stand "outside" oneself.) Neither twin was self-contained and whole; each had pieces of personality that the other lacked. It was only together that they were whole and complete, larger than the sum of their parts.

It is possible to see the symbolism of these twins as related to the conflict between the bright ego and the darker instincts present within the personality that need to be repressed or hidden. This represents a struggle inherent in all humans, of course, not just within Gemini, but that message seems to be embodied in Gemini's myth. Gemini's struggle to do right is a conscious and intellectual one, existing on the top of the mind rather than buried in the subconscious. As an analytical air sign, Gemini is able to dissect his motives coolly and be rational in his search to do right. (Mercury, Gemini's planetary ruler, is completely objective and unemotional.)

Another lesson this myth teaches is that Gemini needs a divine mentor. Pollux cannot reach his brother after death. Thus, Castor becomes a spiritual inspiration and represents Pollux's yearning to associate with the spiritual part of his soul. In the broad sense, this myth speaks of the need of the intellectual part of Gemini to strive toward lofty, heavenly goals through the love and inspiration of an alter ego.

## HERMES, MESSENGER OF THE GODS

The myth of Hermes, the messenger of the gods, very strongly represents the archetype of Gemini's characteristics. From birth, Hermes is clearly very precocious. The story begins with Hermes as a tiny infant. Born in a dark cave, he was the son of the mighty Zeus and a lesser goddess, Maia, who could be the goddess of the night sky. There is some disagreement in the myths about the identity of Maia, although most agree that she was the daughter of the Titan Atlas. Hermes was born to Maia after her liaison with Zeus, but she was forced to keep that relationship to herself, staying hidden in a cave with her baby.

Baby Hermes knew that his father ruled Mount Olympus, and Hermes was not happy to live out his life in a dark cave. Hermes was also troubled to see his siblings (Zeus's other children) living in comfort and with honors. Hermes noted that Apollo, Zeus's favorite son, was living in his father's palace even though he had not been born of Hera.

Bored, Hermes climbed out of his cradle and left the cave. He saw a large tortoise and, being resourceful and ingenious, killed it and scooped out its shell, then strung seven strings of a sheep's gut across its opening. Thus, Hermes invented the lyre. Here Hermes reveals Gemini's most creative and playful quality. Hermes cheerfully began to sing; clearly he knew how to amuse himself, and his love of music reveals a basically happy, upbeat personality.

Next he crept around to look for food and found a large herd of cattle, which he learned belonged to Apollo. Hermes decided to steal fifty of the cattle. Not wanting the mighty Apollo to catch him, Hermes in his cleverness had the cattle walk backward toward his cave. So it appeared by their tracks that they were moving toward Apollo's pasture—not away from it. To disguise his tracks Hermes made himself a special pair of sandals out of twigs, foliage, and the bark from a fallen oak tree.

As an aside, the backward walk of Hermes's stolen cattle seems reminiscent of the retrograde action of the planet Mercury that happens regularly, four times a year, at three-and-a-half-week intervals. In astrology, when Mercury retrogrades, it has a universal and jarring effect on just about everyone. Mercury seems to play pranks on us mortals, causing the areas governed by Mercury—communication, transportation, and commerce—to go haywire. When Mercury retrogrades it also causes forgetfulness, lost computer data, travel to the wrong address, or lost luggage. Plans are overhauled, canceled, or postponed. This is also not an auspicious time for signing documents. Perhaps this is due to Hermes getting his chance to play mischief on us during that time.

Let's consider the significance of Hermes's ability to cover his tracks while he spirited away the fifty cattle. The ability to read animal tracks is an ancient art, one that was often necessary for survival. Those who survive in the wilderness know how to decipher the meaning of various signs—a broken tree limb, the depth or shape of a footprint, bits of wool left on the side of bark. The hunter, like the detective today, knows how to garner the meaning from small clues. As author and mythology expert Lewis Hyde says in his book *Trickster Makes This World*, stories about tricksters and tracking are really stories about "reading" and "writing" (the broken twig is a form of written communication), a very appropriate parable to the Mercury/Hermes myth that is so tied to Gemini. Hermes "rewrote" the event with his clever concealment of his footprints. What's more, Greek mythological stories are filled with people being able to change themselves into different forms—to shed their skins and make new ones— and this is because it was a value they applauded. As Hyde deduces, cleverness was valued more highly by ancient Greeks than rigidity or inflexibility.

Getting back to the story, while Hermes was stealing the cattle, a farmer named Battus saw what was going on, but Hermes quickly paid him to keep him quiet. Not trusting him, Hermes returned disguised and offered a reward to anyone who knew the person responsible for stealing the cattle. Battus immediately spoke up, proving that he was ready to turn against Hermes. Hermes immediately punished the old man by transforming him into stone. This proves that Hermes was shrewd; his razor-sharp mind was operating all the time, just like Gemini's.

The next morning, Hermes stopped to make a fire. He slaughtered two of the fifty cows and roasted them for dinner, and was careful not to leave any trace of the cattle—he burned the hooves and the heads. However, he decided that instead of eating the meat, he would ignore his hunger. He divided it into twelve equal parts and offered up one piece to each of the eleven Olympian gods: Zeus, Poseidon, Hades, Hestia, Hera, Ares, Athena, Apollo, Aphrodite, Artemis, Hephaestus, and added one portion for *himself*. Hermes immediately leveled the playing field—his act was significant because it was the first instance of the gods eating sacrificial meat.

At night, Hermes crawled back into his little cradle and pretended to be asleep. His mother, however, deduced what her child had done and confronted him. Hermes explained that he was not going to spend his life in that dark cave, especially when he saw his siblings living so well on Mount Olympus. Hermes explained that he wanted his father, Zeus, to give him the same honor he gave Apollo.

Meanwhile, Apollo noticed that some of his cattle were missing, so he began searching for the thief. Through a series of omens and other means, Apollo found Hermes. When Apollo arrived at the cave, Hermes was in his cradle. As Apollo entered the room he immediately illuminated it with a powerful golden glow. Baby Hermes looked so innocent and sweet in his cradle, but when Apollo accused him of stealing his cattle, Hermes sat up and began to argue with him (revealing the other, more shrewd side to his personality). Hermes protested that Apollo was bullying him, reminding him that he was just an infant—"born yesterday" (Hermes literally had been born the day before). Apollo was not fooled, but he was nevertheless amused and charmed by this unusual infant. Here we see that childlike innocence that everyone remarks about in Gemini. Using charm, originality, and talent, Hermes easily wins Apollo's support, a talent given to most Geminis too!

Knowing that Hermes would never be an easy child to contain or control and being a bit exhausted by the episode, Apollo decided to bring Hermes up to Mount Olympus. Putting the baby on Zeus's lap, Apollo argued the case for Hermes. Zeus found himself in a bit of a fix. Although he recognized Hermes instantly as his son, he didn't want to admit it because he would have to reveal his relationship with Maia to his present wife. Still, Hermes was a remarkable baby and Zeus too, was charmed by his son's spunky nature.

While Zeus was thinking about his new son, Hermes started complaining to his father that Apollo was getting better treatment than he was and demanded that Zeus correct the situation. Zeus was so amused that he laughed. Here we see Hermes vying for parental favor just as any child would do in any family. It is important to note that the element of sibling rivalry is a dominant theme that runs through this story as well, often a part of Gemini symbolism. Yet Gemini's charm, sense of persuasion, and determination prevail and allow Gemini/Mercury/Hermes to get their way. Zeus was known to love children, so he had a dilemma. He couldn't quite turn his back on one son's situation (Apollo was missing his cattle), nor could he bring himself to punish Hermes. He ordered the brothers, Apollo and Hermes, to make up, and then he told Hermes it was necessary that he return the cattle.

While Apollo was in the pasture herding his cattle, Hermes began to play his lyre. Apollo was enchanted—he had never heard anything as beautiful. He soon forgot his anger about his stolen cattle, for suddenly it did not seem important anymore. Apollo started to negotiate with Hermes for the lyre. Hermes gave Apollo the lyre and in return got the remaining forty-eight cows. Hermes then immediately made another clever instrument, a reed pipe, which Apollo also adored and wanted. For that Hermes negotiated for Apollo's golden staff, and with it was given the prestigious honor of being the god of herdsmen and shepherds. He was also given lessons on how to divine the future.

When Hermes met again later with Zeus, Hermes promised not to steal or lie again if he could be given the highest honor, the role of messenger to the gods. Zeus felt that his mercurial son was indeed swift, clever, and funny too, a good negotiator and well spoken—indeed, he would make a perfect spokesperson for the gods. Among his duties, Hermes would guide souls into the underworld and then return safely. Thus, Hermes was given the rare and important access to roam wherever he wished. Specifically, Hermes could travel freely through three realms: heaven, earthly mortal life, and the underworld.

Hermes received from Zeus a special winged helmet to protect him in all weather, and golden winged sandals to guarantee swift delivery of messages. Hermes was also given a herald's wand, the caduceus, suggesting the link between mind and body in the healing process.

Hermes would be in charge of the safety of travelers, promote all commerce and trade, and negotiate treaties and agreements. The relationship between father and son worked out very well. Hermes became Zeus's constant companion; in fact, Zeus never traveled to Earth without Hermes at his side. Appropriately, his name, Hermes, means "he of the stone heap," referring to the small tower of rocks that travelers use to mark a route on the side of a road for those who will come after them.

Here we see Gemini's mythological heritage as an intermediary guide or a connector of people, things, or events in the world at large and internally as part of the mind as well. Hermes also symbolizes the mind—reason, speech, writing, reading, ideas, and communication—as well as travel and transportation itself. Even internally, within the body, the mind serves as the body's messenger by relaying involuntary and voluntary impulses through the nervous system.

Hermes was also credited with the development of the Greek alphabet, and with the invention of the musical scale, astronomy, gymnastics, and boxing. Hermes is the god that epitomizes youth, travelers, merchants, messengers, and communication, as well as thievery and rogues.

In that respect, the trickster is not altogether a bad character—he is the disrupter of the order of things, the pretender to the throne, or the outsider trying to gain entry beyond the palace gates. In this case, Hermes knew it wasn't fair that he live in a dark cave, but he would have spent his life there if he hadn't challenged the system. Society often benefits when someone slips through the carefully guarded front lines to disrupt the established order. The trickster often acts as a prophet in order to create an accelerated move toward social good, and by crossing lines he reveals boundaries that no one realized even existed. Usually neutral, the trickster isn't necessarily aware of good or evil, but his very actions cause a discussion and a reevaluation.

As we think of the lovable, funny Hermes-type prankster, we bring to mind a wild, creative genius who breaks up static institutions through subversive innovation. Hermes's greatest gifts are flexibility, adaptability, humor, creativity, and vastly improved communication through intellect and language. With those gifts, he has the ability to bring awesome progress to society.

# CANCER PERSONALITY

**Cancer**
June 21–July 22

*Guiding Principle*

"I Feel"

*How This Sign Feels Joy*
Finds joy in home and family, enjoying the
parent-child relationship both as a child or as
a parent, either figuratively or literally.

*In the New Millennium, Your Contribution to
the World Will Be . . .*
Your love of family and perspective on it as a
building block of society will be increasingly
important as people search for new ways to
create community in the world.

*Quote That Describes You*
"TRUE KINDNESS PRESUPPOSES THE FACULTY OF
   IMAGINING AS ONE'S OWN THE SUFFERINGS AND
   JOY OF OTHERS."

—ANDRÉ GIDE, a *Sagittarius*

Cancer, should you find yourself outdoors during a thick snowfall, look up to the sky in the darkest part of night and find your ruling planet, the Moon. Set against a midnight blue sky and surrounded with a thousand shimmering stars that sparkle like diamonds, the Moon will appear at her most majestic loveliness—especially if her face is at its roundest and fullest. As the Earth's loyal companion and alter ego, the Moon has no inner light of her own but reflects the Sun's light with a dazzling brilliance. Under moonlight, the countryside will seem more magical than it ever could be by day. The Moon's role is to enlarge emotion, unearth old memories, stir dreams, and sharpen intuition. Each of these qualities is yours too, Cancer, for you, as the queenly Moon's subject, are her most cherished child. Like the Moon, you are romantic, imaginative, gentle, and at times so private that others call you mysterious, just like the luminary that guides you and protects you.

## SYMBOLS

To the ancients, Cancer symbolized the summer solstice, the time of the year that represents the soul's entry into the body. In our time, Cancer is always associated with the crab. The Egyptians used a scarab beetle as Cancer's symbol, a sacred totem referring to the soul. Similarly, for the Greeks, Cancer was represented by the turtle or tortoise—both the crab and the turtle have a soft underbelly with a hard outer shell. Appropriately, tortoises retreat into their shells when they are frightened or stressed, a characteristic known to be indigenous of Cancers too. After the age of Alexander the Great, a blending of all ancient Mediterranean cultures occurred. This was when Cancer became associated with the crab and with the Moon.

The next time you are at the beach, watch the crab's movements carefully. It does not move directly toward whatever it has decided to capture or attack. Instead the crab moves silently in a zigzag fashion, first going left, hesitating, looking, checking for danger, then quickly darting right, and remaining still, observing, waiting, before speeding forward, then left, then right. And so he goes in an unpredictable, darting mode until he gets what he wants. If it appears his prey is about to disappear and he won't get what he's after, he will attack, snapping at whatever he has his eye on with great precision. If he should lose a claw in the process, Mother Nature will grow him another. Cancer is tremendously tenacious about going after goals, and little, if anything, will stop him or her.

The glyph for Cancer, which looks a little like the symbol for infinity, hints at these intertwining powers of yin and yang. Looking closely at the symbol, it appears to be two full moons attached to a crescent Moon (soul), each attached to the other, in an opposite, interlocking pattern. This symbol suggests procreation and the continuum of life. Your symbol also underscores the feeling aspects of your sign.

### PLANETARY INFLUENCE

Ancient astrologers wrote that the Moon, your ruler, governs the soul and is the repository for memories, habits, and dreams, as well as for unconscious reactions and reflexes. The time of the year of your birth, the summer solstice, is what Mesopotamian stargazers called "the northern gate of the Sun." They believed that was the magical point when the soul entered the body—a very spiritual, sacred moment. Summer solstice falls on or within a day of June 21, and it is the longest day of the year in the Northern Hemisphere. Why would the ancients choose the Moon, a cool, receptive, supportive, and protective nighttime feminine energy, for the ruler of Cancer? Wouldn't a more appropriate choice be the hot, aggressive, masculine energy of the Sun on this, the longest day of the year?

There is a good explanation. The day of the summer solstice marks a turning point in the year because, from then on, *days grow increasingly shorter.* The Sun (symbolizing self, ego, and the individual) begins to lose ground, while the Moon, having dominion over the evening (symbolizing collective consciousness instead of ego) begins to gain in importance. Thus, in the alternating balance of power and friendly cooperation between the Sun and the Moon, the Moon begins to regain her favor. This is why the Moon was chosen to rule you, dear Cancer. Going a step further, being ruled by the Moon but having your Sun in Cancer brings you an extraordinary opportunity to unite both the masculine and feminine energies within you for remarkable completeness and increased possibility for creativity.

The Moon has, since ancient times, been linked to yin energy, signifying a "minus," feminine, charge or impulse—and thus the Moon's influence on your personality makes you receptive, highly intuitive, reflective, and magnetic. One of the hallmarks of Cancer is your ability to absorb emotions like a sponge and reflect them back into the world as effectively as a clean and shiny mirror. When someone around you is sad, you feel his or her sadness with almost equal depth. Conversely, when you are with a friend who is elated, you are too. You seem more in tune with the Earth's inner music, for the phases of the Moon and the constellations of the signs resonate within you.

The Moon does a complete revolution around the Sun in twenty-eight days, remaining in each of the twelve constellations for a little over two days. Because your ruling luminary is busy (no planet in our solar system covers as much ground in such a short period of time), it picks up many different influences, signals, and vibrations from the signs it visits and communicates with during its travels. This, combined with the fact that you are a receptive water sign, is why you are known for your wide range and depth of emotions.

No doubt you have found a way to draw toward you what you need in life and to deflect what you don't. You have probably already learned that you should keep a safe distance from negative people. Should you find yourself overwhelmed with demanding individuals or stressful situations, try to get away for some quiet time to think. Sometimes a gloomy mood is brought on simply by sheer physical or emotional exhaustion—ask yourself if this could possibly be the case.

The Moon has inspired poets, artists, photographers, composers, dancers, and other creative people through the ages. So many myths weave within the Moon's vision that there are simply too many to recount. The cycle begins with the virginal young beauty, the new Moon. At the new Moon, the lunar face is mysteriously veiled, revealing only a small sliver of bright light at the crescent edge. The new Moon encourages the sharing of ideas and the planting of new seeds, and new beginnings.

Two weeks later, the Moon will be at full fruitfulness, reminiscent of a pregnant woman in bloom, radiant, expectant, and ready to deliver her child. The full Moon is a time to reap and to seek completion in our daily affairs. For three days before and after the full Moon we feel its urgency—energy is heightened, and completion of matters will occur then. You may also feel especially stirred at the time of the full Moon. Some people feel extra-high levels of energy, have trouble sleeping, and are jittery or cranky. When Cancers learn to harness this awesome energy, they become highly successful in any phase of life.

After the full Moon, the waning lunar beauty begins to glide back into the shadows. During the last week of the cycle, the Moon seems to vanish altogether, only to reappear again when the cycle is initiated and repeated. The time of the waning Moon is a time to reflect, and to quietly encourage creativity. It is also a time to turn away from the outside world to ready oneself for the coming new Moon. This is a good time to think and to plan but not to act—not quite yet. It is the period of the month that has been compared to the stage of older women as sage or teacher/mentor in the menopause years of life.

The Moon's constancy reassures and comforts us, teaching us that there is, after all, much regularity in the universe. The names of the various months' full Moons have originated in different cultures. The Moon's names echoed certain events, ceremonies, weather conditions, or holidays that fell near the time of a particular full Moon. The names are poetic and some are familiar, such as the term for two moons in one month, the Blue Moon.

There are lesser known names of the various moons, which I will list for you simply because they are so beautiful: There is the Old Moon and the Storm Moon (January), Chaste Moon (February), Sap Moon or Seed Moon (March), Grass Moon and Egg Moon (April), followed by Milk Moon, Planting or Hare Moon (all in May), and the Rose Moon, Flower Moon, Strawberry Moon, or Mead Moon (June). Then comes Thunder Moon or Wart Moon (July) and the Grain Moon or Barley Moon (August). The Harvest Moon comes in September—some have called it the Blood Moon. Following is the Hunter's Moon or Snow Moon (October), Frosty Moon, Oak Moon, or Beaver Moon (November). Finally, just prior to Christmas, the ripe full Yule Moon appears. The December Moon has been called the Wolf Moon (it can also fall in January). The Chippewa/Shoshoni Indians also referred to the various moons with names such as Talking Wind Moon (March), Moon of Big Changes (April and September), Moon of Many Gifts (June), Moon of Thirsty Ground (July), Cold Moon (October), Moon of Many Fires (November), and White Woman Moon (December). These aren't the only names; various cultures gave the Moon other poetic names but it's easy to see how much it has inspired man through time.

The ancient astrologers wrote that the Moon reflects in a horoscope the fine-tuning of a person's character. If true shadings of character can only be revealed gradually, it makes sense that the Moon, a luminary rising in darkness when vision is reduced, should be chosen to be the heavenly body in the zodiac that would reveal one's true inner nature. Also, the Moon is described in astrology as a private, inner-world influence, and, as such, has dominion over the home, your most private place. The Moon's rulership of your sign explains why you, dear Cancer, feel uncomfortable in the role of aggressor, preferring to draw others to you in a more subtle, magnetic way, using charm, empathy, intellect, or, any other of your winsome talents.

Recollections, dreams, and private thoughts all come under the Moon's domain. It encourages you to reminisce, and gives you a remarkable, possibly even photographic, memory. You remember incidents with startling accuracy, as well as the emotions you felt that came with those events, as if they happened just moments ago. Facts and figures remain fresh in your mind too; your ability to access them with ease will astound colleagues. Some Cancers are particularly talented at math, able to add long rows of figures faster than if they used a calculator.

## COSMIC GIFTS

Cancers are highly psychic, intuitive, and instinctive because they are open to the influx of universal forces that channel themselves into the Cancer's mind and sensibilities. As mentioned previously, the Egyptians felt that the sign of Cancer symbolized the entry of the soul into the human body. The fourth house (Cancer's "home") is considered the base of the chart and provides the very foundation of life.

Cardinal signs (Aries, Cancer, Libra, and Capricorn) lead the seasons (spring, summer, fall, and winter, respectively) and as such they are considered quite self-directed and blessed with a pioneering spirit and leadership ability. With a ruling luminary, the Moon, being a passive influence, people see you as a reserved soul who does not need or desire the limelight. When friends get to know you better, however, they will also see that beneath your shy exterior is an amazingly strong individual who wants to succeed no matter what—a self-determination brought to you by the Sun. Within you is the ability to achieve great success in whatever you tackle. You are quite lucky to have the mutual cooperation of both solar (male) and lunar (female) energies for a special sense of completeness. This is a potent blend.

The wheel of the horoscope mirrors human evolution. First, Aries is the initiator or pure life force that says "I am," because Aries' contribution is to bring new things into being. Second, Taurus is the sign that teaches the instinct to accumulate and says "I have." Third, Gemini brings the instinct to learn, and says "I know." Cancer, the fourth house of the horoscope, is the sector of the chart that rules the very foundation and roots of life, one's family, as well as the early bonding experience of mother and child. Thus Cancer says "I feel." This house of the horoscope also rules the physical dwelling of one's home, how it looks and what happens there, throughout life.

Perhaps better than any other sign, Cancer understands and teaches humans to care for others and the need to be nurtured in return. For some Cancers, if they have no baby to nurture, they will nurture a pet or a series of creative projects. While Aries is more focused on the development of self-identity, by the time the zodiac wheel gets to Cancer the proverbial child has evolved and is ready to go beyond concern for "self" to venture into family relationships. In Cancer, the fetus has left the womb (the place where Gemini first becomes aware of its twin) for the family nest. However, Cancer forever "remembers" being surrounded with comforting waters of the womb, its first and certainly most secure "home." Just as siblings (or the lack thereof) shape Gemini's personality, the Cancer personality is influenced most by the mother. She becomes a chief catalyst, more than any other family member.

Actually, Cancer males and females unconsciously re-create mother-child relationships throughout their lives in a much deeper way than is experienced by other signs. Sometimes they play the caring, giving "mother" figure to others. At other times they are needy and yearning to be cared for themselves. However, the mother is a powerful influence, always, on those born in Cancer, but please know that if you had a troubled relationship with your own mother she will not drive your destiny—only you can do that. Many people rise above difficult beginnings to go on to great accomplishments, not in spite of those difficulties but often because of them.

Dear Cancer, have you been accused of brooding or getting snappish? The answer is probably yes, especially when you feel threatened or misunderstood. When you feel like this, unlike a Gemini, who will impulsively talk to anyone who'll listen, you are more likely to find comfort in locking out the world and closing your outer shell. Family and friends may be puzzled by your need to withdraw but attempts to pry open your shell will be futile—they shouldn't try. The Crab won't be persuaded to join the rest of humanity until he is ready. Soon, however, your sunny disposition breaks through those grumpy or sullen periods. Cancer's moods come and go swiftly. Once you center yourself and get in touch with your true feelings you will re-emerge, but not a moment before. Cancers can be amazingly steely about following their own mind despite the pleas of others, for they are a cardinal sign that quietly insists that things are done their way—or not at all.

Like the smart little crab on the beach, you are also a master of subtlety, rarely confronting situations head-on. You feel that if you reveal your intentions to your partners, foes, or competitors, you will be put at a disadvantage because they will be in a better position to defend or advance their position. People close to you say they never quite know what you are thinking—not until you unexpectedly announce your next move. Often this comes in the form of a passionate outburst when you just can't conceal your feelings or motives any longer. "You were not sensitive to my feelings yesterday at the supermarket. When I said I wanted Devil Dogs, you bought what you wanted—doughnuts! You always get your way! You never consider my feelings!" Then Cancer will add something out of the blue: "That's it! I am quitting my job tomorrow!"

Cancer tends to shout out things like this at the strangest times. Who knew you were getting so upset yesterday at the supermarket? Your sweetie tries to convince you not to quit your job. But by now you feel like a ball of screaming emotions and everything in the world seems wrong. Not having those chocolate Devil Dogs put you over the edge, you tell her. You are tired of not getting support from your boss, the people in the office, your neighbors—maybe even the kids. By George, you're going to do something about it! What you need is sympathy, and if you have a wise partner, she or he will give it to you.

You tend to absorb thoughts and feelings instead of throwing them off. Sooner of later the dam bursts, much to your surprise, for you (and certainly those around you) had no idea you were getting so close to the edge. Not surprisingly, this can cause dismay in close relationships: Your sweetheart accuses you of withholding your feelings, of being evasive for no reason, or of letting feelings build up to the point where you can't manage them.

It would be better for you to share your feelings more readily; this could head off lots of interpersonal problems. None of this is done deliberately on your part, but rather you do it unconsciously and instinctively. You may not feel "up" to an argument with your sweetheart, for you may not feel confident that you can win in a game of verbal sparring, which comes so naturally to your preceding sign, Gemini. When you come to know your partner better, you will be more willing to lower your defenses. It is a process that could take years. However, complete disclosure of inner thoughts and feelings is not offered casually by Cancer.

You know that under that hard shell you hide a tender underbelly that is sensitive and easily hurt. You feel as though you have no choice but to defend your vulnerability. While the signs surrounding yours may vent their feelings openly (both Gemini and Leo are "open books"), Cancers have a need for greater emotional privacy.

Ancient astrologers explained that each sign makes up for whatever characteristics are lacking in the sign that preceded and followed it. Your nature is more fine-tuned than that of Gemini or Leo, more delicately sensitive, sympathetic, and compassionate. A reserved, shy sign, Cancer is not the extroverted, gregarious gadabout that Gemini is. Nor would you have the ego-driven impulses of Leo, the sign that follows at the end of July. More introverted and centered than either of those signs, your power is drawn from within yourself rather than from the stimulation and energy of others around you. In Cancer the ego is subdued, and logically so. A strong personality would overpower the balance within a family unit—Cancer instinctively supports the family, rather than compete with its members. And unlike Geminis and Leos, who have many friends, Cancers are more selective about whom they allow to be close. As a result, you put a greater emotional investment into your friends and family. A highly giving sign, you, dear Cancer, have eyes that are usually open to the smallest nuance, the gentlest feeling, or the most fleeting expression of those around you. You intuitively move to respond with nearly psychic compassion to those in need. Highly creative too, Cancer is often able to take simple everyday objects and foods and turn them into something quite extraordinary.

RELATIONSHIPS
The Moon will put extra emphasis not only on home and family but also on your mother. Your mother was important to you because, of course, she was the very first person with whom you had a relationship. Later in life, most Cancers, whether male or female, will find that women in general continue to exert a greater influence on their progress, echoing this primary lunar (female) theme. You may find that women go out of their way to help you in significant ways or that your closest and happiest relationships are with women.

For Cancer, charity begins at home. While you may assume that everyone shares these same instincts, dear Crab, in fact that is not quite true. Aquariuses, for example, are firmly fixed outward toward the world, bent on correcting ills in society, rather than inward toward strengthening their own family. In Pisces, the emphasis shifts to being helpful to the widest collection of individuals possible, from family, friends, and co-workers to subordinates and complete strangers. Pisces kindly keep picking up strays to help and nourish, and whether they are family members or not does not seem to matter one whit.

Your detractors say that some Cancers are too clannish and not caring enough of those outside their families. This is true only of some unevolved Cancer natives. In fact, if you could, dear Cancer, you would shelter anyone without a home, comfort any child without a mother, and bring sustenance to all who are hungry. In your heart, you hope to receive the same kind of unconditional love you send out, the kind of love we typically receive from a mother or a primary caretaker. That memory of being enveloped in love as an infant is carried within you forever. However, you won't be able to give as much until you feel secure, financially, emotionally, and physically. While you may hesitate at first to see if the person suffering truly needs rescuing before diving in, you won't ever turn your back either.

Your sign is known to be wonderfully child-oriented. As parents, Cancers usually do an outstanding job because it is a role they take so seriously and throw themselves into with such relish. You will joyfully watch cartoons, read bedtime stories, or crawl around on the floor with your Lilliputians all evening. Later, as they get older, you'll pay a good game of Scrabble or touch football, or help the kids with their homework. This is the sign that worries most about getting proper child care and who always goes to PTA meetings. Never tell Cancers they dote on their children too much, for you are sure to make yourself quite unpopular.

However, some Cancers can give too much. The Great Mother is strongly embedded in the Cancer archetype. Cancers who do not handle this symbolism in their lives well could overshadow their children's identity with too much of a good thing. Cancer's watery quality brings along with it a need to merge and to blend together without boundaries. Those Cancers get overprotective and even smothering in their attentiveness, and a loss of identity could occur—within you or within the child, or both. With all good intentions, those Cancers could unwittingly prevent their children from growing up independently. But most Cancers *do* learn to let go after a while, confident that their offspring are happy and well adjusted, and let them make a few mistakes on their own. Cancer parents who manage to do this become stronger for it. The bonus is that Cancer parents who do a good job of letting go of their children find that they are free to explore new creative outlets for their substantial talents.

Cancers who have a parent who hovers too much will have to strike a balance between honoring their parent for giving them life and striking out on their own by breaking free, the only way to become truly themselves. Easier said than done, this issue can cause much frustration, even rage, if it isn't addressed.

In the realm of interpersonal relationships, Cancers are wizards at being in sync with the feelings of those closest to them. So exquisite is Cancers' sensitivity that they can sense the tiniest changes within any close relationship, on a daily (and even an hourly) basis. A Cancer will pick up on the smallest static in the air or note a fleeting expression that is imperceptible to other signs. It is Nature's way of helping you to protect and defend yourself with an early warning system. If Cancers pick up a disturbing note on their radar screen, it is deeply disconcerting to them and will make concentration on anything else but the relationship difficult. Nothing will seem, in comparison, quite as important as attending to this, so you do—straightaway.

As a water sign, your feelings in love relationships run deeper than the ocean and as wide as the sky. You want your sweetheart or spouse to match your feelings, and if they can't you will be disappointed. You may quietly ask yourself whether your partner loves you enough or, conversely, whether you are asking too much of him or her. Realize that while it may be natural for you to have such strong emotions, Cancer, it may not be as easy for others to match your intensity. Your best chance for a truly spiritual soul mate is in a relationship with another water sign, whether Pisces, Scorpio, or Cancer. Water signs blend love, sexuality, and spirituality with a rare beauty and grace; other signs can't match the emotional range of water people.

Cancers don't want sex without love; they want a rich, multilayered experience based on authentic emotions. Cancers will show their lovers how to ride the waves of emotions in the sea of love. When you make love, dear Cancer, it will be a sensual, romantic, and very intense experience. And, when all conditions are right, it will include a sincere expression of love over time.

Remember that Cancer rules the stomach, so your lover should keep this in mind. The axiom that "the way to a man's heart is through his stomach" must have referred to a Cancer. (Guy Cancers! This works with women of the sign too.) Cancer doesn't need a fancy restaurant to be happy; in fact, you like a home-cooked meal better. That someone went to the trouble to cook for you is touching and will count for much. Cancer also loves to mix food and sex, so if you have a significant other who is a Cancer, he or she will love it if you mix the two!

Other signs may not be able to dive with you to the unfathomable depths of feeling. However, you may want also to consider dating an earth sign, namely Taurus, Capricorn, or Virgo. You will find that these earth signs lend an attractive stability to your life, anchoring you during life's storms and helping you find your balance.

Yet it will be hard for you to pass up the compatibility of a romantic, sentimental, and sensitive water sign: Pisces, Scorpio, or another Cancer. You are easily slighted, so if you date another water sign, he or she will be tactful and treat you exactly as you like to be treated. In this relationship you will feel confident that your thoughts and dreams are understood intuitively by your lover. Water signs seem to communicate in their own separate realm, as if through infrared beams or psychic powers. As a Cancer, you are a master at reading body language, and so is Pisces or Scorpio. You may wind up finishing one another's sentences and humming the same tunes because you are so in sync.

Cancers are romantics. They love long candlelit dinners, walks by the beach, moonlit cruises, poetry, and reminiscing over old photographs. Cancers are collectors; they love scrapbooks, and they practically invented the keepsake. Cancers love to plan special occasions too, the kind of event that requires lots of preparation. Cancers excel at organizing rituals such as weddings, christenings, graduations, and celebrations of traditional holidays that bring the family together, because they create such a loving, warm experience.

During these holidays the Cancer is always the one answering questions about lineage and ancestral heritage. Cancers must be born with silicon chips in their brains to record all the family relationships. Your sister announces that second cousin Henry is getting married in the spring. The Cancer will always speak up: "Henry is not Aunt Clare's *second cousin* but *second cousin twice removed*." At that point your brother asks how you are able to figure out these complicated relationships and are you sure they are right? Don't challenge Cancers about family relationships. Of course they are always right. They've been on the Internet all night checking out their roots and are getting closer all the time to a complete breakthrough on their geneology, tracing it back to the 1600s. Cancers are also the ones most often chosen to be family photographers and historians simply because they do it so creatively and with such enthusiasm. These are jobs they relish, so don't be afraid of assigning them to a Cancer.

For some Cancers, finding their true family or home situation is a lifelong process. It may come in terms of settling on the perfect house to buy or choosing the ideal place to live—even if this requires a radical relocation. Relocation is never done lightly. Cancers prefer to remain close to immediate family and friends, the social fabric of their lives. Cancers' search for home and family may include finding a birth mother if they were adopted, or finding a child to adopt if they cannot be parents. For some it centers on finding a way to care for an elderly and ill parent with dignity and compassion. Issues surrounding the family often form major life themes for this sign.

Divorce and the subsequent breakup of the home is not an easy adjustment for Cancer because they crave stability. If you are a newly divorced Cancer and there are children, the new stresses and strains of being a single parent could seem just as intense and difficult as the failed marriage. Cancers like being married and would rather marry again than continue the single life indefinitely. Single Cancer mothers have a particularly hard time juggling all they have to do, and they worry deeply about the welfare of their children. Divorced Cancer fathers of school-age children don't fare much better. Unless they are awarded custody, the Cancer dad will find a separation from his children very painful. Those Cancer fathers often become determined (even obsessed) to remain close to their children. In addition, they are usually very careful about keeping child-support payments current, because Cancer fathers fear being "an uncle" to their children, with the "real" job of fathering falling to their ex-wife's second husband. Sometimes Cancer fathers worry too much — children have a marvelous way of knowing in their hearts who Dad is and how much they are loved.

Sometimes, in their zeal to be with their children, male Cancers unconsciously push away a future mate by relegating that partner to secondary status. Of course it is impossible to compete with a Cancer's love for his children, so his new partner is put in a very difficult position. The man is not even aware he is doing this. Is there a solution? If you are a divorced Cancer, listen closely to what your partner is saying. Showing a caring attitude will help a great deal.

Within a romantic relationship there is a danger that Cancer's mother (or mother-in-law) could interfere with a loving Cancer relationship. Male Cancers prize and respect the relationship with their mothers so deeply that they may fail to show their allegiance to their wife first. Unwittingly, they may make their wife or girlfriend feel inferior to their mother. Disagreeing with Mother is nearly an impossible concept for a grown Cancer male to understand (as hard as that is to fathom). Rather than handle the situation easily and in a breezy and yet firm manner, he is likely to make a huge deal out of it, only complicating things further. His passivity might drive away his girlfriend or spouse because he refuses to see the problem he has created.

All that is needed is a little earthy practicality and a casual touch. Cancer, don't create an international incident when there is none. Cancer females aren't immune from this either; they need to separate a little bit from Mom when they marry so their first allegiance is to their husbands.

One more complexity to discuss is that Cancers of both sexes need to appreciate the feelings of their romantic partners when dealing with any family relationships. Cancers always have a tendency to feel that no matter what, blood is thicker than water. Unfortunately, when this is brought to their attention, their usual initial response is to leave little room for reasoning or negotiation. Sometimes all that is required is a small shift in perspective. Therefore, Cancer, try to walk in the other's shoes. You are enormously sensitive, so a tiny effort should ease any difficulties in this area. If your significant other tries to reason with you, listen with your heart.

Cancer is known to be a "worrier," but sometimes you look back a little too much and torture yourself with regrets. This may undermine your confidence. Try to learn from your mistakes but don't be afraid of making more of them. You will win a few and lose a few—the important thing is to learn from whatever happens and not to be too hard on yourself in the process.

You prize stability so much that you will stay in bad relationships or unproductive jobs too long, hoping for things to improve. You may later regret that you waited so long. Your steadfastness and devotion are virtues, dear Cancer. The older you get, the more easily you will see which situations to remain in and which to leave as soon as possible. You might want to ask the advice of a trusted friend—and then listen to it.

## FINANCE

In their financial life, Cancers tend to spend carefully and hold on to what they buy. You love bargains and will go out of your way to find new ones. Cancers always count their change, use coupons, and check receipts for errors. This is one sure way you tend to amass wealth over time. Cancers won't bet on a long shot—it's blue chips all the way. Nor will they invest in anything too flashy, trendy, or iffy—a Cancer venture capitalist will ask all the hard questions about the owners and their past track records. When you buy yourself clothing, dear Cancer, it is usually beautifully made and classic because you like things you know you can wear for years. Make no mistake, Cancer is wise about money, considered among the best and most trustworthy of signs (with Taurus, Scorpio, and Capricorn). Let others tease you—you laugh all the way to the bank!

## CAREER

What professions are best for you, dear Cancer? Although there are many possibilities for you, here are just a few. You make fine executive material, so why not start at the top, as CEO or chief financial officer, or work in accounting, finance, or investing? You would watch the bottom line carefully and come up with excellent cost-cutting measures. Also, on the more human side of the business, Cancers also understand the need for strong customer/client support and are excellent at solving touchy problems (mainly because they empathize so well). A job as a manager of customer support may suit you.

Anywhere you can offer food, shelter, or comfort to others would also be interesting to you. Good career areas include chef, caterer, produce dealer, baker, or restaurateur, hotelier, or retail food-store owner, perhaps selling gourmet or imported foods. You might do very well publishing a book of recipes or working on a food-oriented Web site.

Your natural link to pregnancy, birth, and the care of children means that you might consider being an obstetrician, nurse (especially a labor-room nurse), midwife, or a nutritionist or instructor for pregnant women (such as a birthing instructor for Lamaze or an instructor for the La Leche League, teaching mothers to breast-feed). You would be an excellent nursery school or kindergarten teacher, or work successfully in the toy industry or in any business that caters to infants and small children. You might also be an editor for a parenting type of magazine. With your love of history, you would work wonderfully too in antiques, as a museum curator, or as a historian.

Home and residence are your specialty, so you might become a designer of textiles or of other products for the home, from kitchen supplies to bed linens, from picture frames to rugs. You could be an architect or an interior designer or even a real estate broker. Working as a landscape artist or a gardener might be fun for you too. Finally, you are a water sign, so think about working near water or with liquids. You could make a career in the navy, or be a cruise-ship executive or work in the boating industry. You could run a photo lab or be a photographer. You could run a vineyard or a brewery, or import wine, coffee, or tea, or you could bottle water and soda. Because of your understanding of the range of human emotions and good memory for lines, you could make a superb actor. Your sensitivity would be an asset in any of the arts, including as a screenplay writer or a novelist.

One little known fact about Cancers is their remarkable ability to get publicity and to generate popularity. Because the Moon's energies are directed outward toward the collective unconscious (as opposed to ego), Cancer has a masterful instinctive ability to sense what the public wants and to tune into it. Being a publicity or talent agent might be perfect for you. Others may consider marketing or brand management.

## BODY, MIND, AND SPIRIT

Cancer's home is so important to the Crab that he carries it on his back wherever he goes. When life gets too overwhelming, the Crab simply barricades himself inside by clamping his outer shell shut. That is why it is so vital that Cancers be happy at home, and if they are not, they can become physically ill. In those instances Cancer feels defenseless against a cruel and uncaring universe. Home is sacred, and it doesn't matter how modest or luxurious the abode happens to be. What matters is that it makes Cancer and his or her family feel safe. If the place isn't quite right, Cancer will work at it, over a lifetime if necessary, to make it right.

Most people will agree with Cancer that home represents a haven against the world and a private place that allows us to experiment and grow. We want to feel free, prized for our individuality, and encouraged to take risks by our family, the people who know and love us for who we are. Hopefully, home is a place where you can be genuinely you, and a place for rest and recharge. Although Gemini can live out of a suitcase and constantly travel the globe, Cancer is not likely to be gone too long before a sudden bout of homesickness begins. Crabs want their bed, their favorite foods, and familiar faces around them. Having these simple life's pleasures around them frees them to tackle bigger issues, allowing them the foundation they need to spring into the wide blue yonder.

There are a few telling features of a Cancer residence. First, it will be comfortable and inviting; Cancer wants a warm, cookies-in-the-oven kind of home, something that could remind him of childhood. Your sign does not want to hire a decorator to impose a certain trendy style. They don't want a museum where people are afraid to kick back. Instead, they want an authentic space that reflects their true spirit.

Photographs of friends and family will likely be spread throughout the
house because the people whom Cancer loves are never far from view.
Cancers are a little messy, so if you are visiting a Cancer you may have
to walk over a few shoes in the middle of the living room or pretend you
haven't noticed that mass of papers piled in their den. Cancer also tends
to be fairly territorial, so if you happen to sit in Cancer's favorite chair or
side of the couch, prepare to move.

The kitchen is a key area for Cancer, and in Cancer's home, it will likely
be the hub of activity. Leo, the sign that follows you, may have a fairly
empty refrigerator with perhaps a bottle of champagne and can of caviar
on the shelf on the door. Leos have no time to cook; they're off to the next
dinner party. Gemini, the sign that precedes Cancer, will have plenty of
postage stamps and FedEx air bills in the house but probably no milk
(these worker bees love takeout). Cancer, on the other hand, has enough
food in their cupboards to feed a family of four for a year. Many Cancers
like to cook, whether it's the simple act of whipping up a batch of pan-
cakes for breakfast in bed with your spouse or a soufflé for a Saturday
night dinner to impress guests. For you, puttering with food is fun. Food
links Cancer to the outside world by providing the social interaction that
this sign finds so deeply satisfying. For Cancer, the gift of food says "I
love you."

You have an excellent chance of staying healthy because you like vegetables and fruits and usually drink plenty of water. Watch for possible milk
allergies. While you don't like highly strenuous exercise, you do like to
dance, do aerobics, swim, ski or water-ski, or ice skate (you like all water-
oriented sports). As a Cancer you do have a delicate stomach, so when
you experience tension it is a good idea to switch to milder foods until you
feel better. Cancer women should make sure to schedule regular mammo-
grams. Extra calcium is also recommended, especially for Cancer women.
Since you tend to hold extra water, try to go easy on salt. Another possible area of concern for Cancers include eating disorders. Bulimia and

anorexia are common Cancer problems. Nipping a problem in the bud always makes it easier to fix. Generally, you have a fine chance of staying fit and healthy.

## SUMMARY

In closing, if you love a Cancer, you can be sure your sweetheart will always care for, protect, and defend the family. He or she will build a loving home life, enjoy and provide for children, and remain loyal all his or her life. Cancers understand the need for a strong family unit and won't lightly break up a marriage. They are compassionate, kind, and thoughtful. They invest wisely, don't squander money, and usually accumulate wealth in their lifetime. Few signs love with the depth of feeling and compassion of Cancer, so if you have a Cancer lover, caress your Crab with tender loving care. You'll realize that your Cancer, like the rare and perfect pearl this sign symbolizes, is one in a million.

# THE MYTHS OF CANCER AND
# THE MOON

People sometimes wish they weren't Cancers, saying, "What a name my sign has! Why couldn't I have been called anything else?" Little do they know what a rich and wonderful mythological history the Crab has. The crab itself is a very ancient creature, dating back 500 million years. Appropriately, Cancer is said to be the defender of traditions and is so interested in history and ancestry. Ancient Greeks and Egyptians called this sign the Scarab, a crab-like beetle that has claws. Considered to be holy, the word *scarab* is linked to our word *sacred*. Like the crab, Cancers take an indirect route, allowing them time to reflect, putting new experiences into the framework of past experience. This makes sense, too, as their ruler, the Moon, rules memories. Yet Cancers can be quite stubborn at times—that's their claw, digging into whatever they've latched on to at the moment. The Crab wears his skeleton on the outside, while his opposite sign, Capricorn, wears his bones inside—this increases Cancer's sense of vulnerability and need to be self-protective.

The Chaldeans, one of the first peoples to set down astrologic precepts (see "The History of Astrology") said that Cancer represented the Gates of Mankind, a kind of doorway the soul uses to manifest itself in reality. The fourth house rules not only home and family, but also the very foundations of life. In astrology we call this fourth house the "IC" (Immum Coeli) point on the wheel, which in Latin means "bottom of the heavens." It is quite simply the time when today becomes both tomorrow and yesterday at once. It is the midnight point of a chart, signifying the start of a brand-new day. Experiences we have today suddenly become memories. This is appropriate because the Moon, ruling all dreams and remembrances, rules the Crab.

## HERCULES AND HYDRA

The Greeks offer an exceptionally beautiful myth that attempts to explain how Cancer became part of the twelve major constellations. The story centers on Hercules, the original action hero, and the two Earth Mother goddesses, Hera and the monster Hydra. According to the myth, Hercules had to perform the famous twelve labors assigned to him by Eurystheus, king of Mycena. If he was successful, Hercules would be assured a place among the gods as immortal for all time. As his second labor, Hercules had to battle the dreaded sea serpent, a monster named Hydra. Hydra was a terrifying beast with multiple dog-like heads (some say she had as few as seven heads, but other versions of this myth say she had as many as ten thousand). So awful was she that even her breath was said to be lethally poisonous. Hercules knew that one of Hydra's heads was immortal, so it was clear that he had to chop that particular head off. However, the immortal head was identical to the others, so identifying it was not an easy task.

During Hercules's battle with Hydra, a gigantic crab emerged from the deep and latched on to Hercules's heel. In doing this, the crab was demonstrating his fierce determination to defend Hydra, a mother figure who represented the kindly individual who was responsible for his life. Hercules whacked the crab, crushing it, and kept on fighting Hydra. Hacking away at Hydra, Hercules managed to chop off two of her heads, but two new heads grew in place of each head he cut off. Hercules called upon Iphicles, his friend, to burn each new wound he created using blazing branches so the blood supply would be stemmed and no new heads would grow. It worked! Hercules was finally able to slay the monster by chopping off her immortal head.

The part of the story as it relates to you, dear Cancer, is that Earth Mother Hera noted the efforts of the crab to help Hydra in her battle with Hercules. Hera was Hercules's enemy; so she wanted to honor the crab for his efforts. Using the stars in the heavens, Hera made an outline of the crab and placed it in the sky as the fourth constellation, Cancer, to remain there forever, until this day an immortal symbol of the brave and loyal crab.

## DEMETER AND PERSEPHONE

Other myths that relate to Cancer center on mother figures. The most dramatic is the story of Demeter and her daughter Persephone, a tale outlined in this book in "The Myths of Scorpio and Pluto." In Cancer, instead of focusing on Persephone we center more on the feelings of the mother after she learns that her daughter has been abducted. As the myth relates, Demeter, mother of Persephone and goddess of fertility and harvest, is normally a kind and gentle figure, but she goes on an unusual rampage because of her deep sorrow and her inability to find Persephone. Demeter destroys crops and causes famine for a full year. Zeus in his wisdom feels a need finally to step in and make a deal or risk seeing all life on Earth wither and die.

In the myth, Persephone's mother does not want to let go of her child, for her daughter brings her much happiness. Note here that the mother needs the child as much as the child needs the mother—the two create a circle of love. In the Demeter-Persephone story, in order for Persephone to grow up she has to break free of Demeter. The story studies the pain of that separation. This theme is similar to what many Cancers experience in everyday life on one level or another: a forced separation between parent and child or between members of a family that is temporary (going to another city to work, for example) or permanent (giving up a child for adoption). In the end, it is decided that Persephone will spend half her time on Earth and the other half in the underworld, a compromise that does not please Demeter, for she realizes that life will never be the same again. She accepts it nevertheless as her only viable option. In the story of Mary and Jesus, probably the most moving and well known of all mother-and-child archetypes, Mary wants to protect her holy child from the horrors and pain of the world but is unable to do so. Mother love is usually highly protective. This is a theme picked up and enlarged in the sign of Virgo, but mother's protective love is certainly a theme here in Cancer as well.

Interestingly, in the Demeter-Persephone story, while searching for Persephone, Demeter still was able to take time to show kindness to others. The daughters of Celeus, king of Eleusis, invited Demeter to stay at their palace—they didn't know the real identity of the woman they had invited in, as Demeter disguised herself as an old woman. Demeter taught Celeus and the Eleusinians how to revere her (in the third person) in a well-known series of rites called the Eleusinian Mysteries, perhaps the most popular and most accepted of all Greek rites.

Queen Meteneira hired Demeter to be her baby's nursemaid, a job Demeter enjoyed as she awaited the return or discovery of the whereabouts of Persephone. Demeter loved the baby boy she cared for as well as the boy's parents, so one day she decided to give the child immortality. Each night Demeter put the baby in the fireplace to "burn off his mortality." One evening his mother walked in unexpectedly to see Demeter placing her son in the burning fireplace. She was, of course, horrified—and because she didn't know that the nurse she had hired was Demeter herself, she dismissed Demeter. Thus, Demeter didn't get to finish her series of rites for the child, but even though the boy didn't grow up to become immortal, he did turn out to be a great leader of Eleusis in later years.

Thus we see Demeter in her most powerful role, that of disguised goddess with the ability to bestow immortality, and she is shown at the same time being giving and loving. Like the sign of Cancer, Demeter has the capacity to show great love no matter what private sorrows are being endured.

OEDIPUS

There is one other myth that relates to the Cancer archetype: the Oedipus story. While most people have heard of the tale, they don't remember (or never knew) the details. It is a fascinating story.

In the most basic form, the House of Cadmus was a well-esteemed family in Greece when it was founded. Cadmus had traveled to Athens to locate his sister, Europa, who it is said had been taken by Zeus. At Thebes, a dragon attacked Cadmus. He succeeded in killing it even though the dragon destroyed his entire army. To make a long story short, it is said that Cadmus and five soldiers helped build the city of Thebes. Cadmus later married Harmonia, one of the favorite daughters of Ares (Mars) and Aphrodite (Venus). The family of Cadmus had their difficulties and tragedies, but let's skip to Laius, the great-grandson of Cadmus and Harmonia, who was next in line to assume the throne. Usurpers to the throne forced Laius, still young, to leave Thebes and stay in Olympia. While there, Laius lived under the hospitality of the home of King Pelops. Laius betrayed the king by kidnapping his illegitimate young son, Chrysippus, whom Laius kept for his own sexual pleasure. The young boy Chrysippus soon committed suicide to hide his involvement in this secret relationship.

Laius later married a woman named Jocasta, and they were having difficulty conceiving children. Laius consulted the oracle at Delphi for a cure, but the oracle offered no cure and instead warned if Laius had a child a great misfortune would befall him and his wife, for his future son would kill him and marry his mother. The oracle was very clear about this, on three separate occasions. Laius decided to heed the oracle and remain childless by never having relations with his wife again—but he never told her why. Jocasta, however, not knowing the warning at Delphi, got her husband drunk one night, made love, and conceived a baby son, who was Oedipus by another name.

Terrified of their child (Jocasta by then was told of what could come to be), they gave their baby to shepherds to leave to die of exposure on Mount Cithaeron. The shepherds took pity on the baby and made sure he didn't die. Instead the baby lived and later was cared for by Periboea and Polybus, who loved the child they named Oedipus. The important point is that growing up in his new family's care, Oedipus did not know his true heritage—he thought Periboea and Polybus were his real parents. However, Oedipus didn't look like either one of his "parents," and one night a drunken guest of the family pointed this out to him. Disturbed, Oedipus went to Delphi to ask the oracle about his true roots. Before he could even ask, the Pythia, Apollo's prophetess, became very upset, shouting at him to leave the shrine and predicting that he would one day murder his father and marry his mother. This was horrific news, and Oedipus was terribly shaken by it. He still didn't know that Periboea and Polybus weren't his real parents, so he immediately decided to travel as far from them as possible.

Meanwhile, back at Thebes, things weren't going well for King Laius, who was having feelings of dread he couldn't explain—he needed to know whether the spell on him and his wife was erased yet. The Sphinx (a terrible monster) was killing the citizens of Thebes at the time too. Laius told himself he had to get back to Delphi to consult the oracle once more. The myth here differs on accounts. Some say Laius was going as king to find out how to handle the Sphinx, others say he was going as a man to find out more about how to avoid his fate concerning his son. On the way, when reaching a crossroad, Laius and his attendants saw a young man on the road, whom they asked to move. The young man, Oedipus, refused to step aside. (It is interesting to note here that the word *oedipus* means "swollen foot.") It seems then a wheel either went over his foot or a servant bopped him on the head (or both). This got Oedipus angry enough to kill Laius, who was his true father, although, of course, Oedipus was not aware of this. Laius and Oedipus both tried to ignore their fate and both ran right into it at the crossroads. Laius never knew it was his son who killed him that day.

Meanwhile, at Thebes, the Sphinx was terrorizing the city. It was said that Hera had sent the Sphinx to punish Laius for his behavior toward Chrysippus. The riddle the Sphinx asked any who were brave enough to try to answer it was: What creature walks on four legs in the morning, two at midday, and three in the evening? Whoever answered the riddle would set the city free. Whoever was wrong, however, would die a terrible death, eaten alive by the Sphinx. The Sphinx had just eaten the son of Creon and the nephew of Jocasta. Creon, grieving the deaths of both his son and his brother-in-law, offered a reward: a handsome sum and the hand of his sister in marriage to anyone who would answer the Sphinx's riddle correctly. Oedipus gave it a try—and was successful. He said correctly that the answer was "Man who crawls as a baby, walks upright as a man, and carries a cane in old age," thus ending the Sphinx's reign of terror and getting the hand of Jocasta, whom he did not know was his true mother. (Jocasta didn't know Oedipus was her son either, but she did know that Laius had been killed on the road to Delphi.) Thus, the wisest man of the city, Oedipus, was ignorant of his true parents' identity and committed the very deeds he'd tried so hard to avoid. Despite what Freud tells us about this tale, it seems to carry the message that the sins of the father are visited on the children. The gods seem to be suggesting that those sins have to be paid for—there is no escape. Thus, the story of Oedipus acts as a kind of moral tale to live a clean life or else plan to see one's sorrows visited on one's children.

Some Cancers do have strong and complex family issues to work out over time, and it is true that parents' misdeeds could later cause much sadness in the lives of their offspring. For some Cancers (or those with afflicted Cancer planets), overcoming the grief of childhood sexual abuse or uncovering the truth about a certain family secret can be very painful. For other Cancers there was no "misdeed," only a question of how best to deal with the day-to-day family situation. For example, the question could center on when to take over a family business without hurting the feelings of the parent who founded it. Coming to terms with family issues is a very

Cancerian concern, but one that Cancers are well qualified to handle with expert sensitivity, especially if it is done with objectivity. For Cancers it is hard to separate emotions from facts, so sometimes it is worth bringing in a trusted professional to help sift through the details and to find innovative ways to overcome challenges. The point is, the problem need not end in a tragedy; struggles with family issues could also bring triumph. Unlike the Greeks, who believed in fated destiny, we believe we can and do control our future.

# LEO PERSONALITY

*Leo*

July 23–August 23

### Guiding Principle

"I Create"

### How This Sign Feels Joy

Finds joy in both discovering and celebrating all things unique, as well as through playful, creative acts of self-expression.

### In the New Millennium, Your Contribution to the World Will Be . . .

As the creative artist of the zodiac, your function as a cultural oracle will assume greater importance. It will fall to you to portray the future roles of men and women through art, film, music, dance, drama, comedy, photography, and other venues.

### Quote That Describes You

"THE ESSENTIAL IS TO EXCITE THE SPECTATORS. IF THAT MEANS PLAYING HAMLET ON A FLYING TRAPEZE OR IN AN AQUARIUM, YOU DO IT."

—OSCAR WILDE, a *Libra*

How can you tell a Leo at first glance? This marvelous sign wants to be noticed, so they will make *sure* that you do. It's the lady or gentleman who arrives late, wearing that unforgettable outfit and Leo's favorite accessory, dark sunglasses. As Leo steps out of the limo he or she will bask in the glow of photographers' strobes—those snaps will run in the next morning's papers. Leo's look is widely imitated throughout the kingdom because it is glamorous and, at the same time, *exactly right* for that moment in time. Leos adore large-scale rituals (like coming-out parties), ceremonies (like weddings), and special events (celebrations and birthday parties) because Leos are very aware of monumental moments in their lives. The Leo lady knows how to create an impression that lasts and radiates energy. To find the quintessential Leo male, look closely at the guests at your next party. He is that sophisticated, dashing man in black tie who has just alighted from the helicopter on the host's lawn heading for the drawing room in time for cocktails. Most likely a few key members of his staff surround him. It may be his fine posture or the confident way he walks with a sense of grace and urgency, or the discreet way he converses now and then with aides. Leo must have first declared: "Presentation is everything!" Leo does it best. It is impossible not to notice Leos. Every move they make appears to be, and is, deliberate. Leos conserve their strength and hold it inside so it won't be dissipated; they look self-contained.

Dear Leo, in you there is always that charismatic presence that marks movie-stars-in-the-making as well as successful people in any walk of life. You may not have a limo or a helicopter at your disposal (right now), but no matter what your social status, you possess such dignity that people you meet feel that if you aren't famous yet, you *should be* and *will be* soon. Leo is, after all, the sign of royalty. (HRH Queen Elizabeth, the Queen Mother is a Leo, as was Napoleon, a name that literally means "lion.") Others are always eager to draw some of your power and light. This aura of celebrity you seem to carry with you could stem from your good looks, but more often than not your "aura" comes from your powerful inner poise and self-confidence. Your belief in yourself is terribly sexy and adds luster to everything you do. (Each of us could take a page from Leo's notebook on that count.)

## SYMBOLS

♌ The glyph for Leo resembles the tail of the lion or a combination of the tail and mane. In esoteric astrology, the lyrical quality of the symbol represents this *kundalini* or life force, a serpent power uncoiling from its place of slumber at the base of the spine, ready to arise. It has been said by some that creative people seem to be more sexual than most—this seems to be borne out with Leo. Dear Leo, the passions of your youth will burn brightly throughout your life, even in old age.

☉ The symbol for your ruler, the Sun, is very simple: a circle with a dot in the middle. The circle echoes the shape of the Sun, but the dot is symbolic of the infinite source of divine energy and vitality that exists within every human. It signifies potential, the part of divine energy that created every person on Earth. Leo is about complete self-realization and creativity.

## PLANETARY INFLUENCES

A fire sign, Leo crackles with good ideas and has a strong and whimsical imagination. Leo doesn't want to be like everyone else; you need to "let you be you." No matter what, Leo, you try to do everything with flair, individuality, and style. People imitate you in various ways—you see different aspects picked up by friends and family all the time. It may be a certain way you cut your hair or accessorize an outfit, or it could be your special use of words. You don't mind the copycats; in fact, you find their imitations flattering. In order to get things moving, any Leo knows you have to get somebody's attention first or nothing else will happen. Leos have perfected that process to a science. If it is true that Gemini needs a dial tone as dearly as oxygen (and it is), then in the same way Leo needs the spotlight for the warmth and life-giving energy it provides.

As the second fire sign of the zodiac, Leo is social and gregarious. The sign symbolizes the stage of evolution of man as he leaves the comfort of his family to become aware of his place in society. In Aries, the first fire sign, we find the warrior or entrepreneur; in Leo we find the courageous leader and defender of the populace, the Sun king. Leo enjoys making the rounds of parties and other events that some signs might find exhausting—attending the art opening or the charity fund-raiser or accepting an invitation to speak at the club—and as an extroverted fire sign, Leo will gladly accept a starring role. In fact, a night rubbing shoulders with many new faces isn't tiring for you, Leo—it is invigorating. Going to "in" places to see and be seen is one of Leo's favorite pastimes. Probably the only sign that could keep up with your busy schedule is Libra. Leo believes that when you entertain, you treat your friends like royalty; the food should be superb, and the atmosphere, memorable. You hand-pick guests with special care, masterfully mixing those of various backgrounds to insure that conversation will remain lively and revolve around interesting subjects. What if your job interferes when your boss says a big report is due in the morning? According to Leo, work can wait a while—why waste a perfectly wonderful evening? Leo is more likely to stay out all night and, needing little sleep, show up as the early bird in the morning to get started on the project. Luckily, Leo is a strong sign and rarely runs out of stamina.

## Cosmic Gifts

Much has been written about how Leo loves to get compliments, and this is true. Bless them, but Leos are so vulnerable to flattery that it's charming. No matter how distinguished or famous they become (or how many awards line their mantel), Leos still hunger for a pat on the back. They love to hear that they made a wise decision, look fabulous, or acted in a particularly courageous way. (Leo is, after all, nothing if not stouthearted.) Their authoritative face seems to melt when complimented, and a happy Leo is a joy to behold. You might ask, "Doesn't everybody, of every sign, love and accept compliments?" Actually, no. Scorpio, for example, will wonder about your motives for saying something nice. Pisces will blush and feel uneasy about being the focus of your attention, but will shift the discussion quickly back to you. Cancer will instantly offer food as thanks, while Virgo will smile modestly, note your words, and thank you politely and warmly — but won't fall for flattery. However, Leo will give you a look so warm it could melt chocolate, and this will feel sweeter than a great big kiss. All you want to do is think up some more charming words for them to enjoy.

Is Leo egotistical? Of course! Being ruled by the Sun, the center of the solar system, the most brilliant star in our galaxy and provider of all life on Earth, can do that to a person. If taken to the extreme, Leos can get so self-absorbed that they neglect everyone else's needs around them. Also let's add that Leo can get a little arrogant, act somewhat superior, or even a little snobbish, but normally it's done without thinking. This is Leo's confidence becoming too much of a good thing, but most Leos do know exactly where to draw the line. The vast majority of Leos are joyful, generous, enthusiastic, and warm-hearted people who are deliciously fun to be around.

Leos can't resist a good tidbit of gossip when they get a chance to hear it. Leos are people-persons. Gossip is especially juicy when it's about a famous person or about someone in their circle they admire. As a Leo, you won't care a whit whether Edgar in the mailroom is seeing Ethel in the accounting department after hours. When channel-surfing, a Leo will stop and be temporarily mesmerized by the Robin Leach show *Lifestyles of the Rich and Famous*. That program, which brings you into gorgeous private mansions of successful people, motivates Leo. While the Lion *isn't* wildly ambitious, he *is* competitive (admittedly a bit of a strange combination; it supposes superiority without having to make the hard-driving effort). Not only do you want to be admired, but you want to look up to other people too — you continually search for sources of inspiration.

If you want to know what's hot and what's not, ask a Leo; the beautiful and prosperous people of society draw his or her attention. Leos don't mind if others speak about them either—in fact they expect it! George M. Cohan once said, "I don't care what you say about me, as long as you say *something* about me, and as long as you spell my name right." That sums up Leos attitude in a nutshell, and is a big reason for their success. A Leo won't be ignored.

Ancient astrologers wrote that each sign echoes the progress of human development, so it is interesting to see where Leo fits into the scheme of things. The zodiac begins with Aries, symbolic of the pure life force and fresh beginnings, necessarily, like a newborn, self-absorbed ("Me!"). Taurus is next, covering the baby's growing instinct to acquire things ("Mine!"). In Gemini language and communication begin, and we see the child's first attempts at mastery over words ("Why?"). In Cancer, the sign that proceeds Leo, the child awakens to relationships in the family (especially with his mother), and also explores his immediate family environment ("Mama").

In Leo, the child gets to know his father. As a result, in Leo the child *identifies with* authority figures, as firstborn children are prone to do (the fifth house, which is ruled by Leo, also rules the firstborn). Each sign in the zodiac makes up for excesses and deficiencies of the previous sign. Thus, Leo finds the home-and-family emphasis of Cancer too claustrophobic. Leos' bonding with Father encourages them to become more independent and to separate from parents to explore new relationships and also to learn through play. Leo also wants to have fun and will break free of the family obligations Cancer takes on so willingly. Virgo, the sign after Leo, will make up for Leo's emphasis on hedonistic pleasure by being extremely productive— Virgos are easily the workaholics of the zodiac. The house Leo rules covers creativity, fun, participation in sports and hobbies, and romance. In the evolution of mankind, Leo is the child in the process of self-discovery. Through our likes and dislikes and through creative efforts, we learn a thing or two about ourselves and begin to hear our unique inner voice. Virgo will enjoy the preciseness of numbers and words as well as things they can do with their hands, such as crafts and woodworking. In contrast, Leo works with color, design, texture, fabric, paint, words, or light to create artistic creations of great originality. Finally, falling in love (also part of fifth-house activities) marks an important time in anyone's life. As anyone who has fallen in love will agree, love brings self-discovery because when we are in love we feel cherished for our uniqueness, flaws and all. In the fifth house we learn, then, not only to love others, but also to love ourselves.

Before jumping ahead to look at Leo's approach to love, let's first look at Leo's interests, because they say a lot about your inner nature, Leo. Your tastes are likely to be fairly sophisticated, well developed, and quite urban—Leo wants meaningful experiences in life, and that includes his or her taste in the arts. (Why waste time with second-rate? asks Leo.) Every Leo I have ever met adored music. You will rarely find a Leo with a tin ear, because their senses are almost as exquisitely sensitive as Taurus's, a hard sign to beat when it comes to the senses. Leos' taste in music runs to the popular too, so they enjoy a wide variety of music, from classical to blues, jazz, show music, rock, and golden oldies. Give Leo a sound system or tickets to a concert and this cat purrs.

Leos are the kind of people who will check the art reviews in the newspaper and follow various art movements with enthusiasm; the avant-garde faction in any of the disciplines doesn't throw Leo, because this sign admires originality. A Leo will want to see that the artist's talent is well developed—those whose work is "green" or too amateurish will not score points with Leo. Leo wants to look up to a master. On Saturday afternoons you'll find Aries at a theme park bungee jumping, Gemini is heading out in his or her sports car to points unknown, and Cancer is puttering in the kitchen with a new recipe. Leo, meanwhile, is visiting the latest exhibits at the galleries and museums. Leos love to shop too (whether for designer clothes, artwork, books, or electronics). Poor Virgos, the sign that comes after yours, are no doubt working on their taxes and cleaning out their closets. Unlike Virgo, which likes to get vital tasks done, Leo sees these more mundane activities as a waste of time and doesn't really care if they ever get done. Leo can live with a less than spic-and-span house — or leaves chores for others.

Leo, of all the arts the theater is your favorite. On the stage you are presented with a whole range of emotions and philosophical issues, and you adore the theater because it is life made ever larger. What better way to explore life than on the stage, and as a Leo you want to experience it all. You also want to enjoy the collaborative and multileveled creativity of a gorgeous production, from the brilliant and imaginative costumes and musical score to the dramatic lighting and well-written dialogue. Perhaps because you see yourself as the real-life star of your own life's script, hearing about other heroes' challenges and choices fascinates you. A spirited fire sign, Leo will cry with the play's hero in his hour of defeat as well as rejoice with him in his hour of triumph. Being a vivacious, optimistic sign, Leo prefers happy endings. If the story has some interesting moral, ethical insights, or mythological or historical overtones, this is all the better, for Leos like to think deeply about what they have seen. Epic stories and Shakespeare interest you too. You never know when you might be able to apply those inspirations to your own life's dilemmas. All these elements combine to make a night at the theater Leo's favorite activity.

Leos aren't known to be very versatile or adaptable, but they are very determined. If you are close to a Leo, you will soon find out that they can be quite wedded to their opinions, so don't expect them to change their minds. Their fixed nature makes debating politics or any touchy subject hard; if you are dating a Leo you may want to stay away from certain "hot" subjects. Leos can be quite dogmatic about their strong views on politics. They think it is outrageous to have to pay taxes or to follow so many government regulations. The child inside the adult Leo yearns to be free. They may *intellectually* understand the idea of democracy, where there is "one for all and all for one" but the royal "we" in them makes Leos feel superior and somewhat above certain rules. Of course

Leos know that running things by fiat (even if they are the boss) isn't always possible, practical, or even desirable, but they muse about getting their own way, especially politically. Once they have decided to support a certain political party or candidate, you probably can't change their minds. Like Taurus or Scorpio, if you want to have an influence on a Leo, you will have to get into their thinking process early on. The good side to this quality, however, is that Leos adhere to their beliefs and aren't wishy-washy. Their sense of conviction does attract many admirers.

While others expect Leo to buckle when the going gets tough, Leo does just the opposite. Leos are able to keep their heads and will always show enormous grace under pressure. Remember that Leos may look like pussycats—and most of the time they *seem* like pussycats—but wrong them and they will tear you to bits. Lions and Lionesses do not suffer injustice silently. They are very, very strong-willed, and they will always fight for right.

## RELATIONSHIPS

If you are choosing a gift for a Leo—and, believe me, Leo *loves* to get surprise presents—be sure to get the best quality you can afford within the category you have chosen. If you are buying a vase, for example, instead of any old lead crystal, make it Baccarat or Waterford. If choosing a bottle of wine, spend a little more than usual; Leo will notice the fine selection you made and admire you for your taste. Can't afford gold (Leo's metal)? Get sterling silver, but never anything silverplated. Buying a pen? Choose the classic Mont Blanc or something comparable. You get the idea. You are not purchasing something for a Pisces, who will say it was the thought that counts. Leo rules luxury and feels that the entire idea of a gift is to delight. Unlike Virgo, who would want something practical and useful, a Leo would never think of buying something someone would normally buy for himself or herself, so they would expect you to do the same. Pampering would be an excellent idea—think too of getting your friend or sweetheart an hour (or a day) of indulgence. Start with a massage and you will be on the right track.

Now let's study Leo's zestful view of love. Leos are so enthusiastic about love that they practically live for it. Leo adores the thrill of the chase, the mystery, the notes, the flowers (both to receive and to send), the little tiffs, and even the tearful reunion later (not to forget the passionate love-making that follows). Drama attracts Leo like a magnet. Leos will make memorable lovers who will get the setting and mood exactly right, for like the theater, their other passion, you will be the Leo's heroine or hero in his or her real-life drama. If you are dating a Leo, be aware that they crave adoration. Imagine your significant other as a king or a queen and you will be on the right track—fuss over them and continue to compliment them often to show that your passion still burns brightly.

As mentioned before, Leo is the landlord of the fifth house of romantic love. This same horoscope house rules speculation, gambling, and risk-taking—thus the ancient astrologers acknowledged that risk-taking and romance go hand in hand. Leo understands this instinctively and is always ready to take a chance on love, over and over again if necessary. Leo enjoys the entire process, from first date to wooing (or being wooed), the thrill of the chase, and the final surrender. Young Leos should be wary of being more "in love with love" than with the person they are dating. Thankfully this is a tendency they usually outgrow. Yet the kind of love that Leo rules (and thus understands exquisitely well) is that fresh blush of new love, love that is not yet serious (serious love is ruled by the seventh house of the horoscope, Libra). Love that is experienced in this house is still light and flirtatious—there is time for commitment later (symbolized by the seventh house, Libra's domain).

Does this mean Leo won't marry? Not at all. In fact, Leos have the ability to keep love fresh for a whole lifetime because they relish having fun with their mate so much. Most Leos adore marriage, but it has to be the right kind of marriage. Admittedly, there are some unevolved Leos who do have difficulty with marriage due to restlessness or an inability to remain attentive in long-term relationships. Some Leos will find everyday obligations, overall routine, and lack of stimulation confining. For some, the messy details of dealing with another person's likes and dislikes on a day-to-day basis could prove too difficult for a sign that thinks more in terms of "me" than "we." This will all depend on the Leo and his or her partner and how they relate to each other. My advice to you if you are dating or marrying a Leo is to keep your sense of humor, keep your alliance fresh with plenty of new interests, and, if you have or want children, hire plenty of baby-sitters so that you can devote some quality time for just him or her. Leo loves to be babied.

Realize, also, that Leos want to look up to their partners—Leos want to be inspired, so don't hesitate in going out in the world and staking your claim to fame. Just don't forget to give them the attention they need. Also, make sure your Leo feels needed by you. Leos like to be helpful, and if they aren't they feel useless and unnecessary.

You can be very optimistic about your long-term potential with your Leo. Being a fixed sign, most Leos will stay wed, for they tend to prize stability. Then too there is the possibility of having children, the other part of life that will always be sweet for Leo. Keep in mind that the fifth house of the horoscope, Leo's house, also rules creativity, pregnancy and birth, and care of one's children. Thus, having children is often the most exciting part of marriage. Indeed many Leos say this is their number-one reason to wed. Leos see their offspring as their finest creations, as smaller versions of themselves. Leos will gladly play games or take their kids to the movies or to a natural history museum. As parents, they will want to pour all kinds of cultural influences into their little ones' heads. The Leo mother or father will want to provide piano lessons or ballet instruction so that their children's talent can be suitably encouraged.

Whether just dating or attached, know that Leos like to spend money on their loved one. This sign will not pinch pennies. Expect to sample the best restaurants, shows, clubs, and other hot spots, not only during your early courtship but also throughout your time together. A male Leo will want to dazzle his sweetheart with lavish outings and may add a few wonderful gifts. A female Lioness will surprise her sweetheart too, perhaps with tickets to something special occasionally or by treating him to a great four-star dinner. Is living it up during courtship and marriage a universal instinct for all signs? No. A more frugal sign like Cancer may not want to spend much money or be too worried about leaving family obligations. Ambitious Capricorn will frequently work late at the office, and Virgo and Aquarius will prefer veggie burgers to pâté. But Leo, oh, Leo! Anyone who dates and marries you should prepare for the good life. Your attachment to your Leo could feel like a lifelong affair and is sure to be fun — just keep fanning the fires of love. As discussed earlier, be sure to keep giving Leos plenty of compliments and reassure them about their desirability. Oddly enough, there's a good chance that Leos will forget to give *you* any compliments, so wrapped up are they in themselves. Okay, just know this and then just laugh about it. Chances are you won't need those affirmations as much as your Leo does.

By the way, if you are ever on a date with a male of this sign and he seems a little short of cash, don't offer to pay; his pride will be wounded. If he is going through a tough period, don't offer a loan unless he asks for one. By doing so you may unwittingly be saying that you think he won't be able to get a job any time soon and crush his ego forever. Lionesses don't seem to be prone to this. This may be social conditioning, but Lionesses have pride too. Family members shouldn't assume that she can't get back on her feet without their aid, because chances are she can figure things out quite nicely, thank you. Wanting to be self-sufficient is actually a wonderful quality of this sign, a part of Leo's fierce independent streak.

The regal sign is the ruler of the fifth house of the zodiac, the house that rules children, a logical assignment when you think about how royalty puts great emphasis on bloodlines and progeny. Creative projects come under the same house, and here too there is congruity. Just as kings assure the perpetuation of their family name and power through heirs, similarly, many people find their own kind of immortality either through having children or through their own creative endeavors.

The relationship between father and child is touched on in Leo, but will be further developed later, in Saturn-ruled Capricorn. In Aries, the first sign of the zodiac, father is acknowledged as the source of life but also can be a competitor to be challenged or overthrown. In Leo, father is seen as personal protector who deeply loves his child and is a benevolent, caring figure. Leo is competitive, but not competitive with his child. He teaches his child to be safe (as Daedalus tried to do with Icarus; see "The Myths of Leo and the Sun") and also to make his mark on the outside world, especially through imaginative, creative endeavors. Later, in Capricorn, the father/authority figure theme is revisited. At that time, father (or another key male figure) will be seen as judge, symbolizing the need for man to meet standards to get approval from more critical authority figures.

## FINANCE

Leo likes to mix with the beautiful people and to circulate in the best, most trendy circles. One reason so many Leos become publishers and politicians is because either field will allow them entry into interesting social circles. Finally, Leo rules all expensive things (the ancients actually assigned things of this nature). Many find that great opportunity exists in the "high-ticket" industries of fine wines and champagnes, imported chocolates, caviar, designer clothing, furs, expensive automobiles and jewelry, and any other luxury item you can imagine. If the luxury market sounds good *to* you, Leo, it could be good *for* you too. Go for it!

As anyone might guess, it takes plenty of money to live the lifestyle a Leo expects, and failing a fat trust fund, Leo will have to work for it. Here we come to subject of money — saving it, spending it, and earning it. Oh, boo. Leo hates it when reality intrudes like that. (Silly me for bringing it up.)

Alas, sooner or later Leos will have a day of reckoning if they can't make ends meet. Budgets are so, well, restrictive—and they are almost never popular with Leos. Leos prefer to live a life that is bigger than life. Leos want to spend freely. Within every Leo is a certain set of expectations—including a certain way of life he feels he deserves. If conditions prevent Leos from living that lifestyle, they are patently outraged. Unlike Cancer and Virgo, the signs that precede and follow Leo and who are the original worrywarts, Leos do not concern themselves about how things will turn out, even when they are going through a difficult, harrowing time. Optimism never dies in a Leo. Luck surrounds them and—bingo—they are back in the chips again. Does the Lion seem a bit lazy? At times he does. Unless the Lion is after prey he asks himself, Why get all hot and bothered about doing all these things? Leo would rather see if there is anyone around who will do the untidy deeds for him. What good is it being the ruler if one has to do everything oneself?

Not wanting to work too hard doesn't mean Leo isn't generous. Watch your Leo friends when dining out. Leo's warm-hearted, benevolent spirit makes him reach for the check in any swanky restaurant to treat all his friends. Playing Mr. or Ms. Big makes them very happy, for this is a genuinely magnanimous sign. If Leo ever amasses a fortune, it is almost assured that they will donate part of it, perhaps to add a new wing of a hospital or a floor of a museum. While it is unlikely that a Leo would give quietly or anonymously—Leos like to get credit and to see their name in lights—they will give freely. They make great philanthropists.

Realize that what Leo wants most is respect. Leo is very, very proud, and if you are a Leo you will immediately admit this to be true. Allow your Leo room to save face in any negotiation or battle or you will not get your way. Give them an escape hatch if you need to, but don't ever embarrass them. Having the respect of others means much more to a Leo than anything else—even money. While Aries wants to win—against anybody—Leo wants to be popular. Other signs could recover, but I doubt Leo would. Leo needs to be admired at all costs.

## CAREERS

Leo's energy can be stretched outward toward politics, or inward to express the divine power within, in an artistic manner, as a creator. While we are on the subject of talent, let's look at some of Leo's best as well as the occupations and industries that are luckiest for Leo.

Let's focus on the look of your office for a moment. If you are a Leo you know you like your office as comfortable and as cushy as possible. If your company allows you to bring in furniture from home or order new pieces, you will soon outflank your boss in the pure beauty and design of your choices. Leo likes to add fresh flowers and some artwork, perhaps in the form of a beautiful poster for the wall. They figure as long as they have to spend so much time at work, the surroundings might as well be as comfortable as home.

Also on the walls of your office will be your diplomas and awards, as well as photographs of yourself with other famous people. You won't display pictures of yourself with those of lesser rank—those photos serve the function of uplifting you as you dream about attaining a position of authority. These photographs are trophies in and of themselves. Plenty of photos of your children (if you have them) will also be around the room. As a Leo you are proud of your children.

An interview of various Oscar winners appeared recently in a magazine discussing where each winner chose to display their statuette, if they did choose to display it. Pisces will likely hide it in a box with other memories so it won't remind others of their greater stature and possibly hurt others' feelings. Productive Virgo is likely to use it for a practical purpose (such as paperweight or book end), but no self-respecting Leo would hide that statuette away or use it for anything other than as a reminder of a goal achieved. While Leos might not have it in the foyer as you walk in—they aren't *that* indelicate—they see no reason why it can't be on the mantel in the living room or on their desk in the study. Why not show off a hard-won status symbol, asks Leo. That's what distinctions are meant to do, to reward ability and to delineate differences. Leo is nothing if not socially aware.

Creativity is an enormously important quality of fiery Leo, and usually it needs an outlet. Few things in life have the power to impart the kind of intrinsic satisfaction a creative career can. The Sun, your ruler, dear Leo, encourages new life and gives sustenance to all living things, so it is logical that as a Leo you will have strong creative urges. Around the zodiac wheel, after planting in May (Taurus), the seedlings begin to grow nicely by August. The full harvest won't come up until September (Virgo), so it is time to play and enjoy life, and Leo is more than happy to comply. Leo is not a workaholic like Virgo. In fact, you could say the Lion has a slightly indolent streak. In order to be fully creative, one must retain a young, experimental, and childlike spirit, something Leo excels at.

Many Leos get to show off their talent for color in art and design fields. At the end of July, the Sun is at its brightest and most intense, and so it follows that Leo loves dramatic, rich, ripe, bright color and beautiful design. This artistic talent can be put to use in their work. Leo has an outstanding sense of style that others want to copy; Jackie Kennedy, for example, was a Leo and inspired millions of people around the world. Fashion design is another field where many Leos distinguish themselves; Coco Chanel and Oscar de la Renta are two notable Leos. Other good occupations for Leo include working as graphic designers as well as interior decorators, as art and creative directors, movie directors, Web masters and Web page designers, stage and costume designers, photographers, musicians, dancers, actors, and as other performers. Many of our "divas" are Leos. Madonna and Whitney Houston are two good female examples, with Mick Jagger being the male equivalent. The entertainment industry is incredibly rich in Leos. Ideas are not contained but shared in Leo, a gregarious, warm-hearted sign. Nature bestowed Leo with strong self-confidence and a need for self-expression. These two qualities will assure that your talent comes out!

Leos are legendary at organization, which is why they do so well in business, teaching, politics, publishing, or just about any other field. Leo thinks big, which can be quite inspiring to those who report to them. Decisive, insightful, and intuitive, Leo knows how to set an agenda and stick to it, through thick and thin. However, you are not detail-oriented — Virgo makes up for what you don't have on that score. But because you're such a bright fire sign, others want to follow you, so your ability to rally others enthusiastically is phenomenal. Once Leos harness the power of their determination, they can succeed against all odds. Part of the trick is flicking your inner switch to the "on" position, because some Leos simply just don't use the awesome horsepower idling within them. Another golden quality of Leos is their masterful ability to plan and strategize. Norman Schwarzkopf, the great military hero from Operation Desert Storm, is a good example of a Leo who used this talent to the max. (He was born on August 22, right on the cusp of Leo and Virgo, expressing the best talents of both signs.) Leo tends not to waver, and as a leader continually reminds the flock of the jointly held goals that were collectively chosen. On the personal side, Leo will patiently remind you of your past promises — and make you keep your word. Leos can be wonderful bosses because they are generally so exuberant and enthusiastic about life, and when they shine their light on co-workers they can also help them fulfill their potential. Leos want to see others succeed and will do what they can to make it happen.

Another lesser-known talent held by many Leos is the mechanical ability to fix things. You probably recognize this in yourself, dear Leo. Even as a child you were probably fascinated with how things worked inside and then made the effort to find out. Many Leo children take things apart but later can't put them back together again. Be patient if your Leo child does this, for he is still learning. Both male and female Leos may have thought their talent in this area was "nothing special" until they looked around and saw that no one else has their knack for figuring out how things work. You may not choose to use this skill in your career as an engineer for example, but even if you don't, those around you will be lucky because there are few things you won't be able to fix for them.

Leos make especially fine teachers too. Chances are, Leo, that you are patient, clear, and dramatic enough to make a point in a marvelously memorable way. Also any industry that caters to children should be added to your list of good careers, such as children's programming, movies, or book publishing. All are excellent venues for a Leo. This sign has the natural understanding of children's needs, and Leo's inner child (kept alive and kicking) would know how to interest them. Leo's love of rich color and gorgeous design would make TV, book, or movie projects they work on eye-popping winners.

## Body, Mind, and Spirit

Sexual attractiveness and appearance are extremely important to Leo, probably more than to you than most signs. As we discussed earlier, there is a strong competitive streak in Leos, and they like to see that they are winning the contest. Leo is accustomed to being the leader. This might explain why mid-life affairs appeal to some Leos. Proving to themselves that they are still as vital and good-looking as they were when they were younger is an ever-pressing need and has nothing to do with Leos' feelings for their mate. (Try telling that to a broken-hearted spouse, however.) Leos, male and female alike, do not like the thought of aging, and they are the first to call the plastic surgeon when they notice that they aren't the fairest in the kingdom any longer. They have a playful style and don't see themselves as getting older; it is often a shock when they see this happening. Leo expects to do better and look better than anyone else, and to remain that way nearly forever. While the youngest-looking sign of the zodiac is Gemini, Leos do an excellent job of keeping up their youthful appearance long after others have given up. Leo may work harder on appearance than others do!

You might think that Leos' high emphasis on appearance would turn them into athletes. Actually, no, that is not the case. That would require a big effort, and unlike Aries, Virgo, Scorpio, or Sagittarius (very highly disciplined signs), who will do whatever it takes, Leo would rather sit back and order a pill that promises weight loss and more toned muscle. Sweating on the treadmill is not appealing to most Leos. They abhor any kind of strenuous exertion, especially if the environment is cold. (That means skiing is out, unless there is something else in the horoscope that would suggest it. Taking a run on a warm beach sounds infinitely better to a Leo.) Remember, the Lion doesn't go to the gym unless he has to; he'd rather play a game of basketball, run on a beach, or go hiking.

If you are a Lion, you need to be out in sunshine regularly or risk being affected by seasonal affective disorder (SAD), a feeling of depression some people get most often in winter because they aren't exposed to enough sunlight. Sunlight, it has been found, affects the part of the brain that regulates mood. New studies also point to disturbances in the metabolism of serotonin, the production of melatonin, and the function of the circadian clock. The fix is easy: Be out and about in the fresh air during the brightest part of every day. Take a brisk walk, even if it is just to the bank or the grocery store, to get some fresh air and your measure of sunshine, no matter how busy you happen to be. You'll get your quota of vitamin D in the process. If it's dark and rainy all the time where you live, bright-light therapy is effective.

There are other areas of health to pay special attention to if you are a Leo. For one, it would be wise to do something special for your cardiovascular system. In medical astrology, just as your ruler, the Sun, is the center of our universe, the heart is the center of the human body, and both provide key life-giving properties. Thus Leo rules the heart. Yet it is the heart and circulatory system that are more likely to give Leos difficulties if they don't keep themselves in good shape. Some Leos have only the mildest problems, like poor circulation. Give your body what it needs so that later you won't regret not having paid closer attention to diet and exercise. You are a big-hearted person, dear Leo—keep your heart in shape. The other part of the body ruled by Leo is the spine, so while you are getting fit do some exercises to strengthen your back too. You want to keep walking tall like the powerful creature you are.

## SUMMARY
Leo knows, perhaps better than any other sign, that life is but a stage. Inside every Leo is a star in the making bursting to come out. Dear Leo, keep your eye on that divine power within you, for everything you need is there, ready for you to harness. Even if you have to go down to your toes to find it, it will be there, waiting for you. You were blessed with enormous creative energy and, in effect, you are solar powered.

# THE MYTHS OF
# LEO AND THE SUN

The Sun has no equal in the horoscope—it is the king of heavenly bodies, the brilliant luminary symbolizing all life, vitality, and strength. The Sun also symbolizes our "directed will" or sense of purpose, which allows each of us to make a difference in the world. It is the light that shines within everyone, the divine spirit that is the source of this energy and creativity, given to us by our creator at birth.

The Sun has intrigued just about every culture in every age. In some very early myths, the Sun was depicted as "hero" born of Mother (who was Earth). The four elements that comprised life—air, earth, fire, and water—were characterized as either masculine or feminine. The masculine elements of air and fire were born from the feminine elements of water and earth. Astrology still acknowledges these yin and yang energies, and the astrologer urges that both masculine and feminine elements be blended and balanced for true wholeness within the individual. The story of Apollo, the Greek Sun king, whom we will discuss in a moment, incorporates these energies and forms a good model for Leo. In Leo there is danger of the Sun, considered a masculine, life-giving life force, becoming too unfocused in using its considerable power. Leo has to learn to direct that energy to benefit from it without becoming egotistical or too self-centered (possible pitfalls inherent in Leo).

Why is the Sun thought of as masculine? Repeatedly in certain myths, the Sun figure climbs to the top of the heavens (full daylight, noon). At the pinnacle, the heat of the Sun burns off all moisture, causing the clouds to burst into thunder. In turn, the rain fertilizes the Earth. In mythic symbolism, fire and air are connected to masculinity because the hero-Sun is thought of as impregnating the land. At sunset, the Sun sinks into the horizon and into the depths of night. Here the Sun, our hero, dives into the depths of the unknown, the underworld, and through battling his fears is able to show his mettle and courage. Later he reemerges from the dark unknown and moves back into the light. In astrology as in mythology, "truth" equals "light."

## APOLLO

One of the first myths we think of when we think of the Sun is Apollo, the Greek god, born of Titaness Leto and Zeus. Apollo was a favorite god; as mythologist Edith Hamilton says, he was "the most Greek of all the Gods." Apollo ruled over healing and medicine, mathematics and music, and was also said to have had the gift of prophecy. He was said to be the god of light and truth. Here we see the right brain and left brain united zin Apollo, possessing both the (masculine) rationality of music and mathematics as well as the (feminine) intuitive gift of prophecy. Thus Apollo was able to strike a balance and unite these energies. He is thought to be purely good and beneficent. Although at times he showed cruelty, that was quite rare.

Before building his shrine, Apollo assessed various possible sites. He found that the best place was Delphi, which was considered to be the center of the world. However, a huge serpent, Python, guarded the city, so Apollo first had to slay the serpent. After a terrible battle, Apollo was victorious and indeed did set up his shrine in Delphi, which later was also known to be the city of prophecy. Later, the priestess known as Pythoness would announce her predictions at the Delphi Oracle to those who came to ask her advice. No one *could* question her, nor did they *dare* to. Hence,

Apollo became credited with the laws that were later handed down from Delphi. Over the temple gates were inscribed "Nothing in Excess" and "Know Thyself." Thus, the Oracle tells mortals to keep things in balance by avoiding the excesses of being too willful or overly confident, or arrogance and conceit will follow. The value of self-knowledge lies within one's acknowledgment of both one's talents and one's foibles, and it also encourages the development of one's gifts to their full potential.

This is good advice for any sign, but astrologically it is especially relevant to Leo because Leo can too easily become self-centered. The Sun is, after all, the center of the solar system, while Leo's mythic ruler, Apollo, is the god of truth and (Sun) light. Apollo can bring clarity, focus, and rational insight to a chaotic world. He tempers any inclination toward pomposity or egotism with the more right-brain (or feminine) intuition. He is also the god of math and music, two very rational, precise disciplines. At the same time he is also a prophet and a healer, combining the best of both energies. Thus Apollo serves as a superb role model for Leo.

## HELIOS, THE GREEK SUN GOD

Although Helios is considered a "lesser" god (not one of twelve major gods on Mount Olympus), the image of him as the Sun king is particularly beautiful and poetic. As god of the Sun, Helios was the giver of light. He was the son of the Titans Hyperion and Theia, early deities of the Sun and light themselves. Accompanied by his sister Eos (Dawn) and wearing a golden helmet, Helios was a thrillingly handsome figure. He would begin each day in the east and race a chariot pulled by four magnificent horses across the sky and disappear as he passed the western horizon. During the night he would make his way back to the easternmost horizon, but since the world wasn't thought to be round at that time, Helios would have to go around the perimeter of Earth by riding the river Oceanus in an enormous golden cup.

While he was crossing the sky in his chariot during daylight hours, Helios's penetrating gaze saw everything happening on Earth. Not surprisingly, he became a good source of truth. It was Helios who told Hephaestus that

Aphrodite was having an affair with Ares, and it was also Helios who told Demeter that it was Hades who had abducted Persephone. No one could hide from the Sun's gaze, so mortals often swore oaths by him, knowing that if they broke their vows Helios would know.

The sister of Helios, Eos, the goddess of the dawn (her arms were said to be rosy), rose each morning from a golden throne in the east to announce the impending arrival of her brother, Helios. Despite her name, Eos epitomized not just the light of early-morning dawn, but all of daylight. She rode with her brother in the chariot of the Sun throughout the day. Eos was to fall in love with Astraeus ("Starry"), the son of Crius (a Titan) and Eurybia, daughter of Pontus and Gaia. She was to give birth to the three winds, including Zephyrus (west), Boreas (north), and Notus (south). This coupling also produced Eosphorus (the Dawn Star), as well as all the stars in the heavens.

## HERCULES'S TWELVE LABORS

Hercules is a wonderful hero for all time and the mythic hero most people think of first when they think of Leo. Hercules sums up all the best in Leo: courage and determination to succeed against all odds and as protector and inspirational leader. His slaying of the Nemean lion, the first of the twelve labors of Hercules, is thought to be particularly relevant to Leo, for Hercules keeps control over his passions and confronts his fears, the key elements that allow him to overpower the ferocious lion. In this, the first labor, the lion was said to have a special skin, impenetrable by either stone or metal. Indeed Hercules soon discovered this because his club, arrows, and sword turned out to be useless against the beast. He quickly concluded that direct combat would be necessary. Hercules sealed off one of the two entrances to the lion's cave. Attacking the lion unarmed, Hercules wrestled the lion to the ground and choked him to death.

Then, using the lion's claws to cut off its skin, Hercules made a cloak from the lion's hide and a helmet from its head. Hercules wore this outfit when he came to see King Eurystheus to get his second assignment in the series of labors he had to perform. Hercules so frightened the king by wearing the lion's skins that the king ordered him to leave his future trophies outside the city gates. After this first labor was completed, the cowardly King Eurystheus hid in a jar buried in the earth whenever Hercules came by and had his messenger announce all the subsequent orders to Hercules instead of doing so himself.

In the first labor, Hercules "became" the ferocious lion by donning its hide. He could do this because Hercules confronted what he feared, the lion, and by so doing took on the courageous animal's spirit. In his subsequent labors, Hercules killed various monsters and giants and captured various beasts. He had to capture two prized objects and complete a task of humility, cleaning the stables of Augeas. After his twelve labors were successfully completed, Hercules found another use for the lion's hide. When a band of giants was attacking Mount Olympus, Hera prophesied that none of the gods would be able to defeat them. She predicted that success would come only to the mortal who wore lion skins. Zeus therefore sent Hercules to the battlefield and, after again donning the lion skins and the helmet, he single-handedly killed the giants.

Lions appear in many action stories, the oldest one being the Babylonian story of Gilgamesh, where the hero is in search of the herbs of immortality to bring his friend, Enkidu, back to life. Like Hercules, Gilgamesh had to go through a series of tests as well. His very first was to battle a pride of lions (see "The Myths of Aquarius and Uranus"). Gilgamesh slays them, thus triumphing in his first rite of passage, which seems to suggest, like the Hercules myth, the need to conquer fear and also to tame wild passions within and without, a recurring theme of the sign of Leo.

Astrology distinguishes between the fearless warrior and competitor with father figure (Aries, the first of three fire signs) and wise Sun king (Leo, the second fire sign), and the philosopher-king (Sagittarius, the third fire sign). Leo should not overestimate his ability or become so exuberant that he harms himself by foolishly denying certain realities. This idea is brought to bear in the classic myth of Icarus, which follows.

## ICARUS, THE YOUNG MAN WHO FLEW TOO CLOSE TO THE SUN

Icarus was the son of Daedalus, the master craftsman, and together father and son had built a labyrinth for the Minotaur for King Minos of Crete. The labyrinth had a series of passageways so complex it was virtually impossible to escape it. However, Daedalus showed Ariadne how Theseus could escape. When Kind Minos learned that the Athenians had found a way out, the king became enraged and knew Daedalus must have been the one to help them. He imprisoned both Icarus and Daedalus, and thus, oddly, the labyrinth became a trap for its own creator.

Daedalus had an idea. While there was no easy way out by land or water, air and sky were relatively accessible. He would make two sets of wings out of wax, strap them on himself and his son, and they would fly out of the maze. He got to work and when the wings were finished, Daedalus warned Icarus not to fly too close to the Sun or the wax wings would melt. He also warned his son not to fly too low, either, because the sea could wet the wings. (Find a midcourse of moderation, was the message of father to son.) Exhilarated by flight, Icarus flew toward the Sun, forgetful of his father's words. As a result, he crashed into the sea and the waters came over him. His father was able to make it safely to his destination in Sicily. Finding his son missing, Daedalus began calling out for Icarus. He could not find him even though he searched everywhere. In this story, too much willpower — too much exuberance or enthusiasm — can be one's downfall (quite literally).

In Leo, as a great ruler, there is a need to outsmart and face the beast, which personifies the perpetrator or enemy. If a king was not able to protect his populace in battle, the opposing power would take over, so war represented the survival of the fittest, both physically and spiritually. The Egyptians, for example, had a system that kept their kings strong and fearless. Not only did they insist that their leaders keep their bloodlines clean (physical fitness), the Egyptians also made sure their leaders had the proper character to carry out divine will by conducting a continual series of tests on them (spiritual fitness). The Egyptians weren't willing to wait for an invasion to find out what their leaders were made of.

As you see, the need to test one's physical and moral capabilities continually is very much part of being a Leo, for like Hercules, once you slay that lion (or dragon) you rise triumphant and forever carry that power within you. It gives new meaning to the saying "Whatever doesn't kill you makes you stronger," don't you agree, dear Leo?

# VIRGO PERSONALITY

*Virgo*

August 24–September 22

*Guiding Principle*

"I Produce"

*How This Sign Feels Joy*

Finds joy in being organized, productive, and discerning and in improving both body and mind, because the need to bring things to an optimal state is strong.

*In the New Millennium, Your Contribution to the World Will Be . . .*

Born at the time of the harvest, you excel at production. With the influx of vast amounts of information upon humanity, it will be Virgo's role to show us what is valuable and what is not.

*Quote That Describes You*

"PERFECTION IS FINALLY ATTAINED NOT WHEN THERE IS NO LONGER ANYTHING TO ADD BUT WHEN THERE IS NO LONGER ANYTHING TO TAKE AWAY, WHEN A BODY HAS BEEN STRIPPED DOWN TO ITS NAKEDNESS."

—ANTOINE DE SAINT-EXUPÉRY, a *Cancer*

At the department-store counter a Virgo woman moved closer to the mirror and squinted as she applied lipstick. Checking the color of two different shades, she didn't seem like she wanted help, but the salesgirl asked anyway. Was there perhaps something she could do to help? The young woman, who had remarkably gorgeous skin and a soft, fresh, just-showered look, replied, "Well, it's between these two colors. I've tried them both using your cotton swabs" (of course she did; cleanliness is vital to Virgo). She added, "I can't quite decide which one is the *perfect* one for me. I like this one but fear it says 'The library closes at six.' The other one seems to say what I want—'Baby, let's boogie!'—but I am not sure it is as flattering as the other one. Maybe it's *too* trendy. What do you think? I am simply too shy in most social situations, and if this lipstick can help me come out of myself, well, then, it's done its job."

The salesgirl, not expecting such a practical and well-articulated response from an obviously reserved young woman, assured her that either lipstick shade would look beautiful. At the risk of stating the obvious, the salesgirl assured her customer that her looks were quite striking. I am sure the customer was *not* aware that she was quite a head-turner; Virgos are rarely aware of the full extent of their assets, particularly when it comes to their looks. Virgos take exquisite care of their health—male or female, they have what everyone wants: true radiance from good health and good character, qualities that can't come out of a tube or a bottle. They tend to be quite fit, often with slim, enviable physiques and also great skin.

Meanwhile, in the men's department, almost the same scene is going on at another counter. In this case, a young, slim Virgo male is searching through the counters of various brands, styles, and colors of pure cotton long-sleeved shirts and various prints and styles of ties to find the ones that look "just right" with his new designer suit. Virgos of both sexes adore fine quality and great cut—it is no coincidence that Virgo rules over the city of Paris. Virgo rules fine tailoring and a good fit with handsome details, like quality buttons and a well-chosen lining. While Leo, the sign

that precedes Virgo, will look for the newest, most unique designer wear
to engender respect and admiration among friends and colleagues, Virgo
buys items of quiet elegance that will last several seasons. A more practical sign, Virgo wants a fashion *investment* rather than a fashion *statement*.
Virgos do not waste time or money if they can help it. The pieces they buy
always look new, even when they are several seasons (or years) old,
because Virgos are so fastidious.

Our Virgo man has been in pursuit of a perfect wardrobe of shirts and ties
for about forty-five minutes, but his salesclerk knows better than to interrupt
him. He has seen this customer before and knows he is always polite and
well spoken, and must have a good job, perhaps as an editor of a men's
lifestyle magazine. It must be ninety-seven degrees outside, but this customer
looks cool and crisp. The customer is obviously intent on finding something
special, so the decision will require deliberation. The body language of the
man seems to say, "Don't approach me yet—let me be." Thus, this clerk
will decide, rightly, to hang back. When Virgos are on a quest for perfection,
it is always best to let them ask for help rather than intrude on their concentration. Virgos do not like disruptions.

Dear Virgo, the ancients assigned your astrological traits and talents by looking at the season of the year when you were born. Your birthday comes at the
end of summer, at the bountiful time of the harvest. This gives you a strong
tie to the land, agriculture, health, and nutrition. The fruits and vegetables
that were growing under Leo's golden Sun are now ready to be picked from
the garden in celebration of summer's bounty. The hot, lazy days of summer
are winding down and soon the days will be chilly, and noticeably shorter. It
is time to return to life's routine chores. The tempo picks up, as it is time to
reap the crop. If it is left unattended, fruit will wither on the vine. Provisions
will be needed for the sustenance and survival of the community during the
approaching winter. The harvest now has to be picked, culled, sorted, pickled,
canned, or stored. There is not a moment to lose! Thus, dear Virgo, the season
of your birth gives you a powerful urge to be productive.

A Virgo will feel urgency to attend to projects and finish them on a timely basis. You are outstanding at organizing any and all activity, no matter how complex. Virgo's critical and thoughtful nature makes your sign especially talented at sorting, grading, and classifying, an ability you apply to everything you do. (When those fruits are picked from the tree in the harvesting process, you are Nature's helper in choosing which bins to assign them—for eating, canning, cooking, or for compost.) You are also highly task oriented, recognizing the simple beauty and grace that flow from performing duties nobly. It must have been a Virgo who said "Anything worth doing is worth doing well." You take comfort in attending to the routine and necessary details of everyday life. This appreciation and pride in productivity are part of every Virgo and form the foundation for many of your other talents.

Most people think of the time of Virgo's birth, September, as the psychological start of a new year—it is a time to go back to work or school refreshed and ready to tackle new goals. Your ruler, Mercury, the planet of thinking, gives you a strong love of intellectual activities. At the time of your birthday it is time to go back indoors, get serious, and hunker down to the job at hand. Perhaps for this reason Virgo is thought of as a serious, cerebral sign with strong self-discipline.

## SYMBOLS
Both Virgo and Pisces share the same astrologic axis and therefore both complement and contrast each other symbolically. All signs that are linked on the same axis are thought to work together in special ways. In Virgo, we find the yearning for the heightened perfectionism of the individual, a move to purity and grand self-improvement. In Virgo's opposite sign of Pisces, the focus shifts away from the individual and from the Virgo concept of service to others, to one who sacrifices all for humanity in a more indefinable and all-encompassing name of universal love. Thus, the "virgin" element of the Virgo symbolism refers to the pure, innocent state that is in the process of transformation into a wiser and more developed

individual, symbolized by Virgo's harvest. The self-absorption apparent in Leo, the sign that precedes yours, gives way to an understanding of the need to serve mankind at large.

There is another interesting contrast between Virgo and Pisces. Virgo is the image of the virgin holding a stalk of grain while Pisces symbolizes the fishes. Some astrologic scholars were struck by how the grain and fishes echo the ancient biblical story of the miracle of the loaves and the fishes. Thus there would be plenty of food for everyone, not only to nourish the body but also to nourish the soul by being accepted with hospitality, too. It is one of Christianity's miracles, and illustrates how, both in Pisces and Virgo, the need to share and care for others is strong.

The stages of motherhood are elegantly portrayed in the signs of Taurus, Cancer, and Virgo. In Taurus, woman is a fertility figure—filled with life, round with pregnancy. For Taurus, an earth sign, love is physical. In Cancer, the image is one of resplendent mother with child. Thus, in Cancer the emphasis of the mother role is on her as nurturer and loving caretaker. By Virgo, the sixth sign of the zodiac, the mother realizes she must now let go of her child so her child can grow freely as an individual. In Virgo, an earth sign, mother love requires a sense of reality and practicality—she can no longer keep her child with her—and she must trust in her child's judgment and encourage its individuality as she lets her child fly free.

The glpyh of Virgo is similar to that of Scorpio, so much so that new students of astrology often mix them up. Virgo's symbol turns inward, denoting reflection and the inward development of the self, while the Scorpio symbol turns outward, suggesting a more aggressive need to influence the world.

Both Gemini and Virgo share the same ruler, Mercury, and it is interesting to note the similarities and differences between those signs. If you have not yet read about Mercury and Gemini in "The Myths of

Gemini and Mercury," please do so, for the references in that chapter
relate to you too. Mercury's glyph links the circle (spirit), over a cross
(matter) with a small crescent over the top of the circle (soul or emotion).
Additionally, Mercury, as Hermes, was known to carry the caduceus, the
symbol we use to this day for the medical community and for healing.
This symbolism underscores Virgo's strong mind-body connection, which
is so integral to their personality.

## PLANETARY INFLUENCES

Mercury is the planet of intellect and rational thinking, the planet that will
always urge a search for truth in an objective and unemotional way. As a
result, both Gemini and Virgo produce outstanding journalists, writers,
and editors as well as other communicators who can transmit thoughts particularly clearly. Virgo, an earthy, practical sign, has the added benefit of
being highly organized, detailed, deliberate, and thorough. These are qualities Gemini lacks because Gemini is an air sign. There is a strong similarity, however, in that their joint rulership by Mercury allows both signs to
thrive on continual activity. Have you ever actually watched how much
your Virgo friends accomplish in the course of a day? They (and Gemini)
get mountains of work done—much more than most signs. Both are very
flexible and adaptable too, although differences persist. For instance, while
both are book worms, Geminis (an air sign) will collect ideas for their own
sake simply to communicate them, while Virgo (an earth sign) will be more
motivated to find a practical application.

Mercury, ruler of both signs, is a planet that moves very quickly, so it's
a good bet you have difficulty sitting still very long. Mercury rules the
nervous system of the body, so, not surprisingly, Virgo often runs on
nervous energy. Both Virgo and Gemini are said to have a better chance
of staying slim than just about any other sign. Both fidget continually so
it is not likely that weight would stick on their bones. But Gemini rules
the hands and shoulders, while Virgo rules the digestive system, which
explains why Virgo has difficulty digesting food (and why Gemini doesn't).

Mercury's influence over Gemini and Virgo is asserted very differently. Mercury is quite comfortable in the first mutable sign, Gemini, because that sign suits the planet's need for speedy motion, plenty of conversation, and the gathering of much information. In Gemini, Mercury encourages investigation and exploration of all types of data and encapsulates the Gemini spirit of youthful curiosity. In Gemini, there is no particular need to use the information, because all data is interesting to Gemini. Instead, for Gemini, an air sign, it would be important to broadcast that information quickly into the world, as if by the four winds. In the earth sign Virgo, Mercury's influence is more grounded and stable and encourages Virgo to search for practical ways to use the information that has been discovered. Virgo is discerning and detailed, thus the quality of the communication counts more, including such details as the inflection in one's voice, or if writing, the spelling and grammar used.

Mercury was always said by the ancients to be unemotional, rational, and objective in its thinking. Indeed, Mercury is never more than twenty-eight degrees away from the Sun, a masculine energy. Thus, the Sun imparts part of its masculine rationality, clarity, and brilliance to Mercury.

Mercury's influence of the second mutable sign (and the second earth sign), Virgo, is evident in Virgo's awesome communicative powers, whether in writing, speaking, perceiving, or reading, and is also seen in Virgo's impressive analytical abilities. Virgo's keen talent for organization and critical discrimination is clearly superior to Gemini's, whether dealing with purely conceptual ideas or more tangible physical properties.

Virgos enjoy using their hands, whether for work or for leisure-time activities. Their small motor skills are remarkable, and many Virgos use their hands in their leisure-time activities to do woodworking, refinishing, knitting, crocheting, sewing and smocking, needlepoint, or to type or play a musical instrument like the violin or the piano. One mother of a small Virgo daughter told me that her child would come to her with her hands outstretched, saying, "Mommy, I want to do something with my *hands!* I am bored!" The child is talented with puzzles, paints, sewing (the little girl loves to make doll clothes), and clay pottery. Her wise mother keeps giving her child lots of different materials. Never underestimate how important using the hands is to a Virgo, especially a little one.

Virgo also finds beauty in the order of mathematics and in words too. Virgo is also usually good at spelling and vocabulary and loves word games and puzzles, like Scrabble, crosswords, and jigsaw puzzles or anagrams. (Of course even your leisure time is spent productively, dear Virgo.) Virgo enjoys accumulating trivia as well as matching wits with friends or watching TV shows that test mental agility and the ability to recall obscure facts. Technical jargon can be fun for a Virgo, but using it too often can be confusing to others. (If the person you are speaking with looks a bit bewildered, slow down and explain yourself again.) Virgos are attracted to detail like a magnet because it serves as food for their hungry, ever-active brains.

When Virgos get up in the morning (you can bet your Virgo friends are up at dawn without the benefit of an alarm clock), they are full of energy and raring to go. They are the ones you see *leaving* the gym as you are getting there at 7:00 A.M.—they are already done and on to the next thing on their list. They are keeping the temples of their bodies pure and strong because they have the inner drive to do so.

## COSMIC GIFTS

As we move around the zodiac in order, from the beginning sign, Aries, we see the progression of man's development mirrored in the signs. In Aries we find the newborn, symbolizing the life force. Aries will specialize in all initiations and new actions requiring courage, and thus encourages entrepreneurial activity and fresh starts. In Taurus, the first earth sign, the baby learns to explore the world through the senses and to acquire things of value and to build wealth and security. Gemini brings an understanding of and mastery over language. By Cancer, the child gets to know his immediate environment through the support of his family unit, especially through the support of Mother. Next comes Leo, and the child gains knowledge through play and creative enterprises and finds encouragement through bonding with his father. As the child grows older, Leo encourages growth through the experience of romantic love. Next comes your sign, Virgo, and here the evolution of the individual's development is enhanced through service to the community and the understanding of the need for work and responsibility. If Leo is the symbolic king within all of us, Virgo discovers the beauty and nobility of the humble servant, who is also within us all too. The growing child now learns the importance of order, structure, and routine as part of life, all covered by the sixth house of the horoscope ruled by Virgo.

The constellation Virgo is the image of the virgin holding a shaft of wheat, symbolizing your quest for a purity of mind, body, and spirit. Modest and unassuming, Virgo is known to have strong personal integrity and strength of character with no pretensions. The time of your birth is the time not only to harvest the crop but also to separate the wheat from the chaff. Hence, Virgo has an innate talent for discerning what to value and what to reject. Unlike Libra, as a Virgo you don't waffle; your practical nature makes decision-making quite a straightforward process. If your world isn't exactly black and white, it certainly isn't thousands of shades of gray, either. This ability to see things in clear, pragmatic terms helps move you forward decisively.

Virgo is a mutable sign, meaning a sign that marks the end of a season. Just as Virgo marks the completion of summer, Sagittarius ends autumn; Pisces, winter; and Gemini, spring. A mutable sign does more than just conclude a season. These signs have an ability to break up and dissolve established conditions resynthesizing their components into new forms to help prepare us for the next trend. You have the special distinction of being the only earth sign of the mutable signs, giving you the ability to find a fresh, practical, and often tangible application for the various concepts and ideas you discover. Being highly analytical by nature and conservative of resources (both are gifts from Mercury), you apply yourself well and come up with innovative ways to streamline work methods to achieve verifiable results.

Your credo is to find, analyze, purify, refine, and improve whatever you focus your highly analytical mind upon. Virgo transmutes his mind and body by resynthesizing the parts and rebuilding them into a greater, stronger whole. To Virgo, any area can be made better: one's performance on the job, a relationship, one's mind or body—there is no end to the possibilities. Virgo is always on a quest for self-improvement.

Highly productive, well organized, detailed, tidy, strong, self-disciplined, and goal-oriented are all apt descriptions of Virgo. But despite outstandingly positive qualities, Virgo remains one of the most misunderstood of all signs. Some astrologers have painted Virgos to be cool, critical people who aren't much fun to be around. In truth, Virgos are warm, kind, and often very funny because their wit is so sharp.

While it is true that Virgos wouldn't generally like to while away hours watching sitcoms, soap operas, wrestling matches, or just plain sleeping, they are not spoilsports. Your typical Virgo would prefer to watch or read a mystery, a documentary, or a serious drama because they are drawn to things they have to decode or otherwise figure out. Virgos don't like things that are too obvious or basic—they naturally seek out complexity. They also happen to be very giving, always looking for ways to be helpful to their friends, and like their opposite sign, Pisces, Virgos have a hard time saying no.

The perfectionist tendencies of this sign can admittedly be troublesome because Virgos might be tempted to take this quality too far, never being satisfied with their work, their looks, their relationships (among other things), and so they seek ways to make them better. Sometimes Virgos hide behind their perfectionism. They convince themselves that their work is never good enough to show, that they need more time, and that they never achieve what they could or should, but those Virgos are less common. However, if this sounds like you, dear Virgo, don't let your quest for perfection become an excuse not to reach for goals. A quest for too high a standard of perfection can make a Virgo too timid or wary to take a risk, so dreams never seem to lift off. How sad! Those Virgos continually say that they need more time but their real reason for stalling is that they want to avoid being judged. In fact, they *have* been evaluated by their own critical inner voice, certainly more harshly than they would by most anyone in the outside world. Those Virgos remain stuck in a certain limbo, trapped in a cage of their own making. Those Virgos avoid risks, and so they fail to enjoy life to the fullest. Perfectionism requires plenty of energy, energy that could be put to better use, dear Virgo. Recognize the difference between the good kind of perfection and the bad kind.

The need for perfection could also take another turn, one toward obsession, when you drive yourself off a cliff in an "all or nothing" quest. In those cases the Virgo has become too fanatical. An example might be in an exercise junkie, a person who works out at the gym for hours every day. When life intrudes on some of that fitness time, the compulsive Virgo becomes upset and frustrated because he or she is too inflexible to accommodate a change in routine. Life spins out of control. Relationships and jobs can suffer when one goal or activity takes precedence over the rest of life. This is not a common problem, but it does happen from time to time, usually when a Virgo is under stress. Virgo, you are so strongly goal-oriented, but there is always the danger that you can get so fixed on the leaves of the forest that you don't see the trees. Sometimes you need to step back and study the whole scene.

Let's mention one last downside to Virgo's reality-based, earthy personality: Sometimes this sign can overvalue what can be proven and becomes too much of a crusader for scientific evidence because they find any sort of ambiguity too hard to accept. Learn to trust your intuition more, dear Virgo, for not all things can be correlated with facts and figures.

While basic skills of learning are covered by the horoscope's third house (Gemini's sector, ruling lower education), the sixth house, Virgo's domain, takes learning a step farther into more general life lessons and the process of personal responsibility, lessons often taught to us by our parents. They also include such things as the importance of being on time, of getting homework done, of taking on responsibility willingly, such as a first job (like baby-sitting or being a paperboy). This house of the horoscope also covers skills that are used not only for jobs but also generally for living. These might include learning to drive, swim, dance, play a musical instrument, cook, do woodworking or home repair, use a camera or a computer, or the Internet. These are skills that may or may not be taught in school but are nevertheless useful to learn as one grows up. The sixth house of the horoscope, which Virgos "own," rules the conscious mind—alert, aware, perceiving, and ever questioning reality—as well as the physical body, which sums up so much of what Virgo is all about. This sector of the chart rules the procedures we take to improve health (the first house of the zodiac, under the rulership of Aries, rules vitality), explaining why Virgos are so interested in improving their overall physical fitness and well-being.

The sixth house, ruled by Virgo, does *not* govern ambition, career, prestige, or reputation in one's chosen profession (or the world at large). Those are in Capricorn, the tenth house of the chart. Virgo is the house that prepares the individual for such matters. This house teaches Virgo the value of good study and work methods, as well as the proper relationship to have with colleagues, specifically co-workers and underlings (but not bosses). This is probably why a Virgo is as gracious to the mail-room boy as he would be to the company CEO—Virgo does not make such social distinctions. This same sixth house teaches cooperation, devotion, concentration, and purity of intent, qualities Virgo has in abundance.

Virgo also understands the concept "For everyone there is a purpose and for every purpose there is a proper place and time." Appropriateness of action is a quality that Virgos exude in their everyday actions, and this is why Virgos are so intent on learning proper manners and everyday courtesies, protocols, and ethics to apply in various situations. Without an understanding of the practical wisdom taught in this house of the horoscope, an individual would be lacking a sense of purpose and basic learning and social skills necessary to get ahead. Virgo understands that these skills form the necessary foundation for everything they hope to do.

Pets come under the sixth house, which may echo the agricultural roots of this horoscope sector, for certainly at a farm there would be many small animals to play with and feed. Caring for a pet is often a child's responsibility. Not surprisingly, many Virgos adore pets and are very good to them.

If you call a Virgo on a Saturday at 2 P.M. and he picks up the phone and sounds soft-spoken, never, ever ask if your friend was sleeping. Believe me, your Virgo friend was *not* sleeping. Virgos will be insulted at this suggestion, for they take pride in their twenty-four-hour, seven-day-a-week, ever-present energy. So far this day, your Virgo lark saw the Sun rise at dawn, has read the morning paper, has vacuumed all rugs, written that important memo for his boss, done some e-mailing, picked up his dry cleaning, gone to the post office, and shopped at the supermarket. When you called, he was waiting for the week's laundry to be done in the dryer. He is using a soft-spoken voice because everyone *else* in the house is in bed. He is probably giving a dinner party for ten people tonight. Sleep? Pleeease! We wish. Virgos have more energy than the butcher, the baker, and the candlestick maker all rolled into one.

You've heard Virgo is the neat sign—true or false? True! It is nearly impossible for Virgos to allow dust balls to collect under the bed. Virgos need to feel calm, and they do this by having a clean and orderly environment. To Virgos, neatness suggests peacefulness and is a mirror of one's inner state. It is proof positive in this topsy-turvy world that everything will turn out to be logical, rational, and orderly, just like the interior of their spic-and-span apartment. Virgos will stay home and clean out their closets cheerfully for the sense of joy they get when they open them each time; they will even occasionally turn down invitations to visit friends' country houses or to go to parties in order to get tasks done. A Virgo new mother has to leave the house in order to rest and let go—when she finally gets a chance to sit down while the baby sleeps, all she will see is the rest of the work she hasn't had time to attend to yet. (Remember: Virgo is task oriented, a trait that goes back to the harvest and the need to be timely and productive.) For that new mother, a baby-sitter is worth the cost for the sitter is the only hope that she'll ever get any rest.

Most Virgos like the thought "A place for everything and everything in its place." However, while this emphasis on neatness is a wonderful quality, it can be too demanding on those they live with. When doing housework or office work, Virgos can become overly compulsive (the towels have to be folded "just so"), stealing precious energy from other areas. Leave time for fun, dear Virgo. Having said this, though the majority of Virgos are neat as pins, a few seem to live a scrambled life. The mess in their office might be truly surprising if they have been working for months on a project. Still, ask for something, anything—for example, a certain document or fact—and Virgos will be able either to retrieve it from their head or from under the rubble on their desk instantly and effortlessly. Virgos rarely say they don't know something or can't find something—in their rather formidable heads, the world is always neat and tidy.

## RELATIONSHIPS

In matters of the heart, if you love a Virgo you'll soon discover that learning to relax is their biggest challenge and impediment to getting them into the right frame of mind to allow love to flow. Virgos need transitional time between work and play.

Are Virgos too critical of those they will and won't date (or marry)? Yes, a little, especially about appearances. Virgos may even suggest that they go shopping with their sweetheart to see that he or she present themselves more appropriately. They may suggest a different hairstyle and comment on various colors or styles of clothes. Male Virgos don't want to see too much makeup on their sweeties (Virgo likes the well-scrubbed, natural look). Virgos value a clean-and-pressed image too; dirt repels them. As we've said, they are particular. If you are a Virgo, try to be more forgiving and more accommodating, or you may be playing solitaire forever.

Manners, courtesies, and an aura of gentility will always matter greatly to this sign. Don't expect to get away with bad language, or be late or rude and still be popular with your Virgo. This will remain true whether you are just dating or even married—Virgos want to see polished manners. When you are courting you need not spend a great deal of money—Virgo is happy with being with you and won't be impressed with flashy or expensive evenings. Even in marriage Virgos won't want you to spend too much on them for gifts or evenings out. Their practical nature makes them abhor waste, and they are not impressed with flash. Perhaps because they work so hard for their money, Virgos are thrifty, and they like to see that quality in a mate as well. Highly self-sufficient, the thought of running out of money scares them. They never want to be in a position where they depend on anyone for sustenance or support—not even a mate—and will try to keep a small nest egg set aside for emergencies.

What Virgo does want in love is to see enduring values. Respect, true and loyal love, faithfulness, thoughtfulness, and a sense of responsibility top their list. These qualities may seem a tad boring until you think about trying to have a real relationship with someone who lacks them. Virgos' earthy, feet-on-the-ground sensibility is always clear about the simple values they cherish. It is a rare Virgo who is impressed with superficial things. The most compatible signs for Virgo are other Earth signs like Capricorn, Taurus, and Virgo. Water signs (Pisces, Cancer, and Scorpio) will also blend very well with Virgo and help support their emotional needs. High on their list is the need for an intellectual equal, and Virgos will search high and low for someone who can communicate with them on a deep and substantial level. Virgos will enjoy dating and mating with someone who can share their enjoyment of discussing current events, books, and the arts. (Before a play or show, Virgos will read the reviews and later enjoy deciding whether they agree with those critics.)

When it comes to making a commitment, Virgos will ask themselves: What will this person be like later on, when the children come? Can we survive the day-to-day wear and tear of life? Do we both make enough money now to live without fear? These are the types of questions that run through this sign's mind, and although they may sound unromantic, in fact asking those questions ensures a stronger union once a commitment is made. Virgos won't let the stars in their eyes cloud their judgment.

Finally, if you are going to make love to a Virgo, tidy up the bedroom. They'll be repelled or made anxious by the clutter if you don't. Assuming that you have done this, the next thing to remember is that Virgo is a verbal sign, so the more you talk, the hotter things will get. Words have amazing power to stimulate them. Virgos will communicate superbly to you, so all you need to do is listen closely to their whisperings. They will tell you everything you ever wanted to hear.

## FINANCE

Virgo is a prudent, bottom-line customer. No risks for you, dear Virgo, that's for sure. Ask a Virgo what she spent today and she'll pull out a spreadsheet. You have a whole basket of receipts to back it up—for the taxman, of course. After all, detail is your middle name. When an item breaks down, you have the receipt to prove that the warranty is still in effect—good work, Virgo! This never fails to save you money. Your friends kid you about your organizational zeal, but you are laughing all the way to the bank so don't change your ways one bit. When it comes to shopping,

Virgo carefully compares manufacturers and prices and knows all the benefits and drawbacks of each product. If you're buying an expensive item, you probably check magazine articles for test results before you sign on the dotted line. Virgo, your ability to do research and attend to detail is your greatest strength when it comes to handling finances. Virgos pay their bills on time and aren't into heavy consumerism or a flashy lifestyle. You do demand value for your money, simply because you are such a workaholic. Wasting your hard-earned cash is the last thing you want to do.

Your biggest expenditure is usually a health-club membership, health insurance, vitamins (Virgos like to stay healthy), or computer equipment (Virgos like to write and also enjoy being organized). Being an earth sign, you are realistic about money. You know what you can afford, what is sensible to pay, and when to say no to a new purchase. Because you spend wisely, you always have enough money when you need it. Virgos understand that fiscal stress is draining and unnecessary. This sign puts a high value on productivity and tends to banish anything that gets in the way.

Your biggest impediment to getting ahead professionally is assuming that others are more qualified for a job than you are. That's rarely true. Nine out of ten times, you have more on the ball than they do. You need to toot your own horn about your achievements, dear Virgo. Occasionally send out a status report, so your boss can keep informed of your progress. If you are self-employed, draw up a press release and get a story written about your company in a local newspaper.

Your agile mind operates with crystal clarity. You know that if you should find yourself in a financial jam, you can rely on your intelligence and analytical ability to find a resourceful solution.

## CAREER
Now let's turn to Virgo on the job. Work is Virgo's ultimate security and a Virgo without a job is in a state of unrest, like a Cancer without a home. If

you don't have a job, finding a new one becomes a full-time occupation in itself. Virgo will not rest until all those résumés are sent out, every person has been contacted, and every lead has been tracked down. If you are a Virgo you are no doubt nodding, recognizing yourself! Virgos can go between relationships, but cannot go without a job, for work gives Virgos a strong sense of identity, confidence, accomplishment, and most importantly, a channel for their abundant energies. Oddly, the right position calms Virgo down. Virgo is truly one of the zodiac's original workaholics, and you will put in long hours without complaint. You will even cheerfully do the assignments at the office nobody wants to do, if only because someone's got to do them. Leave something incomplete? That would be a no-no in your world, Virgo.

When things go wrong elsewhere in life, you will tend to dive into your career because it brings you a kind of satisfaction that is lacking in other areas. Work can be healing and therapeutic by giving you a secure and comforting routine to cocoon yourself within when the world seems much too harsh. Toiling quietly in solitude is Virgo's favorite style, and it helps you put the pieces of your world together. Virgos need to be needed, and nowhere else do they feel as needed and as treasured as they do on the job. If done with a sense of balance, work can help a Virgo recover a stronger self-esteem when adversity strikes.

Having a steady income is important to you too, Virgo, because you are an earth sign—security issues matter a lot. You are not a particularly entrepreneurial sign (wild risk is a bit scary to Virgo), but if you find yourself self-employed, you would have both the stamina and the self-discipline to make it a success. More often, however, Virgo enjoys working either as a representative or an agent to others (thanks to Mercury, your ruler, the ultimate go-between for the gods) or as a support to one or more higher-ups, providing the critical detail and backup to the team. Virgo also enjoys to be "hands-on" (Mercury rules the fingers and hands, after all), which is why this sign might *not* want the job of manager.

A whiz at streamlining systems, Virgo will find the best way to accomplish a job, and by that I mean with the least amount of effort, in the shortest amount of time, and at the lowest cost. Virgos never cease to amaze co-workers and bosses with how good they are at multi-tasking and how much they get done in the average day. Some Virgos keep lots of lists, but some don't like them at all. A high-strung sign, Virgos may get too nervous if they are continually reminded about all they have left to do. Other Virgos simply memorize all the tasks they have left; the photographic memories they tend to have can come in quite handy. Make no mistake — Virgos make sure nothing slips through the cracks.

Friends scold Virgos for staying late and working weekends, they keep saying, "Get a life!" But Virgos will reply that they have the life they need, thank you. Don't tell Virgos that they work too hard or too much, for it is where Virgos get most of their satisfaction. Later Virgos always see a pay-off for their steadfast devotion to their careers. You won't likely see too many Virgos who are overnight successes — they tend to like to climb Mount Everest the hard way, step by step, up the steep slope. Like the tor-toise, progress is sometimes slow but they always make it to high positions of respect and responsibility. Scrupulously honest and ethical, Virgo wants to win accolades by earning them the old-fashioned way. Virgos don't like or understand office politics, and they usually try to avoid those situations.

Rather than be boss, Virgos are often happiest on the sidelines, carrying the clipboard, setting up flow charts and deadlines for others to use. Their middle name is Detail. Soon they have everything organized. No other astrological sign can match their attention to minutiae; absolutely nothing escapes their discerning eye. Ask a Virgo a simple question and you'll get a dossier on the subject. A little motto that Virgo lives by is "Always sur-prise people by giving more than they ask for, more than they expect!" This comes under the heading of being *thorough*, an ever-present Virgo goal. Sometimes Virgos feel that their thoroughness is a curse they wish they could turn off. They never feel that good is good enough!

A Virgo does not need much supervision, either—you can be sure if you hire a Virgo he or she will complete your assignments with care. In fact, Virgos will keep polishing their work until it gleams, or until you say "It's okay, you can stop now!" (They have trouble letting go.) At work, Virgo reports are always in on time and are comprehensive. Virgo likes to keep a pencil and pad next to the bed for ideas that come during the night—Virgo's mind never rests long. Things keep occurring to them whether they are awake or asleep. Geminis, Sagittariuses, Leos, Aries, and some Pisces especially need a Virgo around to be sure nothing gets forgotten. If you ask a Virgo to do a simple favor such as go to the bank for you, you will get back the stub of your check stapled with the bank slip. Everything is done letter perfect or not at all. If you have specific instructions for a young Virgo helper, he will write them down in a small notebook and consult his notes often. Virgo aims to please, finding joyful nobility in the completion of small and large tasks. Can a Virgo ever rise to CEO? Of course! When they do, they make fine leaders because they are so good at goal setting and are so sensitive to those who report to them. Virgo makes a modest, hardworking boss who serves the community well. Virgo wants to learn, examine, pull apart, study, and generally sink their teeth into things to search for ways to improve them.

Virgo is both visionary and yet practical. This is a winning combination because it encourages them to make their visions happen in real life, in real time. Virgos will never accept things as they are, but only as they can be—this is evidence of their critical side, which is so often misunderstood. Underneath that razor-sharp intellect beats the heart of an idealist who wants to make a difference by making the world a better place. While the first earth sign, Taurus, can best understand things that can be seen and touched, Virgo can go far beyond the basic physical world to the realm of concepts, dreams, and ideas.

Virgos serve without credit or thought of personal reward, especially when the job involves doing something for someone else's welfare; it is evidence of a very soft spot they have inside. For example, a Virgo and a Leo stop to help at the scene of an accident. They are gratified to have saved someone's life. A reporter at the scene asks their names. Leo will give his name clearly and distinctly and perhaps even offer a business card to be sure the reporter prints the proper spelling. Leo is very giving and may even offer to pay for any treatment if the accident victim can't afford to do so himself. Leo won't shrink from taking credit—he will welcome it. In contrast, Virgo will wave off the reporter, modestly saying he was happy to help and hastily explain that now the patient is resting comfortably, he has to be on his way. Virgo will duck any accolades because he is ultimately unassuming. In Virgo's mind, he did nothing unusual or out of the ordinary, certainly nothing more than anyone else would do under the circumstances. Virgos will always react with modesty and without fanfare.

If there is one profession that sums up Virgo, it is the medical profession. Doctors need to soothe, comfort, and heal others; this inclination is very powerful in your sign. Mother Teresa, a Virgo, embodied the best attributes of the sign: the tireless servant to those in need, one who went far beyond regard for oneself to look after others. Other occupations that are right for Virgos center on those that heal and improve the health of the body. Virgo could likely excel at being a dentist or a dental hygienist, a chiropractor, X-ray technician, EMS ambulance technician, blood technician, or biochemist. Think about becoming a physical therapist, laboratory scientist, public-health official, or pharmacist. Virgo adores small animals and pets, too—consider being a veterinarian, a pet-store owner, or a professional dog walker. Some Virgos find that they enjoy careers such as nutritionist, fitness expert, coach or trainer, greengrocer or owner of a health store. Other Virgos would like becoming a skin-care expert, massage therapist, or operating a service for grooming, such as for manicures, pedicures, and facials (all are Virgo-ruled activities).

Highly intelligent and verbal, Virgos have a powerful ability to get to the core of truth, and they make superb writers, research analysts, and communicators. Whether they choose to be a reporter, journalist, or anchor newsperson on TV or work in a more creative sense, as a novelist, screenwriter, playwright, film director, or producer, Virgos would find any of these roles fulfilling. Virgos deal well with complexities, and hence would be able to mold all the pieces of the plot together into a cohesive whole in a way other signs would find difficult or overwhelming. They would also make superb editors, fact checkers, library scientists, researchers, copywriters, journalists, public-relations executives, advertising executives, or TV, film, or advertising agency producers (Virgos work tirelessly and forget nothing). Virgos are very precise, so they can put their penetrating way of thinking to good use by being a critic for books, restaurants, films, the arts, or any other area you can think of. Teaching would also be a good field for Virgo, as would be an educator who sets standards and tests. Your rulership by speech-oriented Mercury makes you fine linguists, lecturers, and speech therapists.

Your flair for numbers and your ability to be precise and accurate could be put to good use as an accountant, bookkeeper, mathematician, statistician, market research analyst, census bureau taker, or insurance analyst. Think too of being a software designer or code writer (where detail really counts), or a manager of information systems or of information technology. Add to that list cost controller, tax auditor, management consultant, or time management expert. Virgos make excellent corporate planners and strategists too.

Thanks to the rulership of Mercury, who was mythological Hermes, the ultimate intermediary for the gods, Virgo does well when working as a middleman, whether as a broker, agent, sales representative, or even as a messenger (or the owner of a courier service). They tend to prefer staff positions (as opposed to line positions), such as being a top-level executive assistant. Consider also training to be an architect (where following rules and codes matters), astronomer, mechanic, or civil, mechanical, or electrical engineer. Virgo is well suited to be a computer technician, inspector, handyman, or repairperson, or even a watchmaker. Also, because of Virgos' proclivity for purity and cleanliness, they might consider running a valet service or a cleaning service for private homes and commercial businesses. Virgos' small motor skills are superb. Their attention to the most intricate detail and their interest in crafts and handmade things gives them the ability to be a fine dressmaker, tailor sample maker, or, in the fine arts, possibly working as an illustrator or a graphic designer.

Finally, Virgos' superb sense of organization would make them specialists in disaster relief, emergency civil preparedness, or working for the Red Cross. It is the Virgo who is flown into wreckage sites to rebuild from scratch, for nothing fazes a Virgo. No matter how chaotic a situation, Virgo will coolly and calmly put the pieces back together to make everything hum again. In a hurricane- or tornado-strewn area, Virgo decides where the tents will go, how water and food will be distributed, and how to keep people's spirits up. Virgos will be superb in the rebuilding phase too, for they are the ultimate producers of the zodiac. Virgos are also healers, for they have a strong link to medicine and health, and would be caring and sensitive toward the victims.

## Body, Mind, and Spirit

Many people may take good health for granted, but not Virgo. You will rarely see a Virgo consume junk food; in fact many Virgos are vegetarians. Light eating is better suited to their rather delicate digestive systems. They are known to be particular about what they dine on. I bet it's for Virgos that those nutrition charts are printed on the backs of all those food packages. Virgos like to control their diet, making sure they are getting enough nutrients, and, because they run on nervous energy, they almost always feel better when they take time to work out. Exercise gives them a positive way to channel their energies.

It is remarkable how Virgos can remake their bodies to perform better as time goes on. It is common for Virgos to experience health difficulties sometime during the first half of their lives and those very weaknesses fuel their determination to be fit and problem-free in the second half. Thus, as Virgos age they actually can (and often do) get stronger. When Virgos are faced with an obstacle or a problem, they want to be sure they leave no stone unturned in finding out more about what they can do to help themselves. Their penchant to do meticulous research, to read every article, book, or Web site they can find, soon leads them to many options. It is no wonder that they find a way to manage, improve, or stamp out any physical difficulty they encounter. Virgo is not generally a vain sign but rather is motivated by doing things right and being the best they can be. This is why Virgos live so long, and so well!

Virgos have to treat their digestive systems with care—when life gets tense, you should eat very gentle foods. Giving your system a rest is the best thing you could do. Some Virgos experience difficulty with irritable bowel syndrome, others get more serious illnesses, perhaps in the colon. If this sounds at all likely, seek help sooner rather than later. Also when you do take medicine, Virgo, ask the doctor or pharmacist about possible side effects. Your sensitive body absorbs medicine quickly, sometimes too quickly, and that could leave you feeling off balance. Your insistence on being informed is wise. Many Virgos prefer homeopathic remedies to traditional drugs. If a natural cure exists, Virgos will likely find it and prefer it.

Have you wondered why your sign rules the lower stomach? Most astrologers will tell you that just as Aries rules the head and Pisces the feet, the parts of the body proceed from head to toe on the human body in orderly fashion in sync with the zodiac. That is true. There is another reason, however. As we discussed, Virgo's symbol is of the virgin holding the shaft of wheat. In the same way that wheat is separated from the chaff, your intestines separate nutrients from the foods eaten and decide what your body needs and what to eliminate, an appropriate symbol for Virgo.

Did you ever wonder why Virgo is considered the neat, squeaky-clean sign, always interested in clean hands and good hygiene? Because you are considered the most health-conscious sign in the zodiac—that's why!

Some Virgos are prone to food allergies; it might be worth a test by a qualified doctor if you think you have an allergy. Virgos also can be susceptible to eating disorders. Although this is often the case with Cancer, it is also true among some Virgos (especially young Virgos). In other cases, Virgos are simply picky eaters and can't seem to gain weight but can't figure out why. Those who do gain weight tend to be harsh on themselves with too-stringent diets—sometimes Virgo's strong self-discipline is too much of a good thing (something even Virgo will admit). Lighten up, dear Virgo— Rome wasn't built in a day.

Are some Virgos hypochondriacs? Some are, but not *that* many. However, you have to admit, dear Virgo, that you are more interested in your health than most signs and it follows that you monitor how your body feels from day to day more closely than other people. Sometimes it is easy to imagine that you have an illness, particularly if you've been reading about that ailment. Yet on the other hand, when a doctor is truly baffled, it is easy for him to label you (or anyone else) a hypochondriac, a maddening experience when it happens. For some reason, most Virgos have felt the injustice of being wrongly accused of being a hypochondriac at one time or another. If you feel you do need medical care, get a second or third opinion and don't stop looking for help until you find it.

SUMMARY

Virgo could serve as a symbol of the modern man or woman. The plethora of information that might overwhelm ordinary mortals won't faze Virgo in the least. He or she has a masterful talent at both organization and communication. Remaining highly productive is their lifetime goal, and to that end Virgos continually judge the quality of their daily output. Some call Virgos critical, but in truth it is simply evidence of this sign's fierce idealism. Born at the time of the harvest, Virgo was meant to bring everything they touch to its fullest potential. Virgo's earthy, practical nature is an asset, for it allows this sign to actualize dreams. In love, the Virgo man or woman is privately, personally passionate. Through the years, Virgos will remain true-blue and your love will deepen and ripen, like the harvest their sign symbolizes.

# THE MYTHS OF
# VIRGO AND MERCURY

Virgo, the sixth sign of the zodiac, has a rich mythology.

## ASTRAEA

One of the loveliest concepts is the Greeks' and Romans' association of
Virgo with the virgin Astraea ("Star Maiden"), who was the daughter
of Zeus and Themis (Divine Justice) and sister of Pudicitia (Modesty).
During the Golden Age while she lived on Earth, Astraea shared with
mortals her thoughts about justice. Some reports also suggest that she
spent quality time with peasants in the country. As the myth goes, after
a while, it was clear to her that mankind had lost its penchant for high
ideals, so Astraea, disappointed, returned to heaven and took her place
among the stars, where she would remain forever in the constellation
of Virgo.

## ISIS

To the Egyptians, Virgo is the goddess Isis with the sun-child Horus on
her lap. This image is similar to and predates the beautiful image of
Christianity's symbol of Mary with her child, Jesus. In both images, the
mother is given enormous respect and reigns supreme, but she also is
about to experience a terrible loss when her child goes on to find his or
her own path in life.

## MERCURY RULES VIRGO AND GEMINI

The planet Mercury, so-called messenger of the Gods, rules both Gemini and Virgo because there are only eight planets and two luminaries (the Sun and Moon) to be assigned to all twelve signs; some had to share a planet. The ancients never saw much physical evidence of quick-moving Mercury so its assigned tasks, moving information, communication, and transportation, seem logical. If you haven't yet read "The Myths of Gemini and Mercury," you would do well to read the chapter now. As discussed there, Mercury had qualities that made its subjects clever, charming, original, curious, quick, versatile, and adaptable. Certainly these are all very applicable descriptions of both Gemini and Virgo.

Virgo, not Gemini, would be assigned the healing qualities of Mercury — we recall that Hermes had the caduceus or healing rod — as Virgo's earthy quality would be deemed more suitable for this role. Virgo is the sign that would forever be more concerned with health and healing, and the influence that the mind has over the body ("mind over matter") and vice versa ("The spirit is willing but the body is weak"). Virgos work on healing themselves — indeed, some say Virgos work to "perfect" themselves — and then go on to help heal others. Thus, the tangible, physical side of Mercury's influence is readily seen in Virgo. Virgos deal with their bodies (by eating right, exercising), minds (reading and watching plenty of intellectually stimulating fare), and spirits (through prayer, reflection, or meditation). In Virgo there is a depth of effort in these areas we don't generally see in Gemini.

The medieval alchemists spoke of Mercury as an element of spiritual transformation. "Mercurius," as they referred to the element, was androgynous, both male and female in nature, symbolizing the inner spirit of all living things. Mercury was thought to have the ability to change earthly reality into something more. Just as the harvest is a symbol of change — the seed moves from being planted to full fruitfulness and greatest potential — in Virgo there is a yearning to perfect oneself, not only in mind but in body too. Virgo's rulership of the lower stomach (the intestines) symbolizes a need to internalize and digest life's experiences as well as the information this sign discovers. The sixth house, Virgo's house of the horoscope, is one of service; therefore Virgo strives for self-improvement not as a vain endeavor but to serve others better. Mind, body, and spirit all blend masterfully in Virgo (of course, assuming excesses are avoided and balance is achieved).

## HERMES, MESSENGER OF THE GODS

The Egyptians saw Mercury's role as similar to Thoth, one who transported souls, and the Romans saw Mercury in a similar way, as Hermes (see "The Myths of Gemini and Mercury"), messenger of the gods. In the latter role, Hermes moved freely and quickly between heaven, Earth, and Hades; neither god nor mortal had the ability nor the access to travel as freely as Hermes did. Thus, the mind (Mercury, Thoth, or Hermes) is able to go wherever it wants to go; it is truly free. Similarly, this symbolism reminds us that the mind knows no boundaries. We center our thoughts on everyday, real-life matters but simultaneously our mind is also able to grasp dreams and emotions, yearnings and regrets, the future and the past. The mind, like Hermes's Mercury, acts as our guide to our inner and outer worlds and helps us discover our very souls.

In a Greek myth, Mercury united with Aphrodite and their baby was called the hermaphrodite—neither male nor female but symbolically both. So in the death of male-female, in the uniting of both hemispheres of the brain, we have something more: rational thinking and intuition in one. It is a transmutation that unites all into a whole where the result is greater than the sum of its parts. Refinement, communication, self-improvement, and a full transformation for the better are what Virgo is all about, and for your yearning to refine, perfect, discern, and serve we all owe you a debt, dear Virgo.

# LIBRA PERSONALITY

### Libra
September 23–October 22

*Guiding Principle*

"I Balance"

*How This Sign Feels Joy*
Finds joy in collaboration, including relating, harmonizing and the graceful balancing of energy with another in an eternal search for truth, beauty, and justice.

*In the New Millennium, Your Contribution to the World Will Be . . .*
Your talent for bringing about the peaceful resolution of conflict and your outstanding ability to forge relationships will be increasingly prized by people everywhere.

*Quote That Describes You*
"THOSE ARE EVER THE MOST READY TO DO JUSTICE TO OTHERS, WHO FEEL THAT THE WORLD HAS DONE THEM JUSTICE."

—WILLIAM HAZLITT, an *Aries*

There is a persistent rumor that people born under the sign of Libra are better-looking than the rest of us. Although this idea may defy logic and may even seem preposterous, like most rumors, this one has some truth to it. People of this sign do, more often than not, have a gentle expression, a classic oval-shaped face, and refined features that have a pleasing symmetry. Usually, young Libra women mature early and even if they are quite slender they have alluring rounded curves, with no angularity. Male Libra cuts a dashing figure, with a self-possessed confident stride that is irresistibly magnetic. Both male and female Libras often have radiant skin with a faint flush of health, as if they had just returned from a weekend of fresh air and vigorous exercise in the country. Venus, planet of grace and beauty, is the guiding planet of this sign and is mainly responsible for Libra's good looks.

Libra's true attractiveness may be related more to our *perception* than of anything we can point to specifically. They have such winsome personalities that even if they aren't classically beautiful or handsome, we see them that way nevertheless. Venus, as ruler of Libra, allows this sign to sparkle no matter what the prevalent standards for beauty happen to dictate. Actually, Libra seems to defy rigid standards of what is and is not considered beautiful or handsome. This sign always possesses a certain something that attracts people even if they aren't quite able to put their finger on it. A "wrong" nose, a mouth a little too full, eyes too widely spaced— whatever the feature—somehow seems right when added to the whole face, which transcends the sum of the parts. This is Venus, Libra's ruling planet, in action spinning its magic spell.

Socially, Libras are winners. On everyone's must-invite list, Libra seems to know everyone and certainly everyone wants to know Libra. The list of names in their well-worn, dog-eared Filofax is impressive and extends to people beyond their immediate vicinity and even to people across the country and around the world. An engaging sign, wherever they go or whenever they pick up a new interest, new friends follow them.

The progression of the signs of the zodiac is said to mirror the stages of man's life, from birth to old age. By the time we reach the seventh sign, Libra, the growing individual starts to work in tandem with a significant other whose tastes and opinions must be acknowledged, integrated, and balanced into the whole of a relationship. This is considered a very important point in astrology, because the seventh house shows a key development in the individual, which is the individual's ability to share and to collaborate. Working individually and independently can get you just so far, but to progress farther in a spiritual and material way a helpmate is necessary. Later, in the next sign, Scorpio, the idea of intimacy and sexuality is introduced and developed further, but for now Libra tells us that finding "forever, ever" love or, at the very least, being able to form enduring relationships, is the first priority.

**SYMBOLS**
Symbolized by the scales, Libra has a special ability to judge and weigh differences between people, things, and events—whatever you are studying—no matter how small. Libra invites comparisons, whether of weight, order, size, color, form, tune, or time, and, further, makes judgments and comes to conclusions about them. In Libra the importance of individuality lessens while loving cooperation and union with an alter ego becomes more important.

♎ Libra is born at the time of the year when daytime and nighttime hours are perfectly equal. In the Western Hemisphere, Libra marks the coming of fall. From that point on, nighttime increases as daylight fades. The glyph of Libra is two straight lines with a hump on the top line, a symbol of the horizontal bar of the scales. Alternatively, some experts believe the glyph symbolizes the Earth's horizon, with the Sun seen rising (or setting) in the center.

♀ The astrological glyph for Venus is represented by a circle over a cross. The cross is said to represent matter, and the circle over it, the soul. In this image we see that the soul has the power to transform matter into beauty.

Each sign makes up for what the sign before and after it lacks, and here Libra clearly makes up for Virgo's workaday impulses and fervent need to complete a multitude of tasks. Virgo has little time for socializing, for the harvest needs to be gathered, sorted, graded, stored, and possibly transported. The crop has been harvested in Virgo, and in Virgo man learns self-discipline as well as to work in an organized, efficient manner. Virgo also teaches the value of serving the community. In Libra, it is a time to relax and to bring the romance that began in Leo to greater maturity, for in Libra love turns to commitment. On a practical, day-to-day level, the harvest has been picked, the food sorted and stored, thanks to Virgo. In Libra, any food that is considered surplus can now be sold. It is time to weigh it and to negotiate a price for its sale, the cost depending on supply and demand. In the next sign, Scorpio, the need for self-discipline, spiritual intensity, and solitude will return, and with it will come a turning away from gaiety and socializing. For now, however, it is time to enjoy the fruits of one's labors, consider one's current relationship, and perhaps take time to find a lifetime mate.

## PLANETARY INFLUENCES

On the surface, Venus seems like a cream puff of a planet because its job is to spread love and pleasure everywhere. Upon closer inspection, however, one sees that this planet's true role is quite vital: to create an atmosphere of love that will lead to commitment and thus insure the propagation of the species. Venus also guarantees that man will not eat bread alone. Life is meant to be enjoyed, not just endured.

When it comes to love and marriage, Venus cannot do the whole job alone. A whole battery of planets will have to come into play. This lovely planet is thought to be especially effective when working in tandem with her mythological lover, Mars. When Venus and Mars are lined up at bene-

ficial angles, new love can more easily result. Mars adds that special
spice of flirtatious, sexual chemistry that makes the magnetism between two
lovers even stronger. For a truly good relationship to be sustained, however,
more planets will need to come into play. Perhaps foremost, the Moon will
provide emotional satisfaction and a sense of security. The Sun will hopefully
bring ego gratification and the determination to make the relationship
work. Mercury's role will be to provide good communication, and Jupiter
will be called upon to add optimism, spiritual connectedness, and possibly
the financial base to make the union plausible. Hopefully, from the start
there will be no adverse aspects from other planets, particularly from
Saturn and unpredictable Uranus. (If in an angry position relative to
Venus, Uranus can pull the plug rapidly by causing all sorts of upsets
and sudden reversals.) When a relationship reaches a more mature stage,
Saturn brings commitment and ensures that both parties are realistic and
are ready for responsibility. Finally, as the couple's love matures, Neptune,
the planet called "the higher octave" of Venus, will bring love to a richer
level, from a mood of "I just wanna have fun" to one of compassion, altruism, and inspiration. Libra, more than any other sign, knows what it takes
to create a loving relationship. Libra also realizes that having every one
of the elements in perfect form is unlikely and not even necessary for a
relationship to be successful.

Venus has no "thinking" side to its nature. Representing pure feeling,
Venus brings no sense of morality or ethics to matters of love, nor was it
supposed to do that. In the horoscope, "thinking" would be left to
Mercury, said to be rational and objective in influence. The planets provide
a certain purity of purpose in their respective equal but separate areas of a
horoscope. If each planet were muddled with attributes of the others, no
one planet would be powerful enough to exert the required strong, pure
influence. Don't misunderstand—Libra happens to be naturally quite intellectual because of its air-sign modality. Ideally, within a horoscope chart
the two planets work together to provide the person with a balanced outlook. Mercury helps us to know right from wrong, and provides other

functions of thinking, but Venus will furnish that intangible quality of allure, charm, and attraction so necessary to bring people together.

## COSMIC GIFTS

There is no doubt that Libras swim quite deftly through society because their people skills are impressive. Bless them, this sign provides some of the strongest glue of society because they enjoy making introductions, mixing and matching people in imaginative ways for business or friendship. Yet it is in their role as matchmaker that they really shine. From a young age, these precocious social butterflies exhibit a special ability to understand the motivation of others as well as an ability to spot talent within their friends. Libras will encourage their friends' talent, even help them profit from it. When the course of social interaction hits a snag they can be counted on to find more than a few imaginative solutions to end the strife and help people come together again.

Libra invented networking, for they enjoy helping people make new friends. Don't hesitate to ask a Libra for help in this regard; they love making "people soup" by bringing all the right folks together. If they don't know the right individual to help you, chances are they know the name of someone who does. And that introduction is a gift that could actually change your life. When Libras recommend a friend to you, take their advice because they are experts at putting people together.

Libras are courteous, thoughtful, generous, tolerant, sophisticated, and polished. They are also civilized and refined and have a sixth sense about what is and is not appropriate in social interaction. Good manners are important to this sign. If a Libra accuses you of being rude, be on alert; it is one of the worst sins on their list. Libras feel that being treated in an impolite, uncivil, coarse, or vulgar manner is inexcusable, because it offends the gentle teachings of their ruler. It was probably a Libra who wrote the first etiquette book (and the first "netiquette" rules too). Thoughtful and considerate, a Libra won't trample over other people's feelings.

Being an air sign, Libra shares a communicative spirit with Gemini and Aquarius. These signs all like to stay on top of what's happening around them. Libra was also certainly bestowed with strong analytical ability, and they will soon draw others into debate. Defending one's position with this fast-thinking sign may not be easy, because Libras, like all air signs, are gifted with words. Libra is, after all, in search of truth, fairness, and justice, and will go to any length to find them.

Indecisiveness or vacillation is admittedly a Libra trait, yet it can be more of an asset than a liability. The next time you weigh something, watch the scale, Libra's symbol, flutter as it searches for the proper readout. It will rest only a second or two as it searches continually for its perfect, proper balance. A Libra always desperately wants to come to the right answer; so if you are a Libra, you will always study each side of an issue, never quite sure that you have come to the proper conclusion. Other signs criticize you for this vacillation, but to your credit, Libra, you know that nothing is ever simply black or white. You try hard to see the full complexity of any issue, and examine the pros and cons. For this you should not be criticized but applauded.

Impartiality and justice for all is uppermost in importance to Libras in all walks of life. Even when they were children they would say, "But it's not fair!" as if they are born thinking that life should always provide equality, harmony, and proportion. Their goal is to find the win-win situation, the perfect middle ground, the imaginative solution. Libras enjoy playing the role of peacemaker and will jump at any opportunity to do so. They disdain any kind of conflict but are oddly drawn to it too. If they notice two strangers arguing, it is not unusual for soft-spoken Libra to stop and ask the battling parties, "What's going on?" Of course their question is often met with chagrin, but that doesn't stop Libra from meddling occasionally. Libra doesn't mind being caught in the middle, for that seems to be their natural place. This sign is symbolized by the mythological goddess who holds the scales, blindfolded, called Blind Justice. Sometimes Libras' insistence on being fair gets them into hot water if their friends expect partisan support, but Libras' objectivity simply won't allow that. Still, they will find a way to smooth things over if they ruffle a few feathers.

## RELATIONSHIPS

Social Libras are not "stay-at-homes"; being cooped up makes Libra a little stir crazy. Having a continual stream of people in their life increases their energy and zest for living. When phoning your Libra friend, be advised that you'll probably get his or her answering machine. They can go out night after night and never feel the strain of late hours, even as they grow older.

Overall, being a close friend with Libra is almost always a warm and stimulating experience. They are generous and will go out of their way to help you. Libras believe in the value of new experiences, so they have plenty of ideas about things to do, and almost all of them are unique, enriching ones. When a Libra listens and speaks to you it is as if no one else were in the room—or on the planet! Be mindful, however, that Libras will expect the same from you. If you don't give it to them they will keep reminding you by saying things like "You're not listening!" Any lack of attention to them is noticed—and disapproved of—in short order.

These Venus-ruled children of the zodiac have a big advantage in matters of the heart. Especially at a first meeting, Libra's self-possessed manner and unflappable poise usually make hearts thump harder. Confidence is a strong aphrodisiac. Libra is called the marriage sign, because Libras have the mating ritual down pat. To be wined and dined by a Libra male is indeed a memorable, joyous experience. Libra females tend to be "*Rules* girls" who wait for the man to make the first move and play the mating game with skill. After all, Venus's main job is to send Cupid on a mission to sling arrows into the hearts of unsuspecting lovers everywhere. Cupid knows that romance needs a push in the right direction if it is to take off. Being Cupid's favorite, Libra thoroughly enjoys being in love.

You might be tempted to think that Libra is a highly emotional sign because of its rulership by the love planet. But that is not true at all. Libras' heads rule their hearts. This sign doesn't like the feeling of being swept away in the sea of love. You will note a little aloofness, especially during the dating period. Venus's influence on this sign makes Libra a little lazy, so most Libras are brilliant at finding ways to get people to come to them; Libra wants to be the beloved object of affection, not just a lover. But love has to be on their terms for them to be happiest. Libras ask, "Why sweat when others will gladly come to you?" It works; few can resist Libra's mighty magnetism.

But wait, you might say, didn't we just say that Venus is the planet of love and romance, charm and beauty, unencumbered by thinking, morality, and intellect? That is true. Venus is all feeling, no thinking, sometimes even a little narcissistic, because this planet is thought to be receptive, not aggressive. And while Libras could be called vain, they are not self-absorbed. This may be a fine line, but Libras are always thinking about their partners. Venus draws others in but does not act in an outwardly aggressive manner (more about that in a minute). Truly, Libra is a study in finely honed contrasts.

But it is not the Venus influence that makes Libra so analytical and brainy when it comes to love, but that Libra is classified as an air sign—and air signs often think until their little heads hurt. Air signs simply analyze things so much, down to the tiniest detail. It is a rare Libra who will shed tears on his pillow about love gone wrong, as this sign recovers more quickly than most. Not only that, but you will rarely see a Libra desperate for love. As much as Libras want love, it has to come on their terms or they aren't interested, something we spoke about earlier. It is not that they are cold—goodness, no! They have open, good hearts and are willing to give much to their sweethearts and mates. Instead, it's their strong intelligence that tells them, "If she (or he) doesn't value me, I'll find someone else who will!" Strong self-esteem is what you see operating here, and I suppose that is healthy. And while Libras like to keep the upper hand, they do so in such a charming way that the object of their affection is more often than not content to hand over the reins.

Libras value relationships so much that rarely will you find a Libra alone. If you do, they are in the process of leaving a relationship, but they won't likely be single for long; a new love is right around the corner. Just as the little Cancer Crab is lost without a home, Libra feels out in left field without a significant other. Yes, some young Libras, males particularly, due to social conditioning, can get caught up in the dating game and turn their heads at every passing woman. However, soon even that grows boring and they are ready to settle down.

In love, once Libras have found a soul mate, they will want commitment and that usually means marriage or some other formal agreement. But doesn't everyone? Sagittariuses, Geminis, Aquariuses, and some Aries, for example, enjoy their single status and will try to prolong it as long as possible. Pisces, a sign focused on creativity, may also choose to keep their options open for a long time. The most compatible signs for Libra are the other air signs, Gemini or Aquarius, or another Libra. Fire signs that blend well with the air element include Sagittarius, Aries, and Leo. Still, these signs can pose some problems if they are not inclined to early marriage. There may be a delay before both parties are on the same schedule. "Let's get engaged!" you might say to your Libra love, but he or she may suddenly hesitate. They notoriously flutter their scales when trying to make a decision. Libras do need plenty of time to ponder, so don't be surprised if your sweetheart says he or she has to think things over one more time.

It is interesting to note that Libra does not rule the fifth house of true love, children, and creativity, but does rule the seventh house of committed relationships. Love has become more serious as it has traveled around the zodiac, finally landing in Libra's seventh house. All joint ventures, both personal and business, fall into this same seventh-house sector.

When Libra is referred to as the marriage sign, it might be wise to remember that marriage was a very different institution back when the ancients developed astrology thousands of years ago. The concept of marrying for love was not the main reason couples came together—most marriages were arranged. It would not be until the Middle Ages that love and marriage were considered seriously, as in works such as the King Arthur stories of Guinevere and Lancelot. Later, Shakespeare immortalized young romantic love with Romeo and Juliet but also conveyed the message that although romantic love was ecstasy, it often brought disaster. Thus, romance, fun, games, puzzles, leisure activity, and all speculation—including risk—were placed in the fifth house of love. All business partnerships, mergers, treaties, and marriages (joint ventures involving a contract) were placed in the seventh house and are ruled by Libra.

Since there are not enough planets to rule each sign, some planets rule two signs. In Libra's case, Venus is shared with Taurus. In Taurus, Venus's love is expressed in a highly erotic and earthy way, while in Libra, Venus expresses herself in a more spiritual, detached, idealized, and intellectual way, for Libra relates more to the mind than the body. There are other differences. Taurus is a fixed sign and Libra is a cardinal sign, and while fixed signs are known to be determined, they are also quite inflexible. Libras have a more proactive and energetic outlook than Tauruses, which helps them shape their destiny aggressively. Taurus tends to be a more reserved, retiring, "feminine" sign, while Libra is a more active, "masculine" sign. As an air sign, Libra is more probing than Taurus and much more interested in being in charge of a relationship, but this is expressed subtly, a thought we will come back to in a moment.

To find the right soul mate, young Libras should spend some time alone to get to know themselves better, but that's unlikely because to Libra socializing is as delicious as candy. Even as children Libras never seem to want solitude. Even when they do homework they want a buddy. This is because Libras, no matter what their age, do their best work in the presence of a friend or a coach. Libra is considered a "double-bodied sign," like Gemini or Pisces (twins and two fish); Libra has the set of two scales and likes to operate in a dualistic mode. In fact, Libras define themselves through partners, for they learn a great deal about themselves through their interaction with someone they trust. They especially like having a significant other who is willing to act as a sounding board for their many projects. It is through comparing oneself to others that Libras begin their journey of self-discovery. Noting what their significant other lacks, they begin to value their own strengths.

All this talk about love and marriage might lead you to think that Libra is an overly emotional sign, but this could not be further from the truth. Libras do not like messy emotions, so a water sign, like Scorpio, Pisces, or Cancer, may not be quite right as a partner. Water signs will want Libra to plunge to the depths of the sea of emotions, which is why Libras are better paired with air or fire, signs that stay on the surface. The Earth signs, Taurus, Capricorn, or Virgo, may not fare any better with Libra, for the relationship could collapse under their weighty practicality.

Once married, Libras seem much more content, and they are willing to do what it takes to make the marriage happy. However, Libras should be aware that there is always the danger that they can be too willing to keep the peace, compromising too much in the name of love. In their effort to please, Libras can become too compliant or accommodating, and in the process they may lose sight of their own needs. In some cases they may mistakenly believe that somehow they are required to give as much as they do and wind up later disillusioned or disappointed with their relationship. There is an easy fix for this dilemma. If you are a Libra, you hold on tightly to your identity and decide ahead of time where you will draw the line with what you will and will not compromise.

Despite an overall look of softness and gentility, as said earlier Libras like to remain at the helm of a relationship to set its pace and overall direction.

This will hold true regardless of whether their relationship is personal or business. Libras can be bossy, but they manage to get their way by pouring on their charm, and few will be able to resist.

Libras, as a cardinal sign, fear being dominated by their partner, so they unconsciously turn the tables to be sure they wind up in charge. They admire strength in a partner but do not want to be strong-armed. If you are married to a Libra, you'll never win by shouting, "You have to do this my way because I say so!" Libra will smother you with so many questions and debates that you'll wonder why you ever thought you could get away with that in the first place. The ideal situation is a partnership where both parties have an equal say. Yet even though Libras want to be in charge, they will do it in a gentle yet firm manner. They will cleverly, sweetly, and charmingly gain control, and you may never know what hit you.

Lucky is the child who has a Libra parent, for they are often ideal at the job. Fair and just, they will listen to both sides of every dispute between their children and try to come up with a happy solution. Libra parents will expose their children to the arts early in life, whether that be tickets to *The Nutcracker*, the circus, or the children's Philharmonic, bedtime stories by prize-winning children's authors and poets, or great music playing on the stereo. Libra tastes are eclectic and sophisticated, so there will be plenty of variety. If a child shows interest in playing an instrument or learning to dance, lessons will be arranged. Libras want to teach their children about the finer things of life, giving them an allowance and teaching them how to spend and save too. Something fun is always going on in a Libra's family. Libras will give much to their marriage and family, because they are so strongly focused here.

### FINANCE

Venus isn't just a "pretty-me" or "love-me" planet. Venus is considered a financial planet in a horoscope, and thus, Libras are considered excellent at handling money. They manage large budgets of others in a wise and trustworthy manner, whether funds of people they know or finances at the company where they work. Even though Libras love to shop for beautiful things, they also like to have money in the bank. With some fancy footwork they manage to have both.

Libra has a surprisingly strong practical side when it comes to saving and handling money, another blessing from Venus. Certainly this sign will need a stash to afford the finer things of life that they value. Yet they take every opportunity to use their superb bargaining skills to haggle over a price—they simply assume that everything is negotiable. (They surprise us by being right!) One of their favorite investments is gold or gems. Don't expect to see Libra run away to marry a rock star when there's a substantial, feet-on-the-ground banker who is willing to be a good provider and help raise the children. When it comes to finances and shared resources, Libra can be very practical.

## CAREER

If law is the art of compromise (and more than a few Libras have told me that is exactly what law is), then Libra is its best administrator. Their love of justice makes them naturals in the role of attorney, judge, paralegal, legal researcher, bailiff, clerk, bondsman, sheriff, or any other legal job, such as copyright or trademark expert. Being clear thinkers and clever strategists, Libras are a progressive, innovative group that has no difficulty moving with the times. Unlike fixed signs, change does not faze them; in fact, they would like to position themselves on the cutting edge of all that is new and interesting. Libras excel in any profession where skill at negotiation will be prized. If you are a Libra, consider the positions of a labor negotiator, arbitrator, agent, union leader, or representative.

As we said previously, Libra is strongly interested in the arts. Good professions also include museum curator, art gallery owner, and professional critic for the movies, restaurants, art, music, books, or theater. Add to the list the jobs of party planner or promoter, publicist, artist or art teacher,

art historian, designer, illustrator, musician, composer, conductor, piano
teacher, sound technician, opera singer, or voice-over expert. We also
find a preponderance of Libras working as florists, gardeners, and bridal
consultants, and as jewelers or jewelry designers. Consider too the job
of editor of art books, antique dealer, or talent agent. Libras make great
department store buyers, too, especially of clothing, jewelry, home furnish-
ings, accessories, and just about any product that pampers. As a manager
or boss, when it comes to giving credit to their underlings and co-workers,
Libras never fail to give it freely, which is one reason they are so in demand
to work with. Libra is quite aware of others' feelings and treats people
with respect.

There are other careers Libras may be interested in trying, particularly in
the beauty field. Libras make outstanding hairstylists, makeup and
wardrobe stylists, even outstanding designers or marketers of new cosmetics or fragrances. As we said, they have good looks, so many become mod-
els, although acting belongs mainly to Leo, the entertainment sign, or
Pisces. Libras could also consider owning a modeling agency or a spa,
being an interior designer or a textile designer, or they could work in any
capacity in the cosmetics business. Libras would like careers that deal
with the skin too, from massage to reflexology, or studying for work in the
field of skin care, from being a dermatologist to owning a salon for facials
and manicures or pedicures.

## BODY, MIND, AND SPIRIT

Libra is on a quest to beautify the world, and it is a rare Libra who does
not worship one of the cultural arts. Their ruler, Venus, is also in charge
of the decorative arts, as well as luxury and pampering. Venus rules paintings, music, candy, flowers, love letters, dance, jewels and gems, fragrance
and cosmetics, fine clothes and luscious fabrics. These Venus-ruled things
aren't necessities, but what would life be without them? Venus sharpens
the senses too, for this lucky sign. Libras are often gifted musically and
often play an instrument, compose music, or are particularly sensitive to

the beauty of music when it is performed well. It is not surprising that both male and female Libras have been known to use the power of fragrance with the wizardry of an alchemist. Whatever they happen to dab on, it sure is effective.

A Libra hallmark is how sparkling clean they always look. You can always spot Libras by their just-stepped-from-the-shower appearance. Even if everybody else is keeling over in a heat wave, they manage to remain crisp and cool as a cucumber. Libra rules the skin, so it is no wonder that they love fine fabrics that feel great to the touch. This sign wants the best natural fibers close to them, from the richest and thinnest silks and suede to imported cottons, satin, and soft, elegant wools.

In medical astrology, Libra rules not only the skin but also lower back, veins (of course—the vessels that go to the heart), and kidneys. The rulership of the kidneys seems especially appropriate, for the kidneys act as a filter or go-between for much of the body's functions, just as in life Libras often find themselves acting as a conduit. Libra represents the equilibrium, distillation, sublimation, and filtration of bodily functions. The lower back is considered this sign's area of greatest weakness, although difficulty with veins or circulation could also be bothersome. Libra is also sensitive to nephritis and bladder difficulties. Better health can be achieved with frequent checkups, by following a good diet, and by getting proper exercise.

Each of the air signs uses its connectivity in different ways. Gemini uses it to be knowledgeable about current events but is not known to be particularly into fashion or being part of the social "in" crowd, like Libra. Aquarius is interested mainly in all new developments in science, computers, electronics, and high technology, but couldn't care less if others think they are hip, or popular enough to be invited to the "right" parties. But Libra, ruling the seventh house of the horoscope of relationships, cares a great deal about social status. Libras need society's approval and will commit much of their energy to get it. Being fashionable counts. For starters, that means being up-to-the-minute in dress, going to the hottest restaurant, and knowing about popular books and other cultural events. Libra loves to set trends and is society's leading stylemaker.

Being one of the beautiful people sets Libras apart as special, but it also requires that they walk a fine line between expressing their identity and losing it in their fervor to be part of the look and trends of the moment. It is one thing to be trendy but quite another to be a fashion victim. This sounds like lots of pressure, but Libra is up to the test and is adept at avoiding the pitfalls. This sign has a flair for innovating looks and also for adapting them into a uniquely individual style. No wonder they spawn so many copycats!

Being inwardly critical and somewhat competitive makes some Libras seem snooty at times. If you are wearing a hopeless dud of an outfit, Libras will stare at you with a mixture of superiority and pity, perhaps simultaneously rolling their eyes at your sorry state of affairs. They will silently ask themselves, "How could she have left the house like that?" not realizing that some people have things other than fashion on their minds. Thankfully, Venus gives Libras tact, but their expression will be hard to disguise. In Libra's mind, being dowdy is disaster, and ugly should be outlawed. Dear Libra, if this describes you, perhaps you shouldn't try to convince your sister to see a plastic surgeon after all. She may take it the wrong way and think you are hopelessly shallow. Libra has standards, but putting emphasis on style over substance can cause you to be misunderstood by some. Not many Libras fall into this trap, thank goodness, but these extreme examples do indicate the way things could go if Libra's scales begin to flutter out of balance.

Leaving the classics to Taurus, Virgo, Capricorn, Cancer, and Scorpio, Libra wants the newest styles and understands that presentation is everything. Leos like fashion too, but Libras are different, elevating their designer wear into something totally unique yet also quite elegant. Rather than wear anything flashy or bright, Libra tends to choose the paler pastels or neutral hues, while Leo prefers rich color. Venus softens and refines whatever it touches and does not need a lot of money to look great. Libras engender admiration but, more than that, they also manage to attract loving feelings. Libras' sunny disposition effectively disarms their detractors. They have convinced us that Libra is the most fun sign to be. They may be right.

## SUMMARY

An idealistic sign, Libra teaches tolerance of others' points of view and effective collaboration with people of diverse backgrounds and viewpoints. This concept, initiated in Libra, will later be broadened and expanded by Aquarius, but unlike Aquarius where the emphasis is on groups, in Libra the spotlight remains on working in close, personal, one-on-one relationships. Libra assists the work that Aquarius will do by strengthening the grass-roots level of society, by making marriage and contractual business alliances strong through mutual cooperation.

If you are a Libra, be proud. You are the elegant sophisticate in the social thick of things; whether male or female, your charm and stylishness are legendary. You are positively brilliant in putting the right people together in such a way that things start to click. Intelligent, analytical, peace seeking, and a superb collaborator, partnerships are your specialty and you can teach us all a thing or two about cooperation. You are loyal in love once you discover the devotion you crave in return. You enter committed relationships comfortably, seeking to maintain an equal partnership, grounded in mutual respect and admiration. Lucky is the person who weds a Libra, for this sign will be willing to work on their marriage to keep it ever fresh. The world would be a dreary place without you, dear Libra. Although you never purposely want to be different from the group, you must admit you are an original. *Vive la différence!*

# THE MYTHS OF
# LIBRA AND VENUS

With its twinkling scales set in the velvet blue sky, Libra is the only sign
of the zodiac symbolized by a physical, man-made object. At first you might
think, How odd to have a mechanical object symbolize a sign ruled by graceful, diplomatic Venus. Yet the image of the scales crystallizes perfectly the
concept of the balance of forces that are operating at the autumnal equinox,
when day and night are exactly equal in hours. Ruling the natural seventh
house of the horoscope, Libra's scales perfectly sum up this sign's sensitivity
to the give-and-take in all kinds of relationships. A mechanical scale is,
after all, a precise instrument, so Libra is considered cool, intellectual, and
aesthetic. Less physically erotic than Taurus and less emotional than a
water sign like Pisces, Libra is more involved with the classic idealization
of beauty. Libra also strives to balance the real world of materialism with
the inner world of spirituality, the two eternal opposites. Being more social,
Libras are particularly aware of the consequences of their actions, for by
the time the wheel of the horoscope reaches the seventh sign, man has come
out of himself and is aware of a significant other whose needs and desires
also have to be acknowledged. Through others we see ourselves better, and
thus, Libra crystallizes this concept of relatedness; all kinds of serious
committed partnerships would be of enormous importance to Libra.

Your symbol of the scales, Libra, had a very sacred significance to the
Egyptians. We know that the Egyptians believed that when a person died,

the goddess of law, Maat, would place the human soul on one side of her scales and a feather on the other side. If the soul tipped the scales even slightly, she would deem it not ready to enter the afterlife. Such a soul would need to reincarnate with the hopes that the person could show himself evolved enough to release the extra "weight" of the soul to prepare it for the afterlife.

The Egyptians were, in fact, the first ancients who recognized Libra as a constellation unto itself. As the zodiac was being formulated, the Babylonians didn't know Libra, for their zodiac had only eleven signs. In those days, Libra was then still part of Scorpio's claws. The Greeks saw this same group of stars as a set of scales held by the goddess of justice, Astraea, but they associated Astraea with Virgo. The Egyptians noticed that Libra's beautiful star group rose on the horizon in the night sky in the spring, so they associated Libra with the New Year's baby called the Divine Child, or Chonsu. (The onset of spring, not January 1, commenced the new year for the Egyptians.) As we discussed in the chapter on Aries, spring coincided with Aries because Aries rose on the horizon at dawn. Libra, as Aries' opposite sign falling six signs later, rose on the horizon each evening, exactly twelve hours later, at sunset.

In early art, Venus, Libra's ruler, was symbolized as an Earth Mother, the rotund symbol of pure fertility. Who can forget the Venus of Willendorf our art-history teacher first showed us? That Venus is the very oldest Venus figure to date, thought to go back to 30,000 to 25,000 B.C. and discovered in a cave in Willendorf, an alpine village in Austria.

## VENUS AS GODDESS

The Greek author Hesiod (circa 800 B.C.) completely refined that image in his work *Theogony* by providing a vision of Venus as one of love and beauty. The lovely Renaissance painting by Botticelli *Birth of Venus* presents a more modern view of this popular goddess of love and beauty. Venus has intrigued poets, painters, musicians, and other creative people for centuries, probably because love and sex are such deep and abiding human needs.

Hesiod begins his *Theogony* with a description of the world emerging out of chaos. It chronicles the birth of the twelve Titans, whose parents were Uranus (sky) and Gaia (earth), a mythological couple who are said to have spawned all life. When Uranus showed himself to be a tyrannical ruler as well as a bad father (one who had a habit of hiding all his offspring inside his wife, Gaia), Gaia asked her children to help stop his actions. Her youngest, Saturn (as Cronus), responded to her plea by plotting to castrate his father with a sickle. After successfully completing the act, Saturn threw his father's genitals into the sea, scattering the seeds of sky and heaven everywhere, including the ocean.

Out of the primordial waters of creation of the sea, amid the white mist and the foam of the sea, Venus, born of those seeds, emerged radiant on a scalloped shell. In Greek, her name is Aphrodite (literally "one who comes from foam"), and it is said that as she alighted from the water green grass sprang up under her feet. Venus's attendants, the three graces—Eros (love), Himeros (longing), and Pathos (regret)—groomed and pampered Venus, after which they escorted her to Mount Olympus, where she joined the other deities.

## VULCAN, VENUS, AND MARS

Another myth tells us something about Venus's relationship with her husband, Vulcan. Vulcan was a kind but unattractive artisan who was said to have been the god of metallurgy. Rather wrapped up in his work, Vulcan often neglected Venus. Although Venus was beautiful, she required frequent validation of her attractiveness but because Vulcan was so preoccupied, she did not get the affirmation she so dearly needed. Venus felt neglected, but not for long.

Gentle, receptive Venus found herself in a mutual attraction with macho, aggressive warrior Mars, a classic, sexy combination if there ever was one. Opposites attract, and this pair proves it. Vulcan, suspecting that his wife was in love with Mars, set a trap to see if he could catch her in her infidelity. First, Vulcan announced to Venus that he would be away on certain days, assuming correctly that Venus would invite her lover to their palace as soon as he was gone. To catch the lovers together, Vulcan went to work to create a net of golden chains that he later posted high in the bedroom's rafters, hidden over their bed so he could lower them over the unsuspecting lovers once they were in an embrace.

Sure enough, as soon as Venus thought Vulcan was out of town she beckoned Mars to come to her home. Before long they were making love. Vulcan seized the moment by quickly lowering his chains of love over the nude lovers, who continued their lovemaking as they were trapped in his golden net. Then Vulcan took the outrageous step of inviting all the gods and goddesses of Mount Olympus to see them in their shame. However, the goddesses, siding with Venus, refused to come, although nearly all the male gods arrived to stare. Yet inviting the gods may not have had the effect Vulcan intended. Mercury told Mars (Apollo) that he would happily volunteer to change places with him because having Venus in an embrace sounded pretty good to him. Compassionate Neptune finally put a stop to the carnival atmosphere by demanding that Vulcan release the pair immediately, and so they were.

Today astrologers know that when loving, receptive Venus is in a certain positive angle to sexy Mars in a horoscope, sexual sparks result. These two cosmic lovers are certainly known to turn up the heat and intensify the magnetism. As we discussed in the chapter on Libra, however, Venus and Mars alone are not able to sustain a relationship, nor is it their job. To do that a host of other planets will be needed to help lovers carry the relationship to a deeper level if they so desire. In the meantime, that important first spark felt when we first fall in love is often left to Venus and Mars. (Mars also rules firecrackers and incendiary devices—among other things.) Venus not only encourages a capacity for love, but will also encourage self-worth when it is at a good angle to other planets. Being hedonistic, however, Venus does not think much about the future, because Venus simply wants to have fun. Imagine if Venus did not exist; there would be no love affairs, no passion—maybe no babies! Venus encourages each of us to love ourselves too, which some experts say is necessary before any lasting relationship can begin.

Plato was one of the first philosophers to make the distinction between love and friendship and clarify that there were indeed two kinds of love possible between non-family members. Plato put forth in his *Symposium* the view that Venus, as described by Homer and Hesiod, represented two distinct goddesses who personified different kinds of love: sexual (romantic) and non-sexual (platonic). In Plato's view, the latter was infinitely better. Plato also wrote that a spiritual friendship could not exist between men and women because there would always be a sexual influence, no matter how the parties involved might protest and say they are "just friends." Thus, in Plato's view, platonic love could exist only between men. In fact, to Plato, homosexuality was one of the highest forms of love because it did not depend on sexuality. Specifically, Plato wrote, sex between men was optional, but between a man and woman, the relationship must always be sexual (if only beneath the surface). Of course, this is quite a controversial view and one of those classic questions that might not find universal agreement, but it is interesting to think about.

As we saw in the myth about Vulcan's chains of love, Venus wasn't perfect—she was married, but nevertheless entered into an affair with Mars. Venus could also be insecure, jealous, and somewhat vengeful. In the story of the Judgment of Paris that follows, two sides of Venus's character emerge. One, portrayed by Aphrodite, shows her insecurities; the other, portrayed by Psyche, characterizes her more positive side, the part of her that idealizes equality and subsequent devotion in marriage. While there are several versions of the Judgment of Paris, all have basically the same plot.

## THE JUDGMENT OF PARIS

The myth called the Judgment of Paris is one of the most appropriate myths to explain the psychology of Venus and Libra. In the story, almost all the gods and goddesses were invited to attend the wedding of Thetis and Peleus. When Eris, the goddess of discord, was not invited, she became angered and tossed a golden apple inscribed with the words TO THE FAIREST to the goddesses at the wedding. Hera, Athena, and Aphrodite fought over the apple. Finally, Zeus, exasperated, dispatched Hermes (Mercury) to escort the three goddesses elsewhere to continue their disruptive argument, so the trio went to Troy. Paris, a Trojan prince and renowned as the most handsome of mortal men, was asked to decide which goddess was the fairest and the one most deserving of the golden apple.

Hera governed childbirth and marriage and was the wife of Zeus. It was Hera who offered Paris the world. Athena, the virgin goddess of wisdom, practical arts, and war, was thought in other myths to be responsible for Libra's quest for fairness, as well as Libra's well-known cool and brainy approach to life. Alternatively, Athena offered Paris a position of power and assured Paris that if he chose her he would celebrate victory. Aphrodite (as Helen), the goddess of love, offered Paris herself as the most beautiful woman in the world. Paris didn't blink. His choice was easy. He chose beauty over career or power. His prize was the breathtakingly beautiful Helen, but unfortunately Helen was already married to the Greek king of Sparta, Menelaus. Paris's insistence on claiming Helen touched off the Trojan War. Ironically, issues concerning love or beauty often surface in the lives of those with Libra Sun signs and form a recurring theme.

## EROS AND PSYCHE

In the Greek myth about Eros and Psyche we learn that Aphrodite (Venus by another name) was outraged to learn of another woman, named Psyche, who was much more beautiful than she. Aphrodite was jealous and protective of her turf, not only out of vanity but also from a practical standpoint. She realized that a rival beauty might cause citizens to stop worshiping her and instead worship her rival (Psyche). Aphrodite called on her son Eros for help. (We know Eros as Cupid, who creates love by shooting arrows that cause mortals instantly to fall in love.) In this instance, however, Aphrodite ordered Eros to kill Psyche.

Eros set out to find Psyche and encountered her blindfolded and tied to a rock. Just as he was preparing to execute her per his mother's instructions, he accidentally shot himself with one of his magic arrows and fell in love with this nymph-life creature. He untied her, married her, and secretly took her to his castle to live.

Fearing for her safety, Eros demanded that Psyche remain blindfolded whenever they were together so that she would never discover his identity. He could not reveal to her that he was Cupid, the god of love. Psyche's sisters pressured her into finding out the identity of her husband anyway, by suggesting that perhaps her husband was a monster and that was why he would not allow her to see his face. It apparently didn't take much to convince Psyche, and soon she confronted Eros without her blindfold. Stunned by his wife's betrayal, love literally and figuratively disappeared when Eros leaped out the window. Psyche grieved the loss of her husband and begged Aphrodite to return her lover. Aphrodite relented, but only on the condition that Psyche would complete a series of nearly impossible tasks chosen by Aphrodite to humiliate and frustrate her. Aphrodite was secretly confident that Psyche would never be able to fulfill them. However, Psyche did complete her tasks to the letter, thanks to help from the animal kingdom (just like Cinderella in the fairy tale). Aphrodite had no choice but to bring Eros back.

Each of us reenacts the mythology of Eros and Psyche when we fall in love. Like Psyche, when we experience new love we tend to be blind to our lover's flaws but sooner or later realize that we need to see our lover in the bright light of day. Some degree of disillusionment almost always results, marking a moment of truth for that relationship: to stay or to go? (Nobody ever said the road to love was a smooth one.)

## VENUS RULES LIBRA AND TAURUS

As discussed, Venus rules not only Libra but Taurus too, and the differences between how Venus asserts her qualities in Libra and in Taurus are fascinating. In Taurus, a fixed earth sign, Venus expresses her most possessive side. Tauruses don't trust what they can't see, touch, taste, hear, or smell for they are a practical sign: Tauruses use their senses to get more information and tend to be motivated by pleasure and comfort, so if someone (or something) feels good, sounds good, and looks good, they say "Go for it."

By contrast, Venus in Libra exerts a more delicate, ethereal, and much more intellectual influence. Grooming and looking polished are extremely important to Libra. Manners count too, especially in matters of love. Here Venus epitomizes an elegant, refined, classic, and glamorous idealized standard of beauty and of love as well. With Libras, at least half (or more) of the relationship takes place in their mind. Libras' idealization of love and beauty could be so lofty that it may feel unattainable at times. For Libra, Venus is the gorgeous movie star on the silver screen, the model on the cover of a magazine, or the new lover we put on a pedestal. Despite that, ultimately Libra is the quintessential marriage sign, always happiest when wed to the one they love.

# SCORPIO PERSONALITY

### Scorpio
October 23–November 21

**Guiding Principle**
"I Probe"

**How This Sign Feels Joy**
Finds joy in ferreting out others' talents that have been heretofore hidden, awaiting their intense light of discovery.

**In the New Millennium, Your Contribution to the World Will Be . . .**
You are sharply perceptive and highly intuitive, and therefore gifted at unraveling mysteries. As the zodiac's detective, you'll know which answers are and aren't plausible. With so much data to digest in the future, the world will prize your insight.

**Quote That Describes You**
"THE SACRED CALL IS THE TRANSFORMATIVE. IT IS AN INVITATION TO OUR SOULS, A MYSTERIOUS VOICE REVERBERATING WITHIN, A TUG ON OUR HEARTS THAT CAN NEITHER BE IGNORED NOR DENIED. IT CONTAINS, BY DEFINITION, THE PUREST MESSAGE AND PROMISE OF ESSENTIAL FREEDOM."

—DAVID COOPER, *astrologic sign unknown*

Imagine yourself standing on a ship's deck as you cruise quietly over the ocean at night. Notice how very still and black the water appears. It is impossible to peer into it, making you wonder, perhaps, about how deep it goes or what might lurk just under its surface. Intuitively, looking at its vast, black mysteriousness, you might feel danger. At night it seems that almost anything could jump out of it, causing your imagination to run wild. On moonless nights like these, there won't likely be many volunteers to visit the sea's treasures, not until daybreak at least.

Scorpio is a water sign, so, appropriately enough, studying this element's qualities will give you a hint of Scorpio's complexities. Water often holds its secrets jealously. Similarly, a typical Scorpio manages to mask his or her emotions well, often not giving a clue about the dramas that exist below the surface. As the axiom goes, still waters run deep. Indeed. If a Scorpio needs to defend his position, you will soon discover that the Scorpio depth of feeling can be bottomless, running all the way down to the very floor of the ocean.

Should you want to dissuade Scorpio of an opinion, be aware that Scorpio is a fixed sign. Don't expect your Scorpio to be a pushover, for Scorpios cling tightly to their views. Their depth of feeling is a good quality too; you will never find a more devoted friend or lover. Scorpio is a highly discriminating and selective sign and as such Scorpios let few into their inner circle. Once they do, they stand by their intimates through thick and thin.

At times Scorpios can seem a little stubborn and resistant to change, even though this is the sign that governs transformation and evolution. Oddly enough, Scorpios do not like change at all—they would much rather keep things as they are, just "so." As a fixed sign, Scorpio's talent is not in being flexible or adaptable (those qualities belong to mutable signs of Pisces, Gemini, Virgo, and Sagittarius) but rather in steadfastly remaining true-blue to goals. Scorpio's role will be to remind the rest of us not to forget our commitments. Your sense of purpose and self-discipline are inspirational, dear Scorpio, and it is evident in everything you do. It is a big factor in your success in your career, personality, and in your relationships.

Now imagine the vast ocean suddenly provoked by wind and rain. Watch the deep waves move in a series of fairly quick, undulating rhythms. Imagine rough, high seas with swells that would make a grown man shake with terror. Notice the formation of furious whirlpool eddies capable of swallowing not only a human being but also an entire ship. Imagine this and you have encountered another facet to the inner emotional power of a Scorpio. Like a hurricane or tidal wave, Scorpio will not submit easily to efforts to be tamed or confined. While scenes of a Scorpio in a whipped-up emotional frenzy are rare, you can be sure that a deep passion swirls just beneath their cool and calm exterior, whether you see it or not.

We are still looking out upon the imaginary ocean, and the fearsome storm has cleared. The Sun now warms the water gently. The scenes (and the emotional environment within Scorpio) will now change dramatically. The water is now filled with frothy whitecaps, bright and inviting, similar to a scene in an Impressionist painting. The water, which only recently seemed terrifying, now looks enticing with sensuousness that beckons one to take a quick skinny-dip. Reflecting the sky like a clean mirror, the ocean is now a brilliant azure blue and sports a clear, translucent surface.

Standing on the edge of a boat as you survey the scene's beauty, instead of fear you feel exhilaration. If you squint hard to protect your eyes from the glistening water, you might see a school of pretty fish swim by. The storm's rage is gone and the water is peaceful, capable of calming you in ways no other element can do quite as effectively—just like any Scorpio you might know. The sounds near the ocean are just as comforting and refreshing in its near silence and tranquillity except for the occasional ring of the captain's bell, an errant gull cry, or the rapid ripping sound of the boat's flag flapping fast and furiously in the fresh wind. Today the ocean seems as pure as holy water, so different from the swells of yesterday.

The wide range of moods that water can evoke aptly sums up the wide spectrum of Scorpio's emotions. If you know and love a Scorpio, you already sense this to be true. If you are a Scorpio, you know you expect others to dive to the depths of your inner ocean and soar like an eagle to heights they never knew they could scale. When friends or lovers can't quite match your range, you feel frustrated and disappointed. A Scorpio is both the flood and the drought, at once bone dry and drenched—and often nothing in between. Your penchant for extremes is the very quality we love most about you, dear Scorpio. You, of all the zodiac signs, have deeply passionate feelings. When people meet you for the first time, this part of you never shows. It could take years of knowing you to see just how deep those feelings of yours go and what you are all about.

Though Scorpios don't forget their inner storms after they pass, tending to hold on to those memories tightly, it does seem a bit unfair when Scorpios are labeled resentful or cunning by astrologic texts. Yes, Scorpios can be that way at times but more often than not they are the kindest and most compassionate of signs. As members of the water family they also possess a tremendous capacity for insight and sympathy. Just looking into a Scorpio's large and soulful eyes usually gives them away, for it is easy to see their good, true heart and their noble intentions.

Challenge seems to bring out the very best in Scorpios. Scorpio is born at the time of the year in the Northern Hemisphere when leaves fall and nourish the land with fertile compost. In late October, days grow dark, the sky broods and is moody with dark streaks of purple, and the Earth rests and rejuvenates. Like Persephone, Scorpio plunges down into the under-world to live for a while and then re-emerges, stronger than before, after a period of meditation or perhaps a struggle with inner, conflicting needs.

Being the sign of extremes, Scorpios can choose which path to take to make use of their powerful energies. A small number of underdeveloped Scorpios sink to the bottom by choosing a life of crime (your ruler, Pluto, represents the dark underworld and challenges), but a far greater number of you soar like an eagle to the mountaintops. You do this by using your awesome strategic powers and masterful intelligence to accomplish feats of great significance to mankind. Your guardian planet, Pluto, also rules spiritual regeneration and renewal.

Ruled by the eighth house, the entire cycle of birth-death-rebirth seems natural. Scorpio is often thought to be a religious sign, usually capable of finding a deep reservoir of strength from within their spiritual beliefs. Being closer to the mysteries of death, Scorpio seems to understand life in a way that eludes the other signs. Scorpio is a sign that is often curious about religion and philosophy and often enjoys learning about other people's spiritual insights and odysseys. While Sagittarius is interested in learning philosophy in an intellectual way, Scorpio gravitates to it in a vastly more intuitive, instinctual way. The water signs often know things without knowing why they do—they just do.

## SYMBOLS

The astrologic symbol of Pluto is one of two glyphs. Some astrologers use a large capital "PL" encapsulated into one symbol, representing the first two letters of the planet's name or the initials of its discoverer, Percival Lowell. The other symbol astrologers use to depict Pluto is a cross with an upturned crescent above, and a circle floating in the cup-shaped crescent. In astrology the use of a cross always means "matter." The crescent is read as "emotion" or "soul," and the circle expresses "spirit." The symbol suggests that the soul and spirit triumph over matter, as is fitting for a planet that rules transformation. Matter forms the foundation of Pluto's symbol, becoming a necessary pedestal for spirit to perch upon. In ancient times, before Pluto was discovered, Mars was considered Scorpio's ruler, and to this day is Scorpio's secondary ruler.

The symbol of your sign, Scorpio, is an M with the final slash of the glyph pointing upward with an arrow. Some astrologers feel that the raised arrow suggests the tail of the scorpion pointing upward, ready to strike. Scorpios are known for their memory; they never forget a transgression. If you rile a Scorpio by wronging him, know that he will find a way to get you back. Some astrologers feel that the glyph's raised arrow symbolizes a serpent ready to strike; this suggests wisdom, for many cultures associated snakes with special insight or knowledge. Alternatively, the arrow could also be thought of as a phallic symbol. Every sign rules one part of the body, and yours happens to be the reproductive organs. This is appropriate because of Scorpio's natural governorship of the eighth house of the horoscope, ruling not only sexuality but also the entire birth-death-rebirth cycle.

Scorpio is the only sign that has three symbols, and each sums up what you are all about in its own way. All the symbols are sometimes a little bit scary to others because all three are creatures that defend their territory aggressively. The symbols are the scorpion, the snake, and the eagle (or phoenix). Like scorpions, Scorpios are known to use their sting, but the truth is that they do so only when they feel deeply threatened and only to protect the very future of their species. For this purpose, namely the safety of species, the scorpion is willing to give up its own life. It is a well-known fact that by using their sting scorpions will perish in the process, so the creature does not resort to this action without perceiving the situation as one of great imminent danger. Thus, revenge is often a self-sacrificing act for Scorpions and is not in their long-term interest. The vengeful side of lesser-evolved Scorpios is often a self-inflicted wound, not very productive but a way of acting out inner rage that seems to have no available channel of release. Evolved Scorpios harness the energy of their rage and direct it to the common good, such as through community programs designed to correct an injustice.

The snake is an interesting symbol because it reminds us of the Garden of Eden and the sexual side of Scorpio, the part that echoes the vast inner regenerative and reproductive strength of your sign. The snake sheds its outer skin regularly, continually becoming transformed and renewed. In mythology, the symbol of the snake is fascinating because some ancient cultures believed it to hold great wisdom. Please refer to "The Myths of Scorpio and Pluto" for more detail.

Last there is the phoenix, rising from the ashes of defeat. It symbolizes the hope of Scorpio and of all of mankind that no matter how dark things get, strength and determination will always surface to overcome forces of darkness. When Scorpios are down for the count they, like the phoenix, always find a way to rise up again, out of the depths of destruction. Of all the twelve astrologic signs, Scorpio and Aries are thought to be the most determined not to give in to failure. Scorpio has always been associated with deep, intuitive, and even instinctual wisdom and also with mystical, supernatural powers.

## PLANETARY INFLUENCES

If you are a Scorpio, you are also able to find alternate uses for available resources in very original ways. After all, your ruler, Pluto, is called the planet of "hidden treasures" or "unearthed wealth." Your sign holds sway over things that move from darkness to light and you have a talent for uncovering latent, hidden energies and treasures and finding ways to unleash their fullest powers. You also have a way of discovering secrets and making the most of those as well!

An interesting point about your affiliation with Mars as a secondary ruler is that it often brings much physical noise to the life around you. Mars rules both Scorpio and Aries. But in Aries, the energy is expressed more directly, spontaneously, and rapidly. In Scorpio, energy is expressed in a more sustained and less outward manner; it tends to circulate in a more subtle, hidden way, beneath the surface. It is more focused and intense than Aries' energy too, with an ability to sustain for a longer period because of your capacity for endurance.

Yet there are similarities between Aries and Scorpio. Both signs are well suited to engaging in any strenuous endeavor that requires much faith and determination to succeed, from literally going into battle to succeeding in any effort that requires one to overcome much resistance, such as a job in sales.

Inside every Scorpio is often a little rebelliousness that can't quite be contained. This can be a good trait if expressed properly because it causes Scorpio to question authority rather than to submit to it blindly. There is a harmless feisty side to Scorpio that is indicative of inner strength. Parents of Scorpio kids can help their child direct his overabundance of inner energy without stomping on his spirit or letting it run wild. Scorpio's tendency to act up is often part of a self-contained personality that refuses to be led by others. Of course there are Scorpios who simply drive themselves over the far edge of the cliff, but if their rebellion is channelled correctly, it can indicate an emerging, self-directed, entrepreneurial spirit. To take on big risks in life, one's personality has to have a little bit of an edge.

## Cosmic Gifts

Your ability to breathe life into endeavors and relationships, sometimes even long after others have given up on them, is connected to this theme too, dear Scorpio. This is one of your finest and most extraordinary talents. You see potential in situations others fail to see and, being a savvy, clever, and resourceful sign, you seem to know instinctively how best to stage a rebirth. This is an important quality. For example, on a large scale, it's the picture of a leader who is able to bring a dying company back to a position of strength. On a personal scale, this talent could be seen as a husband's realization that to save his marriage he must turn over a new leaf. Once a Scorpio has set his mind on any goal, his follow-through is impressive. No matter how difficult the goal is to achieve, Scorpios' fixed nature makes them plow forward to see it to completion.

Your ability to endure and ever transform is very helpful when facing a
health crisis. Pluto often gives this sign a remarkable ability to heal their
bodies, sometimes much to the surprise of their doctors, who thought the
case was hopeless. This also relates to rebirth from an impossible situation. Scorpios often find ways to rebound miraculously because their
inner reserves are that strong. When a Scorpio trains his mind on achieving something big, nothing will stop him—not fatigue, not physical or
emotional pain, not lack of funds (as a Scorpio, you will find them if you
need them). You are the sign of enormous self-determination, the original
comeback kid. Pluto is the "higher octave" of Mars, bringing the energy
of Mars to a more refined state. Instead of exhibiting Mars' way of pushing energy rapidly outward and competitively onto the world as Aries
would, your co-rulership of Pluto gives your energy a different edge,
allowing you to draw your energy inward and to kindle a remarkable
transformation within yourself.

You also know when to cut your losses, because in controlling power, one
of your gifts is to know what to eliminate. Concentrating your energy is
important, for as anyone knows, being overloaded is often not productive.
Pluto rules trash, waste, loss, decay, evacuation, and elimination. Pluto's
pure power covers the extremes of the spectrum, from atomic energy,
passion, and sexuality to metamorphosis, procreation, purification, and
reproduction. Besides the reproductive organs, other parts of the body
that Scorpio rules are the organs of elimination, the colon and the bladder.
Harking back to Pluto, your guardian planet advises you to give up what
you don't need in order to focus your energies best.

As any creative person will tell you, in the chaos of creation, a certain
amount of waste comes as part and parcel of the birth of anything new.
Scorpios, in their intensity, sometimes have trouble eliminating and
offloading their passions or anger, but with a little practice and enlightenment this can be solved. You have a strong ability to reinvent yourself in
many ways. As a matter of fact, Scorpios are said to experience three sep-

arate chapters in their lives, each radically different from the others. Whether spread equally over the course of a Scorpio lifetime or coming in quick succession, these chapters are a testament to Scorpios' ability to deal well with endings and to know intuitively when it is time to start a brand-new phase.

## RELATIONSHIPS

When we study the axis of Scorpio and its opposite sign Taurus, we realize that both signs represent the human concept of desire in different ways. Taurus stands for personal desire, but Scorpio signifies and focuses on shared desire between two persons or two or more entities, whether in a physical, sexual, personal, or business sense. One of Scorpio's talents is to find a way to share available resources, working collaboratively to create something new and beneficial to all parties involved, and to the world. Few people can laser-beam energy in as strong and concentrated a way as Scorpio can. Thus, Scorpio will always be one of the signs most closely associated with the creation of new life.

Of course, all this focused energy can and does tend toward obsession. In love, you can be possessive and even jealous, which, depending on the point of view of your sweetheart, can be charming or maddening. Scorpio expects an all-or-nothing kind of devotion from partners because that is what they give. If you fall in love with a Scorpio, you will soon find that he or she loves you back with an intensity that few signs can match. Indeed, it is likely to be the kind of love that inspires legends. The love you will receive from Scorpio will be unforgettable. Perhaps you, as the object of a Scorpio's love, will be encouraged to give in kind.

You may have wondered why Scorpio is known to be the sexy, magnetic sign. Sexy Scorpios come in all shapes and sizes, but they have one thing in common: an inner confidence that is detectable ten feet away. The nice part is that any Scorpio can create this aura, not only the ones who are born good-looking. If you are a Scorpio, you know you can draw people to you in a rather strong, magnetic way even though your sweet "prey" (meant in an affectionate way) aren't quite aware why they are so compelled to be with you. Your innate sexuality, although subtle, is always whirling below the surface, pulling others in with a strong undertow.

Scorpio, you love sex and it shows in many subtle ways: in your manner, your laugh, even the way you lightly touch someone on the shoulder. One of your most memorable qualities is your pair of bedroom eyes, capable of melting anyone in your line of sight. That famous penetrating Scorpio gaze is quite legendary and alluring (in a male or a female), capable of getting you just about anything you want. Use your power well, dear Scorpio!

A Scorpio in a loveless, sexless marriage is probably in the worst possible situation. Sex is important to this sign. After all, you are ruled by the eighth house of sex and you do have a need to express passion. Yet to Scorpio love is forever. If Scorpios find themselves married to someone who has become distant, it can be a tough situation indeed. No matter how difficult it would be to bring your mate closer, it is worth a try, even if this means seeing a counselor.

Some Scorpios may choose to sublimate their awesome sexual powers for use in creative projects. You seem to prove true what has been said by social scientists: that creative people have much more sexual energy than the rest of the population. (Not surprisingly, Picasso was a Scorpio.) Whenever Scorpios throw themselves into their work with characteristic single-minded purpose, their creativity has enormous potential for greatness.

A Scorpio's need to merge, intellectually, physically, and emotionally, with another person is always exceptionally strong. In business, it leads to deal making and we will discuss those applications in a moment, but let's discuss personal relationships first. Once Scorpios are sure they're in love, they will almost always want to "possess" the other person. As a Scorpio, chances are you will be ready to make the big commitment fairly soon. If your sweetie isn't ready, you will reject his plea to allow him to continue to play the field while you both date. When you are sure about a lover he had better be sure about you. This is part of the all-or-nothing devotion that is so much a part of your Scorpio personality. If you are smitten you will agree to wait a while, but only up to a point. After that, you are likely to shout "I'm outta here!" and once you do, nothing will bring you back.

Protecting your privacy seems to be an opposing personality trait, yet both qualities exist side by side—your need for privacy and your need to partner wholeheartedly and completely (once you have decided on someone). As a Scorpio you know you prefer to have your dear one around you in your everyday life most of the time. However, Scorpio is a taciturn sign, so you feel no need to make idle conversation. In fact, you find small talk pointless and a waste of energy. It is typical of Scorpios to lock themselves in their den with the door closed for hours on end. Or to bury their heads in a book or newspaper, barely murmuring a "Good morning" or "How was your day?" to their mate. (Sound familiar?) When Scorpio does communicate, it is often with a nod, a smile, a grunt, a lifted eyebrow, or hand signals, but not words.

Your lack of interaction could make your sweetie think you don't care about him or want him around, but this couldn't be farther from the truth. You do care—actually quite deeply. You just don't show it too well! Scorpio, you have to admit that you do like to be alone a great deal of the time. Too much social activity feels draining, so before long you'll start to beg off the invitations to find the time to recharge and regenerate yourself. This isn't a good or bad trait—it's just what it is.

To understand your thinking here, know that Scorpio considers information to be a precious commodity, something of great value, not to be shared or treated casually. As a result you give out data only on a "need to know" basis, and even then it is doled out skimpily. This taciturn side, the side that keeps you mum in order to retain some semblance of control over your life, can be hard for other signs to understand, especially in matters of love and friendship. Your quiet side is understood only by those who have the same tendencies you do, but if you are dealing with a chatterbox Gemini, for example, a sign that is an open book, your need for distance could cause conflict and hurt feelings. A Gemini lover may accuse you of the sin of omission—not of saying something untrue, as Scorpio is usually quite insistent on truthfulness, but of deliberately withholding information to gain some sort of advantage. This can happen in your relationship with just about any sign—you do have a very different slant on "information management."

There is no doubt that you like to keep your distance from the rest of humanity much of the time. This seems so much like your ruling planet, Pluto, which is found in the far regions of our solar system, so far away that it seems almost as if it is spinning alone in its own universe. Likewise, Scorpios want to prevent being overly influenced or contaminated by other signs, perhaps to retain their purity of purpose and a strong integrity within themselves. Apparently this requires a great deal of vision and inner strength. Your intense need for privacy also fits your overall personality description because your sign rules, among other things, passion, sexuality, and reproduction, also a rather intimate and private portion of life. Scorpio is not known to be a promiscuous sign when it comes to life, love, and sexuality. In fact, Scorpio is fiercely faithful.

The area of secrets and confidentiality relates to the subject of privacy and comes under the domain of Scorpio in a horoscope. If you have a secret and tell it to a Scorpio, you are safe, yet they won't tell you their secrets. You've heard the joke: "I can't tell you or I'd have to kill you"? It *is* something like that. Scorpio takes any and all confidences and secrets very seriously. Tell Scorpios they can tell no one, and under threat of physical pain they will not divulge your secret. And if you divulge theirs, forget it. Your friendship is over. They will have difficulty ever trusting you again. It is often true that to Scorpio your revelation of the secret is worse than anything the secret could contain. We know that sexual fidelity is very important to Scorpio. Vows are taken very seriously by this sign. Keep in mind that Scorpio is a fixed, loyal sign, given to keeping its word and to insisting on complete truthfulness.

Recall too, that on the other hand, Scorpio is a sign that enjoys being in the thick of power. It is also a fairly practical and street-smart sign, its members dealing quite well with reality, in other words knowing what can and can't be changed. At the same time, when Scorpios give their word, it is forever. In love and in business, the signs that are most compatible with you are other water signs (Pisces, Cancer, or Scorpio) or with the rock-solid, practical earth signs (Taurus, Capricorn, or Virgo). Earth signs would attractively steady your highly charged energy, while water signs would practically be able to read your mind in a very fluid, instinctive way and make you feel in sync. Water signs really are best, with earth following right behind. Keep in mind that you should look at your whole chart, for there could be reasons to consider nearly any sign of the zodiac compatible, depending on your unique configurations.

In business, Scorpio has perfected the art of the deal and is also very cognizant of the need to maintain and secure territorial boundaries. Scorpio's motto in business is "To suspect everyone and trust no one." Don't laugh; they live the motto. Even though the average Scorpio is quite high-strung, you would never know it; they play poker well, having practically raised it to a science. If you are a Scorpio, you know you don't blink thanks to nerves of steel, which help you deal with enormous pressure. The ancients knew that Scorpio could withstand much pain on the path to success in life—on any level, be it physical, emotional, mental, or financial. This is true because of your co-ruler, Mars; the warrior planet gives you determination that does not quit.

## FINANCE

The eighth house is Scorpio's natural part of the horoscope, the house that rules death and renewal but also financial affairs other than those related to salary and earned income, specifically legacies, loans, royalties, commissions, mortgages, insurance, and taxes. This emphasis on "other people's money" explains why this sign produces some of the zodiac's finest deal makers and negotiators. If you are a Scorpio, chances are you are blessed with a capacity to be quite shrewd and street smart. You are known to do your homework before coming to the bargaining table, bringing along a whole dossier of information on your proposed partner (or opponent). Scorpio leaves nothing to chance.

You know that revealing how much you want something gives away your power, something Scorpio is not about to do. You are marvelously good at masking any kind of jitteriness, instead projecting a calm exterior yet at the same time a strong intensity, perfectly blending intent and desire. For sure, Scorpio is a sign that understands not only raw, untamed power but also the need for control of that power. You have nerves of steel and are always willing to get up from the table and walk away nonchalantly, even if you want the deal badly. This is how you usually get what you want. Your ruler, Pluto, rules vastly powerful multi-faceted global companies, and when your ruler is active in a chart, there is usually some huge corporate Medici at play in your life. Working with powerful people or entities does not throw Scorpio; in fact, you like it, and you may find yourself involved with large companies all your life.

Although money and deal making are important, the key element to Scorpio is garnering respect. Water signs are signs of spirit, so the emotions enveloping the situation are just as important (or more so) than the attainment of money. Scorpios will walk away from the bargaining table if it becomes apparent that the other person is not showing proper respect and deference to them and their party. At that point the game has suddenly

become pointless. If this happens, Scorpios are apt to pick up their mar-
bles suddenly and leave, content that there are other fish in the sea to try
to reel in because this deal is not worth the trouble.

Society tries to keep innovation at bay by setting up obstacles to test one's
resolve. Most Scorpios feel it is worthwhile to try to persuade VIPs to
look at their situation as an individual one that exists outside the general
rule. Though the saying "Rules are meant to be broken" is often true, this
doesn't mean you enjoy breaking the law. Scorpio is a sign very involved
in the whole human mediation of proper crime and punishment. This is a
very positive typical Scorpio viewpoint, for it means that Scorpios feel
intuitively that they can change just about anyone's mind if the argument
is presented in an appropriate and persuasive manner. A true Scorpio
keeps alive all his optimistic expectations and options. Who has not been
in a business situation with a novel idea that is met with plenty of opposition
that seemed not to make sense? Scorpio's ability to succeed in the face of
all odds is legendary.

Related to this concept is your ability to set up your own yardstick of
success, dear Scorpio. Your sign must have coined the term *personal best*.
Scorpios don't like to be compared to others but rather to themselves,
ever trying to outdo whatever victories or breakthroughs they have
achieved previously. This quality means that they are less likely to be
influenced by prevailing attitudes but instead listen to the dictates of their
own heart. Scorpios are often amused when other people feel compelled to
give feedback, compliment or criticism, on their performance. Inside, they
are probably musing, Who died and left you boss? Who are you to tell me
about *my* performance? This awesome confidence and self-containment
will help you achieve much. You are less likely to go on an emotional roller
coaster, where your stock rises and falls with other people's changing
appraisals. You zoom forward with your eyes firmly fixed on your goal
and you know that what you think of yourself counts most.

You are fiercely competitive too. Scorpio never hands over power willingly; their mantra is "Power is never given; it has to be seized." Scorpios' ability to set their own terms, standards, and goals rather than allowing their competitor to set them allows them to win. Being competitive and at the same time one's own person may seem like a contradiction of terms, but both fit quite neatly side by side in the Scorpio persona.

Not being a talkative sign can be quite an advantage in that few can figure out what you are thinking. You will get to know everything there is to know about the other person as they chatter on, but they will rarely know the smallest details about you. Superb listeners, Scorpios pay attention not only to others' words but also to their body language and facial expressions. Your sign rules the roots that go under the earth and all things hidden from view, and this makes you shrewd and intuitive. Your nose is sensitive to what's going on around you. This is a quality you use daily, personally, in relationships, and in your career. Scorpios make master detectives or investigative reporters, excelling in any field that requires that one makes a discovery, because they have a sixth sense about knowing when things don't seem to be adding up. This same talent helps Scorpios make scientific discoveries because they see missing links under the surface. Your acute sensibility warns you if others are not telling the truth. Should you discover this is the case, you will be especially determined to get to the bottom of the situation to uncover whatever has been concealed, no matter how long it takes. For sure, Scorpio has incredible endurance and patience.

Don't think you can get away with deceiving a Scorpio, because you can't—they will catch you every time. But that is not all. It isn't only their ability to see detail that makes Scorpios shine, but it is the way they understand how people tick. Human motivation is their specialty. Virgos might have a slight edge over Scorpios in spotting small clues and details, but Scorpios are better at putting "two and two together" once they find those clues.

## CAREERS

There are many professions that bring out the best Scorpio traits and talents. Scorpio rules the sphere of detective work, spying, and subversive and concealed activity, as well as central intelligence. (Incidentally, Fox Mulder and James Bond have classic Scorpio traits.) Scorpios also make great policemen or other law-enforcement officials. District attorney, prosecutor, judge, or lawyer are all suitable careers too. Scorpio attorneys are said to be particularly persuasive in their opening and closing arguments because they address succinctly the key arguments that matter most to the jury.

Jobs that demand courage and the ability to sustain physically demanding situations are perfect for you too, as well as those that require an ability to pare down and prioritize. Accordingly, think about a career in sales or, because you have such self-discipline and courage, a career in the armed forces.

The worlds of both business and government defense would value Scorpio's talent as a strategist. Like the champion chess player or the general about to enter a battle, you plan carefully by considering all the moves of your opponent ahead of time. Scorpios do nothing without great preparation.

Your sign's dominion over the eighth house makes you talented with any activities that involve making a profit. You could be good at raising venture capital, managing large budgets, negotiating deals, working with tax and other financially oriented laws, and other such activities. Consider banking, estates, trusts, insurance, accounting, tax law, real estate, or working in the stock market, as these are areas you might enjoy and excel at.

Another career path Scorpio is strongly linked to is the medical profession, due to the strong transformational ability of your ruler, Pluto, and its link to the healing arts. The eighth house, being the house of endings and renewal, rules surgery (the doctor removes the part of the body that is no longer needed). Thus, in consideration of the sign's co-ruler, Mars, the planet that rules sharp instruments, Scorpios often make superb surgeons. All parts of medicine are likely to be favorable areas for you. Scorpios make good chemists, pharmacists, biologists, biochemists, researchers, diagnosticians, pathologists, obstetricians, fertility specialists, radiologists, and acupuncturists. Don't forget the realm of the mind, either, as Scorpio is superb at understanding human motivation. The careers of psychologist, psychoanalyst, and hypnotherapist would also be excellent.

Consider work in the security industry, whether as a surveillance specialist, locksmith, or bodyguard. Scorpios can excel in the mining industry, unearthing valuable metals, ore, fossil fuels, or gemstones, an echo of Scorpio's leader, Pluto, which rules what is hidden or underground. Finally, your water-sign element brings success as a wine, liquor, or beverage merchant, or working in any area of the cruise-line industry.

## BODY, MIND, AND SPIRIT
Scorpios find time alone quite energizing and a necessary step to get centered from time to time. Gifted with a high metabolism and plenty of strength (as I said, your co-ruler is Mars, the active warrior planet), Scorpios need strenuous outlets for their considerable energy. Jogging, sprinting, or training for a marathon could allow you a peaceful oasis in the midst of a busy day. Choose a workout that allows you to set your own course and work at your own pace. Weight lifting might interest you too. Although you're highly competitive, in the health and fitness arena, you aren't known to be too concerned with how you stack up against others. You work to please yourself, which is a quite healthy attitude.

Make no mistake, with a ruler like Pluto—the great and powerful transformer—Scorpios are quite robust and blessed with remarkable endurance. Pluto is also called the planet of obsession. You have been known to drive yourself too hard because of the very high expectations you have of yourself.

Be sure to give yourself enough rest, dear Scorpio, and try not to get so wound up with your work that you skip meals.

Looking and feeling sexier while making love could motivate you to stay fit and healthy all your life. You generally don't crave rich foods or sweets. In fact, the simpler and plainer the diet, usually, the better. Some Scorpios have a delicate stomach, so that might explain why you gravitate toward classically and simply prepared dishes. With this diet and so much exercise, you usually manage to stay slim.

Astrologically, the part of the body that Scorpio (and Pluto) rules is the reproductive glands, bladder, and rectum, and therefore these can sometimes become areas of concern. This can translate into prostate or testicular difficulties for men, for example, or with reproductive organ (ovaries, uterus) problems for women. Having regular checkups is important, for the problems can be identified quickly. It is probably a good idea for Scorpio women to choose to give birth in a hospital rather than a birthing center, should the need for medical advice arise suddenly during labor. Generally, however, your sign is a strong one, dear Scorpio, so you certainly have the inner reserves to overcome nearly any obstacle.

## SUMMARY
Scorpio is a sign that is all about power and the containment of and control over it. This comes from your guardian planet, Pluto. You do not waste energy; instead, you focus it sharply on whatever you train your mind upon. This is why Scorpio accomplishes so much and why you seem to emit energy from a powerhouse within. Instead of squandering energy (as some signs do) Scorpios hold it in and dole it out gingerly, with forethought and care. Other signs have trouble keeping up with you because, like the element, plutonium, you never seem to run out of power. Like plutonium you can't bury, burn, or destroy your energy, and it's been well documented that your sign's brand of determination could blast through concrete walls. Many Scorpios are very exacting perfectionists too, because they like things done thoroughly and well.

Scorpio's strength will always be in the emotional realm. Of the other fixed signs, Leo radiates creative energy, Taurus has the ability to take money and build endeavors of material strength, Aquarius contributes to the world in terms of innovative and scientific ideas. Scorpio's talent is in laser-beaming emotional, spiritual energy, and as such, it is the most mysterious. Scorpios' ability to hold a grudge for years or to get revenge is well documented. At the same time, their ability to make a promise or commitment that stands the test of time, no matter what unexpected obstacles fall their way, is also very much part of Scorpios' persona.

# THE MYTHS OF
# SCORPIO AND PLUTO

October is the time of the year in the Northern Hemisphere (where all the myths of astrology spring from) when the Earth begins to darken. The trees lose their leaves and begin to nurture the Earth. In ancient nature-religions it was thought that in the autumn the gods or goddesses start to spend time in the underworld and that spring would not return until the gods and goddesses returned to Earth too.

Appropriately for Scorpios, a sign that rules the cycle of life, death, and birth, the holidays of Halloween (October 31) and all Soul's Day (November 1), are celebrated by many cultures at the same time of the year as their birth. The first known celebration of Halloween was the Feast of Samhain Eve, a Celtic holiday, which was a time when the curtain that separated the living and the dead was thought to have been lifted, allowing free access between the two worlds. In Latin America, there are also holidays during the first two weeks of November (also within the Scorpio time period) that commemorate and honor the dead.

In most myths, heroes have to prove their courage and determination. No journey was thought to be as scary or perilous as that of a visit to the underworld (or "the world of the dead"). Hades, king of the underworld (symbolized by Pluto), never welcomed visitors, and those who did make a trip to see him never returned—at least that was the case for most. Anyone who managed to come back was surely deemed a hero.

## PERSEPHONE AND HADES

The story of Persephone is filled with symbolism, and it seems to echo so much of the themes of Scorpio. Persephone was the sole daughter of Zeus and Demeter. Zeus, of course, was the most powerful of all Olympian gods, ruler of heaven and Earth, the gods, and all humans. Zeus's wife was the goddess of fertility and harvest. Hades, god of the underworld, eyed the lovely Persephone, who was a virgin, and quickly fell in love with her. It didn't take long for Hades to decide that she should be his wife. One day when she was out playing in the meadow among the flowers, he abducted her and brought her to the underworld.

In another account of the same myth, Hades appears in a chariot driven by four black horses racing across the plain with thundering force. Hades grabs Persephone with one arm and deflowers her then and there, leaving the field scattered with petals of every color. At the time of the abduction, Persephone was with a companion. She cried out for help, hoping that either her friends or her mother would hear her but, according to the tale, Hades had acted so quickly that nobody saw the incident and consequently no one was able to help her. For the record, it seems that Zeus, Hades' brother (and Persephone's uncle), knew about the proposed abduction before it took place but didn't do anything to prevent it. After Hades grabbed Persephone the chariot disappeared into a mysterious opening in the Earth, which quickly swallowed them up without a trace.

When Demeter, Persephone's mother, arrived to pick up her daughter from the meadow and didn't find her there, she became terribly distraught. Over the next nine days, Demeter searched all corners of the Earth for her daughter, not stopping to eat or sleep. Demeter was naturally quite upset—furious, actually—and at the time she still had no idea what had happened. In her path she was destroying crops, land, and cattle, searching everywhere for her daughter. It soon became apparent that if Demeter kept this up, the Earth would be left completely barren — she was on a rampage and, stopping at nothing, she soon would destroy all mankind.

Demeter finally found out from Hecate, the goddess of the dark Moon, that Persephone had been abducted, but couldn't be sure by whom. Demeter and Hecate consulted the Sun god, Helios, who sees everything through his brilliant light. He confirmed that it was Hades who abducted Persephone and told Demeter exactly what had happened. Demeter was horrified, and although Helios tried to persuade Demeter to accept her daughter's fate as the bride of Hades, she would have none of that.

In fact, Demeter refused to go back to Mount Olympus. She was also enraged because she suspected that her husband, Zeus, had had an opportunity to prevent the abduction. Turning herself into a mortal, she roamed the Earth, forbidding the Earth to bloom in fruit, vegetables, or herbs. After a year of famine, Zeus realized that he would have to step in and do something dramatic to save the Earth. If Demeter continued on her present path all living things would die, and there would be no mortals to adore the gods. Zeus was clearly worried.

First, Zeus tried sending a whole series of gods to reason with Demeter, but to no avail. She steadfastly refused to make any deals until she had her daughter back. In the end, Zeus finally realized that Demeter was not going to give in. Therefore, he sent Hermes, messenger to the gods, to see Hades to negotiate on his behalf. Hades agreed to release Persephone as long as she had not yet tasted the food of the dead. Persephone had been so sorrowful that she had refused to eat.

Just before she was to leave the underworld (probably feeling quite happy and relieved), Hades tricked Persephone by coaxing her to eat a single pomegranate seed. (Some versions of the myth differ at this point,

saying that Hades' gardener stepped forward to report that she had
already eaten seven pomegranate seeds during her stay.) No matter which
version of the myth you accept, all accounts agree that anyone visiting
Hades could not leave if they have tasted food from the dead—period. As
you see, there was suddenly a big problem.

Rhea—mother of Zeus, Demeter, and Hades—came up with a solution
that everyone involved agreed to, if reluctantly. Persephone would spend
six months (some versions of the myth say three to four months) in Hades
and spend the balance of the year on Earth with her mother, Demeter.
During the cold months, when Persephone resided with her husband,
Hades, she would rule as his wife, Queen of the Underworld. Demeter
kept her promise to restore the Earth's fertility and she also returned to
her rightful place on Mount Olympus. Also, in accordance with the terms,
during the time Persephone left the living to become Hades' bride in the
underworld, the Earth fell cold and barren until her return in the spring,
when the Earth would warm and all the foliage, fruit, and beauty of life
would return.

Pluto, besides symbolizing rebirth and rejuvenation, also symbolizes loss
and the things that we give up to make room for growth and maturity.
Often when one experiences a strong Pluto transit, something we feel we
cannot possibly live without is torn from us. There could be the death of a
loved one or a loss of a situation (such as a job) or a relationship that has
gone on for a long time and now finishes. Endings are part of life and
although we sometimes feel we cannot go on after experiencing that loss,
we in fact grow stronger because of it.

Additionally, Pluto covers buried and repressed thoughts and ideas that
reside in the subconscious. (Neptune also governs the subconscious, but it
has a different role, that of supervising dreams, inspirations, and aspira-
tions.) In the myth, Demeter gave up her daughter, Persephone, and

experienced terrible loss and pain in the process. Demeter also grieved for her daughter's loss of innocence, thus the myth speaks of the separation of mother and daughter, so necessary if the daughter is to grow into a woman. With Persephone's return both to Demeter and to the living, the myth symbolizes the cyclic spiritual re-awakening, joy, and new life we feel in the spring. When Persephone returned to her mother she was changed, and both mother and child understood that. Like Persephone, the Scorpio nature has an extremely bright side that co-exists with its opposite dark side. Scorpio has the ability to choose which energies will predominate, good or evil.

### ADVENTURES OF GILGAMESH

There is another powerful myth that pertains to the sign of Scorpio, a very old Sumerian tale that dates back to 2100 B.C. and is therefore one of the oldest hero stories known to mankind. It is the adventures of Gilgamesh, which is also recounted in this book, in "The Myths of Aquarius and Uranus." The tale is too long to tell here, but the gist is that Gilgamesh, a Sumerian king, took a journey that required that he cross dangerous territory and mountains guarded by two lions (Leo), a bull (Taurus), and the scary "Scorpion men." The myth focuses on Gilgamesh's ability to test his mettle. After he battled the two lions, he next had to walk through a thirty-six-mile tunnel that had no light what-soever. Coming out of the tunnel's darkness into the land of gods, he was rewarded for his trials and tribulations. He came upon a magical place where glittering jewels hung on the branches of trees. This journey through darkness has been compared to a journey into the depths of Hades, which is prevalent in many later myths and concerns the ability of the character to face inner demons and find meaning in life.

The ancients felt that the only way to wisdom was through experience gained through hardship. Going to the depths of our being can, for some, be a painful experience if one needs to deal with disturbing, private, inner

psychological issues. Yet the strength of Scorpio shows you the way out—
Scorpios have more inner strength than most—and as such, a well of
energy is theirs if and when they need it.

Snakes have always been interesting creatures, and they appear in the
Bible and elsewhere in all kinds of myths and rituals. Snakes regularly
shed their skin each time they grow to renew themselves—an apt symbol
for Scorpio. If you read "Scorpio Personality" you know the snake is one
of three symbols (scorpion, snake, and eagle being the three) most closely
associated with your sign.

## SNAKES AS SCORPIO SYMBOL

In early days of Crete, the snake was thought of as holder of life-and-
death secrets as well as the symbol of sexuality. In other stories, the snake
has wisdom to share, as in the story of Cassandra of Delphi, who was considered a prophet with a gift of foreseeing the future. According to that
myth, Cassandra had been left overnight in error at the sacred temple of
Apollo Thymbrius by her parents. While she slept at night, snakes licked
her ears to purify her soul and give her the gift of prophecy, a gift she was
to keep over her lifetime.

Snakes were also used in religious ceremonies (the link between Scorpio
and religion and spirituality is very strong) because it was thought that
the snake held the secrets of life and death. Snakes' venom was used in
various rituals because it was thought that they could bring on a halluci-
natory state, including the ability to see visions. Some ancients felt that
ingesting snake poison would help heal them. Older cultures also believed
that by ingesting venom one could visit the dead to learn the secrets of
health and healing before returning to the world of the living. The link
between healing and snakes is a persistent theme that comes down to
us to this day; we are reminded of the symbol of caduceus used in the
medical profession, that of a pole being twined by two serpents.

Finally, Scorpio, the second water sign, differs from Cancer, the first water sign, in one very powerful way. Cancer deals mainly with the family and the nurturing of the children, while Scorpio breaks the bond between parent and child (as in the story of Persephone) to form a true and closer relationship with one's mate. The Pluto guardianship of Scorpio stresses the need for oneness through sexuality or merging. This theme of bonding closely with another needs to be controlled; it is as if Scorpios subconsciously realize that, in their intensity of merging with another, they might lose their identity and so they clutch at it dearly, striving for some kind of mastery and control over the situation or relationship.

Sex, pregnancy, birth, and death are silent forces that touch the core of life's mysteries and occur deeply within us. The water that surrounds us in the womb echoes Scorpio's intense and emotional inner life. It harks back to the sexual act itself, perhaps the most intimate and private activity of our lives. Scorpio is considered a "feminine" sign (yielding a negative rather than a positive charge), and as such it increases intuition and the understanding of universal wisdom in Scorpios of both genders. Scorpio's intuition is a survival mechanism that prevails, a deep well to draw from whenever he or she needs it, forever.

# SAGITTARIUS PERSONALITY

## Sagittarius
### November 22–December 21

*Guiding Principle*

"I Aspire"

*How This Sign Feels Joy*

Finds joy in expanding horizons through
travel and the gathering and preserving of
information to ascertain that data is accessible
to all, globally.

*In the New Millennium, Your Contribution
to the World Will Be . . .*

As the philosopher of the zodiac, your role is
to study the rich spectrum of human events
in order to understand the collective human
consciousness. Now, more than ever, your
exceptional ability in this area will be encouraged and admired.

*Quote That Describes You*

"I LOOK . . . NOT INTO THE NIGHT, BUT TO A DAWN
FOR WHICH NO MAN EVER ROSE EARLY ENOUGH."

—HENRY DAVID THOREAU, a *Cancer*

Thinking back to high school or college days, can you remember your favorite teacher? Perhaps it was a college professor who taught you theology, political science, ethics, logic, or sociology. Because of his or her penetrating way of presenting the material, in truth, this teacher could have taught just about any subject to you in just about any grade. Chances are that when you first visited his or her class you didn't have very high expectations, but once you heard this person speak, your attitude changed. You couldn't wait to go back to hear more. He or she probably encouraged you to ask questions you had never considered and then dared you to find the answers. If you are lucky, you may have one or two such teachers in a lifetime. A teacher like this can help you discover latent talents and impart the confidence to develop them to the max. Great teachers pull us out of ruts and shake us up a little. Chances are your favorite teacher is a Sagittarius, for this is a description of what this sign does so well. Inside every Sagittarius is a certain largeness of mind, heart, and spirit that is positively contagious, and completely unforgettable.

Teaching is usually in Sagittariuses' blood. They express this marvelous quality whether in the formal sense, working as a college professor or a mentor or boss to a gifted underling, or in a more informal way as a friend or parent who offers insightful advice and encourages you to see the big picture. Sagittarius will always encourage others to ask the hard questions rather than simply accepting what seems apparent on the surface.

## SYMBOLS

Sagittarius's constellation, found in the Milky Way, is that of the centaur: half man and half horse. Astrologers feel that this symbol encapsulates man's ability to rise above his animal instincts, at the same time retaining some of the animals' superhuman power and strength. Fire signs are renowned as highly intuitive and innovative as well as spirited and creative. In this constellation the centaur holds a bow and arrow and points it upward toward the heavens, indicating the supreme optimism of this sign and the need to keep aiming high to lofty goals. It is true about

Sagittarius that as soon as they reach one goal they are well on their way to attaining another one.

♐ If there were one truth about this cheerful sign's personality, it is that expecting the best can indeed be a self-fulfilling prophecy. The Sagittarius astrological glyph echoes this role as archer, because the glyph is that of an arrow with a cross bar at the bottom. This symbolism seems to represent the eternal struggle between dreams and reality, but it also hints at the awesome power of the warrior in battle. The arrow points upward, thus the warrior is ever sure of eventual victory. If ever there was a sign that said "Yes, I can do it!" it's Sagittarius.

♃ Looking at the symbolism of your ruler's glyph will reveal some very important symbolism of Jupiter and Saturn. Jupiter's glyph is similar to Saturn's, but it is written exactly in reverse (see Saturn's symbol in "Capricorn Personality"). This makes sense because each planet has opposing influences. Saturn restricts and limits, while Jupiter expands and brings abundance. In Jupiter the half-circle (crescent) rises above the cross, meaning that although mind and matter are linked, the mind is able to rise above the material world. Jupiter's role is to expand from the center outward, while Saturn's job is to draw the outward inward, toward the center. Jupiter is big and airy, and Saturn is small and dense.

Jupiter represents the soul's need to grow, improve, and experience more. It also embodies the human need to succeed and, in matters of health, to experience a feeling of well-being. Faith is also part of Jupiter, as the crescent (feelings) rises over the cross of matter. Saturn's glyph is just the opposite—the cross of matter sits above the crescent of the soul. In other words, reality in the material world dominates Saturn's realm, while in Jupiter's sphere faith conquers all. Both needs have to be balanced. For example, Jupiter's growth, if left unchecked, could become grandiose, inflated, and expand out of control. And while Saturn keeps all in the realm of reality by balancing Jupiter's exuberance, if left unchecked

Saturn could deflate too much, too quickly, becoming overwhelmed and depressed—too "stuck"—to be able to move forward.

## PLANETARY INFLUENCES

You are lucky, Sagittarius, for you are ruled by Jupiter, the planet considered to be the great benefactor of fortune, prosperity, compassion, faith, and true happiness. In astrologic lore, Jupiter is the planet that protects and cares like a kindly parent, rewarding hard work, kindness to others, and faith in ourselves, in others, and in our creator. There is also a scientific basis in this role of Jupiter as protector. Scientists tell us that Jupiter has been deflecting harmful asteroids from Earth for years. Its megagravitational field pulls those asteroids off course and deflects them back into space.

Jupiter brings expanded opportunities and lucky breaks by creating fresh opportunities and new contacts. Jupiter generates continual hope in a world filled with trials and tribulations. Jupiter's massiveness coaxes us to think big and also to be more optimistic and enthusiastic. Jupiter will not only increase the favor and generosity other people show us, but it will also indicate the scope and nature of our generosity outward, toward other people in the world, as well.

In matters of health, Jupiter is also known to increase vitality, strength, and radiance as well as resistance to disease, for Jupiter has been attributed to have healing qualities too. For those with a chronic or serious illness, a Jupiter transit to key planets has the ability to bring help in the form of a doctor who is likely to understand your condition, a person who could prescribe the right treatment for relief or a cure. This is truly a mighty planet, and the ancients wrote that Jupiter was able to extend her influence beyond the physical plane and into spiritual realms. Ancient astrologers called Jupiter the planet of faith and miracles, and they saw evidence of this when Jupiter was magnificently aligned with other planets in what astrologers call a rare and special aspect to other planets. With qualities like these for a guardian planet, it is easy to see why Sagittariuses are said to be such powerfully upbeat people.

Earlier, in the chapters devoted to Leo, we discussed the influence of the Sun, Leo's ruler, in the horoscope and in regard to Sagittarius, and we speak of the influence of Jupiter as the sign's guardian planet. Both the Sun and Jupiter are beneficial influences in a chart, and because they share some similarities, it might be easy to confuse the contribution each makes to a horoscope. Let's consider their similarities and differences and see what roles they play.

In a chart, both Jupiter and the Sun have the ability to help each of us find favor from highly placed people in authority and will also encourage good health and strong vitality. Yet the Sun (center of our universe and ruler of Leo) is more individual and personal in its influence, for one of its jobs is to locate unique qualities and quintessential talents. The Sun also helps to build self-confidence. Jupiter's blessings, on the other hand, are thought to arrive through the interaction between you and other people who are willing to help give you a chance to further your goals. Jupiter can also give you special magnetism to attract a romantic attachment, friends, and generally a warm feeling of acceptance. In other words, Jupiter's role is social, bringing fortunate experiences to you from the outside world, while the Sun is personal, allowing us to develop talents to full potential. Jupiter often brings a financial benefit to you too, that, through gifts, cash, or windfalls, will allow you to follow your bliss more easily. Leo's ruler, the Sun, when well positioned, promotes inner confidence and pride in one's uniqueness, which in turn allows you to press forward because you feel you deserve success. When you are confident, others become more willing to help you.

Your ruler, Jupiter, increases good judgment; it is in charge of laws, morals, and ethics, so this planet is also thought to cover the government's role as guardian of the people. On a more personal level, Jupiter helps you build your personal view of the world and your place in it, a view that integrates your hopes and dreams and your spiritual or religious beliefs into a unified personal philosophy of life. Whether created consciously or unconsciously, this philosophy forms the blueprint from which you work, providing you with principles, morals, and ethics you can draw from to guide you in every big decision. This is very special and is sometimes referred to as one's fundamental "character."

## COSMIC GIFTS

A horoscope is a kind of map that not only tells you about yourself but also, in the larger sense, traces mankind's development and progress throughout life. The sign of Sagittarius, in the ninth house of the zodiac, is where man has taken care of his immediate needs related to himself and his parents, siblings, mate, and children. By the ninth house, man has evolved and matured enough to take a broader view of his place in the universe. At this point in development he needs to shape his religious beliefs, make plans for education, and decide about his own morals and ethics. He is getting ready to decide on what his greatest contribution to the world should be, and should he need to read and study more to make that contribution, he gains it here, in this house. The ninth house forms part of the "mid-heaven" point, or the apex, of the chart. This is where leadership qualities start to blossom. Study and scholarship—whether through learning or teaching—would play an enormously important role to your very meditative and essentially intellectually creative fire sign. It's a tall order but one that is ultimately fulfilling.

If you are a Sagittarius, you think big, due to having Jupiter as your ruler. Jupiter just happens to be the largest planet in the solar system, and it is often called "The Great Benefactor" or the "giver of gifts and luck" in a horoscope. Astronomically, if you grouped all the planets in the solar system (excluding the Sun, which is a star) together in one part of the sky, Jupiter would be bigger than all the other planets put together! The massive size of Jupiter, along with the ancient astrologers' association with blessings and fortune, gives Sagittarius a sparkling personality. Sagittariuses are generous, jovial, cheerful, hopeful, inquisitive, risk-taking, and, yes, downright lucky too!

Sagittariuses are known to expand whatever they do, and they extend their knowledge beyond the outer limits of what anyone else thinks or dreams is possible. Your brand of optimism is so fresh and intoxicating that if you could bottle it, people would line up to buy some. At times, everyone wants to be you, Sagittarius, especially in tough times, when your unsinkable attitude keeps people around you buoyed up—and you are there to teach others how to land sunny side up. You bring logic, reason, and scholarship to all that you tackle, and when faced with changing conditions you are flexible enough to keep coming up with alternative plans. It has been said that there is always a crowd around a Sagittarius, listening to his or her every word. Little wonder! Your ideas are well chosen and carefully thought out, and the world can never get enough of them.

Intellectually, you are one of the zodiac's deepest thinkers and greatest philosophers. A creative fire sign, Sagittarius is not afraid to ask the mysterious questions of life, whether in the religious, philosophical, moral, or ethical sense. Sagittarius works hard to dispel glib theories, wanting to see ideas thoroughly fleshed out, for a Sagittarius will always strive for purity of truth and wisdom. Think of yourself as the zodiac's keeper of keys to the libraries of the world, containing all the knowledge of civilization through the ages. You know that those libraries need to be protected and preserved, for they contain the truth of the ages. Maintaining the standards of this knowledge is a tall order, and it's one that Sagittarius does not take lightly. Anyone who has ever written a book knows that a publisher will insist on seeing several concurring sources for information presented in the material. Sagittarius, the sign ruling publishing, understands this kind of factual accuracy at all times.

Most Sagittariuses like to do scholarly work. In fact, astrologers agree that this sign produces "homework people," students and teachers who are highly motivated and involved in their work. Sagittariuses like learning and classroom situations so much that they are known to be the sign that is most likely to come back for advanced degrees, seminars, or refresher courses throughout their lives, no matter how many years have passed since completing their formal education. Their curiosity about the world is broad, deep, and continuous. It is the Sagittarius mother who returns to school at age forty to get her law degree or the Sagittarius worker who quits his boring job and goes back to school for a degree in computer science so he can make an exciting career switch. Sagittariuses will never let a lack of education prevent them from moving forward—they have the will to get it and they find the ways and means, as the whole area of education is lucky for them.

The Sagittarius need for adventure through travel is also very strong. A fire sign needs freedom; it is not an element that is contained. Thus, if you are a Sagittarius you have a strong need to go to where ideas live, flourish, and change. You were born with a deep wanderlust and curiosity about the various continents of the world. Through visits to various cultures your sign matures and grows. The ancient astrologers felt that foreign travel is just another form of becoming educated and represented a valid way to expand one's horizons and to consider new possibilities. If you don't have a set of matching luggage, dear Sagittarius, you should think about saving up for one soon because it's a good bet you will be traveling most of your life.

Ultimately, Sagittarius longs to solve some of life's greatest mysteries. Always in the back of your mind are questions like Where did I come from? Why am I here? What will be my main contribution to my generation? How can I contribute best to the world at large and make sure my time on Earth is well spent? Sagittariuses are always aware that life holds some higher purpose, and finding that good is a pressing need. If a definitive answer is not possible, Sag wants to create a working theory, for now, and test it over time. Even in a cursory first meeting with Sags, it would be hard to miss that special earnestness of purpose that each of them exudes.

Sagittarius is well suited for these academic quests because Sagittarius rules the natural ninth house of the zodiac. This house occupies a special place on the horoscope wheel, for it is the house of the philosopher, teacher, guide, mentor, or sage. That same house rules publishing, broadcasting, international communication in general, and all kinds of higher education and certification. It rules the judicial system, government, spirituality, and international travel and commerce, too. Matters related to morality and ethics are also the domain of this sector of the horoscope.

Sagittarius's polar opposite is Gemini, a sign that occurs in June. Like many opposites, Sagittarius and Gemini actually have many things in common. Looking at Gemini's traits is useful because both Gemini and Sagittarius share the same axis; by contrasting the two, we will learn something about Sagittarius. Like Gemini, Sagittarius is not considered an especially emotional sign. Instead, intellect dominates. Gemini and Sagittarius happen to be mutable signs, so both are quite flexible and versatile and they love to play with a wide variety of ideas. There is no chance that either sign would get stuck on one method, for both are known for their ability to come up with imaginative alternative courses of action, even (or especially) when under stress. When you want someone to think on their feet and come up with fast solutions, call a Gemini or a Sagittarius. If, during the course of an argument or debate, it becomes apparent to either the Gemini or Sagittarius that the idea needs adjustment or refinement, they will adjust that position right away. The prospect of a loss of face does not worry these signs; they simply want the right answer. In fact, the egos of both these signs are attached not to any one truth but to the *process of discovering* that truth. In other words, finding the truth is the fun part. Sagittarius is not prideful, like Leo. This is a critical point, Sagittarius, because without the need to defend your position continually to protect your ego, you free yourself to rework your theories continually as you get feedback and reconsider and refine your position.

Yet there are also some big differences between Sagittariuses and their cosmic partner. Called the zodiac's scribe, or journalist, Gemini collects facts and tidbits of information on a daily basis. Gemini was also given the sole job of naming things in the universe. This is a key role, for unless society has a name for an idea, person, or concept, it tends not to "see" (i.e., perceive) it. Like the reporter on the evening news who reports what happened during the course of the day, Gemini (a current, trendy sign if there ever was one), finds *all* news equally interesting. There appears to be almost nothing Gemini doesn't want to investigate; this sign's job is not to discriminate among the various *kinds* of information it gathers—their job is simply to get it.

Sagittarius, on the other hand, needs to step back and find the symbolism or meaning in the detail that Gemini finds. In the scheme of things, Sagittarius gets to prioritize and make judgments about the material Gemini finds. Thus, if Gemini is the reporter on the scene, Sagittarius is the bureau chief back at the newspaper writing the editorial view. Sagittarius's job is to try to make sense of what happened by putting a philosophical spin on it.

Sagittarius pokes fun at Gemini because Sag feels that Gemini is too scattered, continually darting here, there, and everywhere. Sagittarius says Gemini is too interested in every morsel he hears, reads, or discovers. Sag says: "Gemini, you should focus on one area of interest and stop being a Jack of all trades." Of course there is some merit in this advice. However, Gemini's retort to Sag is that Sagittarius *needs* the detailed information he digs up. Therefore, Gemini says, Sag shouldn't rag on him so much. Further, Gemini points out that Sagittarius can become too theoretical, spending too much time closeted in his ivory tower. Gemini, being the polar opposite of Sagittarius, can see Sagittarius clearly and says he should spend a little time out among the masses, where he (Gemini) circulates in his daily rounds. Gemini's criticism has merit because sometimes Sagittariuses can become so lost in theory that they ignore what is going on around them, even to the point of missing the obvious; at times Sagittarius could use a shot of reality.

Of course both signs are valued. What makes Sagittariuses special is their insistence on making sense of all the information that Gemini finds. Sagittarius pulls data apart, questions everything, and turns things inside out in an effort to find the philosophical truth that overrides the event. Among the options that flow from this process, they meditate and debate, working hard to find and draw the proper conclusions.

In fact, the ancient astrologers felt that it would fall to Sagittarius to delineate and preserve the many different contributions of knowledge by the various civilizations in the world. Sagittariuses weave what they learn into a cohesive whole in order to hear the whisperings of human consciousness over the course of time and geography. They manage the libraries, storing the accumulated knowledge that can be used by anyone for the common good.

Where others might focus on the differences among nationalities and religions, Sagittarius sees similarities. You choose to celebrate differences among the cultures instead of bemoaning them. Your sign understands that as world citizens, united we stand, and divided we fall. Sagittarius, along with Aquarius, is particularly sensitive to the need to stamp out prejudice and to increase tolerance among people the world over.

Sagittariuses increase awareness of their concepts not so much through artistic efforts (Leo's domain) or through commerce (Aries' base), but through publishing papers, commentaries, books, articles, or theses, by lecturing, or through one-on-one encounters during their travels. It is not surprising that Sagittarius, the sign so involved with the weighing of morals and ethics, would also be designated to develop laws and rules of conduct for society. That is a tall order, but nothing is beyond Sagittarius's scope, because with bountiful Jupiter as a ruler, this sign knows that anything can be achieved no matter how awesome the goal.

Reading thus far, have you come to the conclusion that Sagittarius might be a bit of a stuffed shirt? If you think this is a possibility, think again. In fact, this sign can be quite the humorous prankster. Most Sagittariuses are ready to burst someone's bubble at a moment's notice, in the most naughty, devilish—yet adorable—way! Jupiter, Sagittarius's ruler, is a derivative of the word *Jove,* from which the word *jovial* is derived. This jolly, optimistic, and truly happy sign has an enormous potential for laughter—especially the variety that is cleverly ironic or witty in some way.

Sagittarius is a mutable sign and, thus, quite flexible. Mutable signs are the last signs of each season and are said to deal well with transitions. Thus, Gemini ends spring, Virgo ends summer, Sagittarius ends fall, and Pisces ends winter and all share this talent for adaptability and versatility. Mutable signs like yours show their mettle in extreme situations, such as natural disasters. You are so resourceful that chaos doesn't faze you. You are able to think under pressure and continually changing conditions and even lead others to safety. You use this talent all the time in your everyday life but you probably don't give yourself enough credit for it.

The symbolism of all the astrologic signs is based not only on ancient mythology but also on the seasons found in the Northern Hemisphere at the time of the year when the sign appears. (As said elsewhere in the book, the symbolism of the signs applies to people everywhere no matter where they were born or live.) At the end of November through the first three weeks of December, night falls early over the chilly, leafless land-scape. We start to draw indoors as cold winds swirl; by this time of the year in certain regions of the globe, there is no doubt that winter is on the way. It can be a lonely world outdoors, yet as dreary as it is outside, it is bright and cheery inside. It is time to share good food and family tradi-tions, hear new and familiar stories. We take time to read, write notes, cards, and e-mails and re-establish our connections to those we love. It is time to reflect and make plans for the future.

By the time Sagittarius's birthday comes around, many people of the world begin to get ready for the biggest, most luxurious, and most joyful holiday season of the year. Jupiter's rulership of this sign is so appropriate. Lavish displays of food suddenly appear; year-end party invitations show up. Santa Claus, the warm, happy, rotund, jolly, and generous provider of gifts, is a perfect symbol of Jupiter's generosity. Most people shop for gifts mainly through the month of December and are finished by the time of the winter solstice, when the sun enters Capricorn. It is a time to think about the blessings the universe has bestowed, and it is a time to say thank you to one and all who have shown kindness throughout the year.

Many people begin to focus on their own most cherished religious beliefs, principles, and values, which are all Sagittarius qualities. The anticipation of the holiday season brings joy and optimism too, and a renewed effort to link peoples of the world into one family of man, in genuine hope for peace and goodwill. This all makes sense, because Sagittarius teaches that when one man suffers all of mankind suffers, and unless all are protected, all are diminished.

In astrologic symbolism as daylight grows shorter and the night grows in importance, it means there is greater emphasis on the collective (the mass populace) and less on the concerns of the individual. Thus, the collective concerns of society, universality, is paramount in Sagittarius, reaching an all-time high. When the winter solstice arrives at the start of Capricorn on December 21, the shortest day of the year, it marks a turning point, and the days begin to grow longer; the "day force" lengthens and the "night force" shrinks. Emphasis reverses back to the growing emphasis on the individual.

In astrologic lore, each sign balances the qualities of the sign that precedes it. In Sagittarius there is a strong desire to be released from Scorpio's powerful intensity. In Scorpio, feelings are directed inward and are strongly private, but in Sagittarius there is a freer, more outward manifestation of feeling and thought. There is none of the stewing of Scorpio in Sagittarius, and where Scorpio is a somewhat skeptical sign, Sagittarius is trusting and easygoing. Where Scorpio is a loner and taciturn, Sagittarius is sociable and talkative. Power and control are important to Scorpio, but they are not an issue to Sagittarius. Passion and possession mark Scorpio, but Sagittarius wants none of that, instead opting for independence and freedom. And while Scorpio may conceal his motives to protect his position, Sagittarius's motives are clear and almost naively honest.

The interest of Sagittarius in the universality of man can be demonstrated in astronomical terms too. It is said that the middle of our galaxy is found at exactly twenty-six degrees of Sagittarius. Thus, the degrees thought to be at the center of our galaxy—twenty-six Sagittarius—arrive late in that sign, on Sagittarius birthdays that fall on precisely December 18. (Each sign encompasses twenty-nine degrees; after that the constellation moves on to the next sign.) Thus, as we get to the darkest part of the year, within hours of the winter solstice, we are tied to concepts so huge and universal that the only apt symbol for these ideas would be the entire heavens above.

From Earth, the center of the Milky Way is placed at this precise point of twenty-six degrees Sagittarius. The Milky Way, a dense band of 200 billion stars that stretches across the sky in a glittering streak, has been the subject of many myths, including one that calls this lovely sprinkling of stars a road to heaven. This pathway has been said to link the world of dead souls to the world of the living. The Romans gave it its name, Via Lactea, while the Greeks called it Galaxias Kuklos ("Milky Circle"). Plato said it hemmed the two halves of heaven.

There is a lovely tale of the Greeks that calls the Milky Way a stream of divine milk. In the Greek myth Jupiter liked to have affairs with mortal women, which is why Sagittariuses, particularly males, are said to like to sow wild oats in their youth. The sons of Jupiter's indiscretions could be immortal only if nursed by his wife, Juno. However, Juno was not thrilled at the prospect of nursing the illegitimate children of Jupiter's mistresses, and when it came to Hercules, Juno simply refused. Trickster Mercury put Hercules at her breast one night while Juno was sleeping, and when she woke up she pushed the baby away. But it was too late; Hercules had nursed enough to become immortal. When she pushed the baby away, Juno's milk spilled and created the Milky Way for all time. Such a lovely image!

We have been talking about upbeat sides of Sagittariuses, but they do have one small feature that drives everyone around them a little crazy, and that is their tendency to put their foot in their mouth by being too straightforward. Alas, that arrow seems to be ever pointed at someone. Sagittarius, you do have strong opinions and you are also alarmingly frank. Always in a bit of a rush, you don't have the patience to take the time to dress up what you've got to say—it just tumbles forth. Being on the receiving end of Sagittarius's bluntness can be quite painful.

If you are a Sagittarius you know that you can wind up distancing the very people you care about. This could be evidence of Sagittarius's continual need to slip into teaching mode, if only unconsciously. Sag, you simply can't resist improving others. (However, if anyone dares to criticize *you*, you become outraged.) You may be blunt, but you do tend to get results. Those comments always contain a nugget of truth, which is why they are so startling and not easily dismissed. When you aim your arrow it can cut to the quick. However, pals forgive Sagittariuses because they exude a genuine goodwill. Jupiter gives you the ability to be magnanimous, perhaps even generous to a fault. And in relationships of every kind you strive to be fair, even if words just "tumble out" in somewhat the wrong way.

### RELATIONSHIPS

When it comes to romance, you like to maintain your space. As we said, Jupiter, your ruler, loved women and was often so busy romancing them that he had little time to conduct work from his base on Mount Olympus. That's why Sagittarius is prone to sow wild oats for a while before settling down. This tends to be more likely in the males than the females of this sign, perhaps because of cultural conditioning. It is your need for space and variety exerting itself. Not all members of the sign are like this, but many are.

Getting married is a step you would never take lightly or enter into quickly. In fact, you will delay commitment as long as possible. Being tied down to reality or to people or places doesn't interest you, at least initially. Most Sagittariuses get married late in life. Some astrologers go so far as to refer to Sagittarius as the "bachelor sign" because freedom and independence is something you hold dear, just the opposite of Scorpio, a possessive sign that likes to "have and to hold." You are far less emotional than Scorpio and in fact fear that over time you will feel claustrophobic in a relationship. Spontaneity is a Sagittarius must, but you know that marriage and family might restrict individual expression. Sagittarius can feel trapped by *any* pre-existing commitments they make (even business ones), so your sign always, even unconsciously, likes to keep its options open.

Thus, if you are in a good relationship, you will still keep partners waiting as long as possible. But there is another, perhaps overriding, concern delaying your venture into marriage, which is that you want to form a clear idea of your identity first. Many people say that married couples tend to become more like each other over time, so rather than start blending before you even have had a chance to know your true identity, you may choose to marry later, after your personality, and your philosophy, are more sharply defined.

In choosing a partner, you seek an open-minded person with sophisticated tastes and views like yourself. You admire those who have high moral values and strong integrity and who are not prejudiced against other racial or religious groups. You also seek someone who can debate various issues in an exciting way. In that regard you are like your opposite sign, Gemini — you want a stimulating partner. Not surprisingly, many Sagittariuses are attracted to partners who have a vastly different background and, with your eclectic approach to life, that type of partner fits nicely.

Once you do marry, your excellent ability to communicate helps you keep your partnership strong. The fact that you marry later in life also bodes well for future success—by the time you tie the knot you know what you want from the relationship. Happily, when Sagittariuses marry, they tend to stay committed. Sagittarius is a playful sign, so when you finally have your own children you make an ideal parent, too, curious, thoughtful, funny, ever young in spirit. Sagittariuses adore taking their children to places of interest and exposing them to a wide variety of fun activities as well as mentally and culturally enriching exhibits and shows.

Keep in mind that at times you may have to make allowances for your partner. Few people can move at the speed of light, as you do. Ideally, you want a partner who can travel with you and share your wanderlust so that together you can conquer the world. You want to experience Paris in the spring and the snows of Kilimanjaro in the winter, see Asia in the fall and explore Antarctica in the summer. If you look hard enough, dear Sagittarius, this partner does exist, and you can bring along your little ones as well.

In terms of where and how you like to live and your adventuresome instincts, Sagittarius loves the open road. Before tying the knot, many a Sag needs to listen to the call of the wild by going on an adventurous trip or two while they are young and unfettered by children or other responsibilities. The sign of Sagittarius is associated with huge, open spaces, big sky, and other grand features of nature. You tend to resist the confines of being in a crowded city. Too much civilization makes a Sagittarius long to break free. Sagittariuses are always plotting to go on camping or ski trips, safaris, and other adventures that bring them back to nature.

Domesticity is not something that comes naturally to you, no matter what your marital status. You are notorious for slipping out of dreary chores. Oddly, you'll do an entire thesis, working for months, years even, to get a degree, but when it comes to do doing mundane chores like cooking dinner or doing the laundry you'll be missing in action the minute you're asked to help out. Much of your mate's frustration is that you tend to be quite messy. You like to spread out and that comes, again, from Jupiter. The reason you aren't into earthly matters is that your head is often in the clouds, meditating on the truly big matters of life, dear Sagittarius. That's why your sweetie forgives these little indiscretions. If you can find the extra cash, hiring a helper to work with you to tidy up your space would keep lovers' spats about communal neatness to a minimum.

## FINANCE

Financially, your sign's unease with the concept of restriction can make you spend money wildly and extravagantly, and this could create a touchy area in your relationship. There is always a tendency toward extravagance. You often wonder, How much can I push my luck? This is due in part to the influence of Jupiter expanding everything it touches. You have a certain optimistic attitude that your bank balance will always be replenished no matter what you spend. The ancients used to write that Sagittarius is the sign of the gambler, but that label need not be a literal one. You could just as easily be a risk-taker at work by suggesting ideas and concepts that are well ahead of their time. If you can direct and control your downside, Sagittarius, you could find yourself quite well off. Sagittarius is not born with the street-smart shrewdness of Scorpio in financial matters, so maybe you should have a good Scorpio adviser. For one thing, Sagittariuses are a bit too open and not proprietary enough about their ideas in business dealings. Remember to protect that intellectual property of yours. If you can combine your awesome intellectual and creative talents with financial savvy, you could be king of the hill. Just don't break the bank first. On the flip side of this, you are never stingy. You share whatever you have with family and friends, and it is hard not to be touched by your good heart, dear Sagittarius.

## CAREER

Sagittariuses adore animals and will often have large, interesting dogs as pets. Of course, this is the sign of the centaur, so horses are also a natural for you. Many Sagittariuses know how to ride and even compete in riding and dressage events. Your sign rules other large animals, exotic ones like elephants, lions, and bears. To be closer to the wild, Sagittariuses choose to work with animals like these in their career. Good jobs for Sagittarius would include zoologist, veterinarian, riding instructor, animal trainer, breeder, jockey, and rodeo star. Want a truly exciting career? Venture into the wilderness or the snow-capped Poles for an extended stay to study animals in their habitat, or become a safari leader. If you want a job that's a little tamer, you might want to run your own pet store or animal-grooming service. You could also offer a dog-walking service.

There are other careers that might be right for you. Being a fire sign, you have a certain star quality or presence and a corresponding need to perform in some capacity, whatever arena you choose. However, Sagittarius does not rule classic theater (that's Leo's domain). Let's look at what that "stage" could be for you. As you might expect, many of the best vocations for you revolve around your nature to think big. Because you make such a good student and are not averse to many years of study, you might consider one of the professions, such as medicine, dentistry, law, or teaching. Sagittarius is often a sign that produces deep thinkers, scholars, researchers, philosophers, and others who enjoy weighing the pros and cons of a subject and thoroughly exploring it. Thus the judicial system may beckon you. Consider being a judge, district attorney, or other officer of the court. Your ruler, Jupiter, was the Roman god of laws and justice. Your sign also produces some terrific politicians, so consider a run for office.

Your sign makes superb journalists, foreign correspondents, writers, magazine, book, or newspaper publishers, and political science commentators (especially regarding foreign affairs). Languages may interest you, so consider being a linguist or a language translator. Many Sagittariuses are also leading inventors.

You have an outstanding feel for broadcasting and the Internet, so consider working as a producer, content provider, anchorperson, or radio or TV talk-show host. You speak well, so consider sales or public relations too. Your sign is playful and jovial, so your career doesn't have to be serious. If so inclined, you could become a highly successful sitcom writer, columnist, or even a stand-up comic. (Keep in mind that your material will probably be popular overseas.)

For many Sagittariuses, the spiritual nature runs very deep. Thus you may consider a life devoted to a religious order, working, for example, as a priest, nun, pastor, or rabbi, or as a theology professor, scholar, or philosopher. You might also enjoy working for a foundation or not-for-profit international organization like UNICEF or other United Nations organizations content in knowing your work is contributing to a good cause. Your innate understanding and sensitivity of other cultures would allow you to excel as a foreign diplomat, ambassador, international banker, or financier. Consider too becoming an importer or exporter of goods or services or building a Web site to conduct global e-commerce. Your interest in other cities of the world and travel would also make you a superb international corporate event planner, travel agent, tour operator, pilot, airline steward, or, if you want something really off the grid, explorer.

Speed and big machines with lots of power (fast cars, private jets, and so forth) intrigue you. Therefore, consider working in the transportation fields, including aviation (including airfreight) or the automotive, trucking, or shipping industry. Design sleek, elegant (and expensive) cars, or invent newer versions of gasoline-free automobiles. Another good career choice would be engineering.

Finally, you might also consider being a professional athlete or sportsman. As we discussed earlier, many Sagittariuses like athletics and seem to be naturally talented in this area. Focus on sports that are included in the

Olympics and aim to represent your country. You are attracted to the idea of taking on a worthy competitor and because your sign is usually quite robust and muscular, with the right training you could go very far. Even if you choose not to become a pro, you should investigate sports for fun, because you probably enjoy exercise very much and it will help you reduce stress.

## BODY, MIND, AND SPIRIT

Athletics usually play a solid role in the life of a Sagittarius. This sign expresses the very best of the Greek ideal of sound mind and sound body. Fire signs like to compete to test their innate physical and emotional strength, and Sagittarius is no exception. Indeed, Sagittariuses often need to express their enthusiastic energy. Without a channel for it, Sag gets quite restless or high-strung. (Fire-sign Aries is said to have athletic ability too, but the fixed modality of the second fire sign, Leo, tends to make its energy combust internally rather than externally. As a result, Leo's energy tends to engender unique and individual creativity rather than athletic ability.)

While not all Sagittariuses enjoy sports, almost all enjoy pitting themselves against challenging conditions. This allows Sagittarius (and Aries) to experience the delicious feeling of victory that is so important to these signs. Indeed, Sagittarius (like Aries) is considered fearless. The symbol of the Olympics is a flame, an appropriate symbol for games that unite nations in the spirit of brotherhood and an international theme that also underscores the qualities of Sagittarius.

Medical astrology tells us that Sagittarius rules the liver, hips, and thighs. However, because of Jupiter's rulership of your sign, you seem to have a little too much of a penchant for foods high in fat. Try to keep those cravings down, dear Sagittarius, or you could find your cholesterol levels climbing too high. Control alcohol consumption too, to protect your liver. The main difficulty Sagittarius experiences stems from overactivity or mishaps from participation in strenuous sports. You are a bit of a daredevil and, being rash, you tend to try sports that would be hard for anyone. Easy does it! In older age, take calcium to avoid problems with broken bones (particularly of the hip and femur).

Energy is expressed a little differently within the members of the fire-sign family. Aries is known to be spontaneous and particularly entrepreneurial. This sign has quick, short bursts of intense energy. Aries are the only fire sign that need no outside trigger to propel them into action; their initiative stems from within. In Leo, the fire element is directed inward (rather than outward to the world) because of the fixed nature of the Leo sign. Therefore, the fire element of Leo is thought to be particularly innovative in an artistic sense, especially talented with color, music, and design but not too athletic. Their fixed nature makes Leos a little too fond of comfort. Sagittarius, being both fire and mutable energy, is breezy and continually moving; imagine a fire being fanned. A highly communicative sign, Sagittarius has a need to disseminate information to the world after the material has been processed. So rather than sell ideas (Aries) or magnetize others (Leo), Sagittarius persuades through reason and attracts through transmitting truth. The fire element in Sagittarius begins to become changeable, less indelible, and more transmutable. Yet in terms of physical energy you have much endurance and therefore can go the long distance.

Fire signs generally don't like people telling them what to do. Fire needs room to breathe and grow, so they do best when they are independent, either self-employed or running their own departments with a high degree of autonomy. What fire signs like yours generally fear most is dull routine. Rules, regulations, bureaucratic systems, and political infighting drive this sign more crazy than most.

Sagittariuses are in danger of burnout because they can be attracted to too many new ideas, become scattered, or dissipate their energy by being too unfocused, thus absorbing too many divergent thoughts at once.

Sometimes you lose track of what you were seeking in the first place. You also can be tempted to try shortcuts and later will have to backtrack when projects and papers aren't up to snuff. Sagittarius, be discerning so that you can direct your sweetest energy to achieve the greatest good.

## SUMMARY

Critics say you can be overly confident, even defiant, uncompromising, outrageous, arrogant, brusque, or boisterous at times. Yet in the end, sincerity, honesty, and hopeful perseverance more than balance these quirky qualities that show up from time to time. You may be frank, but you rarely miss the mark. Your clear mind, logical reasoning, and need for scrupulous ethics balance these qualities by the bushel. So, Sagittarius, we will just have to take the whole package you present to us—and that's just fine. Inside you beats a very generous, giving heart. You make people think more deeply than any sign of the zodiac and while, much to your dismay, your honesty can sometimes hurt, your sense of right could ignite nations to your cause.

# THE MYTHS OF
# SAGITTARIUS AND JUPITER

In mythology, Jupiter comes from the Latin word *Diu-pater*, literally, "God-father." In ancient times, this description surely fit. Jupiter was considered the chief lawgiver, spiritual head, and overseer of Rome. Before that, Jupiter was Zeus, a Greek god and ruler of the heavens who was symbolized by the largest planet of the sky. Both Zeus and Jupiter brought spiritual enlightenment to men everywhere and, like the beacon of light they were, showed the way to finer ethics, morals, and spirituality. In Rome, Jupiter was always seen sitting on a throne, holding a thunder-bolt in one hand and a scepter in the other, with an eagle perched on his shoulder. Jupiter also ruled marriage, and was thought to give special protection to the nuptial couple as well as to the children and the family as a whole. (Astrology bears this out too, in that Jupiter is exalted when found in the home-and-family caring sign of Cancer). The Romans adapted the Greek gods to their culture, and the meaning of Jupiter remained the same.

It's been said that people who have Jupiter prominent in their charts (or who are Sagittarians) are in some way able to control their own universe, much in the way that Jupiter ruled the cosmos as a chief sky-god on Mount Olympus. People with a well-placed Jupiter usually find themselves in the upper echelons of society, and when they grow up they seem to take part in making some of the laws they use to rule their personal universe, and this could describe you, Sagittarius. Of course, like any planet, Jupiter does have its drawbacks. Jupiter creates excess of abundance, which can make one lazy, a bit rotund, or even arrogant—indicating that too much of a good thing can be a problem.

In addition to being ruled by Jupiter, Sagittarius is symbolized by the centaur, a creature considered half man and half horse. Mythically, centaurs were considered highly intelligent (human), but their bodies belied animal instinct. Most centaurs were considered violent because they often started brawls and other disturbances. However, Sagittarius was not to be symbolized by just any centaur, but a very special one named Chiron, the wise and kind and the most holy of the centaurs. He was said to be a healer, philosopher, and teacher.

## CHIRON, THE WISE TEACHER

Chiron, according to the myth, was accidentally and unintentionally wounded in the heel or thigh (stories conflict) by one of Hercules's poisoned arrows. In a twist of irony, the great healer Chiron was not able to heal himself, even though he was a deeply respected healer, because the wound came from Hercules, thought to be magical. In terrible pain, Chiron longed to die, but because he was immortal he could not give up his life, not unless he chose to do so quite deliberately. Chiron finally did give up his immortality, but he did it in a way that gave his life special meaning.

Chiron told the gods that he was ready to exchange immortality for death on the condition that his death would cause the release of Prometheus from his pain and torment. Prometheus (meaning "foresight" and considered humanity's great awakener) was a Titan who was chained to a rock by Zeus in punishment for challenging the gods. Prometheus had stolen fire from the gods to give to mankind, in compassion for mankind's helplessness. Zeus had condemned Prometheus to eternal pain by ordering an eagle to tear out his liver. Each day Prometheus's liver would be restored, and each day the torment would be repeated when the eagle would tear it out again. Chiron ended this cycle by demanding that Prometheus be returned to Earth to continue his service to mankind in exchange for Chiron's giving up his life. As the tale goes, the only way Prometheus could be freed was if an immortal god agreed to give up his immortality and descend into Hades. For a while this looked like a highly unlikely circumstance, but when Chiron proposed to do just that, it turned out to be a miracle for Prometheus. Prometheus, considered the savior of man, was released and returned to Earth. Out of respect for his kindness, the gods honored Chiron by having his image placed in the sky in the constellation of Sagittarius, a rightful image for Chiron, who made the ultimate sacrifice for universal good (a characteristic Sagittarius impulse). Chiron, as the great centaur, is considered part of the driving force behind Sagittarius.

Sagittarius and its polar opposite, Gemini (a sign found exactly six months earlier), are signs that rule travel and mobility. So, to a freedom-loving sign like Sagittarius, a wound in either the heel or the thigh restricting mobility can be very frustrating. Anyone who has been ill would relate to this theme of being "brought down to Earth," trapped within a body that is not functioning properly. In the myth, when kindly old Chiron was alive he chose to live in a cave in Mount Pelion, where he meditated and studied medicine (the type of medicine we associate with herbs and homeopathy), as well as the subjects of music and mathematics. He was no recluse — Chiron would often venture out of his cave to share what he had learned with others. Some of his famous pupils were Jason, Achilles, Aesculapius (the great physician), Actaeon (the great hunter), and Aeneas, all of whom he trained for battle. Chiron taught medicine to Aesculapius, child of Apollo, and he eventually surpassed the talents of his teacher and was deemed patron god of the healing arts. Chiron aptly crystallizes the sharing spirit of your sign, dear Sagittarius, and your constant quest for excellence through higher education.

# CAPRICORN PERSONALITY

### Capricorn
December 22–January 19

### Guiding Principle

"I Accomplish"

### How This Sign Feels Joy
Finds joy in achieving honors for their contribution to the community, through leadership, vision, and the setting of practical goals and priorities for others to follow.

### In the New Millennium, Your Contribution to the World Will Be . . .
You have the gift of knowing how to build complex organizational structures. Your ability to lead, as well as to create and maintain an orderly chain of command, will be respected and abundantly rewarded.

### Quote That Describes You
"AT THE AGE OF SIX I WANTED TO BE A COOK. AT SEVEN I WANTED TO BE NAPOLEON. AND MY AMBITION HAS BEEN GROWING STEADILY EVER SINCE."

—SALVADOR DALÍ, a *Taurus*

Capricorn has a dream, and it is all about power and success. In your fantasy you can see your name engraved on a plaque on your door, the sterling silver case that holds your business cards, and the view of the glittering city that serves as a backdrop to your corner office. All three secretaries who report to you have roses on their desks and take or hold calls, manage your packed schedule, and keep you moving from meeting to meeting. People who visit you might notice the awards you have won discreetly lined up on the sideboard behind your desk and the many photographs of you with your family or shaking hands with world leaders. Can this dream come true? Of course! You are a Capricorn, so it's not a matter of "if" this will happen, but "when."

Yours is the sign of ambition, and because you visualize your goals in such minute detail, you often achieve them. You certainly have all the right qualities to get ahead. You are rational, reliable, resilient, calm, competitive, trustworthy, determined, cautious, disciplined, and quite persevering. Your underlings see you as a tower of strength, and indeed you are. You manage to sidestep all the potholes to success because you make such deliberate, careful career decisions, as if they were a series of well-thought-out chess moves. Because your working life provides so much of your sense of identity, it is vital that you find a career that satisfies your need for growth and that makes good use of your talents. You work very hard and some call you a workaholic. If you are a Capricorn, you laugh at those critics and say that your work is your play, and that, dear Goat, is true.

Capricorns know that job security is only as strong as their most recent victory and that there is no free lunch. This is the mature attitude of a realist. Unlike Sagittariuses, who can talk themselves into anything, Capricorn is an old soul who's "been there, done that" and learned that there are no shortcuts. A purist, you have little patience with those who sloppily apply a quick fix instead of taking the long view and do things right in the first place. You don't waste time wallowing in wishful thinking, either.

## SYMBOLS

♑ The ancients designated this Goat as a symbol of one who climbs to the top of the mountain to spread the knowledge of the sea and of creation to all of mankind. It is only "recently" (since the Greeks) that Capricorn's symbol became a goat. In ancient days the goat was revered for being sacred, and it was used in the most important sacrificial ceremonies. The goat was special in another way: It was an animal that could survive when the soil was very poor or the conditions quite adverse — much like Capricorn. The Goat tends to be solitary, content to climb the mountain in a somewhat lonely (rather than gregarious) manner. The reward is the view from the top, which is well worth the trip for the Goat.

♄ Capricorn's ruler is Saturn and its glyph is a cross over a crescent, meaning that for Saturn, matter and reality dominate spirit. (With Jupiter the reverse is true: Spirit soars above matter in the symbol, for the crescent or soul is formed on top of the cross symbolizing matter.) Thus, each planet, Saturn and Jupiter, forms an opposite and complementary approach to life, allowing alternate means to integrate soul and spirit into reality.

## PLANETARY INFLUENCES

The winter solstice occurs on December 21, and from then on the Sun (and daylight) begins to grow in importance. Hence, on the solstice a symbolic point of fullest contact with "universality" is reached. Darkness is always symbolized by the collective unconsciousness, whereas increasing light was and still is considered to symbolize the self. Thus, the increasing light that occurs at the time of Capricorn calls for the transformation and renewal of the individual's spirit, which is accomplished through the wisdom of collective consciousness that came to fullness during Sagittarius/Jupiter.

In late December, Jupiter relinquishes his baton to Capricorn's ruler, Saturn, a planet the Greeks called "the Sun of the night." (In fact, some astrologers today believe that Capricorns do their best work in the evening, when they feel brightest and most energetic.) Whenever Jupiter and Saturn are found in important helpful aspect to one another in a chart, they are thought to have the ability to help mankind move toward important, positive change. Symbolically, in December and through most of January, man leaves Jupiter's period of optimism and is now asked to take stock of his actions and to make plans for the future. Saturn's rulership of Capricorn tells us that our mission is to take responsibility for our lives through disciplined actions.

The tenth house, which rules your sign, is one of "philosopher-king" — that lofty place in the horoscope that allows you to put your deepest philosophies into action as a leader. Everyone on Earth has the possibility of being a king in some area of their life (on whatever scale they choose), and it is in this house that you choose your domain for your ultimate career contribution to the world and what you would forever be known. This success or destiny point is not usually revealed until one becomes older and wiser (around age forty or fifty or so). It hardly ever arrives earlier (although, admittedly, for some people it does). There is the suggestion that one needs to work toward this goal and earn the role. (The ascendant is where you begin your quest, and it describes your personality, while the mid-heaven point, which is another term for this tenth-house cusp, is where you "arrive" in terms of status and reputation in the community.) This tenth house, owned by Capricorn, rules fame, status, rewards, honors, and ultimate achievement, so we see that the taking on of responsibility and making commitments leads to the joy of a having a fine reputation and community respect.

As we already know, the Sun symbolizes authority, and to Jupiter, a helpful, affirming father, Saturn represents still another side, that of the stern disciplinarian. Some astrologers assert that Saturn's role in Capricorn's chart (or, indeed, its placement in any chart) seems to hint at the need to correct the shortcomings of a significant "father" figure, one's parents, boss, partner, mate, or other such key individual.

The horoscope isn't just a symbol for an individual but also a sort of map of the stages of mankind at large. Thus, by the time we get to the tenth sign, Capricorn, man is ready to make his contribution to the world. Up to now, man has learned about himself and his identity. He has had time with his close and distant relatives, probably has experienced love, friendship, and possibly even marriage and children. In Sagittarius, the ninth sign, man may have had a chance to get a good education and/or to travel afar. By the tenth house, it's time to give something back to society, and in Capricorn this happens in spades.

## Cosmic Gifts

Goats have the faith that all accounts will be totaled, tallied, and balanced and their hard work eventually rewarded. When it is, it will be a bright and happy day indeed. In your world everything is right and just; work is rewarded and actions have direct consequences. Not naive, you are determined and driven by a vision of destiny that you feel an urgency to fulfill. This feeling sustains you despite the powerful obstacles you face on the climb up Mount Everest. A lovable side to you is that you are modest about your accomplishments and may even become surprised when others make a fuss over you. While you love to get recognition, you are, unlike Leo or Aries, not one to brag.

You know in your heart that although your opponents may be picked by pundits as clearly the probable winners, they will run out of steam long before they reach the finish line. You have the inner confidence to know that your patience will be rewarded, so you bide your time. Like the tortoise, you pull out ahead in the long run and win more times than not. You are interested in winning not one battle but the whole war. Consistent and purposeful, when you set your sights on a goal you are sure to achieve it, for you have enormous inner fortitude. Some old astrologic texts say that Capricorns are pessimists by nature, and while this may be right in some isolated cases, by and large I feel that most Capricorns are a cheerful lot, their serious goals notwithstanding.

Astrologically, each sign makes up for the excesses of the sign that precedes it. Thus Sagittarius's blind optimism is tempered in Capricorn. Capricorn also works to stem the extravagance of Sagittarius with prudent controls and cost-cutting measures. If Sagittarius is bent on getting education, Capricorn is bent on using it. Yet Capricorn is pragmatic enough to know that getting good marks alone won't guarantee success; drive and ambition do. Consistency is important, and here again Capricorn wins, for the Goat is steady and sure-footed. As Boy Scouts Goats were taught the motto "Be Prepared," and this sign is prepared for everything.

Capricorn never has a problem with delaying gratification for a later, larger goal. Duty will always come before fun. Says Capricorn, "How can I relax at a party when I am still thinking about all the work on my desk? I would rather stay and work." Yet you set such a high standard of performance that others begin to *expect* that high level of output. No boss is likely to say "Nice job" often enough to you, so be sure to take a moment to congratulate yourself, dear Capricorn. There is another obvious pitfall in working such long hours: You may later feel that you missed important parts of life, regretting that you did not spend more time with family and friends. Finding the right balance will always be a Capricorn challenge.

History interests you, and being armed with a solid knowledge of the past helps you plan for the future. You instinctively understand that the conditions you face today are simply an outgrowth of events and decisions you (or others) faced yesterday. By tracing the source of your difficulties and using history as your guide, you can plan more effectively for the future. However, your love of the past can become a drawback too. Capricorn can get too enamored of tradition and not put enough emphasis on innovation. However, history cannot be used as a blueprint for all circumstances, and in unique situations you may lack the strength of conviction to make bold changes.

You need to keep a powerful view of the future. In ancient days, kings were thought to derive their powers directly from the Sun or from God. Thus, the high, lofty, and often lonely position held by the king engendered enormous respect on the part of his subjects. However, the ancients knew that at some point the king would become the old king. At that point he no longer derived his power from such lofty sources; his power came from a worn-out tradition. Applications to this rule are played out in life today in a multitude of ways. It will become obvious to the subjects that it is time for a new king, but it is very important that the would-be king be sure of his timing when staging his palace coup. In so doing, the new king needs to generate his own spiritual and practical foundation from which to base his authority. Today this is called a candidate's platform, and it is done within companies too, not just played out in politics. If the new king does not represent a new philosophy he will never form the proper base from which to rule, and, worse, he will unwittingly perpetuate the regime of the old king. If that happens, he will, either consciously or unconsciously, accept the worn-out, tired tradition of the old king instead of supplanting it with fresh, new ideas.

Keep this thought in mind, dear Capricorn. Your sign can be a little too mistrustful of new methods and ideas. The next time you are tempted to say "It's not broke, so why fix it?" (as your fellow sign Taurus is also prone to say), stop and think. You may have to force yourself to march assertively into the twenty-first century. While Goats are not known to be born visionaries like Pisces, Aquarius, or Aries, you do have the talent of knowing how to give other people's ideas breath.

Producing, building, and expanding on the ideas of others are your true genius and your ultimate contribution to the world. When Aries are ready to start another business but don't have a clue about how to grow the one they already have started to the next, more established level, whom do they call? A Capricorn, of course! In meetings, if someone voices a very good idea, every instinct in you wants to act on it. The Goat will say,

"Let's get a budget together and a team, and let's agree on some deadlines." You know how to get results. What good is an idea if it never gets acted on? you ask. You are right, dear Goat. You are superbly organized and know how to get teams to work together effectively, even when the goals seem impossible to accomplish. A whiz at hiring people, you have a legendary talent for assigning the right person to the right task. Your practical mind won't let emotions get in the way, either. Like your ruler, you reward those who earn it, not out of friendship but for putting in the right effort. Capricorn's big fear is letting someone down — so it simply doesn't happen.

You can put your finger on what's missing in any project and compensate for it by adapting the resources you do have to whatever needs to be done. Resources are never squandered; your sign gives new meaning to the word *conservative* (as in "one who conserves"). Saturn teaches us to make do with what we have, and this certainly is the case at your birth time, when winter presents a more severe and less bountiful atmosphere.

Mental concentration is powerful in your sign; if you are a Goat you know you can laser-beam into any project (personal or professional) without danger of becoming distracted. Should a marching band parade through your office or den you would scarcely notice because you focus so intently on what you're doing. Saturn helps you hold an enormous amount of detail at once, and because you get into what you're doing, you can continue for very long hours without needing a break. Family and friends marvel at this in you. Hopefully you have an office that is as comfy as home, because you spend so much time there. Goats are not quitters or procrastinators, either.

Perhaps this strong commitment you exhibit comes from the fact that Capricorns are choosy about which projects they take on in the first place. This sign knows not to overcommit time or energy (as Gemini is prone to do), or money (as Aries, the high rollers of the zodiac, might). You tend to be realistic but not overly optimistic (as Sagittarius is said to be). Capricorns don't even let their egos get in the way of a big or tough decision (like Leo is prone to do). Instead, this sign refuses to get mired in detail (as Virgo is known to do).

Make no mistake: Capricorn thinks big. The ancients wrote that you are capable of undertakings of enormous magnitude, so there are few things that are beyond your ability. If you want to manage an empire, it's yours for the asking. Capricorn also has stamina, and while Aries (another cardinal sign) has incredible short bursts of energy, Capricorn has the endurance of a long-distance runner. Think of your energy as coal, a source of fuel your sign rules. Slow and steady, and ever so warm, it lasts and lasts.

One of your most attractive sides is that you have the wackiest, most off-beat, and funniest sense of humor of most any sign of the zodiac. It's been said that to laugh about something we need to take the subject of the joke very seriously—that's your territory, Capricorn. Not surprisingly, some of our very finest comics are Capricorns. Sometimes you use a self-deprecating humor that leaves us falling over and holding our sides with laughter. At other times you apply a crackling wit so dry it takes a second to "get it," but when we do we beg for more. Even cynical or sarcastic humor cracks us up when it's delivered with your special timing.

Humor can also help you take disappointments in stride, and you know that disappointments are part of life; you are quite philosophical about dealing with setbacks. In fact, you are one of the best signs for "getting back on the horse" after being thrown off. However, the side of Saturn that rules fear could, at times, lower your self-confidence. When you find it shaken, you must stop, back-pedal, and give yourself a good pep talk. A Goat without confidence is a lame Goat indeed, for self-esteem is the magic cloak that allows you to do your great deeds. Depression is said to be an occasional byproduct of Saturn, but more often than not what you may be experiencing is the result of pure exhaustion or not eating right. You do work long hours, so try to stay healthy and then see if your spirit brightens. If not, seek medical help. Chances are there is a good treatment waiting for you. This is one time when being the stoic tower of strength is foolhardy.

## RELATIONSHIPS

As the original Spartan of the zodiac, Capricorn, you can be too hard on yourself, especially when you think you've been lazy. Your staunchest critics are not your bosses or your stockholders but yourself, and you should know that you can make unreasonable demands on yourself. You tell yourself that you don't need compliments, but you do—everyone does. Capricorns have moments of self-doubt and low self-esteem just like everyone else. And because you think *you* don't need continual affirmation, you tend to forget that others need it, and this can hurt their morale. Don't forget to praise family, friends, or employees when praise is due.

Reading your moods can be hard for those around you. People often don't know how you are feeling, dear Goat. You could be thinking warm thoughts, but your natural reserve may veil those feelings. This might give another person the impression that you don't like him, which isn't the case at all. This is further compounded by the fact that Capricorns are never as at ease in social situations as they are in business ones (where the rules are clear). It is hard for you to relax in a social situation. However, if you just speak up a little, others will be able to pick up on this more quickly.

Like their polar opposite, Cancer, Capricorns' motto in romance is "Love me, love my family." Rest assured that the Goat's supportive clan is not far away. This is actually a very endearing quality about you, Capricorn, for in the same manner that you respect your own family relationships, you will also respect your own sweetheart or spouse. Visits to your spouse's sister's graduation or mom's birthday party will be embarked on cheerfully. If you have a sweetheart who is a Capricorn, you will soon see that family members are always somewhere in the background, calling and sending notes or gifts. The Goat enjoys being in the warm circle of children, parents, siblings, aunts, uncles, cousins, and other blood relatives. Capricorn rules foundations, and certainly these individuals provide a powerful emotional base for you.

As this sign matures, Capricorns tend to be very aware of themselves in the context of their ancestorial lineage, and this is a part of their overall love of history. Studying their roots is a fun pastime for Capricorns, and chances are, if you are a Goat you have already checked out your family name on the Internet. Capricorns, of all signs, are cognizant that many generations had to live and die to give them life. They are not about to blow the opportunity to make a strong contribution in their lifetime. Even when young, Capricorns are aware that someday they will be someone's great-great-grandma or -grandpa. When the future children of the family inquire, generations hence, about who they were and how they lived, Goats want to be sure they will turn out to be a fascinating member of the family tree. And of course they will be.

Even though shy, Capricorns enjoy enlarging their social circle and, with their polished manners, understated elegance, and serene demeanor, they fit in everywhere. As a Capricorn, people almost always assume you have an esteemed, even pedigreed, family, even if you don't. And you expect to find the same genteel ways in a mate. A boorish person who is sloppy in manners or who uses bad language won't stay in your circle very long.

Some say Capricorns are social climbers, but that charge may be a harsh one too. Certainly Capricorns do not try to keep up with the family next door. It is actually the other way around: The "Joneses" have to work hard to keep up with you! Still, if a Capricorn has "made it," it will be tempting for him or her to flaunt it a little. That tendency shows itself in several ways. Never given to things flashy, Capricorn will buy an elegant, quality automobile in a neutral color complete with a luxurious leather interior and lots of extras that may not be apparent but are still lovely to have. They like to wear (or give) expensive, real gold jewelry and generally shop at the best retailers. Women of this sign may even want a fur coat, as environmentally "out" as that might be. She'll explain, "Darling, it's warm and will last for years!" Not all Capricorns are that way, of course, as some are very environmentally aware, but Capricorns as a rule are a bit status conscious, as any of this sign will admit if pressed.

No matter how wild they may have been in their teens or in college, inside every Capricorn is a respectable person who would never run off to Las Vegas to marry a rock star. Capricorns think ahead, and they have no plans to suffer from life's vicissitudes if they can help it. They go for purposeful, practical, and powerful partners, who, like them, are bent on success. Capricorns' mamas apparently taught them that it is as easy to marry rich as poor, so your sign tries to marry "up" in society, and if no likely candidates are around in their twenties, Goats may hold out for a while to find someone better. In fact, it is common for Goats to want to get their career underway first, so delaying marriage is no big deal.

Certainly, Capricorns want a winner on their team. Should you later find yourself tied to a mate who has no ambition or is completely irresponsible, things will go downhill quickly unless that individual starts to show some spark. However, on the other hand, having a high-powered, successful mate could cause other problems. With the Goat's propensity to have a brilliant career, it would also be nice to have someone back home to take care of things. This is true whether you are a man or a woman—many women would love to have a "house husband" to help with the kids. It's hard to keep a household going when both partners are high-powered.

When it comes to looking for love, keep in mind that all work and no play can make you a dull Jack or Jill. You may initially feel a little out of place at parties, unless they are career-related mixers and cocktail parties, because even when you are out socializing you usually need a clear goal.

Purely fun parties tend to be a little open-ended for you at best, or at worst a waste of time. Instead of giving up on the social scene, personal introductions may be a better way for a shy Capricorn to meet new romantic partners.

You are very reserved, and sometimes you wish you could break out of this imprisoned state to relate more honestly and freely with those you care about. In any emotional relationship it is tremendously important that you feel safe. Unlike other signs, who are less unguarded, you would rather be safe than sorry. You will want to see some evidence that the other person has the same feelings for you before you will risk and declare your own feelings. If you have any fear that the other person may take advantage of your goodwill or is not on the same wavelength, you will hold back until you sense a greater feeling of loyalty, devotion, and support. Capricorns are cautious and protective of their emotions; they are not about to wear their heart on their sleeve. Best romantic partners include the other earth signs, Virgo and Taurus, and other Capricorns because they instinctively understand this impulse. Water signs—Pisces, Cancer, and Scorpio—would be next best, for water and earth signs mix together quite well.

With Cancer on the cusp of your marriage house, it's clear that you want a caring and nurturing family person for a mate, someone who is a bit more emotionally demonstrative than you are. Choosing someone like that would make good sense, for you would get the enduring romance you secretly crave, and your mate would get the solid rock of a mate he or she desperately needs.

Once Capricorns have found someone special, they like to involve their mate in their career. For a man that means crowning his wife First Lady, and for a woman it means marrying her prince, who will cheerfully work with her to build their castle (or empire) together. Capricorns enjoy bringing their mate to business conventions, dinners, or parties, and since the higher a position they assume in their company the more socializing is expected, Capricorns are right to choose a partner who is up to this role. Hopefully, their sweethearts realize that this will be expected of them over time and are looking forward to fulfilling this special role. If not, there could be trouble down the road, for Capricorns also marry their job.

There may be an age difference of eight or more years between you and your marriage partner, Capricorn, especially if your Venus is in Capricorn too. Male or female Capricorns are not averse to marrying an older mate because they feel, rightly, that age alone should never separate soul mates. Often these marriages turn out to be highly successful; Capricorn tends to be very clear-headed in matters of romance.

Once married with children, the role of provider is one that you take seriously, and this is true whether you are a man or a woman. There are plenty of women who found themselves suddenly left without child support from spouses who had no sense of responsibility at all. The only danger is that Capricorns can get into a strong self-sacrificing mode, especially after children arrive, making it hard to relax and think about themselves. The only way to break this cycle is to hire a baby-sitter and simply slack off for a while; it is time for a well-deserved break.

Yet no matter how dire the family circumstances (should they become that way), Capricorns won't give up their goals of sending their children to college and providing life's little extras along the way. Even if their partner isn't up to it, Goats manage to give their offspring new clothes and a pair of cool sneakers, some toys and a fun vacation, if only a modest one. To Capricorn, a promise is a promise, and to a blood relative like a child the promise to care for and protect is sacred. Some Capricorns are called on to help an elderly relative at some point, and if so, the same is true. Nothing stops them from being a provider, for love energizes them enormously.

Sexually, some suppose that Capricorns are cool, but again, this is often assumed to be true but in fact isn't. While you don't like dramatic, outward displays of emotion, you have no problem being intensely sensual and erotic in the earthiest sense behind closed doors. In fact, old astrologic lore states that the zodiac signs symbolized by animals with horns (Aries, Taurus, and Capricorn) could be the most frisky and erotic of all. So the world shouldn't be fooled by your modest, shy exterior.

As mentioned earlier, Capricorn values fidelity and loyalty. However, because Capricorns tend to live their lives "backward" (being serious in youth and youthful in old age), you could be tempted to roam a little in older age, mainly because you may experience a sudden need to make up for lost time and to cut loose a little. If this happens it would be just after a big career victory, when you find yourself with time off and in the mood for a sweet romantic distraction. Hopefully this will be only a passing phase you can recover from quickly. Love of family and children and the need to honor past obligations are likely to keep you from upsetting the apple cart.

### FINANCE

Practical Capricorns wear a T-shirt that reads LIFE COSTS. MONEY HELPS. You are practical enough to spend carefully; you know you'll need a comfy nest egg for emergencies and you like brand names and tend to trust well-known retailers. Quality is what you are after because you like to hold on to things year after year. You know you work too hard to throw money out the window. Always on the prowl for a clever bargain, you buy things wholesale, on sale, or at a reduced price whenever possible. You also happen to be a superb negotiator. When it comes to credit cards, you are very careful to maintain a good name and will take steps to be sure that your credit rating is never tarnished.

Capricorn enjoys investing in stocks and bonds, but would not likely be the risk-taking day trader Aries is more prone to become. Capricorns put their money in sturdy global companies with solid earnings, firms that offer an achievable vision of the future. The Goat also likes investing in gold, silver, or other precious metals or diamonds and other gems too, for you know they will always have value. For the same reason, earth-sign Capricorn also likes to put money in real estate.

While Capricorns are known to be very thrifty, even a good quality can sometimes go to extremes. When this happens, though rare, Goats' need to conserve could turn them into miserly old Scrooges. Appropriately enough, this tale is told at Christmastime, Capricorn's birth time of the year.

### CAREER
Ruled by the tenth house of the horoscope, which is devoted to achievement, honors, fame, and recognition, Capricorn is known to produce effective leaders. Capricorns care dearly about their reputation and will give their work the loving detail they feel it deserves. The trappings of success — money, power, and possessions — usually follow, in heaps.

Capricorn "means business"; your sign rules large budgets and as a sign actually governs the world's biggest global, blue-chip companies. Hence, Capricorns always do better working in large organizations than in small ones or being self-employed (which is Aries' domain). You like the benefits and vast resources a sizeable company can provide. However, if you decide to start your own business you have the energy to make a good go of it. You would do well by forming a strong strategic alliance with a bigger business in order to grow your own firm. You also do well working in large companies because the idea of a chain of command appeals to you. This makes sense because your ruler, Saturn, governs the skeleton of the body, the structure of a building, and the organizational chart of a company. The new management idea of a flat organizational chart that expands outward with fewer people reporting to others and that is more "open" (no doors, no offices) doesn't appeal to you.

You are detailed, practical, and financially prudent too. Members of your sign often serve a financial function (even if that's not their main job), and if you are given this responsibility will manage finances in a trustworthy manner, treating funds with the same care you would give to your own money. Along with Taurus and Scorpio, Capricorns are considered among the most talented financial managers in the zodiac.

A perfect job for you would be to work as a CEO or something close to that, such as chief operating officer, chief financial officer, or treasurer. You are highly mathematical too, so you would also make a good chief of technology. Add to this list economist, financier, mathematician, account-ant (CPA), stockbroker, financial columnist or adviser, or insurance or real estate broker or developer.

Being an earth sign, Capricorns make excellent architects, contractors, builders, surveyors, or real estate developers. Try estate planning or work for a landmark commission and save valuable old buildings from destruction. Since you care deeply about "doing the right thing," you would make a great public leader. Consider running for office or becoming a civil servant. Capricorn is also a sign that likes to see law and order upheld, so consider being a law-enforcement professional or detective.

Saturn is your ruler, and it rules the aged, so you may choose to go into geriatric medicine or run a nursing home. Saturn also rules bones and teeth, so some Capricorns choose to be dentists, orthopedic surgeons, or chiropractors.

Capricorns know how things work or want to find out and are often blessed with mechanical talents. Consider being an engineer or auto mechanic, repairman or computer technician.

Capricorns also love history, so add archaeologist or anthropologist to the list, or aim to be the curator of a historical museum. Perhaps you would like to be a documentary filmmaker or an author of historical novels. Or you might become an auctioneer or dealer in valuable old documents, coins, stamps, furniture, artwork, porcelain—or anything else of value from the past.

Saturn has a link to agriculture, so you could make a fine farmer or a bio-chemist, especially one who finds ways to grow more nutritious foods or to feed overpopulated nations. Capricorn rules caves and things buried in the earth too. Be an excavator, gemologist, geologist, mineralogist, coal miner, or stone mason. Other good fields include leather tanner, time keeper, watchmaker, or jeweler—even an undertaker. Some are drawn to religious callings, so think about becoming part of the clergy.

A little-known side to Capricorns is that many are highly talented in the arts. So consider being an art director or an illustrator. Study music to play in a classical orchestra or learn to conduct. Study to be an art restor-er or furniture refinisher. Capricorn rules things of value from the past, so these professions could be fun for you. You have a great sense of humor, too—become a sitcom writer or a stand-up comic, or write a regular humor column in the newspaper.

## BODY, MIND, AND SPIRIT

Dear Capricorn, have you ever noticed how both men and women members of your sign prefer neutrals (even on weekends)—whether black, beige, brown, camel, charcoal, or pale gray or white—underscoring their dignified and low-key yet sophisticated look? That's because Saturn is keeping you understated and elegant, just like winter's palette at the time of the year when you were born. It gives you a very powerful look too. All those navy blue suits and white shirts. Those all-black uniforms, even at parties. Some people may be a little timid about approaching you. Let them be; it's time to let you be you.

Often for Capricorns childhood is delayed or "missing," for whatever reason. Many members of your sign grow up quickly, feeling mature beyond their

years, because they are asked to assume a big burden or responsibility
early in life. This makes the Goat, like firstborn children, always taking
care of others and learning to be leaders before other kids they knew
mastered reading and writing. Other Capricorns are born with health
deficiencies, obstacles that would deter others or make them lower their
sights. But hardships just spurred you on. Those challenges may have
turned out to be blessings in disguise because they have fueled your drive.
The good news is that Capricorns almost never hit their stride until later
in life, so, happily, the older you get, the sweeter life will become.
Certainly those life's rewards (whether personal or professional) you
were so dogged about achieving start to come your way after forty, and
they should start a very gratifying time for you. In a cosmic twist of fate,
the Capricorns actually start to look younger and sexier as time goes by,
a lovely development indeed! So while young Goats may look older than
they are, the reverse is sure to happen as they age. If you think you are
living life a little backward, you are—but aren't you glad? Also, there are
probably more Capricorn centurions (people who live to be 100+) than
any other sign, because Saturn rules longevity. This more than makes up
for the slightly tougher-than-normal start to your life, dear Capricorn.
The Goat can laugh at our society's obsession with youth. They realize
that "kids" (those under age thirty) have value and a contribution to
make, but Goats also know that people get a whole lot more interesting
after age forty or fifty.

You may be surprised to hear that Capricorns don't feel entirely comfortable with celebrating fresh beginnings and new ventures. They are always
worried that they won't live up to the potential the threshold of the event
represents. Instead, Capricorns will enjoy resting on their laurels (if only
for a second) *after* they have accomplished what they set out to do. So
while they may be vaguely uncomfortable celebrating their wedding day
(often torturing themselves with the thought, What if this doesn't work
out and we spent all this money and had all this fuss made by friends and
family?), at their thirty-fifth wedding anniversary they're ready to kick up

dust. Goats will nervously celebrate a career promotion, but five years later, when they have proven their worth by writing that book, or making the cover of *Time* magazine (or whatever the goal is), they can revel in their success.

By now you must be aware that Saturn, your ruler, who influences so much of your personality and outlook, is the planet of responsibility, hard work, limits, delays, sacrifice, and determination. Before you say, "Oh, great! Why did I have to get stuck with a ruler like that?" wait a second! Saturn just happens to rule the apex of the horoscope, the part of the chart called the tenth house of honors, awards, achievement, and fame. Saturn is all about reality, the parts of life you can see, hear, taste, touch, or smell, and she makes you quite clear-eyed. Saturn always gives tangible rewards when challenges are met. You of all people know that nothing worth having comes easily.

The knees are the part of the body that is associated with Capricorn. Some Goats have a scar on their knee or limp from an old sports injury. If you play football or other sports, protect those knees. Capricorn also rules bones, nails, and teeth, so it would be wise to make sure that you get enough calcium and that you see a dentist regularly; not to do so would be pure folly. Do some regular weight lifting too, to keep bones strong and healthy, especially as you age. Rheumatism and arthritis might become a problem, but hopefully modern medicine will continue to find innovative ways to relieve pain, and a cure may be very close. To ward off stiffness and creaky joints, get plenty of exercise, Capricorn, and be sure to stretch, stretch, stretch all through your life. Sitting at your desk for long hours is not good for you.

Skin also comes under the domain of Capricorn, so use plenty of SPF 15 sunscreen, not only to protect your skin from disease but also to keep it from wrinkling. The ears (i.e., hearing) could be another area of concern, as they too, are ruled by Capricorn. While no one can completely control hearing loss, do what you can to protect your ears by keeping the volume of your music in earphones moderate.

## SUMMARY

You set an enormously good example for the rest of us. The Goat would rather climb the mountain than spend his days in the valley, for the Goat craves fame and usually achieves it in his lifetime. Others tell the Goat not to work too hard but, ruled by practical Saturn, this Goat is a realist. You know that anything worth having is worth fighting for and won't be won easily. Capricorns would always rather *earn* their stash than *win* it. Make no mistake, the tenth house is one of the philosopher-king, allowing you the stage to put in motion your deepest moral and ethical values and to inspire us all. Your mate sees you as sensible, sexy, supportive, steadfast, and passionately devoted. For these reasons and so many more, people can't help but admire you deeply.

# THE MYTHS OF
# CAPRICORN AND SATURN

Many cultures of the world, as far back as 3000 B.C., have found the time of your birth, dear Capricorn, highly significant, and in fact Capricorn is one of the oldest constellations, dating back to records of the Babylonians, several thousand years before the birth of Christ.

Your symbol, known in many ancient Mediterranean cultures, was not just any goat but a very special goat named Ea, one that had the head and half-body of a goat and the tail of a fish. In Babylonia, the god Ea was a man who wore a fish's skin and was also called the "antelope of the subterranean ocean." His domain was the life-giving water that flowed beneath the Earth, which was considered the power behind the Tigris and Euphrates Rivers. Thus, Ea was an amphibious creature who could inhabit the worlds of both water (dreams, emotions, and the collective unconscious) and of land (reality and the material world), bringing a psychological link to the two. Ea had another role, that of a wise teacher to the people of Sumer. Not much is known about Ea, but in Mesopotamian art goats and antelopes ate from the Tree of Life.

The concept of nourishment is echoed in the two signs Cancer and Capricorn, signs that lie on the same axis. The people in ancient days lived in a mainly agricultural economy and thus the seasonal rise and fall of the Nile River was considered very significant, for it represented both

abundance and sustenance for the populace who lived along its banks and
who depended on the river's life-giving properties. In ancient calendars, in
May–June the Nile swelled to fullness just as Capricorn was rising on the
evening horizon, a time that signaled to fishermen that they had to get to
work because the fish in the waters would be plentiful. By controlling irri-
gation and providing successful abundance for the populace, society
remained orderly, quite a Capricorn concept.

## PAN AND TYPHON

A fascinating myth about Pan also relates to Capricorn as the goat-fish,
one who is part of the life-giving waters of life. Pan, who was the son of
Hermes, was a happy-go-lucky, musical god with a goat's horns and
hooves. He was thought to be the god of shepherds and goatherds and
companion of woodland nymphs. All wild places were his home, and he
was especially associated with lovely places of thick foliage, forests, and
mountains, places where he would play his musical instrument, the reed
pipes he made himself. It is said that his music was as beautiful as the
song of the nightingale.

At one point Pan leaped into the water to avoid the monster Typhon
just as Jupiter was helping to disguise Pan as an animal. (The word
*panic* is supposed to have come from this legend.) The result was that
the part of Pan that was above water remained a goat, but the portion
that was submerged in the water became a fish. Thus, this myth embodies
Capricorn's yearning to find a balance between struggle and freedom,
depths and heights, and hardship and victory. Capricorn's glyph reveals
this story, too, showing the two horns of the goat with a loop on the right
side, which represents the knee so necessary for climbing the mountains
of life (knees are also ruled by Capricorn). The glyph ends in a curve
that symbolizes the fish tail of the mysterious sea-goat. As an aside, the
story of Pan is where Capricorn is said to get its playful and sexy inner
nature—certainly Pan was no slouch when it came to partying and fun.
This energy is thought to be balanced by Saturn's demands for

respectability. However, it is there, hidden inside the Capricorn personality to be enjoyed.

## SATURN AS AGRICULTURAL GOD

In old Roman days Saturn did not have the serious connotations it does today. In ancient Rome Saturn was thought to be an upbeat agricultural god, and at the time of the winter solstice the Roman festival of Saturnalia (December 17–24) took place. Celebrating Saturn, the god of the "sowing of seeds" and of harvests, the festival was anything but restrained—there was uninhibited partying and eating and a celebration of Nature's gifts. Masters waited on servants and reality was generally turned inside out in a giddy, topsy-turvy time.

At this festival Saturn was portrayed carrying his sickle, which was, quite remarkably, transformed into a symbol of a curved horn of plenty or cornucopia, overflowing with fruit, flowers, and grain. (The sickle was used to cut grain, which in Rome was a sacred ritual.) Thus, the idea of material abundance was associated with Capricorn, and inherent in this symbol is the message "As you sow, so shall you reap." Saturn is therefore an ultimately fair influence in a horoscope, and it underscores the idea of karma; in other words, you get out of life what you are willing to put into it.

In order to understand how differently the Romans viewed Saturn, we need to flash back to an early time, to ancient Greece and the Greek mythology of Saturn, whom they called Cronus. Cronus was one of the Titans, the first race of gods who ruled the world before the immortal Olympians took over (and who were to be ruled by Zeus). He was not only Zeus's father, but also the parent of Hades, Demeter, Poseidon, and Hestia.

## CRONUS AND HIS WIFE, RHEA

Fearful of an omen that warned him that one of his sons would challenge and supercede him, Cronus dutifully ate each newborn baby his wife, Rhea, presented to him to make sure they would never grow to maturity and overthrow his regime. Here is an image of an old ruler who does not want to give up his throne even though it is becoming increasingly apparent that he is tired of life and can no longer rule effectively. This follows the concept of the old king discussed in "Capricorn Personality."

Rhea felt that she could not stand by and watch her children be eaten by her husband without taking action. After Zeus was born, Rhea wrapped up a stone in swaddling clothes and presented it to Cronus, pretending it was their newborn son. As she hoped, Cronus quickly gobbled up the rock without so much as looking at it. In the meantime, Zeus was scurried off to Crete to grow and mature in secret. Later, Zeus fulfilled his father's fearful omen by becoming Cronus's cupbearer and poisoning his father's drink. Cronus instantly regurgitated all of Zeus's brothers and sisters, much to everyone's relief. A bloody battle ensued, one that Zeus and his siblings won. The Titans were relegated to a place in the underworld called Tartarus. Zeus was made the powerful new leader of the new race of gods, the Olympians.

This tale seems to play out the adage that "what you fear most is what ultimately comes to be." Yet Cronus was no stranger to insurrection— he himself had supplanted his own father by castrating Uranus with his sickle (see "The Myths of Aquarius and Uranus"). The Greeks did not recognize Cronus after Zeus took over, but the Romans found Cronus interesting and brought him back as god of agriculture. Saturn was shown homage throughout the year, but at Saturnalia homage was made to Cronus as the biggest holiday because it was the reaping of the harvest of corn and grain by cutting it down with his symbol, the sickle. The cutting of the corn was then a sacred ritual, a special time when the stalks were cut and the corn (like Cronus's children) eaten.

The word *cronus* means "time," and parts of Cronus's name are found in words we now know, such as *chronological* or *synchronicity*. Today, as the year nears its end we see a version of Cronus as an old and worn Father

Time wearing a black cloak and carrying a sickle, but now he is a symbol of the cruelty of time or one who would judge our actions when time is done. Father Time is also the tired old year, who relinquishes his tenure so that a beautiful bouncing baby, the icon for the new year, can take over. Father Time is associated with old age, death, and transition. At year's end we look back and make New Year's resolutions for the coming year, promising to give up bad habits. Appropriately, we respond in January to Saturn's admonishment that "less is more."

The saying "As you sow, so do you reap" is perfectly applicable to your sign, dear Capricorn. Saturn makes you a realist who values actions over words. It is no wonder that you wind up being not only a success but also the one chosen to teach and to lead as philosopher-king, as only the Goat could do.

# AQUARIUS PERSONALITY

**Aquarius**
January 20–February 18

**Guiding Principle**

"I Innovate"

**How This Sign Feels Joy**
Finds joy in change, in replacing old,
outworn social and scientific structures,
methods, and notions with improved and
more relevant innovations.

**In the New Millennium, Your Contribution to
the World Will Be . . .**
Your innovative and technology-oriented
point of view is the key to humanity's understanding of what lies ahead. The Aquarius
principle that "information should be free"
will touch many and liberate all.

**Quote That Describes You**
"DISCOVERY CONSISTS OF SEEING WHAT
EVERYBODY HAS SEEN AND THINKING WHAT
NOBODY HAS THOUGHT."

—ALBERT VON SZENT-GYÖRGYI, a *Virgo*

The most striking quality about you, Aquarius, is your amazing eyes. They often are a beautiful crystal blue or other light color, with a depth of expression that seems bottomless. Those of us who meet Aquarius feel ourselves "falling into" those eyes, not wanting to unlock our gaze from yours. Paul Newman, born under this sign, is a good example of legendary Aquarius charisma. Most members of your sign are famous for looking at their subjects with what seems to be X-ray vision. Dear Aquarius, when you look at someone, it is as if you are able to see straight through them to their soul. Who is to say you can't? Aquarius is known to be one of the most psychic signs, and you know certain things without knowing quite why you do. It is not surprising that your eyes, the tools of your vision, seem somehow different from everyone else's.

Of course, not all Aquariuses have those characteristic light eyes that sparkle like gems in Tiffany's window. Each sign has certain physical characteristics first suggested by the ancients, but there are exceptions. Oprah Winfrey, for example, is an Aquarius, who has chocolate brown eyes that are bigger than saucers and are so warm and engaging they could melt polar ice caps. People want to tell Oprah their secrets because they sense that her heart is open and that she genuinely wants to help. She proves that it's the Aquarius expression that matters most and is often so engaging. Your eyes dazzle, Aquarius, and they make people sit up and listen to what you have to say. Socially, on a more personal level, the intensity you exude has such strong sex appeal you've practically branded it.

## Symbols
Your symbol is the image of a male (in some very old text it was a woman), kneeling, holding two jugs in a downward, pouring gesture. The jugs contain life-giving water, which symbolizes mankind's collective knowledge, which he pours into the cosmic ether for the benefit of all. The Hebrew name for Aquarius is Delphi, or water urn, signifying that the pouring-out of the water was related to cleansing, for atonement and for purification (similar to baptism). Aquarius allows fresh, life-giving

water (knowledge) to flow to the parched Earth (ignorance), which is in need of its nurturing (enlightenment).

In the image of your sign, the figure kneels so he serves; he is not a pompous leader but sees himself as an equal of the people. This sense of democracy and identification with common man is particularly strong in Aquarius and is the secret of your success and why you often are chosen to play a leadership role. You are fueled not by the need to be admired (as Leo is) but by the need to contribute something of lasting value to the community, whether it be in your immediate surroundings or on the world stage.

The glyph for Aquarius looks like two wavy lines, and although many think this is water, it actually suggests air currents. Your ruler, Uranus, rules electricity—a fitting force for you because this energy, quick as the speed of light, is like your element air, powerful yet invisible. Uranus has always been associated with flashes of inspiration and invention.

The glyph of your ruler, Uranus, reveals your talent. Uranus's symbol looks like an "H," but instead of two straight lines the H is made up of two crescents (moons), left and right, that face outward away from each other. The crescents are united by a straight line (the middle of the H), suggesting Earth's horizon, and below that horizon is found a small cross (the cross always suggests "matter" in astrological symbolism). Below that cross and attached to it is found a small circle (in astrologic language, the circle is read "spirit").

The linked crescents suggest a union of the perspectives of both the collective consciousness (groups of people) and the individual. Thus, the cross suggests that while the spirit is busy working within a material world, it is still controlled by the mind. The symbol further suggests that intellect can be rejuvenated and refreshed by man's spirit. Man has dominion over the material world and has the power to make it a better place.

This symbol is appropriate because it transmits that your best work is done in groups (the two crescents on either side) to create a whole that is bigger and better than the sum of the parts. With Aquarius there is no lack of ideas or lack of dedication to ideals. The symbol of intellect (the semicircles or moons) indicates that the higher (divine) mind works well with the so-called lower (common or everyday) mind.

Aquarius's metal is uranium, a radioactive element. Looking up the word *uranium* in the dictionary, one learns that it is used in research, as a fuel, and in nuclear weapons. Uranium owes its name to Uranus, the planet that was discovered eight years prior. The similarity of these two names Uranus and uranium, reminds us that science gives us both great and terrifying inventions. On the upside, science gives us rocket travel, unimaginable medical advances, and all kinds of everyday conveniences like telephones, faxes, and television sets. But science also brings us war and methods of mass destruction. Ever present in the Aquarius mind is the compulsion to act with responsibility and prudence, a concept learned through the former ruler of Aquarius, Saturn. While some signs, like brawny Aries, hope to win physical wars, Aquarius wants to come out on top through logic, objectivity, and intellect in an ultimately peaceful way.

## Planetary Influences

Ruled by the independent planet Uranus, Aquarius is idiosyncratic, imaginative, resourceful, quirky, inventive, ingenuous, and original, and a lot more than that. It is hard to describe such an independent sign, for few Aquariuses will ever agree on those descriptions.

You have never felt a need to agree with the crowd in order to be popular. You don't care very much what other people think about you, and that only adds to your power and mystique. Like Scorpio, you design your own yardstick of success. Your cool aloofness, always present to some degree, is read as "mysterious" by your fans. This, combined with a usually high confidence, is often very sexy. Uranus, your ruler, is known to give you a need for detachment and a need for as much independence as possible because too much closeness makes you claustrophobic. Leaving blanks open allows the rest of us to fill them in.

To best understand you and your ruling planet, Uranus, we must first look to Mercury, a planet positioned closer to the Sun that also governs objective thinking and intellect. Mercury's effect is completely unemotional and rational—its job is to search for the whole truth and nothing but the truth. (That is why Gemini, ruled by Mercury, is considered such a superb journalist and why Virgo, also ruled by that planet, is so detailed and such a perfectionist, in search of all the facts.) Like a heat-seeking missile, Mercury will seek and destroy everything in its path until it finds unbiased veracity. Mercury rules information gleaned by observation, perception, reading, speaking, and listening that is revealed through everyday conditions.

Uranus, in astrology, is considered the "higher octave" of Mercury, allowing mortals to bring the beauty of knowledge and intellect to a more original, inventive, and creative level. In a chart, Uranus rules the higher mind, a planet that helps you deal not only with what is but also with what can be. While Mercury reflects the gathering and learning of information on a daily basis, Uranus is different. Uranus rules the vast amounts of information that are accumulated over a long period and are manifested as intuition.

If Mercury is the messenger, student, reporter, or journalist on the scene, Uranus is the sage, wise teacher or judge. You can see how fortunate you are to have such a powerful guardian planet—and you can also see the corresponding responsibility you have to use your power well. With Uranus bolstering your every move, it is the reason an Aquarius is so experimental, inventive, and even, at times, psychic.

Thus, lucky for you, Uranus is the great synthesizer, taking all information beyond the individual level to include the collective consciousness and gathering it into a package to create something completely new and different. Most importantly, that "something" is individualized and custom-made for the situation, being unique in every way. This describes your ability, Aquarius.

Uranus also rules chaos, so as an Aquarius you are fairly comfortable with ambiguity, a quality that allows you to be creative and inventive. Within a soft structure (or no structure at all), you are more easily able to build things according to your own inner vision and view of the world. You see chaos as a good thing; it is a bubbling, creative cauldron to be poured and molded into something useful and innovative.

## Cosmic Gifts

You tend to need more change and serendipity in your life than most. You get bored easily and when things get dull you deliberately shake them up. Aquarius doesn't need a calm environment—commotion suits you just fine. Uranus teaches you that you have a bigger job to do too, and that is to take established structure and question its value. Thus, Uranus teaches you to upset the apple cart when necessary. Unlike Pluto (which works its changes very gradually), Uranus works in a very sudden and rebellious way, thus this planet is called the Great Awakener.

You can be a bit unpredictable at times, although if asked you will say you never act in an impetuous way. To you, everything you do is logical and thought out; you have no idea why people think you act randomly. You know it's time to change before the rest of us do. Uranus gives you thunderbolts of inspiration and compels you to act in ways that others are not quite ready for. Nothing about your guardian planet is subtle, nor should it be. This planet needs you to help the world wake up and smell the coffee. While your ruler can coax you to act in disconcerting ways, you can provide the world with a sense of sudden liberation too, after you have helped break the chains of restriction.

The worst thing to say to an Aquarius is "We have always done it this way." You don't care about what was done previously. You leave that role to Capricorn (defender of tradition). Your ruler's reputation as the planet that breaks the bonds of debilitating conditions and liberates from old thinking is well known. Thus, Aquarius, your job is to dispel old standards and, if necessary, stand them on their head. Uranus makes you an iconoclast in the true meaning of the word, one who smashes (or at least questions) time-honored icons of society. As an iconoclast you give the world an exhilarating vision of new, altered states.

Yet Saturn, the planet that was considered Aquarius's ruler before Uranus was discovered in 1781, has a different but related role in Aquarius's development. Saturn teaches us that man needs discipline, order, structure, form, and lasting foundations to feel secure. Uranus tests both a structure's strength and its usefulness, leaving intact forms that are still functioning effectively. The fact that Saturn was the former ruler of Aquarius suggests that when you, in your zeal for progress, strip away society's security, you have a responsibility to rebuild what you dispose of with something just as stable if mankind is to prosper as a result of these changes. Your sense of social responsibility is strong, however, which is why you are so perfectly suited to leading mankind into the new century.

Your sign has been called the sign of genius, for your ruler is capable of bringing thunderbolts of sudden inspiration and understanding to the rest of us. In the dictionary, *genius* is defined simply as "an extraordinary intellectual and creative power." We know from Thomas Edison that genius is also "1 percent inspiration and 99 percent perspiration." As an Aquarius, a fixed sign, you have exactly the kind of dogged determination needed to stick with a project. The Swiss philosopher Henri Amiel wrote how he delineated talent and genius: "Doing easily what others find difficult is talent, doing what is impossible for talent is genius." This applies to you, Aquarius, for genius is often the gift of Uranus.

Being misunderstood is something you have had to get used to, and it does not deter you. All great minds suffer ridicule at one time or another, and, luckily, you have the ability to shrug this off. In fact, you probably learned to wear your eccentricity as a badge of honor. As E. B. White put it, "Genius is more often found in a cracked pot than in a whole one." You don't mind being labeled radical. The rest of the world will always have trouble keeping up with you, Aquarius. You may be surprised and frustrated to see how long it takes people around you to catch up with your view of tomorrow.

Like most air signs, you approach everything with the same marvelous curiosity. This could involve something fun and silly, like figuring out a way to get your doorbell to chime the first few notes of Beethoven's Fifth, or something serious, like finding the cure for cancer. While Gemini will ask questions about things that happened, Aquarius wants to know how things work. You like to take things apart, whether it is a molecular cell (as in biotechnology) or a computer, to drill down to find its essence. And yes, while it is true that some Aquariuses can become too stubborn, rigid, or dogmatic about what they believe, most are not. Your most wonderful quality is your openness to the world.

Aquarius rules not only all things newly invented, but also all things that are not yet fully understood. For that reason, astrology comes under the domain of Aquarius. The mathematical properties and recurring cycles underlying astrology are particularly fascinating to you. You like to take apart things you don't understand, bit by bit, and then re-synthesize them in a totally new and fresh way. Aquarius astrologers are usually exceptionally talented for that reason. Truly Aquarius is an intellectual sign, but realize that if you live in your head most of the time, you may forget you have a body that needs care and exercise. Aquarius rules blood circulation, and if you notice that your circulation is poor (one sign being that you feel chilly much of the time), regular cardiovascular exercise would be an excellent idea. Aquarius also rules the ankles and, to a degree, the shins and calves. These are areas that might give you difficulty, so keep your joints nimble and flexible through stretching.

Being ruled by Uranus, the planet of electricity, you are also susceptible to nervous tension more than most and should factor in some regular downtime. Most of the time you like surfing the Net, playing computer games, going to the electronics store to shop for new toys, or watching *The X-Files* or *Star Trek* re-runs on TV. Since you love to play, Uranus keeps the kid in you very much alive. You must try to find a little time to attend to this child. You seem to get oxygen from time off, and it helps you find breakthroughs in your normal work.

Inherent in being an Aquarius is the occasional feeling of being a loner, and you probably felt like a square peg in a round hole at some important time in your life. Even as a child you may have felt different from the other kids or even from your siblings. This psychological separation from peers at a young age didn't hurt you. In fact, that very lack of peer acceptance only fueled your development as an independent thinker, and possibly as a leader too. To be outstanding in the truest sense, it is often very necessary for one to stand outside the circle.

You hold a great deal of minutiae in your head at once. Sometimes people say you are forgetful, but they simply don't understand that you are busy concentrating on things that matter most. You will remember all the tiniest details of a complicated mathematical formula but forget to pick up milk on the way home. Shopping for milk won't help you save the world, but spending time to formulate a new algorithm just might. When you are concentrating on something important, your fixed nature bores into the subject like a drill through concrete. You simply won't stop until you've turned over every stone.

When first meeting you, sometimes people assume that they must have seen you on television or have a feeling that you are about to become very successful. People say this to you continually, but you often aren't sure why. It could be that your demeanor is usually noble or especially refined and that you carry yourself especially well. If you aren't headed for stardom in the media, you can be sure it is within your community or company. If you want fame, it is possible for you.

If you do make it in the world, you will surely wear your success modestly. Pretentiousness is not something you tolerate in yourself or in anyone else. Being a highly and superbly communicative and analytical air sign, your climb to prominence will be built on a firm foundation of solid credentials, for Aquariuses tend not to do things by the seat of their pants. Being a fixed sign, you work hard and never give up, remaining ever mindful of your main goals.

You feel very strongly about human rights, social justice, and humanitarian issues. You do not tolerate prejudice in any form. Many Aquariuses find time to volunteer for philanthropic causes, for your sign tends to jump into action when seeing something that needs to be redressed. If it weren't for you, one wonders who would mobilize action to save the planet from oil spills and ozone contamination, and who would focus attention on the need to protect the rain forest. It was probably an Aquarius who started trash recycling and who won the fight for equal pay for equal work. You demand humane treatment of animals and lobby for more shelters for the homeless. Aquarius is on the forefront of prison reform, toxic waste cleanup, and research on the possible danger of electromagnetic fields. You name it, whatever ills society happens to be blind to, Aquarius will notice and point them out, and get something done about them.

One of your great gifts is that you don't see the differences among people but rather the similarities that bind them together in brotherhood. Aquarius has a strongly idealistic, altruistic bent with a strong destiny to work with groups of people who are linked by commonalities. The common denominator of the group could be those who work within your profession, or who share a common interest, such as people who want to learn more about computers or who want to help a certain charitable or political cause. Your understanding of man's similarities as a member of planet Earth extends to all ethnic, religious, and cultural groups—you always manage to see the common thread. You have psychic ability too, something your rational mind can't quite figure out but that you have to admit is truly remarkable.

You find answers to complex questions in unorthodox and creative ways. As an Aquarius, you will do whatever you need to do to shake up your thinking, often using random thought processes. This could mean studying unrelated fields to find possible parallels. Through perseverance (you are a fixed sign) and "accidents" you hit upon breakthrough discoveries. Incongruent facts and statistics fascinate you and you enjoy assembling them in new ways. You might also look to your horoscope to do some creative brainstorming. Or you might find yourself opening the dictionary and finding the fourth word in from the first sentence on page 179 (or whatever), forcing yourself to find any association between that word and your problem in order to open up your mind. The method you take doesn't matter as much as the result. Making new and sometimes weird associations helps you crack problems in creative ways. Forging new paths will always be your forté.

One especially strong quality about your sign is your uncanny ability to spot social trends long before the rest of us do. In marketing or product innovation, or in medicine, the sciences, art, or politics, Aquarius is light-years ahead of the rest of us. Often, however, because you are so forward thinking, you are misunderstood or your judgment is mistrusted. Other people may give you a hard time. You do your best work when you are not second-guessed by a committee and are allowed to follow your intuition. Eventually you do prove yourself to be an astute seer, having a pulse on the market and social consciousness before anyone else does.

## RELATIONSHIPS

Gregarious and outgoing, Aquarius has many friends and contacts (you seem to know everyone), but you allow only a few into your inner circle. Again, this is evidence of your need to keep a little distance, an inconsistency that puzzles people. (With so many hubs of people buzzing around you, who would suspect that you need plenty of space and privacy?) The unemotional, highly intellectual side of Aquarius makes you come off a bit distant and elusive at times. This is that mysterious coolness that others find so frustrating about you and yet at the same time are so attracted to. You are known to be "of the world" (a leader who responds to the crowd) rather than be oriented toward particular individuals on a personal scale. There are exceptions, of course, but by way of explanation, here is an example. While Pisces might be more oriented to help an elderly neighbor who now lives alone and who suffers with arthritis, you would be more likely to set up a foundation for worldwide arthritis research, mobilizing groups of people into action.

Friendship is something an Aquarius cares about deeply and doesn't take lightly. You tend to have friends for years, and over time your bond grows stronger. There is very little you won't do for a friend in need, for when an Aquarius loves in friendship, it is forever. Your warm, affable way makes you the star in any group. You probably withdraw from that ever-buzzing circle of people around you in order to think. You would not likely turn into one of those people who are so busy putting out fires that they never seem to get to plan their life. Not being too wound up about what is going on every moment allows you to focus on tomorrow, your favorite time zone.

In love, as in everything else you do, you reveal your innermost personal style. When you first start to date someone, you often like to be friends first before going to the next step. Your brain is always working and you never lose your head in love, so you tend to want to know your partner fairly well before moving forward. You prefer to enter a relationship holding the other person at arm's length until you have had a chance to figure him or her out and decide how you want to proceed. You want to see if this person will hold your interest and if he or she has things in common with you. Sex is important, but to you there are other vital ingredients in a relationship too. (Of course you do love experimentation in all of its forms, so some less-evolved Aquariuses might be on a continual and promiscuous search for new partners.)

Most Aquariuses look for an intellectual equal (this is a tall order), someone who is up to debate and discussion and who is interested in current trends. Others can gain your respect even if you don't agree with them. You do expect whomever you date (or marry) to have carefully formed opinions backed with research and defended intelligently. You will listen to the other's point of view to find out if there is any merit to what he has to say, and indeed, you will defend his right to say what is on his mind. With Gemini on the cusp of your house of love, you need to converse with your lover, and if he or she won't engage you in debate soon the fun will disappear from the relationship.

In terms of attraction, having a grand mastery or skill over a certain subject is the one quality you find irresistibly sexy and a real turn-on. This special knowledge or talent could relate to a person's profession, a pet project, or a life's passion. When you see someone exhibiting exceptional excellence along with a measure of joyful pride and enthusiasm, you find yourself falling in love, hook, line, and sinker.

Many members of your sign are known to have difficulty with the concept of marriage, either early in life or later, when you realize that the kind of togetherness that some marriages require is simply not your cup of tea. Marriage is an institution, and you have difficulty with anything established or conventional. You also don't like to fulfill other people's expectations; a sense of freedom and space is important to you. If you are in love, you will find a way to be with that person but you may take years actually to feel ready to apply for a marriage license. The whole idea of merging personalities or lifestyles with another person is a bit of an anathema to such an individualistic and independent sign, and quite scary, for you too. In your case, you do have to look to find that special person who understands the real you.

While many people marry for material or security reasons, you don't. You don't have a materialistic bone in your body, so the pooling of money and the amassing of resources have never been a big attraction. (What drives you are self-fulfillment and the ability to create or invent.) You feel that money and security are a poor excuse either to wed or to stay wed should the union become turbulent. Your idealistic nature tells you that a relationship should be based purely on love. Marriage might not agree with you because of your need to create a lifestyle that suits you, and this may conflict with your mate's ideas of what is best, or "normal." For example, your mate may want to eat dinner with you at roughly the same time each night. But since routine is something you resist at all costs, this could pose a problem. You dislike doing anything at the same time each day. You may have a job that requires an idiosyncratic schedule, but more often than not it is simply that you run from any kind of redundancy. You feel that spontaneity is the spice of life. You also dislike having to check with your mate before making plans (in your mind, it's a waste of time) or having to call him or her if you are running late (you don't want to stop when you are concentrating). Relationships bring constraints that may be hard for you to deal with. This is fine if your mate understands your sweet soul, but if not, prepare for a rough ride.

There is also the fact that you are highly self-controlled and rarely show your intense inner emotions. This can be hard in a relationship when your significant other wants to see those feelings. You tend to show only a calm, placid exterior most of the time, even if you are quite stirred inside. At the same time, your idealistic side wants to "do the right thing." If you fall in love but later discover that person to be wrong for you, you will move to end the relationship quickly but you will tend to do it in somewhat of a cold, practical manner. Your heart could be breaking, but you won't show it. This is simply the way you are as an Aquarius, very private and very practical when it comes to feelings.

## CAREER

Careers you would excel in include working in any capacity in radio and television broadcasting; the Internet; computers and other electronics; telecommunications and wireless systems; digital, artistic, and X-ray photography; or other areas of invention and high technology. You are a good communicator and know what people want to have or know about next. Therefore, consider writing, journalism, marketing, or advertising. You would also do well working in any of the sciences, including the biosciences, in the space program, as a mathematician, or as an astronomer. New Age professions are ruled by Aquarius too, so you have superb potential to grow into a talented astrologer, for example.

Consider, too, the social sciences, where you would put your humanitarian sensibilities to good use, perhaps by working for a not-for-profit charity or as a social worker. Finally, Aquarius works well in medicine, art, and other areas where you can push the envelope on new discoveries or develop your individuality through shock or surprise.

Money does not motivate you; rather, making a contribution or inventing something new does. Yet even if you aren't after money, the universe usually cares for you financially anyway. Other signs take for granted the "package" that society gives us at birth, but not Aquarius. Inside most

Aquariuses is an altruistic heart beating with a passionate need to give back to society. You also subscribe to the credo "Information must be free," especially when it comes to your beloved Internet, which you enjoy so much. You won't find many slick Aquariuses in the cyber-scam market because you aren't built that way. You veer away from things that exploit others. Your sense of right won't allow it.

Your role is to paint the broad strokes of your vision to inspire others. Your charisma is well known. Others will naturally want to follow you. Being an objective, rational thinker who loves to play with new ideas and concepts, you see what is missing in the marketplace quite readily. Combining that talent with the fact that you see yourself (rightly) as a "can-do" person, you roll up your sleeves and mobilize others to help you find a fix. Since you don't like dealing with details very much, you leave those to the Virgo or Taurus people around you, and it is just as well. This is what you are meant to do.

## FINANCE

Ruled by erratic Uranus, you don't like to feel contained or constricted in any way, so creating a rigid budget would not sit well with you. The way you keep track of checks written is, like everything else, a little unusual. Rather than be bothered with entering all your checks and deposits regularly into computer financial software (or add these items up with a calculator) you tend to keep an intuitive running balance in your head. This might unnerve your spouse or roommate, but soon you show the world that you are able to do this with remarkable accuracy, managing to remain above reproach!

You have been known to go through extreme cycles of saving and spending, such as when you have a goal in mind and miserly save every penny you make and then go out and blow it on one big purchase. Don't take this to mean that you are extravagant or that you often live beyond your means. Quite the contrary, dear Aquarius, you are not a big spender.

Pretentious status symbols offend your democratic, "one-for-all-and-all-for-one" style. Whereas a Taurus or Leo will crave a beautifully prepared dinner in a four-star restaurant or enjoy owning an expensive watch, you would more likely see such spending to be a waste of money. A modest, nutritious meal might be more healthful and a plastic digital time piece more utilitarian.

On the other hand, you aren't a tightwad, either. You see great value in tools that help you communicate, explore, or enjoy the world around you in a fun or convenient way. You also like things to be functional and well designed, and for those things you will occasionally spend large sums of cash. You enjoy your electronics—things that give you pleasure on a daily basis.

Like Aries, if you believe in an idea, you will fund your own business to launch it. Being a fixed sign, you are not a quitter, making you perfect for self-employment. On that count, if you use your love of technology in your work, you could find a financial bonanza. Aquarius easily senses future market trends, and that ability gives you an amazing edge. You like to work hard and you concentrate exceptionally well too—that sort of intensity helps you succeed.

When your bank balance does one of its characteristic roller-coaster rides, you know how to find more income. While financial success is not usually your main goal (contributing to society is a more compelling motivator), when your ship finally does come in, it usually brings a bounty in direct proportion to the extraordinary effort you have put in. Financially, you tend to take full responsibility for your actions, and this is a good trait. However, this quality might make you hesitant to seek expert advice when you need it, viewing your need to reach out as a weakness. Don't let pride stand in your way, dear Aquarius!

If you do come up with a good idea, be sure to get a patent or trademark early on. Don't let others take advantage of you! You can be so intent on perfecting your idea that you may lose sight of the need to protect your-self. Investing wisely in the right technology stocks is another way you could amass wealth.

## BODY, MIND, AND SPIRIT

There is always something memorable or unusual about your physical appearance and sets you apart from others. You may be exceptionally tall or lanky, or have a slightly asymmetrical face or walk in a certain way. If looking different didn't happen naturally, you took steps to make it happen. When you were five years old you probably cut your own hair, and when you grew up you shaved your head, or you style or color your hair fashionably or even aggressively. This is true whether you are a male or a female. Hair is only one way you might set yourself apart—there are dozens of other ways, like tattoos and body piercings.

You also decided early on that nobody was going to tell you what to wear or how to look; you were going to decide that for yourself, even if it defied convention. At black-tie events, it's the Aquarius who wears a tux with a pair of sneakers. Female Aquariuses refuse to become fashion vic-tims; they dictate looks and start trends. Aquarius is not a follower. You have thumbed your nose at society at some time or other, and it is not unusual for you to go to extremes. As an Aquarius, you know you are compelled to go against the grain. You simply won't do what everyone else expects you to do.

## SUMMARY

Aquarius's role is to be "out there"; neither males nor females of this sign are known to be particularly strong homebodies. The extreme example is the tireless volunteer who champions children's rights for her community but who is never home for own children. Realize that as an Aquarius you will have a very demanding role on the world stage, and very few things will get in the way of fulfilling that priority. Plan to get proper help and to set aside time for the people who love you and need your presence. Your life was never meant to be simple or straightforward, and it will be busy. The good news is that your ability to problem-solve is rarely stymied — you can surmount any obstacle if you train your mind to it.

Marriage can work out well if you have the forethought to select a mate who understands your need for space and for developing your talents to their full potential. Certainly life with you can be very exciting. Once smitten, no matter how friendly or flirtatious you might act in any given social situation, you are likely to remain true-blue to your partner because, being a fixed sign, stability in a relationship is something you value.

You are inventive, original, independent, and intuitive, as well as creative and imaginative, dear Aquarius, don't ever change. Your vision is our deepest hope for a better tomorrow.

# THE MYTHS OF
# AQUARIUS AND URANUS

By studying the myths that surround your sign, we can see many of the recurring themes that were thought to reflect your personality, Aquarius. In Greek mythology, Uranus is connected to the higher divine mind that is said to have invented the world. Uranus is symbolized as heaven or "sky" and is the original, most important mythological figure associated with creation. Uranus sexually awakened Mother Nature, whose name is Gaia, or Earth, by having an incestuous relationship with her. According to the myth, Uranus used thunderbolts and lightning to impregnate Gaia with the fertilizing seed of rain and, in doing so, Earth and sky were united, awakening life itself. As the father of the Greek story, Uranus set off the chain of events that led to life's unfolding.

Uranus soon found the offspring that he had had with Gaia were a difficult brood. Gaia had given birth to monsters, three one-hundred-handed giants and three Cyclops, as well as the twelve Titans (a term that would come much later, also said in the myth to be the first rulers of the universe).

## THE THREE CYCLOPS
The three Cyclops Gaia and Uranus had later became god-like figures in their own right, famous for being highly innovative smiths who forged thunder and lightning. The trouble with them was that they soon proved to be arrogant, willful, and yet powerful children who continually had dif-

ficulty relating to authority figures (said to be an Aquarius tendency too, by the way). Fit to be tied, Uranus threw his children into a dark underworld, where he hoped to contain them. All this while, Uranus was frustrated and disappointed—he felt that none of his children were perfect.

## CRONUS CONFRONTS HIS FATHER

One day, Uranus decided to bury his children one by one by pushing them back into the womb of Mother Earth (Gaia). As you can imagine, having so many of her children back in her womb proved to be painful. (Gaia would have twelve Titans, three Cyclops, and three one-hundred-handed giants in her uterus.) After a while, the burden was too much and Gaia, also known as Mother Nature, rebelled. Gaia crafted a sickle and then asked her children to volunteer to punish their father for trying to bury them. Most of the Titans did not want to confront their father, that is, none except for the youngest Titan, Cronus (known to be Saturn, the planet of mature responsibility). Cronus turned out to be the most daring child, probably because he despised this injustice most. He used the sickle to cut off his father's genitals, which he threw into the sea.

This violent act caused Uranus's blood to be splattered all over Gaia, causing her to become pregnant again. She later gave birth to the Furies (among other children), and the latter subsequently spawned violence, hatred, and rage upon the world. Uranus became understandably angry with his children and labeled them Titans (meaning "Over-Reachers"), and warned that Cronus's violent act would be avenged. Some good did arise from all this, for Aphrodite, goddess of love (Venus), was born, emerging from the sea foam on a half-shell. Thus, in this myth Cronus (Saturn) breaks free of Uranus's irrational behavior and through chaos ultimately restores order to the universe.

One would think that Cronus (Saturn) would turn out to be a wise ruler, but that was not the case. In actuality, Cronus behaved even worse than his father, Uranus, had. Uranus and Gaia had abilities to foresee the future (thus, as an Aquarius, you do too), and they told Cronus he too would be overthrown by his father, but Cronus loved power so much he didn't want to listen to their advice.

This story continues in the myth of Capricorn, but the point is made: If you think that perhaps the Uranus/Aquarius concepts illustrated here are inconsistent and somewhat chaotic, you are right—these myths capture the spirit of Aquarius (and Uranus) perfectly. In the world of Aquarius, the objective, mature, logical, scientific mind exists side by side with the wild, unruly, unpredictable, and chaotic. To an Aquarius, these concepts are necessary twins, existing as two halves of a whole. Your role as an Aquarius is to unite the irrational with the rational to create something completely new. This myth also underscores Aquariuses' need to foster individual independence while at the same time developing themselves as leaders, ones who are responsible for the welfare of the group.

The Romans asserted quite a different myth as part of the Aquarius model, and they insisted that theirs was the only true myth. The Romans felt that Ganymede, son of Tros, who was king of Troy, embodied the myth of Aquarius best.

## GANYMEDE

Ganymede was thought to be the deity responsible for showering the Earth with heaven's rain, again reinforcing the image of nurturing the Earth with life-giving properties. Additionally, Ganymede is said to have been the most beautiful boy alive, causing Zeus (Jupiter) to fall in love with him. Turning himself into an eagle, Zeus carried the boy off and assigned him to be cupbearer to the gods. In the tale, the gods drank ambrosia, not water, from a golden bowl. (*Ambrosia* is the same as the Sanskrit *amrita*, which means "drink of immortality.") Ganymede's father objected to Zeus's kidnapping his son, so Zeus sent the boy's father two elegant horses, explaining that in return for his work as cupbearer to the gods his son would become immortal. This reinforces the theme of consuming or giving a nourishing liquid and/or herb connected with the myth of Aquarius in one way or another.

Ganymede has been the symbol of homosexual love since the Middle Ages. Astrologers writing about the planet Uranus usually mention that sexual ambiguity is part of that planet's qualities. Uranus seems to be androgynous; not masculine or feminine but possessing the qualities of both sexes. This does not mean that people born under Aquarius, being ruled by Uranus, have a stronger tendency toward being homosexual than any other sign. (Nor does it mean that having a prominent Uranus in a natal horoscope fosters this proclivity.) Astrological text simply tells us that Uranus is neutral, and that it bestows a powerful intellectual talent on the sign that seems to be slightly stronger than the pull toward the physical. The myth suggests why being a committed and loyal friend is so deeply satisfying to you, dear Aquarius. Put another way, the quality of the relationship is just as important (or even more so) than pure physical pleasure. Once involved in an alliance, Aquariuses are just as passionate in their intimate relationships as any other sign.

## The Nile As Symbol of Life

We have seen the Greeks' explanation of Aquarius, and the Roman myth too, so now let's look at the Egyptian interpretation. To the Egyptians, Aquarius represented a power that renews, replenishes, and fertilizes all living things. The people of Egypt revered the life-giving qualities of the Nile, and it has been said that the icon that suggests Aquarius, the man holding pouring jugs, may mean that he is pouring waters of the Nile. At the end of July or in the first three weeks of August, the Nile almost always floods near the full Moon, the time of the year when the full Moon rises in the constellation of Aquarius. (The full Moon always rises in one's sign in the month six months away from one's birthday.)

Further, Egyptians thought the Nile was governed by the god Osiris. The holy shrine, the Temple of Elphantine, was considered among the holiest in all of Egypt and the spiritual gateway of the Nile. (In actuality, it wasn't the head of the Nile.) At that shrine resided a sacred relic, the shinbone of the god Osiris. (Not coincidentally, Aquarius is thought to rule the ankles and lower leg.) On the nearby island of Philae was found a bas-relief depicting Hapi, the god of the Nile, pouring water from two vases, also reminiscent of the symbol of Aquarius as the water-bearer pouring waters of life for the nourishment of mankind.

## ENKIDU

There is one myth that relates to Aquarius that stems from the Babylonians, the founders of astrology. Their name for Aquarius was Gula, which, translated, means both "goddess of childbirth and healing" and "the constellation of the great man." The latter is thought by scholars to refer to the giant god Enkidu, patterned after the sky-god Anu, who was formed to counterbalance the out-of-control arrogance of Gilgamesh. Enkidu turned out to be a kind and loving man, a very likable, freewheeling spirit who lived on the plain among wild animals. Enkidu befriended the beasts by releasing them from hunters' traps. He is often depicted in old images as a man watering an ox. When it came time for Enkidu to fight Gilgamesh, they initially went at one another but soon realized that they were well matched and formed a friendship instead. Thus, according to the legend, as an Aquarius, friendship comes easily to you.

## BOOK OF EZEKIEL

The four fixed signs of the zodiac recur again and again in Babylonian stories. Two appearances occur in the epic of Gilgamesh and in the Hebrew Book of Ezekiel. Here is the myth: When Enkidu died, Gilgamesh went looking for herbs of immortality, but he had to pass many tests to find it. The goddess first sent a bull against him (Taurus), which Gilgamesh survived. Gilgamesh also conquered "the pride of lions" (Leo). He passed through a gateway where the scorpion-men stood guard (Scorpio). Meeting up with the bull, lion, and the scorpion proved to be a kind of gauntlet that Gilgamesh had to run to prove his worth. Those three signs (Taurus the Bull, Leo the Lion, and Scorpio the Scorpion) form, when Aquarius is added, what is called in astrology the Grand Fixed Cross, a very difficult configuration that could be interpreted as a kind of supreme cosmic test. (Each is ninety degrees away from the others, forming a T that will be completed when Gilgamesh meets with Utnapishtim, who is an Aquarius.) Before Gilgamesh could reach the underworld, where Utnapishtim lives—Utnapishtim symbolized Aquarius—he had to do battle with these creatures.

Utnapishtim (Aquarius) seems to be a smart, resourceful, and spiritual guy. Having been warned of the coming flood, he built himself a boat and saved himself in a Noah-and-the-ark-type story. Utnapishtim (Aquarius) was rewarded by the gods for listening to divine advice, and was given eternal life guarding over the herb of immortality. His friend Gilgamesh did finally manage to find the herb he sought, only to lose it later. Thus, the moral of the story is that mankind still had a way to go (and much to learn) before being granted immortality. It is, in its own way, a story of hope, friendship, and victory over challenge.

Hopefully you have found some inspiration in these myths, as they are very revealing of your gifts.

# PISCES PERSONALITY

*Pisces*

February 19–March 20

*Guiding Principle*
"I Believe"

*How This Sign Feels Joy*
Finds joy in compassion, sympathy, and
deepening spirituality through altruistic
acts that ease suffering in others.

*In the New Millennium, Your Contribution to
the World Will Be . . .*
You do not focus on money or status symbols,
but rather on eternal truths and the universality of the human spirit. Your compassion
will inspire us all to rise to a higher, more
evolved state.

*Quote That Describes You*
"Compassion is the desire that moves the
individual self to widen the scope of its
self-concern to embrace the whole of the
universal self."

—Arnold J. Toynbee, an *Aries*

Pisces is born at the coldest and darkest part of the year, a time when spring is still beyond reach. Nature brushes the landscape in a whole range of winter whites and sparkling, icy blues. Many of life's other hues are softened and veiled under sheets of frozen ice. Icicles shiver and tinkle like tiny bells on leafless branches. The silent landscape is barren and perhaps harsh, but there is also a kind of holiness in its spare severity.

If the old bear, leaner from months of hibernation, should lumber out of his cave to look for food now, the howling winds may convince him to go back inside to hunker down a little while longer. Deer, fox, raccoon, and beaver will have a harder time finding nourishment too, but they are not alone. Even humans will note that their provisions are running low. The peaches, apricots, and cherries that were carefully preserved in Bell jars are almost gone by winter's end. Crops will be plentiful eventually, but not quite yet—for now offerings at the market are fairly thin. Winds are kicking up, suggesting that a new season is well on the way, but for now it is time to wait, rest, reflect, and visualize what should come when the weather softens. Cabin fever will give way to dreaming up images to entertain and humor the spirit, thoughts of fairies dancing on the fresh green lawn of summer or of whole communities of Lilliputians singing and playing on the windowsill. Life inside the mind will always be a source of rich inspiration.

Pisces is the twelfth, and therefore the last, sign of the zodiac, born at the end of the astrologic cycle, a time of limiting portions or even fasting, and a time to ready oneself for an entirely new cycle. Old obligations have to be fulfilled, new goals set, and a general state of readiness put in place. The concept of "less is more" that first emerged in Capricorn resurfaces in Pisces, but in a different, more spiritual way. In Pisces, self-denial is not carried out for earthy, practical reasons, as it is in Capricorn (such as to improve one's appearance or to balance one's bank account). Instead, self-denial is for deeper ends, to be worthy of redemption and renewal by cleansing and purifying the mind, body, and spirit. Most religions suggest the need for limiting food for atonement. No matter what their personal religious beliefs happen to be, there is always a sense in Pisces that life can hold a higher purpose and that finding that purpose is paramount.

## SYMBOLS

In the Pisces constellation there are two fish swimming in opposite directions; one swims upstream while the other one swims downstream, and they are tied together with a single cord. In Pisces there is always a choice between opposites, whether to follow the high road or the low road, to go with the current or swim against it, or to express the negative charge or the more divine, positive charge. It also suggests the need to reconcile and integrate both the material and the ethereal worlds into one. Pisces are often surprisingly good negotiators, and the most evolved members of the sign are ever cognizant of the need to keep a grip on reality while maintaining their quest for ever higher spirituality. Of course not all Pisces are evolved. There are some Pisces who are too willing to indulge themselves—for surely this is a sign prone to extremes—but these Fish must eventually learn that they need to practice abstinence to purge themselves of the substances that are not good for their mind, body, or spirit.

Some experts feel the glyph of Pisces may possibly be an Egyptian hieroglyph meaning psychic regeneration. The two fishes symbolize the two hemispheres of the brain, and the line or cord that links the two is said to represent the psychic state or the "third eye" that brings Pisces "second sight."

Pisces is guided by the planet Neptune, the planet of altruism, dreams, spirituality, and faith, and as such engenders great compassion, insight, creativity, and inspiration, as well as a deep sensitivity to beauty. Called the Planet of the Mist, Neptune merges with whatever it touches, for this planet's waters are not easily contained. Its symbol is the trident, Poseidon's pitchfork, symbolizing the threefold parts to man: body, mind, and spirit, the greatest of these being spirit. Neptune can help each of us imagine—and reach for—a better reality.

## PLANETARY INFLUENCES

Neptune was first discovered in 1846, so prior to its discovery Jupiter was considered Pisces' ruler, and, accordingly, many astrologers still note Jupiter as the co-ruler of Pisces in a horoscope. As we saw with Sagittarius, Jupiter is also a spiritual planet, a planet of seemingly boundless optimism, and a strong symbol of hope. If we travel back in time to Olympian times there is evidence that the god Neptune was then considered ruler of Pisces, so there has always been a connection to this sign.

An extraordinary talent of Pisces is that when they strive to express an emotion artistically, whether it be love, despair, loneliness, or any other concept, rather than hold that emotion at arm's length to study it, Pisces brings it so close that they easily, naturally, and unconsciously become that feeling. Neptune, their ruler, teaches this sign to merge, so there is never a wall separating Pisces from the emotion they are studying. Pisces crystallizes ideas by bringing them up from the bottom of the sea of their unconscious. Having Neptune as ruler gives Pisces special insight into the feelings of the masses. Pisces feel their pain, hear their longings, and predict what they are likely to want as time goes on. Pisces are the philosophers and the seers, the sign most in touch with others around them, so much so that they are able to sublimate their own egos in their altruistic quest to serve others for the greater good. Neptune makes Pisces great visionaries too, but, unlike Virgo, who notices every detail on the leaves of the trees (but misses the forest), Pisces sees the forest in its fullest panoramic image (but keeps tripping over the underbrush directly in front of him). Pisces has great foresight but could, at times, use a little more near-sightedness.

## Cosmic Gifts

A horoscope relates not only to one individual but also serves as an overall map, tracing mankind's development and evolution. Ancient astrologers wrote that each sign gains from all the zodiac signs that precede it. Thus Pisces, as a compilation of all the signs that have come before, carries within it the collected knowledge and wisdom of all the signs, as well as some of their wishes and dreams. Like a prism of colors that comes to shine out the pure white when whirled and combined, Pisces has much to draw upon and a corresponding heavy obligation as the zodiac's philosopher. Within every Pisces heart is the desire to leave the world a better place.

By the time the wheel of the horoscope rotates to Pisces, man is viewed as having gained wisdom and now stretches upward to reach his highest possible form of spiritual evolution. In Pisces, man is now capable of stepping outside himself and his own needs to see where his contribution to the world would best be achieved. Deep down, Pisces believes in universal love and the goodness of mankind, and perhaps this is why this sign often seems magically protected by outside forces, such as by guardian angels. Pisces yearn to find their true destiny and, like their opposite sign, Virgo (whose birthday falls six months earlier), Pisces need to satisfy an inner calling to serve and to be helpful to others.

The symbolic beauty of nature at the time of Pisces' birth echoes this water sign's sensibilities and strong emotionality. By middle March, Mother Nature has usually initiated her spring thaw, and the world fills with liquids. This is poetically appropriate because Pisces' ruler, Neptune, as the old powerful god Poseidon, governs all liquids on Earth. So the majestic waterfall and the graceful pond, the fog and the morning dew, the deep blue lagoon and the toxic, black brackish water that can harm, and the holy water that is said to heal all come under Neptune's domain.

In March, winds will kick up and clouds laden with moisture will gather and break open in showers, triggering the melting of the snows. In the meantime, tiny purple crocuses, those perennial harbingers of hope, will push their faces up through the earth and delicately announce their arrival. Brooks and rivers will begin to gush, and the frosty lid covering the lake starts to crack, melt, and dissolve into the lucid deep pool of blue beneath. Sweet sap of the sturdy maple trees will also awaken and begin to flow steadily into wooden buckets hooked securely to their trunks. Pisces, born just prior to Mother Nature's re-awakening of spring, carry within their hearts the ever-present hope of better days to come and are eternally rewarded for that faith.

Until spring comes, however, at the end of February and during most of March, nature is still quite dark and blustery in northern latitudes, so there is little or no impulse to go out of doors. Like the old bear, most of us choose to stay inside, where life is dry and cozy warm. Appropriately, for Pisces what is happening outside, in what people refer to as "real life," will never be nearly as important as what happens in the inner recesses of their hearts and souls.

In Christian religions, sometime within the period of Pisces' birth, the end of February through March 20, marks the beginning of Lent, which is a period of fasting, abstinence, or denial. Lent was started by Christian followers to honor the ritual purification of the blessed mother Mary forty days after the birth of Jesus. Christmas falls on December 25, and Lent starts approximately forty-five days later (corresponding with the sign of Pisces; it is exactly half of a season), beginning a forty-day period that is considered a spiritual gestation cycle. It is believed that any habit can become fully entrenched if followed for forty consecutive days—after that, it's yours. Modern social scientists agree that there is truth in this line of thinking, and it seems to have some basis in science.

Lent begins on Ash Wednesday, usually in late February, and echoes Jesus' forty-day period of fasting and meditation. The day prior to Ash

Wednesday is called Shrove Tuesday, and *shrove* means a confession that is made before penance. (Lent begins on a different day each year, depending upon when Easter arrives. On a lunar calendar, Easter is always the Sunday following the full Moon on or just after the spring equinox).

In ancient days, followers of Lent gave up eggs and fat. That is why the start of Lent is preceded in many places by the Mardi Gras, translated literally as "Fat Tuesday," a day of reveling before followers initiate their period of denial. Today church followers schedule meatless days and relinquish certain self-indulgent habits in order to get ready for the spiritual renewal that occurs at Easter time.

In Pisces, self-indulgent habits are sacrificed not only to heal and to achieve an improved sense of self-worth, but also to show love and devotion to one's creator and for purification of one's soul. This goal differs from Capricorn's self-imposed discipline as a reaction against the excesses of Sagittarius found in December.

In "Virgo Personality" we spoke about the virgin who holds a shaft of wheat, signifying bread. In Virgo's opposite sign (and therefore on the same axis), we now meet Pisces, represented by the fishes. Thus we are reminded of the story of the miracle of the loaves and the fishes in the Bible, which is recounted previously in "The Myths of Virgo and Mercury."

Albert Einstein, a famous Pisces, once said that you could think of life in one of two ways: You could assume that life held no miracles at all or, conversely, that life held nothing *but* miracles. Pisces will always choose the latter way of thinking because they inhabit a world based on bright and beautiful spiritual wonders. When others finally look at life through Pisces' eyes, they are often enlightened. Indeed, Pisces will explain patiently that many of life's gifts are sent as blessings of a caring universe but are also all too readily taken for granted. Your sign knows that if life is lived in a positive manner, everyday miracles will help them toward their ultimate, chosen destiny.

Compassion is one of Pisces' finest attributes, something no other sign of the zodiac, except Cancer, can begin to match. Even compared to Cancer Pisces chooses to go the extra mile. Pisces' need to relieve suffering is so strong that they will go beyond helping friends and family to serving total strangers. Pisces easily walks in others' moccasins. Because they are psychic sponges, Fishes need regular time alone to rinse themselves of others' cares, to meditate and to regroup their energies. Neptune's mist blurs borders, so Pisces, not a sign associated with a strong ego, sees no difference between "I" and "thou." In fact, Pisces' ability to mirror the full spectrum feelings of the people they are with is legendary. When their friends are happy, Pisces are happy too, and when they hurt, Pisces feel others' pain as if it were their own. All is revealed in Pisces' large and expressive eyes, a glistening mirror to what they are thinking and feeling.

People take advantage of Pisces' good nature, and Fishes will readily admit that is true. Yet the Fish will silently smile to themselves as they admit this, forgiving their friends for not being evolved enough to stand on their own. Pisces will often allow others to draw their energy from their pool of strength because it is nearly bottomless and it continues to be replenished. Says the typical Pisces: "If that person needed to take from me, let him, for maybe he needed to do so. May God bless him." Pisces is always the philosopher, ready to forgive and to say to himself: "They know not what they do." Indeed, if there was ever a sign that was prone to turning the other cheek, it is Pisces. Evolved Pisces won't let people with bad behavior drag them down to their level. Most Pisces strive to be above reproach, for this sign tends to be the most spiritually motivated of all.

Pisces deals especially well with ambiguity in all of its forms, and this is why it is called the sign of faith and hope. To Pisces, opposites or inconsistencies are simply a part of Nature, and, consequently, Pisces feels that mysteries are there to be celebrated. Pisces knows that not all things in the universe can be explained and answered in one lifetime, or even over several lifetimes. Pisces pities those who insist on using only their limited five senses to find answers to life's questions. This sign has always relied on another sense, a sixth sense, which has always served them well.

Pisces rules the twelfth house, the part of the zodiac that rules seclusion, dreams, memories, secrets, and confidential matters as well as medical help and healing. It also rules places of confinement like hospitals, rehabilitation centers, and even prisons, for this place in the horoscope governs such concepts as restraint, limitations, silent suffering, and parts of life that remain hidden but are sometimes revealed. Ancient astrologers wrote about this sign's occasional proclivity for self-undoing, and by this they meant the troubles that we all experience in life that are no one's fault but our own. Evolved Pisces can clearly sidestep these potholes, but some, particularly young, impressionable Pisces, often have to stumble once or twice before they learn. Pisces finds that the very best way to deal with depression or a stressful time is to do charity work. This pulls them out of their self-involvement and gives them comfort in knowing they have endeavored to make the world a better place.

Sleep is part of Neptune's rule, and Pisces particularly understands the value of that mysterious sliver of time between wakefulness and slumber, for it is when the subconscious mind speaks to them most clearly. Pisces enjoys life most when the edges have been blurred. In a way, the very thin point between genius and madness is so very Pisces in spirit. This is a twilight zone of time that other signs dismiss or simply do not recall; it is, nevertheless, an altered state that Pisces draw on to enlarge their intuition. When they are too sleepy to submerge or inhibit their emotions, truth springs free. Pisces also find enormous meaning and direction in their dreams, providing them with both insight and a compass to direct their energies. Some signs, particularly the earth signs, Taurus, Capricorn, and Virgo, as well as intellectual, analytical Aquarius and Gemini, need to see and touch, taste and hear all parts of the world around them to make sense of it. This is not so with Pisces. Of course this love of life with softened edges can give some Pisces a need for a crutch, such as for drugs or alcohol, but those Fish are in the minority.

An exquisite quality of Pisces is that they see beauty everywhere, in the
smallest, most common things, in places others easily overlook. Evolved
Pisces also find that their creativity gives more satisfaction than anything
they could possibly buy. Pisces will never do anything purely for money, so
this sign isn't likely to "sell out." Pisces realizes he or she is part of a tempo-
ral world—and the plane that Pisces soars on is far more ethereal. If they
were to win a pot of gold Pisces would build a hospital or start a foundation. Perhaps that's why money finds its way to them when they are busy
thinking about something else, busy creating and weaving their dreams.

When Pisces suffers during a particularly dark period, this sign can literally or figuratively be brought to tears by others' gestures of kindness
toward them. These episodes always make a big impression on Pisces,
and once they see the shining divinity of another person's heart they are
forever changed by the experience. They can no longer be impressed with
superficial standards of grace that one age or moment in time dictates,
and, concurrently, they are even more determined to pass the baton by
helping others in return. Pisces' understanding of true beauty crosses
cultural and ethnic barriers. Through their own suffering this sign comes
to see the white light of human spirit, and, once glimpsed, the experience,
for Pisces, will be unforgettable.

The color violet, associated with Pisces, is found at the end of the spectrum,
and when extended a bit farther, it becomes ultraviolet, disappearing into
the wide, unknowable yonder of complete universality, an appropriate
metaphor for Neptune, the planet ruling things that are both universal
and invisible.

Nature has blessed Pisces with what can only be called night vision. This
is their right-on instinct that serves as a protection, and it never fails
them. The symbols of the other two water signs, Cancer and Scorpio, are
the crab and the scorpion—both creatures can exist on either land or
water. Unlike those, the fish cannot live on land, for it cannot breathe air.

Thus it must remain in water to survive. Further, because the Fish has no claws, horns, or even a way of calling for help with a roar, chirp, or bark, Nature had to give the tender fish a better protective device. Thus, Pisces has the blessings of precognition and sharpened instinct. Friends and family will marvel at Pisces' uncanny ability to read thoughts clearly, as if listening to some unseen radio waves in the air. It's been said that thoughts are in fact vibrations of energy, so it is entirely possible that Pisces, like certain animals, hear at frequencies that are beyond the average person's range. No one will ever be able to figure out how or why this extrasensory perception works, but it does, and it seems to be beamed at birth to Pisces to secure their safety.

As discussed throughout this book, every sign of the zodiac balances the qualities of the sign that precedes it. Thus, Pisces, reacts against Aquarius's cool and purely objective, detached point of view. Pisces knows that facts can be flawed and have their own limitations. Intuition, on the other hand, is almost always on target, for Pisces knows that the heart tends to speak only the truth. If science often questions faith, Pisces does the opposite by expanding and enlarging faith. Pisces want to explore the world by listening to the whisperings of their heart rather than by investigating it through the lenses of a microscope.

Pisces know they will be criticized or taunted by others for being "feeling" people who happen to live in an age that values science. Standing firm no matter how heated the debate becomes, Pisces recognize truth when they physically feel it. The twelfth house of the horoscope, which rules Pisces, also rules the subconscious mind and balances the sixth house, which is ruled by Virgo. Both take up the same amount of space in a horoscope wheel; therefore both have the same potential to bring insight. Pisces knows that the subconscious mind can pick up vast amounts of information under the radar of consciousness, where intuition is born. While the conscious mind begs to know, "What and why?" the subconscious mind whispers, "Simply listen, and the universe will tell you." In this, the last sign of the zodiac, wisdom and insight are born of the understanding that some things cannot be explained away easily and keep the faith that all truths would be revealed eventually.

While Aquarius works very effectively in groups, reserved Pisces often chooses to work directly with needy individuals one at a time. A more lively, outgoing Pisces might be able to work both ways. Both Aquariuses and Pisces are highly sensitive to their fellow man, usually expressing a desire to help in different ways. It is interesting to note that Aries, the next sign and harbinger of spring, counterbalances Pisces' almost complete lack of ego. Thus, Aries underscores the importance of the "self" and individual expression. Aries is the sign of entrepreneurial, pioneering spirit and is known to have strong confidence—something many Pisces lack, particularly in youth. This is how the cosmos intended each sign to serve the world best.

Friends urge Pisces to be more of a hard-head, to draw the line in the course of social interaction, but it is nearly impossible for Pisces to do this because Neptune's mist makes Pisces resist containment or drawing boundaries. If you are a member of this sign you know that doing so could practically make you ill. If you must put your foot down, you dress your words carefully, always trying not to hurt the other person's feelings. This does not mean you are wishy-washy or unsure of your intentions. The Fish can be very determined, even stubborn at times (thanks to Taurus on the cusp of their third house of communication). You always achieve your ends, but in a way that allows you to retain your sensitivity and dignity.

Pisces' ability to mirror emotion stems partly from the way the fish is formed and partly from watery Neptune as their ruler. The fish is one of the oldest forms of life, coming out of the very waters of creation. They have a long spine and, instead of a head, legs, and arms (like humans and many other creatures do) they have an ultrasensitive body. Their fins notice the smallest changes in rhythms and vibrations in the currents of the water they inhabit. Sound is louder and travels faster under water than in air, so the Fish can sense those sounds—even *feel* those sounds— faster than most other creatures on Earth. This underwater sensitivity to sound, brought by Neptune, is undoubtedly why Pisces is known to be so talented with music.

To Pisces, the greatest gift is one's time, given freely, and with good spirit and never grudgingly. Not surprisingly, Pisces have many friends in all walks of life and of all religious and ethnic backgrounds. But aside from their friendships, they are continually finding needy people (sometimes perfect strangers) to help and possibly bring home, much to the chagrin of their partners. The reason for Pisces' clear-eyed priority to help others is the understanding that life is for now but a soul lasts forever. Pisces' focus is fixed not on the mundane, but on eternity.

While water cleanses and purifies, it can also silently poison or harm in other ways. This double-edged sword of Neptune is always there—this planet can inspire hope, empathy, and purification, but it also can bring confusion and deception, and even kill. Pisces always have to walk between the two, never allowing themselves to be engulfed by the waters of Neptune. For some, that's not easy to do. We all have read of certain Pisces musicians and actors, for example, who, overwhelmed with stardom, turn to drugs and drinking as an escape from the pressures of success or the confused emotions they feel as life continues to make demands on them. Sometimes too visionary and not practical, Pisces have to strive for clear thinking and the setting of goals. Once they do, this all-or-nothing sign can rocket to stardom or find the inner peace they crave. In a sense, they can write their own ticket.

Faced with a crisis, Pisces can become overwhelmed and feel like they're drowning in a sea of emotion. Or they may report that they feel adrift in the middle of a vast ocean, lonely and disconnected from the very people they always helped but who are now suddenly missing. As the old saying goes, "Success has many fathers, but failure is an orphan." Pisces may be at a loss about how to make it back home to terra firma, but the answer is that they must try to reach out to others for help. While this sign will encourage others to come to them (always offering on-target advice), they seem strangely hesitant to go to others for assistance, supposing they would be a burden.

It is undeniable, however, that the occasional crisis Pisces endure allows them to find their deepest reservoirs of strength. As Pisces awaken from a dream of illusion, the torrents of life will inevitably force them to confront directly the very things they fear. A highly misunderstood sign, Pisces is too often and too easily dismissed by the other signs as weak. When the chips are down, they soon prove to be stronger than anyone supposed. Pisces' survival skills are powerful, and their instincts, as said earlier, often are amazingly sharp and always help them figure out how to slip out of most of life's tangled nets. And if they have chosen to live life as the good Fish, with a pure soul and good intentions, the universe has a way of saving even those Pisces who have no one but themselves to blame for their misfortunes. (Pisces have been known to shoot themselves in the foot.) Again, Pisces can emerge triumphant if they put their minds to it.

The ocean is highly changeable so mutable Pisces can be moody, but not as much as their fellow water sign Cancer, because Cancers are ruled by the Moon. The sea can be rough, with torrential storms and gale-force winds and terrifying waves, but then, soon after, the waters calm, returning to a clear and peaceful crystal blue. In turn, Neptune gives Pisces the ability to change form in the same way and with the same speed Neptune's waters do. This gives Pisces a fantastic edge of adaptability that allows them to survive under the most difficult circumstances. If one method is not working, the Fish can try another in the twinkling of an eye. Pisces is chameleon-like in that it can adapt to almost any circumstance, even extremely difficult ones, and, as we all know, survival belongs to those who are able to adapt most adroitly to their environment.

Pisces is the sign thought to represent the feelings of humanity—the collective, unconscious emotions of all mankind, the common denominator that unites us all, no matter our age, gender, or nationality. "Great collective" includes the prevailing mass opinions, fashions, trends, and politics of an age. In Pisces, the antenna is up so high that they know precisely the prevailing thought of the moment. In contrast, Sagittarius feels a link to mankind through ideas and the contributions of knowledge made by the various civilizations of the world as a family of man. Pisces links people in a more instinctive way, through the kinship of mutual emotions.

Add to this that Pisces are very right-brain-oriented, quite different from their polar opposite sign, Virgos, who are highly verbal and precise in left-brain functions. Because information tends to enter visually, Pisces is especially adept at reading symbols, body language, gestures, a look, or a glint of the eye more precisely than any other sign. Thus, this creature can sense anyone's true intent, for Pisces, like Capricorn, trusts actions over words. But, unlike Capricorn, the Fish will read body language and voice inflection in addition to interpreting what people are doing, and come up with a very sound idea of what is going on.

Romantic, emotionally sensitive, and extremely imaginative and creative, it is easy to see why Pisces excels in the arts. The realms of photography, film, music, writing, poetry, dance, acting (which is enhanced by the chameleon qualities we discussed earlier) are all perfect for this sign. This is, indeed, the zodiac's poet. They work best when others do not impose structure, for they need to feel free, working where they like and when they like, at all hours. As said earlier, the need to make a strong contribution to whatever they are doing is their key motivator, not the money to be made. Yet Fish are superb negotiators too, for they understand human psychological motivation. People in business continually underestimate this sign, assuming the Fish to be weak or wishy-washy, yet if you are a Pisces you know that this almost always turns out to be an advantage. Opponents keep trying to guess what you are likely to do next, but they are almost always wrong.

Pisces is comfortable in chaos and indeed seems even to thrive on it.
Pisces' ease with disorder, confusion, and general randomness is linked
to their deep wellspring of creativity. Their ability to deal with ambiguity
also allows this sign to make new discoveries. Even those who don't work
in traditionally artistic professions are able to work in the midst of general
clamor and pandemonium, for their concentration is usually superb and
their detail ability sound. Pisces are also able to spot quickly whatever is
missing in an endeavor and to find ways to compensate for that missing
puzzle piece right away. In that regard they are a little like Capricorn.

Unlike the Goat, however, Pisces is an artist, and as such often chooses
to fulfill the artist's function. That is, to portray the roles the rest of us,
collectively, are about to assume before any of us knows consciously that
we are headed in that direction. The successful artist offers a memorable
icon that resonates as especially "right." The grand collective—the masses
of a region, or of the world—views what Pisces has offered and says,
"Yes, that's it, exactly who I am becoming, and who I want to be, and
indeed who I am now!" An artist not only has the role of predicting the
future identity of an entire culture, but he or she may also suggest lifestyle
choices. Thus, the artist has a very subtle but profoundly powerful influence
on mass culture. Fashions, music, and art, the style of homes, the politics
of the times and the books read, all are influenced by the artist in Pisces'
domain. If Pisces chooses not to enter the arts, the other strong pull will
be to medicine, to healing the body, mind, or spirit.

Up to now, we have discussed the serious, spiritual side of this sign, but
Pisces have an equally strong playful side. The five-year-old child inside
is still very much alive, and this explains why their creativity is so strong.
Pisces think the world would be a terrible place without theme parks, cartoons, and fairy tales. The Fish feels that fantasy will always beat reality
for it allows the creative Fish to build the world they see in their rich
imaginations. Reality may bruise Pisces, but a creative project or a little
time in VR (virtual reality) provides a path to another time and space, and

Pisces enjoys being swallowed up in it. Fantasy allows Pisces the ability to be truly himself, to become the person he sees in his mind's eye. While of course this tendency for escapism can pose a danger, for most well-adjusted Pisces it is only good, serving as a protective device for them, a secret place of the mind and heart that allows them to heal whatever wounds they may have.

So Pisces goes to Orlando to see Disney World, to New Orleans, Las Vegas, Tinseltown (Hollywood), or other such "never-never lands" that offer theme parks or other fun ways to forget reality, if only for a while. Going to a place like this can help refresh Pisces' spirit, as long as they don't go overboard. In Pisces' mind it is perfectly possible to fly or even to hurl oneself into space or to inhabit other planets. If you tell a Pisces they can't possibly do this, they'll roll their eyes and tell you they feel sorry for you.

Actually, sometimes Pisces would rather visit places in their mind — as part of their productive daydreaming — than actually go to places in real life. After all, if they go in real life there is always the chance of being disappointed. The realities of the airport, or the parking, or the difficulties of being treated like a tourist can make the trip a nightmare. On the Internet or on a virtual-reality adventure these problems vaporize. Pisces could live for days by falling, like Alice in Wonderland and the White Rabbit, down the chute into the depths of exciting panoramic images. They think pixie dust might actually exist — Pisces will always believe in miracles and magic. Both Michael Eisner, who heads Disney, and Steve Jobs, founder of Apple Computer and Pixar, often speak about the "magic kingdom" or "leading the faithful." Tell *them* reality is better than fantasy and they will both laugh out loud. Of course! They're Pisces!

In the movie *Brazil,* the characters agreed that a still-life picture of the meal they ordered from the waitress was better than having the real thing. To Pisces that makes perfect sense. Visuals are eye candy, and pleasing sights nourish them more than anything they could ever put into their mouths. Pisces continually run out of household staples like milk, butter, soap, and garbage bags. But they won't ever run out of paints and canvas, film and dark-room paper, RAM and bandwidth, or scissors and glue—whatever their creative tools happen to be—for those are too precious to them.

The most important thing to remember is that Pisces has a great imagination, perhaps the richest and purest of all the signs of the zodiac. Alternative worlds of the inner mind and heart are simply too compelling not to investigate. When their third-grade teacher told them, "Someday you will read books that don't have any pictures. You won't need them and you'll never miss them," these little tots wagged their heads, saying quietly to themselves, "No, that's never going to happen, because I love pictures too much."

## RELATIONSHIPS

Let's turn to Pisces' romantic side, as a lover and as a part of a relationship. As you might suspect, Pisces is incredibly tender and magically romantic. Modest, reserved, and possibly even shy, the Fish wants a close, private relationship with someone who will explore the full spectrum of human emotions rather than a lover who will skim the surface of a relationship. This is why neither air nor fire signs (Gemini, Libra, Aquarius, Aries, Leo, or Sagittarius) are generally quite right for Pisces. Pisces always need a loving intensity in their relationships and they want to dive to the bottom of the sea of love to experience love's fullness. Pisces always believe in their ability to achieve a "happily ever after" with someone special. They often do find the love they seek, if only because they are so giving.

There is a very strong reason for Pisces' romantic and giving nature. Neptune is considered the "higher octave of Venus," which means that Neptune brings the beauty of Venus to a higher and more spiritual level. As we saw in Taurus and Libra, Venus rules beauty and harmony, so Venus is happy and tends to increase the sensual pleasures, but Venus may also be a tad hedonistic. Venus deals with the outer world, the fun, parties, and other places and forms of enjoyment, and, after setting the scene, initiates the flirting and the initial spark of chemistry between lovers. Neptune celebrates beauty in the deeper and broader aspects of love. If Venus is earthly touch or feeling, Neptune brings sensitivity into the psychic realm. Venus wants to enjoy love, but Neptune is so encompassing that it will suffer for love and will even sacrifice for it. Neptune's job will be to bring that first spark of sexual attraction to a much higher, more spiritual sphere, possibly to commitment (with the help of other planets). If Venus is concerned with the outer world that one can see and touch, Neptune is more interested in the inner life of heart and soul.

Pisces' dream lover would be a Cancer, a Scorpio, another Pisces, or a Taurus, Virgo, or Capricorn. The Fish longs for someone sensitive and diplomatic, supportive and affirming, because Pisces sometimes need a little boost in the self-confidence department, no matter how successful they happen to be. Their partner should also have an adventurous spirit when it comes to traveling and at the same time be romantic enough to provide the element of surprise and fun in the years they are together. A gregarious sign, Pisces likes mixing in the social scene too, but will need an equal amount of solitude — too much socializing will leave the Fish flustered and in desperate need of rest.

Pisces long to be understood and want to be valued for their shining qualities and flaws alike. A Fish won't ever enter a relationship quickly or cavalierly, but always slowly and tentatively. This sign knows their feelings are easily hurt, so they are understandably self-protective, especially at the onset. Once they know they can trust the other person, they will be supportive and caring and will move toward commitment. Don't be crude or overly aggressive — this sign prefers a subtle and indirect approach. Come across brash and this Fish will vanish in the rocks beneath the sea, and you'll never find it again.

In choosing someone to love, a typical Pisces will seek to balance his or her artistic and sentimental nature with a person of rock-solid practicality who also is steadfastly dependable, loyal, and emphatic in nature. Pisces also likes an industrious partner, someone who works hard and is enthusiastic about his or her work. Be aware that Pisces are often intense about their own work (especially if they have a creative job, which can result in a twenty-four-hour-a-day, seven-day-a-week situation), so they think it's normal for others to be that way too.

In lovemaking, Pisces want to experience the passion of a near religious experience, one where the world drops away and two souls blend into one. This sign has a natural grace and rhythm that makes them simply unforgettable sexual partners. The quality of the experience will depend on the depth of true feelings of both partners—Pisces is looking for authentic emotions. If thunder and lightning don't occur early during the courtship, Pisces will wait a little while to see what develops. After a time, however, if lightning doesn't strike, Pisces will try to find out why. If they sense that their partner simply isn't on the same vibration, they will give up and silently swim away. Scenes are not their "thing," so Pisces' partner may awaken one morning to find this Fish gone. A disillusioned Fish who has suffered heartbreak will need a long time to heal; Pisces does not get over broken love affairs easily.

However, if the relationship is sweetly harmonious and provides a certain spice of excitement, Pisces will open a floodgate of emotion for their beloved. Idealistic, they will always see their partner in the best light. The most compelling phrase their lover ever could utter to Pisces is "I need you." There is almost no way a Pisces could not respond. Pisces want to make a difference in others' lives and will give their love freely in return. They are willing to sacrifice much for their beloved, as well as for the children who may come later. If you are a partner of a Pisces, you will need to encourage your sweetie to think about him- or herself too, as sometimes they go overboard by giving family too much of themselves and can become almost martyr-like in their denial of their own enjoyment. Because Pisces keep their inner child so wonderfully alive, they will make fantastic parents. (The desire for children is usually quite strong, and it's a big reason to get married in the first place.) Pisces will encourage and support their partners to scale heights they would never have tried alone, and they listen not only with their ears but also with their whole heart. Powerful, faithful, curious, playful, and always looking for a little surprise, Pisces bring an enchanting, bewitching quality of romance to their union. Pisces keep that stardust in their eyes, so if you are in love with a Pisces treasure him or her, for you will have found a compassionate, imaginative partner who will encircle you with endless love.

## FINANCE

Financially, Pisces has astounded more than a few members of the other signs by pulling out ahead of the pack. With Aries poised on the cusp of the second house, Pisces are comfortable generating their own income and with whatever that entails, so being self-employed suits them. Pisces are frequently known for success in *two* professions, often at the same time.

*Forbes* magazine recently conducted a poll of the *Forbes* 400 millionaires and billionaires. The results of the poll revealed that Pisces led the zodiac in producing the highest percentage of self-made millionaires and billionaires. The exact percentages were 11.3 percent Pisces with Aquarius in second place at 9.4 percent. (*Forbes* magazine, October 16, 1995, pages 380–382.)

## CAREER

Pisces make brilliant filmmakers, virtual-reality producers, designers, animators, cartoonists, musicians, storytellers, producers, and studio heads. They also make talented photographers and cinematographers, film editors, or film directors. Add the job of special-effects artist, art director, hairstylist or makeup artist, costume designer, prop designer or fashion stylist — the more fanciful the better. You get the picture of what they do well.

To readers who are not Pisces, here is a little warning: Pisces are sensitive. They are also ultraloyal and expect you to be that way too. Pisces do not like confrontation, so if you criticize their creative efforts do so delicately, or they will feel as though you've attacked them or that you hate their creations (you will note that they refer to their creations as their "children"). If you insult them, they won't put up a fuss or argue with you. Instead, they will simply, quietly, and silently swim away and never come back. If they go, believe me, you'll miss them. A life without your Pisces is like a life without Mickey Mouse, Goofy, Peter Pan, Woody Woodpecker, the Jolly Green Giant, the Pillsbury Dough Boy, the Ghostbusters, and Superman all rolled into one. They bring joy to all ages, everywhere, so if you must criticize, be gentle.

Pisces also make great movie stars. If you are a Pisces, know that you probably have exceptional talent because Neptune gives you the ability to morph into many different forms. Neptune has a glittering quality too—think of the iridescent, sequin-like scales of the fish—so if you are Pisces you would take well to stardom, enjoying the real-life role of glamour too.

Neptune rules all things that appear and disappear, so add magician to the list. Indeed, the whole entertainment field is kind to Pisces. You could be a stage-lighting director, theater playwright, or stage director or casting agent. Study to be a costume designer or curate a costume museum. Design video games, virtual-reality experiences, or theme parks. Be a Web designer or a content developer, or design corporate identities. Run a movie studio or an archive of old films. Become a poet, artistic painter, or illustrator. Or author screenplays or richly imaginative novels.

Dance is Pisces' domain. Pisces ballerinas and modern dancers are some of the best in the world. Choreograph dance or instruct others how to dance—these are equally good fields.

You like to help people, so you might like to be a nurse or nurse's aid. Look into medicine that involves long-term care or become a physical therapist. Film is ruled by Pisces, so you might find success as an X-ray technician.

The same instinct that may draw you to medicine (that is, to help those who suffer) might lead you to work for a charity, foundation, or other not-for-profit organization. Join Doctors Without Borders or the Red Cross, for example. Also, Pisces loves animals and caring for them, so you might like a career as a veterinarian or as an official at your city's animal-welfare humane society.

Your sign rules the subconscious, sleep, dreams, and other such phenomena. Consider being a doctor who studies sleep disorders or an anesthesiologist. Pisces also rules the feet, so consider becoming a podiatrist. Your sign is fascinated with the mind, so you could also make a fine psychiatrist, psychologist, psychoanalyst, or hypnotist. Other careers might include being an inspirational speaker, teaching meditation or yoga, or helping others by being an astrologer.

Pisces tends to be the most religious of all signs, and as such you may have a calling to join a convent or religious order as an officiant. You may even choose to be a missionary or run a religious bookstore.

The sea lures you too. Careers that place you near water are ideal. Be a ship captain, cruise-tour operator, or a ship's activity director. You could be a deep-sea diver, oceanographer or fisherman, or join the navy. Raising money to search for sunken treasure might be the most fun of all.

Indeed, liquids are quite lucky for you. Work in the beverage industry: tea, beer, coffee, soda, water, wine, champagne, or traditional liquor, in any capacity. Or work in the oil industry or pharmaceutical industry in any capacity. These are ruled by Neptune as well. Design ice sculptures or fountains. Be a swimming or scuba-diving instructor or a lifeguard for the summer, or become a merchant marine or part of the Coast Guard. Build boats or sell them.

Finally, Pisces make great detectives or even spies, for they know how to keep a secret and, because they know how to make themselves invisible, they can slip under the radar while they do their work. As you see, you have many career paths open to you, and each would use your talents well.

Besides the visual, creative arts, there are other careers where Pisces would excel. As Pisces has a good sixth sense about what the public wants, mass media is a great area for this sign. Pisces is keenly sensitive to the pulse of the public and its changing moods, so would be great in advertising, public relations, marketing, broadcasting, or publishing. Wherever the shifting sands of public opinion and the need for information are important, is the perfect place for Pisces. With Sagittarius on the mid-heaven, success in publishing is a sure thing, as is a job as a travel agent. Pisces' imagination and sense of adventure are strong, and they love to travel. They can successfully paint a bright, alluring, and highly poetic picture of faraway lands that they enthusiastically recommend.

## BODY, MIND, AND SPIRIT

In matters of health, Pisces are less robust than other signs, and hence should take a little extra care of themselves. As mentioned earlier, the world tends to wear down this sign, so solitude is often the perfect anecdote to stress. Neptune can mask an illness, making it harder for doctors to diagnose a problem, so at one time or another Pisces may have to be patient until their doctor locates the source of the problem. Pisces rules the feet, one area that is likely to cause pain. You can always spot Pisces by the old shoes they are fond of wearing. They love them best when broken in, soft, and comfy, perhaps a tad scruffy-looking in an otherwise elegant appearance. Metaphorically, the feet represent foundations, and physically they carry the entire body. The lymphatic system, which cleanses the body of toxins, is also under the rulership of Pisces. This is quite appropriate for a sign interested in maintaining a pure and integrated mind-body-spirit. Pisces loves to drink all kinds of liquids, though water is particularly good for the Fish. Homeopathic remedies are often better for sensitive Pisces than strong medicines, for this sign often experiences strong side effects—their systems seem to soak up drugs faster than most. When stressed, the Fish needs to be either near water (the beach) or in water, because that's where they unwind best. Women Pisces especially love aromatherapy massage; it is also quite healing for them.

## SUMMARY

The next time you throw a pebble into a cool and placid pool, watch how the stone grazes the cheek of the pond and how the circles reverberate in ever-expanding circles. This is Pisces, the last sign of the zodiac, the sign that wraps up all the qualities of the signs that have come before. Pisces never stops believing in miracles and, as a result, the universe provides for them. On November 26, 1994, *Newsweek* reported:

"New (scientific) work in cosmology suggests that humanity is very much a part of the universe. . . . We are part of an ongoing community of being . . . akin to all creatures, past and present, and to nonliving entities too. . . . The very atoms in our bodies were once stardust, ejected when stars exploded." (*Newsweek*, "Science of the Sacred," November 26, 1994.)

Pisces smile a little smile when they hear this, and they whisper quietly, "I knew, for I believed." They have never doubted that mankind is made of stardust and that we are linked together in a common bond. Pisces probably dreamed about this discovery eons ago.

Pisces have a vast and limitless subconscious, a reservoir from which they can draw to create things of poetic art or to come closer to understanding the human heart. Pisces will always be the sign of dreams, weaving their richest tapestries in the depths of sleep. Bless their hearts, where would we be without Pisces to inspire us?

# THE MYTHS OF
# PISCES AND NEPTUNE

The Romans renamed Poseidon, the important Greek god of water and the seas, *Neptunus* (or, as we would say, Neptune) and kept Poseidon's mythology virtually the same. Neptune's name means "husband (or lord) of the Earth." Indeed, he was a major figure, and although he had rather sumptuous quarters under the sea, Poseidon chose to spend more time out mixing with the other gods on Mount Olympus. Neptune was a rather temperamental god, but he was also credited with acts of mercy. His violent side is thought to represent the fury of sea storm and its awesome destructive power.

Note that the reference to Neptune/Poseidon as the mythological governor of Pisces did not occur until long after the Romans, for the planet Neptune was not discovered until 1846. The qualities of the age when a planet is discovered—in this case the Age of Romanticism—was considered significant in assigning the astrologic description of the planet. Until then, ancient astrologers assigned Jupiter to Pisces, a ruler it shared with Sagittarius. (There are fewer heavenly bodies than there are zodiac signs, so some planetary rulerships have to be shared by signs.) To this day, many astrologers consider Jupiter as Pisces' co-ruler. Jupiter's influence is humanitarian and broad in outlook and fits well with the selfless service of Pisces, who tries to work for the good of all.

If we go farther back in time, the ancient Greeks always sensed a link between Pisces and Neptune, so in a way, through the discovery and naming of planet Neptune as the ruler of Pisces, astrologers were simply going back to assigning this sign its rightful ruler. As seen later in this chapter, mythological Neptune has some links to mythological Jupiter, making the mythology of Pisces all the more intriguing—and mysterious.

### ZEUS, HADES, AND POSEIDON DRAW LOTS

As the son of Cronus and Rhea, Poseidon (known also by his other name, Neptune) was Zeus's older brother. Cronus ate all his children except for Zeus (Jupiter) because Cronus feared being supplanted by them, which later happened nevertheless. (Please refer to "The Myths of Capricorn and Saturn.") Poseidon and his brother Zeus set out to overthrow the Titans, the first generation of gods, and were successful. Along with his brothers, Zeus and Hades (Pluto), Poseidon drew lots to see who would get to rule which parts of the world. They had agreed to leave Mount Olympus and Earth as common ground. Zeus won the top-ranking position, reigning over the sky, and Hades was given the underworld of the dead. Poseidon was given the bodies of water of the world. Since Poseidon was upset that his brother Zeus won the more prestigious position, ruler of heaven, there would always be some tension between Poseidon and Zeus.

Neptune was known in Greece to be "the Earth shaker" or the creator of earthquakes, which makes sense in the context of the tension between Poseidon and Zeus. Neptune's rule of earthquakes also makes sense when we consider his reputation for being moody, vengeful, and volatile. You might ask, "Wouldn't earthquakes be more suitable for a planet like Uranus, the planet that rules unexpected happenings, rather than Neptune, which is said to rule mainly Earth's waters?" Many astrologers have debated this question, but the Greeks' assignment of earthquakes to Neptune does have a scientific basis. Modern geologists tell us that earthquakes are triggered by changes in climate that, in turn, cause shifts of weight on the various landmasses. When ice that covers land melts, as it did in the Ice Age, the ocean grows larger. Land becomes lighter and the Earth bounces back, triggering earthquakes.

## NEPTUNE AS CHAMELEON AND PROTECTOR OF ARTISTS

Neptune was the only Olympian god who had free access to the depths of the sea; thus, the Greeks designated him as god in charge of the arts, of music and dance. Because the sea has always symbolized pure emotion it was said to bring special inspiration to all artists, poets, actors, and musicians. The sea symbolizes intuition, memories, and dreams and, according to psychologist Carl Jung, it is also a metaphor for the collective consciousness, including memories and dreams, of masses of people.

Like most sea gods, Poseidon had the ability and the power to transform himself into other shapes and forms, even into different creatures. He did so mainly to seduce potential lovers. Isn't that what the actor, poet, musician, and artist do too: seduce us into watching his art as he changes form? Again the link between art and Neptune is apparent, for the artistic temperament is said to be Pisces' domain.

Neptune the mythological god was not known for his fidelity in love. His escapades were rather well known and somewhat outrageous, and they involved a wide number of nymphs, goddesses, and even mortal women. In one example, Demeter, mother of Persephone, was quite upset over the loss of her daughter. To escape her brother's advances, she changed herself into a mare. Not about to be stymied, Poseidon changed himself into a stallion and mated with her. Demeter bore him a divine horse, Arion, and a daughter, Despoena.

Perhaps Poseidon's mating with Demeter explains why he was later to proclaim the horse sacred. Some myths say that Poseidon (Neptune) actually created the horse by smashing his trident down upon a rock. It is also written that Neptune invented horse racing; Pisces who are not evolved are said to lose themselves in gambling and horse racing when real life becomes too much to bear. However, Pisces' link to the horse is especially interesting because horses are the domain of Sagittarius, which is ruled by Jupiter, the former ruler of Pisces. It seems appropriate for Jupiter to be associated with Poseidon and, by default, with Pisces, through the symbol of the horse.

## ODYSSEUS

In another myth, this one written by Homer, Poseidon was to give Odysseus a very hard time. Because of a long-standing animosity with the Trojans, Poseidon intervened on behalf of the Greeks, even though his brother Zeus expressly asked him not to do so. The tensions between Poseidon and the Trojans stemmed from an earlier episode when both Poseidon and Apollo worked on behalf of King Laomedon, Priam's father. King Laomedon reneged on his promise to pay a certain sum to Poseidon and Apollo for building the walls of his city of Troy. Neptune forgets nothing, and indeed, Pisces is said to have the memory of an elephant.

Poseidon challenged Odysseus, making him lose his way repeatedly, causing great sorrow and delay in his journey over the sea. No one showed more faith and determination than Odysseus, who, in true Pisces spirit, solves problems not through brute force but through creative thinking and a resourceful nature. Odysseus wanted to return home to the loving center of his family and refused to give up. That staunch will to survive is very much part of Pisces' outlook.

## THE FOUNDING OF ATHENS

Another early myth explains how the people of Athens had to choose between art and commerce and how commerce won. The story goes that Poseidon had a number of property battles with other gods over land he claimed as his own but often lost those altercations, much to his consternation. In one of the most notable, he found himself in a conflict with Athena, who would rule over the ancient place of Attica in Greece.

Poseidon claimed the land by piercing the earth with his trident and creating a saltwater spring. By so doing, Neptune was symbolically offering the citizens a life of feeling and artistic expression. Athena later planted an olive tree beside Poseidon's well and in turn offered the citizens a future of economic prosperity. (Olive trees later made the land surrounding Athens prosperous.)

Upon hearing this, Poseidon threw a fit and quickly challenged Athena to combat. At that point Zeus stepped in and put the matter before a divine tribunal and, aiming for neutrality, abstained from voting. The other four male gods voted for Neptune (Hades remained in the underworld so he didn't vote, which was his custom). However, the five goddesses, in a show of solidarity, voted for Athena, giving her the right to the land because of the perceived greater value of her gift, the olive trees. Neptune, outraged, flooded the Attica plain, so the citizens of Athens appeased him by denying women the right to vote and also ended the practice of women carrying their mother's name. Poseidon and Athena both were honored on the Acropolis. The city was called Athens, after Athena. This is said to be a turning point for Western culture, where life would be ruled by economics and other practical considerations forevermore, sadly considered more valuable than a life centered on the arts and emotion.

### VENUS AND CUPID

The Romans had a lovely myth that explained the creation of Pisces' constellation. Venus and Cupid were startled one day by a flaming monster. The two knew this monster could not survive water, so to escape him they transformed themselves into fish and jumped into the water. Before doing so they were careful to tie themselves to the end of a single cord so that they would not lose each other. As the myth goes, Jupiter, the past ruler of Pisces, rewarded their ingenious escape by commemorating their survival in the heavens, placing them among the stars as the two fishes.

Without any aggressive tendencies, Pisces protects himself through intuition—feeling the currents of the waters around him—and by transforming himself in a particularly adept way. In fight or flight, Pisces chooses flight, which often takes a clever form. In this case, Cupid and Venus turned themselves into fish. We are reminded in this myth that Venus is today considered "exalted" when in the constellation of Pisces, for it symbolizes love in its most unselfish and giving state.

# BIBLIOGRAPHY

Applewhite, Ashton, William R. Evans III, and Andrew Frothingham, *And I Quote: The Definitive Collection of Quotes, Sayings and Jokes for the Contemporary Speechmaker.* New York: St. Martin's Press/A Thomas Dunne Book, 1992.

Ashley, Wendy, Lectures for the National Council of Geo-Cosmic Research. Mythic Astrology Workshop Series in New York City. "Cancer & Capricorn," Sunday, January 23, 2000; "Leo & Aquarius," Sunday, February 20, 2000. Tapes available.

Banzhaf, Hajo, and Anna Haebler, *Key Words for Astrology.* York Beach, Maine: Samuel Weiser, Inc., 1996.

Biedermann, Hans, *Dictionary of Symbolism: Cultural Icons and the Meanings Behind Them.* Trans., James Hulbert. New York: Meridian, 1994.

Bills, Rex E., *The Rulership Book.* Tempe, Arizona: American Federation of Astrologers, 1971.

Burt, Kathleen, *Archetypes of the Zodiac.* St. Paul, Minnesota: Llewellyn Publications, 1996.

Casey, Caroline W., *Making the Gods Work for You.* New York: Three Rivers Press, 1998.

Condos, Theony, *Star Myths of the Greek and Romans: A Sourcebook.* Grand Rapids, Michigan: Phanes Press, 1997.

Dreyer, Ronnie Gale, *Venus: The Evolution of the Goddess and Her Planet.* San Francisco: Aquarian/HarperCollins, 1994.

*Encyclopedia Britannica.* CD-ROM. Encyclopedia Britannica, Inc., 1997.

George, Llewellyn, *The New A to Z Horoscope Maker and Delineator.* St. Paul, Minnesota: Llewellyn Publications, 1995.

Goodman, Linda, *Sun Signs.* New York: Bantam, 1968.

Grant, Michael, and John Hazel, *Who's Who in Classical Mythology.* New York: Oxford University Press, 1973.

Graves, Robert, *Greek Myths.* London: Penguin Books, 1984.

Greene, Liz, *The Astrological Neptune and the Quest for Redemption.* York Beach, Maine: Samuel Weiser, Inc., 1996.

Grimal, Peter, *The Dictionary of Classical Mythology.* Trans. A. R. Maxwell-Hyslop. Oxford: Blackwell Publishers, Ltd., 1986, 1996.

Guttman, Ariel, and Kenneth Johnson, *Mythic Astrology: Archetypal Powers in the Horoscope.* St. Paul, Minnesota: Llewellyn Publications, 1996.

Hamilton, Edith, *Mythology.* Boston: Little, Brown and Company, 1942.

Heindel, Max, and Augusta Foss Heindel, *The Message of the Stars: An Esoteric Exposition of Natal and Medical Astrology Explaining the Arts of Reading the Horoscope and Diagnosing Disease.* Eighteenth ed. Oceanside, California: The Rosicrucian Fellowship, 1980.

Hyde, Lewis, *Trickster Makes This World: Mischief, Myth and Art.* New York: Farrar, Straus and Giroux, 1998.

Knowles, Elizabeth, ed., *The Oxford Dictionary of Phrase, Saying, and Quotation.* New York: Oxford University Press, 1997.

Malsin, Peter, *The Eyes of the Sun: Astrology in Light of Psychology.* Tempe, Arizona: New Falcon Publications, 1997.

McDonald, Marianne, *Mythology of the Zodiac: Tales of the Constellations.* New York: Metrobooks, 2000.

*Microsoft Encarta 98 Encyclopedia.* CD-ROM. Microsoft Corporation, 1998.

Osborn, Kevin, and Dana L. Burgess, Ph.D., *The Complete Idiot's Guide to Classical Mythology.* New York: A Division of Macmillan General Reference/A Simon & Schuster Macmillan Company — Alpha Books, 1998.

Parker, Derek and Julia, *The Complete Astrologer.* Michael Beazley Limited/McGraw Hill Book Company Publishers, 1971.

Soffer, Shirley, *The Astrology Sourcebook: A Guide to the Symbolic Language of the Stars.* Los Angeles: Lowell House, 1998.

Toen, Donna Van, *The Mars Book: A Guide to Your Personal Energy and Motivation.* York Beach, Maine: Samuel Weiser, Inc., 1995.

Vaughan, Valerie, *Astro-Mythology: The Celestial Union of Astrology and Myth.* Amherst, Massachusetts: One Reed Publications, 1999.